STUDIES IN ROMANCE LANGUAGES: 37

John E. Keller, Editor

Spanish Poetry of the Twentieth Century

Modernity and Beyond

ANDREW P. DEBICKI

THE UNIVERSITY PRESS OF KENTUCKY

Publication of this book was made possible by a grant
from the Program for Cultural Cooperation between
Spain's Ministry of Culture and
United States Universities.

Copyright © 1994 by The University Press of Kentucky

Scholarly publisher for the Commonwealth,
serving Bellarmine College, Berea College, Centre
College of Kentucky, Eastern Kentucky University,
The Filson Club, Georgetown College, Kentucky
Historical Society, Kentucky State University,
Morehead State University, Murray State University,
Northern Kentucky University, Transylvania University,
University of Kentucky, University of Louisville,
and Western Kentucky University.

Editorial and Sales Offices: Lexington, Kentucky 40508-4008

Library of Congress Cataloging-in-Publication Data
Debicki, Andrew Peter.
  Spanish poetry of the twentieth century : modernity and beyond /
Andrew P. Debicki
    p.   cm. — (Studies in Romance languages ; 37)
  Includes bibliographical references and index.
  ISBN 0-8131-1869-7 (alk. paper)
  1. Spanish poetry—20th century—History and criticism
I. Title. II. Series: Studies in Romance languages (Lexington, Ky.);
37.
PQ6085.D398   1994
861'.609—dc20   93-36928
ISBN 0-8131-0835-7 (pbk: alk. paper)

Contents

Introduction

Any attempt to construct a literary history at the present time must seem problematic. The very notion of a literary history has been questionable, and questioned, for decades. Analytic critics of the 1940s and 1950s (most notably in Spain, Dámaso Alonso) argued, rather convincingly, that traditional literary histories obscured the individuality of specific works and invited readers to reduce complex poems to simplistic examples of movements or trends. To some degree, analytic criticism and *estilística* gained support precisely because of their effort to eliminate such historicizing: works as different as I.A. Richards's *Practical Criticism* and Dámaso Alonso's *Poesía española,* as well as many books of analytic essays, are in some fashion "antihistories," although they did not manage to eliminate the prior genre. But a reading of many positivistic literary histories today confirms the charges made against them and makes clear that those who relied on them for judgments about individual works received inadequate insights. Even the larger patterns that they offered often proved questionable.

Yet we continue to seek, in some fashion, ways of setting literary texts in their contexts and organizational schemes that relate individual poems and books to each other and to currents of life and thought. This need has increased in recent years, as we have again become aware that the meanings of any poem depend on the circumstances in which it is produced and read, and we have tended to abandon the notion of literature as immutable. Though a traditional history of literary works may be impossible, cultural patterns, ideas, styles, forms, and language do develop in time, and their development can shed light on texts. Some of the most useful historical works about Spanish poetry of the twentieth century have been, indeed, studies of poetic principles, of styles, of forms, of intellectual climates (see Ciplijauskaité 1966; Siebenmann; García de la Concha 1987). As we glance back at these and other attempts to situate this poetry, however, we become aware of a second major problem.

Almost all historical assessments to date have implicitly assumed the possibility of finding an organizational scheme that would have objective validity. Many scholars attempted to explain why their scheme was more true than others. Yet from our vantage point we realize that any organizational pattern is an artificial construct. Recent criticism has made us aware how the meanings of poems and books are contingent on contexts and readers; any historical patterns formed by such poems and books would be even more contingent. We can only seek structures that will be useful for given purposes, at given times—and not try to discover a permanent order.

This awareness may, however, offer me an opportunity not available to traditional literary historians. No longer obligated to discover one true historical pattern, I may change the goal and the questions. I can be free to seek whatever ways of organizing materials will make it easier to read twentieth-century Spanish poetry with insight and appreciation. Since I will no longer have to determine which kind of scheme—generational, modal, periodic, ideological—has absolute validity (none do), I will be able to use and combine them selectively and pragmatically. Rather than attempting and failing to construct an objective and permanent literary history, I might succeed at offering the contemporary reader a practical guide to make the task of reading easier. In the process I will also avoid, I hope, the first problem discussed above. Aware of the contingent nature of any interpretation, I will know that any historical generalization will not limit the individuality of a text, but will only provide background to its reading, and thus I will develop my discussions accordingly.

Free from the obligation of trying to be right, I might thus be able to offer a book that is interesting and helpful (see Fish 180). My purpose, then, is to produce an interpretative history, consciously arranging my presentations in order to make the best case for a reading of Spanish poetry of the twentieth century (more general, but parallel to the cases I have made for readings of individual poets in my earlier work). I will try to make it reasonable and nonidiosyncratic enough to invite my reader to share it; beyond that, I leave it to the reader to compensate and modify my judgments.

To introduce my interpretation, I must first set a context and a focus. Spanish poetry of the twentieth century has generally been studied in isolation from other literatures and from its European contexts. This occurred, first of all, because critics defined and discussed two specific movements at the turn of the century: *modernismo*, an aesthetic renewal originating with Rubén Darío in Latin America around 1885 and ending by the early 1900s; and the activity of the Generation of 1898, comprising philosophic and thematic developments in Spanish letters after the disastrous war with the United States. Attempts to characterize, contrast, and relate these two movements led critics into narrow perspectives and kept them from investigating larger patterns, especially the issue of how Spanish letters fit into the development of European modernity.

This inquiry became even narrower because Spanish critics organized literary works by the generations of their authors. Based primarily on the theories of Julius Petersen and established in Spain by José Ortega y Gasset and his followers, mainly Julián Marías, the generational approach produced schemes made up of many short periods and a literary history characterized by frequent reactions by one group against another. It also assumed, at least implicitly, that the works produced by a given generation did not evolve in response to new times and to succeeding generations. Especially when used haphazardly and capriciously, this approach often produced multiple, erratically arranged units, some of which, such as the Generation of 1927, made more sense than others (Generation of 1914, Generation of 1936). As we will see throughout this book, editors and publishers have exaggerated the importance of generations by publishing anthologies of poets of similar ages (usually accompanied by statements of poetics), making readers and critics perceive the field as a collection of such clusters.

The generational approach became even more limiting when it was linked to specific moments in Spanish history. When studying the period after the Spanish Civil War, for example, critics classified poetry by first, second, and third postwar generations; both the fragmentation and the emphasis on an exclusively Spanish event and situation led to isolated judgments and to an ignorance of wider issues applicable to Western literature.

To compensate for this isolation and for the fragmentation of literary periods, I have attempted to situate twentieth-century Spanish poetry in the larger context of European modernity. Mine is not the first effort to do so: Gustav Siebenmann took modernity into account in his history of poetic styles, first published in German in 1965. Sensibly rejecting the dichotomy modernism–Generation of 1898 and pointing to a larger view of Spanish modernity, Siebenmann nevertheless did not examine in detail the modern aesthetic. He also, albeit hesitantly, sought the end of the modern in the 1930s, and he obviously could not see the issue from the (very important) vantage point of developments in the 1970s and 1980s. Hugo Friedrich's study of modern European poetry only took into account one Spanish generation, that of 1927. Neither Siebenmann nor Friedrich, nor any of several Hispanic critics seeking a wider view of modernity, in any event, affected the most prevalent ways of organizing contemporary Spanish poetry. Meanwhile, some good recent literary histories—María del Pilar Palomo's is the best example—while insightfully seeking to define periods that cut across generations, have not taken the issues of modernity into sufficient account.

Through focus and organization, I intend for readers to keep the larger context of modernity in mind as I follow succeeding moments and texts of Spanish poetry. For that reason I have traced, somewhat pragmatically, several rather large periods, within each of which I can suggest some unifying traits, encompassing poetics, themes, language, and style, with various emphases at various moments. I see these periods as working models through which to follow shifts in sensibility, forms, and texts. Within each period and unifying focus, I study poetry published by authors of different ages. This procedure will necessarily yield more of a history of poetry than of poets: it will emphasize general shifts in sensibility and expression and avoid the impression, created by purely generational histories, of separate blocks of writers of diverse ages, independently moving through time.

I will, however, try to take advantage of some of the merits of a generational approach. Writers of the same age, especially when raised and educated in a similar fashion and placed in contact with each other, often reveal common—or at least parallel—concerns, attitudes, and responses. This is especially true of Spain, where significant cultural developments occurred mostly in a few places (mainly Madrid and Barcelona), where most writers knew each other, where a few publication outlets have been dominant, and where a group usually had the opportunity of publicizing its poetic stance in anthologies and special issues. For this reason, I will often examine the poetics of the most prominent generation, usually before studying the poetry published at the time. This procedure, I feel, will help clarify ideas and attitudes that are most characteristic and defining and hence will illuminate, pragmatically, several phases of the development— and transcendence—of modernity in Spain. Especially at certain times, these generational attitudes provide useful background for the work of poets of different ages, all of whom responded, in some fashion, to the prevalent aesthetic.

In constructing literary periods, I found myself, initially to my surprise, creating overlapping ones. On reflection, I realized that this occurred because a new attitude, a new aesthetic, and often some consequent new forms of poetry frequently developed while a prior view and form of expression were still in existence. The period from 1953 or so until 1960 is a good example. Although the dominant poetic mode was then social and testimonial, a group of younger writers, influenced by a new aesthetic of poetry as discovery, published important work. That work, in turn, initiated a new period extending until at least 1970. By creating an overlap between chapters 3 and 4 and treating social poetry at the end of chapter 3 and the new directions at the start of chapter 4, I found I could explore the issues more effectively than if I had forced an absolute break between periods. The decision to allow such overlaps permitted me to fold some of the insights of a generational approach into an organization by periods.

My organization often led me to discuss different works of a given poet in different chapters. This has some disadvantages, mainly that of disguising the cohesiveness of the poet's production. Yet it has the advantage of making clear major developments and patterns in the history of the genre, as these find evidence in the works of many authors. In addition, it often helps underline the significance of a given text or book that might otherwise melt into obscurity when considered alongside the poet's other works. As I noted above, any scheme is contingent and to some degree arbitrary: Is the most important unit the poem? the book? the poet's oeuvre? the books of a period? I nevertheless feel that the method here employed is well suited to exploring the course of Spanish poetry through modernity and into a postmodern era.

In the past I have often criticized literary historians for using a poet's attitude to explain a poetic text superficially, or for reading poems as messages about poetry. Therefore I have tried to keep in mind that a text may contradict its author's conscious poetics. Yet especially as the twentieth century unfolded and as shifts in modern aesthetic attitudes took place, poetic stances had an important relationship to the texts produced, and this relationship needs to be explored. I have tried to do so with caution and common sense, and I recommend the same to my readers.

A necessary danger of any broad history of poetry is the too brief, simplified discussion of texts and the accompanying use of excessively short segments of quotes. I have tried to compensate for this, to some extent, by occasional longer studies. But the only totally satisfactory solution would have been to write a different book, more in the mode of the volumes of the *Historia crítica de la literatura española* edited by Francisco Rico, which combine separate essays. This would have contradicted my purpose of offering an interpretive overview in manageable form.

Dealing with poetry separately from other literary genres obviously narrows one's focus and can prevent one from seeing important relationships between genres. This is especially true of Spanish literature of the last decades, in which techniques traditionally associated with one genre also appear in others. I would argue, nevertheless, that modern Spanish poetry does need to be studied historically by itself, since only in that fashion will its most important features become clear. (The same is true of the fiction and drama of this time, which have indeed been studied historically more extensively and successfully than poetry.)

I have provided translations, with the aim of making this book accessible to readers in allied fields. In all cases the translations are my own; when translating poetry, I have generally tried to render accurately, in prose, the text's most obvious meaning. That should help readers with a slight command of Spanish make some sense of the originals. Occasionally, when line divisions or rhythmic effects seemed especially central, I have rendered my versions in lines of free verse, and/or departed very slightly from literal equivalents.

In many ways, this book is the result of years of studying and teaching contemporary Spanish poetry and of writing critical works on poets and generations. My previous work has furnished me with detailed insights and approaches that have helped me deal with such a large area of literature; it has also made it possible for me to step back and develop more synthetic perspectives. As I did so, I had to make some difficult judgments, leaving out or discussing very briefly a number of good books and poets, as interesting to me as others that are treated more fully. Some of the ones left out have not been accepted into the canon; others did not contribute to the overviews I was tracing. And the desire to deal in some depth with crucial texts, in a volume of manageable size, placed a limit on the number of poets I could discuss. I have, however, given space to some neglected but to my mind important figures.

The reader will note a shift of emphasis as this book develops. In the first chapters, attention centers on major figures and on a few exemplary texts; as I move closer to the present, I mention more poets and books of poetry and deal with many of them rather briefly. I do this with the awareness that all judgments have to be more tentative, and more suspect, as we come closer to our own time. No canon has been defined, however provisionally; and differences in opinion, especially those related to shifting cultural currents as Spain moved into a post-Franco era, have not been resolved. I have relied more heavily on personal judgments but have compensated for this by giving at least some attention to more poets, so that the reader can explore a wider field while developing his or her own interests.

Given the scope of this book and the fact that it draws on many years of my career, it owes a great deal to many people, too numerous to mention individually. Yet I am keeping them all in mind, with great gratitude: it is to them that I owe much of my professional satisfaction. The list includes dozens of students, graduate and undergraduate, at the University of Kansas; the great participants in three National Endowment for the Humanities seminars for college teachers; and colleagues in the wonderful Department of Spanish and Portuguese at Kansas, which has been a most stimulating and rewarding intellectual home for me for many years, and also in other units of the university, at other institutions at which I have taught, and in the profession at large. I am also keeping in mind my wife, children, stepchildren, and grandchildren, who form such a major component of my life.

I would never have completed this project without the support that let me devote the 1992–93 academic year to it: a sabbatical leave from the University of Kansas; a fellowship from the National Endowment for the Humanities; and a residential fellowship from the National Humanities Center, which offered an ideal setting and unsurpassed library assistance. The conclusion was written and much of the revision was done at the marvelous Bellagio Center of the Rockefeller Foundation. I gratefully acknowledge the support of all these organizations. I would also like to thank Dan Rogers for his fine work in constructing the index.

1

The Apogee of Modernity
in Spain, 1915–1928

One View of Modernity

After examining various definitions of the term *modernity* up to the mid-nineteenth century, Matei Calinescu emphasized Charles Baudelaire's use of *modern* to describe an aesthetic sense of "presentness." For Calinescu, this offered a new and fruitful way of characterizing a period of literary and cultural history. Baudelaire's formulation transcended a purely chronological meaning of *modernity* and stressed, instead, a main goal of the poets of one era: the achievement of timeless immediacy in their works (Calinescu 46–58). Baudelaire thus initiated a poetics that was to underlie Western European letters from the late nineteenth century until at least the 1930s.

Baudelaire's conception of modernity is also a good initial vantage point from which to look at contemporary Spanish poetry. The poetics on which it was based governed the writings of the important Spanish and Latin American poets of the late nineteenth and early twentieth centuries. As Calinescu points out, the most famous Spanish American poet of this time, Rubén Darío, consciously attempted to define a "modernist" artistic renovation based on French influences, "combining the major postromantic trends, parnassian, decadent, and symbolist," in contrast to the Spanish literature of the time (69). The aestheticism of the Spanish American *modernistas* was clearly derived from the symbolist conception of the work of art as a unique way of embodying, of making present for then and forever, fundamental human meanings.

This conception indeed constituted a main feature of the symbolist poetics. It was implied in Baudelaire's ideas about "correspondence." Going beyond earlier romantic notions of literary correspondences, Baudelaire described how poets give form to new perceptions by establishing relations between diverse elements (Balakian 51–54). That process of giving form to perceptions, in turn, represents a desire to give permanence to human experiences and aesthetic meanings, to antepose a sense of presentness to the flow of time.[1] "The pleasure we derive from the representation of the present is not merely due to the beauty of the display, but also to the essential 'presentness' of the present."[2]

This notion of the poem as a means of making present and hence preserving elusive meanings becomes even clearer in Stéphane Mallarmé's view of the symbol: "*Nommer* un objet, c'est supprimer les trois-quarts de la juissànce du poème . . . ; le *suggérer,* voilà le rêve. C'est le parfait usage de ce mystère qui constitue le symbole: évoquer petit à petit un objet pour montrer un état d'âme." (869). {"To merely name an object is to suppress three-fourths of the play [or range] of the poem . . . ; to suggest it, that is the goal. It represents the perfect expression of that mystery that makes a symbol: to evoke an object little by little, so as to reveal a state of soul."} Mallarmé's opposition to direct naming in poetry was not merely a way of separating it from everyday expression, but an endeavor to grant it a special role: that of giving form to otherwise incommunicable states of emotion. His "symbol" is a unique way of embodying untranslatable meanings, of making them tangible and present for all future readers and thus rendering them timeless.

This notion of poetry, of its nature as a kind of icon for the preservation and eternalization of elusive meanings and experiences, also underlay the poetics of many Hispanic writers from the latter nineteenth century into the 1920s and even the 1930s. Ricardo Gullón, who developed the broadest definition of Hispanic modernism, indicated that a devotion to poetry as an almost religious task of embodying fleeting experiences binds together all modernist poets, from the late nineteenth-century Spanish Americans Rubén Darío and José Martí to the twentieth-century Spaniards Juan Ramón Jiménez and Antonio Machado (Gullón 1971, 39–40, 166–67, 189). Such a view of the poem as icon also helps explain Darío's interest in rhythm and in music as ways of objectifying meaning (Debicki and Doudoroff 39–41).[3]

Since this view of modern poetry as preservation of meanings was so central to Darío and other Spanish American poets of the turn of the century, and since it connects them both to their contemporaries and to later Spanish poets, it is unfortunate that the term *modernismo* acquired a much narrower definition in Hispanic criticism. Gullón's concept of modernism as the defining impulse of a larger era that lasted from the 1880s to about 1940, and a similar formulation of Ivan Schulman (see 9, 14–15), have been rejected, in Hispanic criticism, in favor of a view of *modernismo* as a specific movement, with two phases: an aestheticist one lasting from about 1885 to about 1895, and a philosophical one extending from 1895 until about 1910. The term *postmodernismo,* consequently, has been used to describe writers between 1910 and 1920 or so, who in turn give way to *vanguardismo* in the 1920s.[4] This narrow view has also motivated many studies that try to differentiate *modernismo* from the Generation of 1898, usually by contrasting the aesthetic renewal of the former to the thematic renewal of the latter (Díaz Plaja 1951). Even Pedro Salinas, while describing the rejection of literalism and pedantry common to both of these "move-ments," treats them as separate (1970, 23–25). All this has produced a canonical view of twentieth-century Hispanic poetry as fragmented into many movements and has obscured the presence of dominant poetic con-cepts and features that underlie that poetry from the late 1880s until at least the 1930s.

If we adopt a broader view of modernism, more consonant with one gen-erally used in Anglo-American and French criticism, we can take more into account the presence and impact of fundamental attitudes that originate with the symbolists, and better define the poetics and the verse of the major Spanish poets of the earlier twentieth century. In this chapter I will focus on the period between about 1915 and 1928, since it was then that a modernist stance led to an extraordinary flowering of poetry, and that poetry would constitute a canon to which later writings would necessarily respond.

We should remember that this period is generally considered the high point of modernism in Western literature. Describing all its strands or tak-ing into account all the different definitions of *modernism* would be impos-sible within the confines of this chapter. I will merely highlight one, which picks up and modifies the symbolist concepts discussed above. From 1912 to about 1917, the imagist poets in England had attempted to capture, in precise form and metaphor, untranslatable meanings and experiences, continuing the symbolist quest for the objectification of meaning.[5] The 1920s marked the composition of T.S. Eliot's *The Waste Land* and *Ash Wednesday,* of many of Ezra Pound's *Cantos,* of William Butler Yeats's late work, of much of the poetry of Paul Valéry in France, as well as the emer-gence of e.e. cummings and Hart Crane in the United States. In the verse of these poets as well as in Eliot's essays, we can see a continuation of the symbolist quest, albeit with a more traditionalist hue. Eliot tried to codify the process of objectifying meaning through the concept of the "objective correlative," outlined in a 1919 essay on Hamlet; he fitted the process of creation and embodiment into a larger view of the literary tradition in his "Tradition and the Individual Talent" of 1919 (Eliot 104–8, 21–30). The notion of seizing experience in form had lost some of the lyric, mystical nu-ances of the early symbolists and had become a systematic critical principle that was to be a cornerstone of the New Criticism. Meanwhile, a complex poetry developed, with new uses of form and allusion that called for new and exact forms of study.

High Modernity in Spain, 1915–1924

Spanish poetry also exemplified the world of high modernity in the decade or so beginning around 1915. Madrid witnessed at this time a gradual opening to artistic currents coming from France that became intensified in the early years of the regime of Miguel Primo de Rivera, which began in 1923. Though the dominant style in poetry reflected the decorative manner of Darío's early work, a search for new directions, coupled with a liberal and cosmopolitan orientation, pervaded the city's cultural establishment.[6]

Very important to the city's cultural life was the Residencia de Estudiantes, directed by Manuel B. Cossío. Cossío espoused idealistic views, derived from the liberal thought of the Institución Libre de Enseñanza (Free Institution of Learning). He dreamed of a society elevated by the arts and did all he could to bring it into existence. From 1910 on, the Residencia housed a number of poets, including Juan Ramón Jiménez, Federico García Lorca, and Rafael Alberti; published important works like Antonio Machado's complete poems to date (1917); and served as a center for poetry readings, artistic events, and lectures by foreign artists and scholars. Meanwhile, beginning in 1915, José Ortega y Gasset directed the magazine *Revista de España,* through which he conveyed his ideals of a European-based culture and commented on artistic currents coming from abroad. In the next decade Ortega directed the famous *Revista de Occidente,* which between 1923 and 1936 published the best work of the writers of the Generation of 1927, as well as older ones. The vitality of the Madrid cultural scene of this era also becomes clear when we read the *Gaceta Literaria* (1927–32), a newspaper-format magazine that reported in some depth on all aesthetic happenings in Spain and in the rest of continental Europe. Parallel developments were also taking place in Barcelona (see Díaz Plaja 1975, 137–41) and in other cities; a number of small magazines throughout Spain reflected the vitality of the literary scene in the 1920s. The most important poetry of Spain's modernity emerged in this climate of renewal.[7]

Probably the best-known poet of these years was Antonio Machado, born in 1875 and generally considered a representative of the Generation of 1898 because of his treatment of the past glory and the current decay of Spain in his *Campos de Castilla* ("Fields of Castile," 1912, 1917). Yet Machado emphasized a universal view of the poet as one who embodies basic human experiences in words. Machado's oft-quoted view of poetry as "palabra esencial en el tiempo" {"essential expression in time"}, his idea that poetry seeks meanings opposed to those of logic, and his definition of the modern poetic quest as a search for values at once individual and timeless all situate his poetics within the symbolist trajectory (Machado 71).[8]

A more detailed look at Machado's poetics reveals many ambiguities, especially in view of his propensity for multiple perspectives and for paradox, and his use of heteronyms. For my purposes, however, what matters is Machado's symbolist filiation. Whatever its outcome, his struggle to define poetry as a way of dealing with temporal existence—a struggle that culminated in the discussions embedded in the *De un cancionero apócrifo* ("From an Apocryphal Anthology" composed between 1923 and 1936)—places him within that tradition to a far greater degree than common critical opinion has allowed.[9]

Machado's actual poetry also fits within the symbolist tradition, as J.M. Aguirre has demonstrated (168–69, 181–87). This becomes clear if we adopt a modernist (perhaps we should say New Critical) perspective and borrow a critical term from Eliot. Beginning with *Soledades, galerías, y otros poemas* ("Solitudes, Galleries, and Other Poems," 1907) and throughout *Campos de Castilla,* Machado's verse makes natural scenes and elements into correlatives of subjective attitudes, always avoiding the decorativeness that had characterized the *modernistas*. In poem 32 from the former book, a tightly presented landscape embodies a negative mood:

> Las ascuas de un crepúsculo morado
> detrás del negro cipresal humean . . .
> En la glorieta en sombra está la fuente
> con su alado y desnudo Amor de piedra,
> que sueña mudo. En la marmórea taza
> reposa el agua muerta. [Machado 95–96]

{The embers of a purple dusk smolder behind the black cypress grove. The fountain, with its winged, naked stone cupid, lies in the shadowy plaza. In the marble cup, still water rests.}

All aspects of the description—the image of dusk as embers, the dark colors, the presence of trees that generally line Spanish cemeteries, the reduction of human life to a mute statue, the still water, the word *muerta*—engender a sense of time passing and suggest finitude and death.

In like fashion, Machado's sixth section of "Campos de Soria," from *Campos de Castilla,* alternates two types of description to reflect its speaker's double attitude toward the ancient city. A distanced and idealized outlook focuses on the city's silhouette and makes us feel its historical grandeur; meanwhile a pragmatic one sketches its decaying walls and deserted streets, populated only by howling dogs. These poems confirm Carlos Bousoño's notion that Machado constructs "bisemic" symbols to objectify moods and to make fundamental experiences out of specific personal referents, in *Soledades,* and out of civic topics, in *Campos de Castilla* (Bousoño 1966, 139–81).

Although Machado's *Nuevas canciones* ("New Songs"), written between 1917 and 1930, contains poems with a more conceptual bent, the poems are also fine ones in which the sense of time passing is expressed in concrete symbols (see Sánchez Barbudo 1969, 382). Aguirre has suggested, in fact, that Machado's poetry actually points ahead to the poetics of the next generation: "El adelgazamiento y la simplificación de su vocabulario tiene mucho que ver con las ideas de la época sobre la poesía pura" (373). {"The tightening and simplification of his vocabulary have much to do with the ideas of the period concerning pure poetry."}

This connection between Machado and the Generation of 1927 may seem surprising, in view of the opposition generally established between them, and of Machado's negative comments about the work of younger poets. In the same essay in which he defined poetry as "palabra esencial en el tiempo," he claimed to disagree with their use of images "más en función conceptual que emotiva" (71) { "in a conceptual rather than an emotive way"}. This only indicates, however, that Machado was not sympathetic to the tighter and more spare poetry of Jorge Guillén, Federico García Lorca, and others of their generation. He could not see that these poets were carrying forward the same quest for the embodiment of experience in verbal form that had been fundamental to his own work.

From the perspective of the 1990s, of course, we tend to question the very possibility of "embodying" meanings in language, without allowing for differences in reader perspectives, for the instability of signs, for historical circumstances. Today it is difficult (or pointless) to argue the permanent value of Bousoño's (or my New Critical) interpretation of the Machado texts. What is true and important, however, is that within the (logocentric) premises of modernity, these texts illustrate the goal of capturing, universalizing, and making present the human experience.[10]

Miguel de Unamuno is another poet seldom connected with symbolism or modernism, given his classification as the dominant figure of the Generation of 1898. Yet if we read his poetry of this period (including *El Cristo de Velázquez* ["Christ by Velázquez," 1920], *De Fuerteventura a París* ["From Fuerteventura to Paris," 1925], and *Romancero del destierro* ["Ballads of Exile," 1927]), we will see a very controlled use of language and form that attempts to seize complex meanings. Given the importance of paradox throughout Unamuno's work, we should not be surprised to find carefully crafted poems (many of them sonnets) in which a key image or personification captures the nuances of an ambiguous attitude and experience. In one sonnet from *De Fuerteventura a París*, Unamuno personifies a palm tree; a series of visual and tactile images make it reflect a human being's affirmative, yet also anguished, thirst for life (see Diego 1962, 73).

More obviously modernist (as well as *modernista* in the narrow Hispanic sense) is the verse of Ramón del Valle Inclán (b. 1866), which—especially in *La pipa de Kif* ("Kif's Pipe," 1919)—produces surprising effects similar to those of his plays and *esperpentos*. Valle Inclán creates distorted realities through imagery and synesthesia; his poems thus reach beyond logic, concept, and message and use language to engender and convey feelings.

In the 1920s Manuel Machado (b. 1874) kept writing well-crafted poems that attempt to capture subjective experiences, continuing a path his poetry had followed for decades before. He was to be recognized by the younger poets of the Generation of 1927 for his ability to convert the effects caused by visual art into verbal expression. His turn-of-the-century sonnet "Felipe IV," alluding to what seems to be a composite of several Velázquez paintings of a Spanish king, appeared in the important anthologies of modern Spanish poetry published in the 1930s and 1940s. The following lines personify colors and objects to produce a feeling of decadence, which offers a classic example of the symbolist quest to freeze sensations in words:

> Es pálida su tez como la tarde,
> cansado el oro de su pelo undoso,
> y de sus ojos, el azul, cobarde.
> Sobre su augusto pecho generoso
> ni joyeles perturban ni cadenas
> el negro terciopelo silencioso.
> [Diego 1962, 139–40]

{His face is pale like the afternoon, the gold of his flowing hair is tired, and the blue of his eyes cowardly. On his august, generous chest, neither jewels nor chains disturb the silent black velvet.}

Several other turn-of-the-century poets, generally classified as *modernistas* because of the way in which they cast muted romantic feelings in carefully crafted verse, also kept publishing into the 1920s. Probably the best known was Francisco Villaespesa (b. 1877), whose abundant poetic production was once given much importance. Today the feelings he expressed seem almost sentimentally romantic, although we take note of the rhythmic and musical effects of his work. The verse of Eduardo Marquina (b. 1879) ranges from a conventionally late romantic (or *modernista*) pantheism to almost pedestrian messages. Probably the most readable in this category today is Tomás Morales (b. 1885), whose poems offer low-key mood descriptions, often based on scenes and motifs of his native Canary Islands. For me, these poets are historically important because they show the prevalence in Spain of a typically modern impulse to preserve untranslatable subjective experience in linguistic form.

More important is the poetry of León Felipe (b. 1884), which in a variety of tones reflects a desire to explore the poetic possibilities of human life. The first volume of his *Versos y oraciones del caminante* ("Verses and Prayers of the Walker," 1920) seems more sensual; in the second (1930) the poet discovers his more original idiom and imagery. Beginning with this 1930 volume, León Felipe makes artistic use of a direct, powerful vocabulary, usually reflecting the moral responsibility of reaching for higher outlooks and contributing to the world's welfare. Generally forceful, sometimes shocking and blunt, occasionally prosaic, this poetry is an antidote to decorative *modernismo,* but it is modern in the deeper sense of seeking the original expression of important sentiments.

The most important poet for the understanding of Spanish modernity, and especially of the period discussed in this chapter, is Juan Ramón Jiménez. Born in 1881, Juan Ramón had been writing, from 1900 until the late teens, sensual landscape poems in which nature images reflected emotive states, and in which a melancholy vision of reality predominated. Critics have linked this early style of Juan Ramón's with Spanish American *modernismo* and with impressionism (Valbuena Prat 537–46); from today's perspective, we might say that it recalls features of late Spanish romantic poetry and the impressionism of Paul Verlaine. It was the next phase of Juan Ramón's work, however, that led Spanish poetry into what we might call high modernism.

The late teens and the 1920s mark the publication of the main books of this "second period" of Juan Ramón Jiménez's work: *Diario de un poeta recién casado* ("Diary of the Newly Married Poet," later retitled *Diario de poeta y mar,* ["Diary of Poet and Sea"], 1917), *Piedra y cielo* ("Stone and Sky," 1919), *Poesía* ("Poetry," 1923), and *Belleza* ("Beauty," 1923). These reveal a new style accompanied by a new poetics. As Antonio Sánchez Barbudo has indicated, they constitute an effort to give verbal form and expression, in the most exact and spare way possible, to a sense of the beauty of things (1962, 11–17, 49–81). This effort exemplifies the symbolist theory of poetry as a quest to embody life's essences, to turn experience into presentness, and to thus counteract time (Olson, chap. 1). As Juan Ramón himself immodestly noted, "Con el *Diario* empieza el simbolismo moderno en la poesía española. Tiene una metafísica que participa de estética" (Gullón 1958, 93). {"The *Diario* initiates modern symbolism in Spanish poetry. It contains a metaphysics that also involves aesthetics."} His poetry continues, extends, and purifies the prior work of Rubén Darío and of the late Spanish romantic Gustavo Adolfo Bécquer, both of whom strove for an art that would preserve and objectify human experience.[11] As Howard Young has indicated, Juan Ramón's verse was influenced by his readings and translations of William Butler Yeats (Young 1980, 159–61, 247–48). We are again reminded of the connections between modernist poetry in Spain and in other European countries.

When read in the context of the symbolist poetics, Juan Ramón's poems illustrate perfectly this goal of configuring and preserving experience. Let us, for the moment, take a New Critical–modernist view of the following text from *Piedra y cielo:*

> Mariposa de luz
> la belleza se va cuando yo llego
> a su rosa.
>
> Corro, ciego, tras ella . . .
> La medio cojo aquí y allá . . .
>
> ¡Sólo queda en mi mano
> La forma de su huída!
>   [Jiménez 1959, 777]

{Light moth, butterfly, beauty departs when I arrive at its rose. I run, blindly, after it . . . I half seize it here and there . . . Only the form of its escape remains on my hand!}

On the most obvious level, the poem operates symbolically: the "mariposa de luz" is explicitly identified as beauty, and its evasiveness stands for beauty's fleetingness. The speaker's efforts to capture it conjure up the poet's frustrated attempts to seize beauty and only produce his apprehension of the patterns of its elusiveness.

Much of the poem's effectiveness, however, depends on the way in which it characterizes a particular event while at the same time carrying forward its more abstract symbolic meaning. "Mariposa de luz" refers, literally, to a specific kind of insect, a light moth, and thus describes an immediate reality. Yet *mariposa* means "butterfly"; it and *luz* {"light"} are also words frequently associated with beauty, and they support the overt symbolic pattern. Similarly, the rose in line 3 both specifies the setting and introduces the most traditional symbol of beauty in Western literature. (Had the poem used *flower* instead of *rose,* it would have been both less visual and less symbolically explicit.) By calling himself "blind," the protagonist evokes the disorientation caused by chasing an elusive insect and also points to the poet's frustrating blindness in his search for beauty. The "form of its escape" refers to the illusion that we can actually see the path of a rapidly fleeing object and at the same time to the evidence of beauty's escape in many poetic works. Juan Ramón's remarkable ability to make the same words support both the literal and the symbolic levels of his poem produces a successful combination of immediacy and significance.

The poem "Mariposa de luz" thus operates as a spare and harmonious whole, in which the specificity of the referents blends perfectly with the larger symbolism. (The rose's concreteness in no way diminishes its symbolic value, nor does the literal meaning of "mariposa de luz" diminish the symbolic overtones of light.) Even the way in which the speaker describes his actions ("I arrive," "I run") integrates his role as protagonist with his quest as poet in search of beauty. This melding of meanings, the absence of any anecdotal detail unrelated to the symbolism, and the tightness of the text all make the text an archetype of the modern poem in the symbolist tradition. (We could easily connect it, for example, with imagist poems, or with texts by Paul Valéry, Guillaume Apollinaire, or even e.e. cummings.) It illustrates the modernist endeavor to objectify a specific event and action, to freeze it into an eternal present. In another sense, of course, it points to the impossibility of its quest, as it portrays beauty's flight.

An overview of Juan Ramón's *Diario de un poeta recién casado* lets us see this same quest on a larger scale. Constructed by a careful interweaving of its five parts, the book embodies a conflict between youth and adulthood, and between the speaker's inward and outward impulses (see Predmore 139, 224–27). It takes a particular human experience, obviously modeled on Juan Ramón's own life, and by means of symbolic and structural patterns attempts to freeze its meaning in form and to extend it to readers of all time. *Piedra y cielo, Poesía,* and *Belleza* pursue the same general quest. As the search develops, it illuminates a desire to reach beyond the poet's (or persona's) limits and feeling of emptiness, to search for some higher sense of being in language (Silver 1985, 85–117).[12] From today's perspective, this quest and desire of Juan Ramón's illustrate both the tremendous idealism and the ultimate impossibility of the whole symbolist-modernist endeavor.[13]

The Poetics of the Generation of 1927

This quest of Juan Ramón's poetry not only defines the modernity of the works he wrote during a period extending from about 1915 through the 1920s but also suggests why he would become a model for several younger poets of the Generation of 1927. These poets, as Dámaso Alonso has indicated, began their poems not by reacting against prior traditions, but rather by relating their work to the aesthetic achievements of preceding poets (1969, 160–62). Their interest in and homage to Luis de Góngora reflected their early desire to elevate art above everyday existence, to give it greater value and universality. Given these goals, Juan Ramón's work would naturally be a model for them; its quest for an essential expression devoid of excessive ingenuity and verbal play exemplified their own ideal of poetry's presentness and timelessness (ibid. 164).

This view of the Generation of 1927 is not new. Having adopted the generational method as the main system for organizing Spanish literary history, many critics have defined something like two decades of Spanish poetry as the realm of this generation, which by consensus includes Jorge Guillén, Pedro Salinas, Federico García Lorca, Vicente Aleixandre, Dámaso Alonso, Gerardo Diego, Luis Cernuda, Emilio Prados, and Manuel Altolaguirre. Discussion and debate have centered on the main characteristics of its poetry, on the degree to which it could be considered aestheticist or escapist, on how it did or did not embody basic human concerns (see Debicki 1981, 29–52). What most prior critics have not seen, however, is that some of the main traits attributed to this generation are part of the general aesthetic climate and are shared by the older and supposedly *modernista* Juan Ramón Jiménez, by Antonio and Manuel Machado, by Unamuno and Valle Inclán. A clearer and more accurate picture emerges, in my opinion, if we first concentrate on several characteristics of all major works published between 1915 or so and the late 1920s that fulfill the poetics of the modernist tradition.

As we draw this picture, we continue witnessing the search for presentness and for aesthetic transcendence in the poetics and the poetry of most writers of the time, who together produced the apogee of the poetry of modernity in Spain. The poetics I have discussed do not constitute the only important current of the time; in the next chapter I will examine a countervailing one, which appears in vanguardist writing and in the verse of Pedro Salinas and Miguel Hernández, which presages a later shift in sensibility during the 1930s, and which perhaps even points ahead to a later move beyond modernity.

For the 1920s, however, the dominant line was the one represented by Juan Ramón and Jorge Guillén. The belief in poetic transcendence and the search for universality in art were dominant postures of the time, rising out of the symbolist tradition and superseding a prior realistic aesthetic. After 1915 one could no longer assert with any confidence the realistic goal of portraying an objective world with accuracy: recent scientific formulations, vanguard literature, and texts such as Unamuno's *Niebla* (1915), with its metafictional questioning of the author by a character in the novel, had made it impossible. A modernist vision of art as elevated above the everyday, and as the embodiment of higher realities, offered writers a countervailing goal. (This goal has been linked, at times, with ideological positions; Christopher Soufas offers valuable insights in this regard, though at the peril of understating formal and aesthetic concerns.)

As long as we situate it within this larger perspective of a dominant modernist aesthetic, a generational perspective can help explain the more specific ideas and contributions of the younger poets emerging in the 1920s. As both Julián Marías and José Arrom have indicated, writers growing up in one place at one time necessarily share intellectual climates, influences, and responses. Marías (drawing on José Ortega y Gasset) and Arrom differ in their application of this approach, but both make a good case for using the outlook of an emerging generation to illuminate a specific period. The poets of the Generation of 1927, all born between 1891 (Salinas) and 1902 (Alberti, Cernuda), in fact best illuminate the various nuances of the high modernist poetic as it acquired a dominant role in Spain in the 1920s and early 1930s. And they articulated it most forcefully and coherently, as they became prominent at this time.[14]

Most of these poets met in Madrid in the early 1920s, studied at the university, took part in various literary events, and were influenced, for the most part, by the intellectual and cultural milieu of the Residencia de Estudiantes. Only Gerardo Diego, and to a lesser degree Pedro Salinas, were deeply involved in the more iconoclastic avant-garde movements of the period, although all of the poets were aware of French and European aesthetic currents and developments. Many of them spent time in France, some for long periods (Salinas between 1914 and 1917, Guillén between 1917 and 1923). Almost all of them had a superb background in Western literature, which they deepened over time. Spanish poetry of the Middle Ages, Renaissance, and Golden Age had the greatest impact on the poets of this generation: it offered them models of the transcendence that they sought in their art and led many of them to a traditionalist posture that paralleled those of Eliot and British modernism. The lectures and studies that several of them did on Luis de Góngora, and the symposia and activities in his honor that the group organized, served as affirmation of a poetry at once artful, polished, imagistic, and significant, a poetry that would represent perfectly the ideal of embodying and making present universal human values. These goals dovetailed with their predilection for Darío, Bécquer, Mallarmé, Valéry, and the imagists (see Alonso 1969; Guillén 1961, 206–7).

Consonant with this program, the generation adopted mentors who embodied the modernist aesthetic and thus presaged its poetic stance. Much as it admired Machado, it was, as I have noted, more drawn to Juan Ramón Jiménez (Guillén 1961, 204). Another guide was José Ortega y Gasset, in whose *Revista de Occidente* and in books published by its press several of them issued their early work. As Guillén later suggested, Ortega might have misunderstood this generation's goals when he described a "dehumanization" of art (ibid. 191). Ortega's universalizing philosophical vision, however, and his view of imagery as creation of a higher reality would appeal to these writers.

This generation grew up inheriting the symbolist vision of art, spent the decade of the 1920s affirming it and attempting to exemplify it, and slowly became the leader of a high modernity until it was modified and replaced in later decades. As time went on, its members acquired increasing influence through their books, through magazines that they founded (Guillén's *Verso y Prosa*, Diego's *Carmen*, *Litoral* ["Coast"], *Gallo* ["Rooster"]), and through academic posts (Salinas and Guillén). The two editions of Gerardo Diego's anthology of modern Spanish poetry (1932, 1934), constructed in consultation with his fellow poets, retrospectively helped define canonical parameters. They included poets from Darío to the members of the generation and through their poetry selections and statements of poetics emphasized what I have called the high modernist perspective. The generation's growing leadership role, in fact, motivated some criticisms and jealousies on the part of older poets, exemplified by

Antonio Machado's negative comments and by Juan Ramón's peevish refusal to be included in Diego's second anthology.[15]

A typically modernist vision underlies various statements on poetics by members of this generation, which almost converge into a program for raising reality to a higher plane and preserving human experience through language. Federico García Lorca, in a lecture delivered at the Residencia de Estudiantes in Madrid in 1927, at the tercentenary of Góngora's death, ascribed the baroque poet's greatness to his way of elevating reality and preserving its essence: "Se dió cuenta de la fugacidad del sentimiento humano . . . y quiso que la belleza de su obra radicara en la metáfora limpia de realidades que mueren, metáfora construída con espíritu escultórico y situada en un ambiente extraatmosférico" (García Lorca 1957a, 70). {"He realized the fleetingness of human feeling . . . and wanted the beauty of his work to rest in a metaphor free of mortal realities, a metaphor constructed with a sculptor's spirit and situated in an extra-atmospheric milieu."}

In a brief essay also written in 1927, Guillén stressed Góngora's ability to organize reality into its ideal shape, making it timeless. Guillén defined himself, in the process, as modern: "[Góngora] acepta su mundo. . . . Debe nada más ordenar sus elementos, conforme a un ideal que los propios elementos están demandando. . . . Góngora, buen clásico, es el primero de los modernos" (Guillén 1980, 320). { "[Góngora] accepts his world. . . . He only has to organize its elements in accord with an ideal that the elements themselves require. . . . Góngora, a good classic, is the first of modern writers."} A similar vision of poetry permeates Guillén's numerous critical writings of the 1920s, as K.M. Sibbald has made clear, and dovetails with his cultural traditionalism and his European outlook (Sibbald 444–47).[16] This vision governed Guillén's poetics for decades and culminated in the following words from an essay commenting on the goal of his own book of poetry *Cántico:* "Y el cántico se resuelve en una forma cuyo sentido y sonido son indivisibles. Pensamiento y sentimiento, imagen y cadencia deben asentar un bloque, y sólo en ese bloque puede existir lo que se busca: poesía" (1969, 95–96). {"And the canticle is resolved in a form whose sense and sound are indivisible. Thought and feeling, image and cadence, must form one block, and only in that block can there exist what one seeks: poetry."} Guillén here sees the poem as an object, similar to a statue or a painting, which maintains its identity for its readers (see Zardoya 1974, 2: 211). This conception of his art, at once idealistic and logocentrically concrete, leads to Guillén's retrospective assessment of the achievements of his own generation: "Reality . . . was not duplicated by mere copying but was re-created in the freest manner possible" (1961, 207).

Pedro Salinas has discussed the relationship of poetry to reality in even more explicit terms. In a 1935 review of Guillén's *Cántico,* he defined a poet's task as follows:

Su labor no puede ser otra sino transmutar la realidad material en realidad poética. Si la poesía de Guillén, siendo tan real, es al par tan antirealista y da una sensación tan perfecta de mundo purificado, esbelto, platónico . . . es por lo potente y eficaz de su instrumento de transmutación. [Salinas 1983, 1: 153]

{His work can be no other than to transform material reality into poetic reality. If the poetry of Guillén, being so real, is simultaneously so unrealistic and gives such a perfect sense of a purified, sleek, platonic world . . . it is due to the powerful and effective instrument of transformation.}

These words clearly derive from a modernist poetic of the work as at once a means of transcending ordinary reality and a correlative for the poet's higher vision of things. Such a poetic also dominated Salinas's criticism throughout his career, though with some nuances that differentiate him from his contemporaries. It culminated in his book *Reality and the Poet in Spanish Poetry* (based on a series of lectures at Johns Hopkins in 1937), which unfolds on the following premises: "Reality is indispensable to the poet, but it alone is not enough. . . . Reality must be revised, confirmed, approved by the poet. And he confirms or re-creates it by means of a word, by merely putting it into words. . . . And the poet is therefore the one who uses language best, who utilizes most completely its power . . . of giving a reality distinct and poetic to indistinct, crude reality" (Salinas 1940, 4–5).

This heightening process resulted, for Salinas, in the creation of a timeless work: "Apenas comienza a existir la poesía, el poeta percibe el poder que en ella late para inmortalizar lo que canta" ("Aprecio y defensa del lenguaje" ["Appreciation and Defense of Language," 1944] in Salinas 1961, 41). {"Barely has poetry begun to exist, when the poet perceives the power that it possesses to immortalize that which it sings."} Yet this very modernist emphasis on poetry's power to embody experience was coupled, for Salinas, with a view of reality as ambiguous and incomplete, as needing to be recast, reinvented, rewritten. This view later led him to write criticism anticipating post-structuralist and reader-response studies. It also connects Salinas to the avant-garde and Vicente Huidobro (see Silver 1985, 128–29) and explains how his poetry ties in with a different strand of the twentieth century (see chapter 2). The focus on the poem as an attempt to preserve meaning, however, leaves Salinas's ideas within the mainstream of modernity.

A similarly modernist view of poetry appears in the early writings of Dámaso Alonso, the outstanding critic of this generation as well as a poet of major importance. Alonso's doctoral dissertation on the poetic language of Góngora, completed in the tricentennial year of 1927, aims to show how the poet's particular style converts traditional techniques into instruments for creating and preserving beauty (Alonso 1935). A like purpose underlies

Alonso's lecture delivered at the symposium in Góngora's honor in Seville that same year, which uses the balance between popular and learned traditions in Spain to defend the universality of Spanish poetry (Alonso 1960, 11–28). Alonso's view of poetry's goal is best summarized in the following sentence of a 1931 book review: "Se produce en el poeta el maravilloso salto desde la materia caduca de nuestra vida a la permanente del arte" (Alonso 1931, 245). {"The marvelous jump from the fleeting materials of our life to the permanent life of art occurs in the poet."}

Similar attitudes toward poetry can also be derived from the verse of Alberti, Cernuda, Prados, and other members of this generation, as Biruté Ciplijauskaité has indicated (1966, 359–64). The following sentence by Cernuda reads like a compendium of the modernist stance: "El poeta intenta fijar la belleza transitoria del mundo que percibe, refiriéndola al mundo invisible que presiente" (Cernuda 1965, 199–200). {"The poet aims to fix the transitory beauty of the world that he perceives, transposing it to the invisible world that he intuits."}

Inheriting and developing to its ultimate consequences the idealistic vision that had come down to them from the symbolists, the Spanish poets of the Generation of 1927 exemplified the logocentric stance of high modernity, by which the verbal work of art objectifies human values and preserves them forever. This stance is also related to the "mystique of purity," the desire to define the poem as a perfect, pure, and perennial reality situated above ordinary life.[17]

The issue of "pure poetry" had triggered an important debate in France in 1925, which in turn stirred reactions in Spain. A lecture by Henri Brémond, advocating, rather mystically, a vague, ineffable purity for poetry, drew a critical response from Paul Valéry and others. Valéry, taking a more technical stance, saw poetic purity as something achieved by eliminating from the poem all impure elements. The controversy was reported by Fernando Vela in the *Revista de Occidente* in 1926 (see Blanch 198–204). The Spanish poets generally took Valéry's side. Jorge Guillén, in a letter to Vela, later reprinted as Guillén's poetics in Gerardo Diego's classic anthology of contemporary poetry, objected to Brémond's vagueness and stressed the need to craft, with precision, a transcendent poem. At the same time he indicated his own support for a poetry that would be pure, but not excessively so, and could construct meaning out of any materials and language.[18]

The importance attributed to this issue and debate makes clear not only the dominant symbolist stance of Spanish poetry at this time but also its concrete goal of capturing transcendent meanings in verbal form. This view of poetry's task can be linked, with some reason, to an antimaterialist and even anticapitalist attitude (Soufas 29–30, 56, 243). For me, nevertheless, it is more important to situate it within the idealism of a highly creative moment of cultural history, in which poets and writers sought, beyond personal concerns, larger goals for their art and attempted to render present, timeless, and universal the experiences they turned into poetry. Their idealism was of course made possible by the relative stability of Spanish society in the decade of the 1920s, by the ease with which ideas and aesthetic concepts circulated, by the contacts between Madrid, Paris, and London, by the upper-middle-class background of the poets. What seems central, nevertheless, is the result: a poetry of great value, even for us who can no longer share the poetics out of which it was engendered.

The Poem as Icon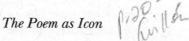

A modernist stance based on the idealistic vision I have been tracing can illuminate the actual poems written at this time by this generation. The attempt to embody poetically an essential vision of beauty, which we saw in Juan Ramón's "Mariposa de luz," also underlies Guillén's *Cántico* ("Canticle"), especially in its first two editions, of 1928 and 1936.[19] We can see it illustrated in "Perfección" ("Perfection"):

> Queda curvo el firmamento,
> Compacto azul, sobre el día.
> Es el redondeamiento
> Del esplendor: mediodía.
> Todo es cúpula. Reposa
> Central sin querer, la rosa
> A un sol en cenit sujeta.
> Y tanto se da el presente
> Que el pie caminante siente
> La integridad del planeta.
> [Guillén 1987, 1: 250]

{The firmament stands curved, compact, blue, over the day. It is the rounding out of splendor: noon. All is a cupola. The rose reposes, central without intending to be, subject to the sun at zenith. And the present gives itself so fully that the walking foot senses the wholeness of the planet.}

We can easily read this text as an attempted icon of perfection. It does not offer a detailed realistic landscape or a logical explanation of why this scene is deemed perfect. Instead, it contains a very precise verbal and syntactical pattern that tries to embody the sense of timeless order. In lines 1–4, a series of adjectives and nouns (*curved, compact, rounding out, cupola*) evoke a geometric scheme that functions as an archetype of perfection. The visual scene described also conveys harmony: a semicircle of sky up above, the sun in the middle, the earth below, with the rose at its center. No action occurs: the verbs, all of them in the present tense, mark stasis rather than motion. Human presence is reduced to the synecdoche of the foot, tangibly (perhaps even sensually) yet schematically embodying the perception of timeless order.[20]

The vision of reality emerging from "Perfección" is confirmed throughout the first two editions of *Cántico*. Guillén organizes his poems in symmetrical groups: the first *Cántico* is divided into five well-balanced parts, the second into seven. (Later editions returned to a five-part structure.) New poems are inserted into various sections, not added at the end of the book. Early poems of sections often refer to dawn, while those portraying dusk and night tend to appear late. Harmonious forms reflect the theme of reality's harmonies.

As I have discussed elsewhere, concrete referents are used to underline universal schemes throughout the work. Metonymic patterns often lead to larger symbolic visions; in "Naturaleza viva" ("Living Nature" or "Living Still Life"), for example, the process by which a tree becomes a perfect table points to reality's orderly continuity. Various structural schemes pervade most of the texts, with a predominance of circular organizations (Debicki 1973, 19–50, 166 ff.). The joyous affirmation that emerges as we read the book is founded on the persona's discovery, behind the events of his daily existence, of larger patterns of life. In that sense, lyric form and expression are the vehicles for elevating human life into a higher and more cosmic perception of presence. Christopher Soufas has argued that *Cántico* offers not a declaration of the innate beauty of reality, but rather a willful transformation of reality, a projection of the persona's attitude (53–62). For Soufas, this is a sign of the rejection of a capitalist milieu; I would call it an example of idealistic aestheticism that emerges from the modernist vision, based on symbolist tenets.

Today's postmodern reader could well object to the premises behind my analysis of "Perfección" and my discussion of *Cántico*. The very possibility of "embodying" any meaning or experience in verbal forms is placed into question by our awareness that signs are unstable, that a perfect correspondence between intuition and verbal expression is an impossibility (see De Man 1971). My analysis and discussion, however, pretend to historical rather than critical validity: they do not argue for a "correct" reading of Guillén, but rather for a sympathetic understanding of the poetic quest and vision that underlie his work.

Federico García Lorca's earlier poetry also reveals its modernist and symbolist filiation. Although his first book, *Libro de poemas* ("Book of Poems") contains mood pieces and vignettes of a personified nature that recall Bécquer and Juan Ramón, it also possesses some compelling images and a theme that will pervade all of the poet's work: the effort to stop time, to expand human experiences, and to preserve such experiences from death and decay. This theme becomes more dominant in *Canciones* ("Songs") and *Primeras canciones* ("Early Songs"), composed between 1921 and 1924, *Poema del cante jondo* ("Poem of the Cante Jondo"), written in 1921, and the *Romancero gitano* ("Gypsy Ballads"), written between 1924 and 1933.[21] In *Canciones* and *Primeras canciones* Lorca draws on the tradition of Spanish popular poetry to create sharp, short texts, often using parallel construction and sharply delineated images to highlight essential life patterns. In "Remansillo" ("Small Pool"), for example, basic colors evoke the basic moods and themes of purity, passion, and death. They may also point, as Soufas has suggested, to the poet's inability to seize more than "the memory of his own desolate image" (172):

> Me miré en tus ojos
> pensando en tu alma.
> *Adelfa blanca.*
> Me miré en tus ojos
> pensando en tu boca.
> *Adelfa roja.*
> Me miré en tus ojos.
> ¡Pero estabas muerta!
> *Adelfa negra.*
> [García Lorca 1957b, 273–74]

{I looked at myself in your eyes, thinking of your soul: white oleander. I looked at myself in your eyes, thinking of your mouth: red oleander. I looked at myself in your eyes, but you were dead! Black oleander.}

In the *Poema del cante jondo* Lorca on the one hand personifies different elements and kinds of "cante jondo" and on the other stylizes various aspects of reality. By so doing he underscores larger themes, above all the power of song and of art in general to magnify and to preserve human experiences. "Las seis cuerdas" ("Six Strings") offers a good example:

> La guitarra,
> hace llorar a los sueños.
> El sollozo de las almas
> perdidas,
> se escapa por su boca
> redonda.
> Y como la tarántula
> teje una gran estrella
> para cazar suspiros,
> que flotan en su negro
> aljibe de madera.
> [García Lorca 1957b, 241–42]

{The guitar makes dreams cry. The whimpering of lost souls escapes from its round mouth. And like the tarantula, it weaves a great star to hunt down sighs that float in its black wooden well.}

The guitar's song embodies the expression of otherwise hidden feelings. Personified, it becomes the agent for their release and for their conversion into artistic form. By stylizing the scene, hiding the guitar player, and transforming the guitarist's hand into a tarantula, Lorca takes focus off any anecdote and places stress on this larger theme. The theme, nevertheless, is vividly captured in the imagery: the inchoate nature of unexpressed feelings is emphasized by the image of the guitar as a deep well, while the miracle of converting feeling to art is stressed by the tarantula's weaving of a star. Image and form produce a correlative and a compelling experience, in a text that, for all its Spanish materials, recalls the poetry of the British imagists.

The echoes of Spanish popular poetry of the Middle Ages and Renaissance ("poesía de tipo tradicional") in Lorca's, Alberti's, Alonso's, and Altolaguirre's verse reflect the goal of seizing meanings in sparse and exact form. Though at the opposite end of a scale from Góngora, popular poetry represented for the Generation of 1927 the other classic Spanish model for the verbal representation of human experience.[22]

Keeping in mind Lorca's underlying drive to render wider meanings in poetic form, we can see the gypsy protagonists of his *Romancero gitano* not as characters in a specific narration but rather as archetypes, as embodiments of a will to beauty that asserts itself against the limitations of ordinary life. Combining metaphor and metonymy, Lorca created visions of exceptional power that testify to his goal of making poetry magnify and preserve the most worthwhile elements of human life. In "Reyerta" ("Fight," or "Feud") for example, a series of extraordinary metaphors convert a scene of death into a vision of beauty: a bleeding man becomes an aesthetic image. "Su cuerpo lleno de lirios / y una granada en las sienes" (García Lorca 1957b, 357). {"His body full of lilies / and a pomegranate on his temples."} In "Muerte de Antoñito el Camborio" ("Death of Antoñito the Camborian"), the protagonist's courage in the face of death engenders images of beauty that again convert him, and the poem, into a correlative of aesthetic values that can be preserved through the art of the poem (ibid. 375–76).

Luis Cernuda's *Perfil del aire* ("Profile of Air," 1927; recast as "Primeras poesías" ["First Poems"] in Cernuda's complete works, *La realidad y el deseo* ["Reality and Desire"]) is dominated by natural scenes and images. These are presented as enigmatic and fleeting, yet containing essential intuitions:

No es el aire puntual
El que tiende esa sonrisa,
En donde la luz se irisa
Tornasol, sino el cristal;
Que de tan puro, imparcial
Su materia transparente
Hurta a los ojos, ausente
Con imposible confín,
Porque su presencia en fin
Tan sólo el labio la siente.
[Cernuda 1964, 20]

{It is not the punctual air that tenders this smile, in which light rises as sunflower, but water; which, being so pure and impartial, so absent and limitless, steals its transparent matter from the eyes; its presence, finally, is only felt by the lips.}

Natural light is fleeting and inexplicable and does not reach the speaker directly. Yet it possesses a vividness that he can apprehend through its reflection, sensually and irrationally. Cernuda uses a mixture of description, stylized metaphor, and personification to heighten the sense of nature's values and mysteries; in the process, he elevates and mythifies personal experiences into universal artistic ones.

Somewhat similar experiences are produced by Emilio Prados's poetry of the 1920s, which also forges correspondences between natural processes and human life. In *Cuerpo perseguido* ("Pursued Body," written in 1927 and 1928) Prados uses syntactic patterns, images, and personifications to make his language reflect the way in which human life fits within the larger patterns of natural cycles. Poem 3 of its first part, for example, juxtaposes parts and features of the speaker to nature:

Quisiera estar por donde anduve
Como la rama, como el cuerpo;
como en el sueño, como por la vida;
igual que sin la frente, sin la sombra;
como la mano, como el agua.
[Debicki 1981, 355–56]

{I would wish to be where I walked, like the branch, like the body, like in dreams, like in life, as without my forehead, as without the shadows, like the hand, like the water.}

The chain of parallel similes reflects the fusion of human and natural elements into a timeless whole. Word and structure again function to embody verbally a subjective attitude and outlook.

Much of the poetry of Manuel Altolaguirre also uses regular patterns of form and image to engender feeling. Like Prados, Altolaguirre explores

relationships between human and natural patterns. His early poems of-
ten adopt the orderly, rhythmic, yet simple schemes of old popular-style
Spanish poetry. Altolaguirre collected and recast his poems in various
editions, including several versions of *Las islas invitadas* ("Invited Is-
lands"). His interest in form and in the concrete embodiment of aesthetic
meaning is also clear from his career as editor and publisher. Altolaguirre
began it by founding, in Málaga, the beautiful magazine and poetry series
Litoral, which issued many important works of the Generation of 1927. He
later founded and directed other magazines and series in Spain, in Paris,
and in Mexico and was personally responsible for extremely elegant, aes-
thetically pleasing publications, which make clear that he and his colleagues
strove for the preservation of poetic experiences in form and in time.[23]

From a formal and stylistic point of view, the poetry of Rafael Alberti is
the most heterogeneous of this generation. His *Marinero en tierra* ("Sailor on
Land," 1925) and *La amante* ("The Beloved," 1926) echo popular Spanish
poetry; via a rich variety of metaphoric techniques and personifications, the
short texts of these books sharply portray feelings of illusion, nostalgia, con-
flict, unrequited love. In *El alba del alhelí (1925–1926)* ("The Dawn of the
Wallflower," 1927) the poems are longer, and short vignettes give way to di-
alogues and dramatic scenes, although the same themes appear. *Cal y canto*
("Lime and Song," 1929) marks a surprising change, as Alberti consciously
adopts Gongorine style and imagery, in an overt homage (and experiment).
Later, in *Sobre los ángeles* ("Over the Angels," 1929), surrealist images portray
a symbolic cityscape, projecting a sense of warring forces and an overall pic-
ture of disillusion and anguish. In the 1930s Alberti developed a revolu-
tionary outlook and began writing social verse.

There are several ways of finding common ground among these stylisti-
cally disparate books. A thematic approach will reveal an underlying conflict
between idealism and disillusionment; a stylistic one can show the repeated
use of certain objectifying techniques (see Salinas de Marichal, esp. 144,
178, 258–60). In an earlier study, I used the concept of an "objective cor-
relative" to shed light on a repeated way of objectifying emotive states (De-
bicki 1981, 265–304). Soufas, noting Alberti's early career as a painter and
his search for "new representational mediums," draws a convincing picture
of the poet's never-satisfied quest in language and in society, a series of
failed attempts and alienations that led, finally, to political answers
(201–38). All of these hypotheses prove useful; in Alberti's case, different
angles of vision yield different answers. Perhaps if we place them in a his-
torical perspective, they can be brought together.

If we think of Alberti's poetry of the 1920s within the modernist tradi-
tion that I have been tracing, we will see the different styles of his books as
succeeding steps in poetry's constant quest for turning experience into pres-

ence, into timeless verbal form. Regardless of any conscious or unconscious intention on the part of the real author, Alberti's heterogeneous poems constitute diverse attempts to verbally draw, and hence detain, an experience. In my earlier study, I examined the following text as an example of an objective correlative:

Limpias

La vaca. El verde del prado,
todavía.

Pronto, el verde de la mar,
la escama azul de la pescado,
el viento de la bahía
y el remo para remar. [Alberti 107]

{Limpias.[24] The cow. The green of the field, still there. Soon, the green of the sea, the blue scales of the fish, the wind of the bay, and the oar for rowing.}

Each stanza embodies a different mood and atmosphere; the poem creates a contrast between a slow, possibly pedestrian effect produced by the land scene and the swift, playful, rhythmic effect of the sea. Caesura, rhythm, and sound emphasize the former, whereas a rapid rhythm highlights the latter. The contrast is made obvious by the juxtaposition of "cow" to "fish," of "still" to "soon." A New Critical analysis could go on and on (see Debicki 1981, 272–73). Yet all it would prove, ultimately, is that a fairly inconsequential scene has served as a basis for a beautifully arranged verbal construct that, if its reader cooperates, makes present an archetypal sensation of contrasting sluggishness and speed, lethargy and rhythm.

If we turn to the Gongorine poems of *Cal y canto*, we will of course note a dramatic shift in style. Yet behind it there is a very similar way of focusing on a scene, transforming it through image and word, and thus making present and concrete a subjective attitude. *Sobre los ángeles* raises other issues: its surrealist filiation and many of its tactics and effects bring in a different way of using imagery to produce experience and mark a shift within Spanish modernity. Yet even in this book, images and symbols configure basic moods and attitudes, as different angels reflect diverse traits, including anger, goodness, and stupidity. Perhaps Rafael Alberti illustrates as well as any of his generational colleagues the quest and the premises of high modernity: to convert human impulses and reactions to form, to verbal construct; to transcend one's own limited experiences by turning them into texts; to turn what is time-limited into the timeless. Futile as that goal may seem to us today, it continues to evoke our admiration.

2

Currents in Spanish Modernity, 1915–1939

A Strand of Indeterminacy, 1915–1928

The idealistic poetics that dominated the 1920s in Spain, and that influenced the major lyric texts of the decade, were somewhat counterbalanced by a different current, consisting of avant-garde writings. This second current was not directly related to the canonical poetry of the decade, and it lets us see another strand of modernity, one that bears a relation to poetic works and movements of succeeding decades and to a much later transition from modernity to postmodernity.

In describing the development of European modernity, Marjorie Perloff saw a continuing tension between a symbolist and an antisymbolist poetics and mode. The former, of course, fits the concept of high modernity that I discussed in chapter 1 and the notion of the poem as an embodiment of the eternal present. The latter, which Perloff traces back to Rimbaud and finds exemplified in Gertrude Stein, Ezra Pound, and William Carlos Williams, views the function of poetry (and of art in general) as process, as play, as an expression of experiences resistant to closure, to organization, to logical definition.

Perloff's scheme raises thorny questions, because many of the traits she attributes to the antisymbolist current of modernity were used by later critics (especially Ihab Hassan and Jean-François Lyotard) to define the *post*-modern. Yet it is not useful to call their occurrence in 1915 or 1922 an example of postmodernity, since that would contradict the underlying chronological implications of this term. More important, and as we will see later, the indeterminacy that emerged in the poetics and poetry of the 1960s and 1970s had a much more all-encompassing effect and a clearer link to various cultural phenomena and thus can be more easily tied to the notion of postmodernity. The strand of indeterminacy of the 1920s appeared more as a minority voice that provided a challenge and a shading to the dominant symbolist mode.[1] It was still generally expressed within an assertion of the independence and the value of art and hence still retained a connection to the main line of modernity. In any event, this strand, though secondary, developed and reappeared in several ways throughout the late 1920s and the 1930s. It did contribute to significant modifications of the dominant symbolist tradition of poetry at that time.[2]

In Spain, a modern yet antisymbolist attitude to literature was already presaged as early as 1908, in the magazine *Prometeo* and the work of Ramón Gómez de la Serna, its editor. Influenced by Italian futurism—Gómez de la Serna translated and introduced Marinetti's futurist manifesto in the magazine in 1910—*Prometeo* took an iconoclastic and irreverent approach to art (Geist 1980, 29; Videla 15–19). In that attitude lie the seeds of the antisymbolist vision: literature expresses a will to perform, not a desire to embody transcendent meanings. Such an attitude also crystallized in discussions among a group of young writers who, from 1915 on, gathered around Gómez de la Serna at the Café Pombo in Madrid. It underlies Gómez de la Serna's *Greguerías,* published in 1919. The *greguerías,* although listed as prose, consist of metaphors like those constructed by *ultraísta* and *creacionista* poets writing between 1920 and 1925 or so, all of whom knew Gómez de la Serna and his work (Videla 21). Explicitly defined as a combination of metaphor and joke by its author (ibid. 19), a *greguería* produces unexpected linkages and is intended to let the reader extend its meanings. Because it stands alone and does not point to larger issues—which for Gustav Siebenmann makes it inferior to a coherent poem (215)—the *greguería* is indeterminate and nontranscendent, in contrast to the symbolist metaphor.

In *ultraísta* and *creacionista* writings and magazines we find the best early examples of the antisymbolist aspect of Spanish modernity. The *ultraístas* came into existence in Madrid around 1918, after the Chilean poet Vicente Huidobro visited there on his way back home from Paris. Huidobro's reports about aesthetic developments in France stimulated a group of young poets, more or less led by Rafael Cansinos-Asséns. They began to meet at the Café Colonial, wrote the first of several manifestos, and planned the publication of the magazine *Ultra,* of which twenty-four issues were eventually published between January 1921 and February 1922. They also took over *Grecia* and *Cervantes* and published poems and essays in a number of other ephemeral magazines. By 1923 or 1924 *ultraísmo* had pretty much faded away. The same magazines also published works by Huidobro and by the Spanish poet Gerardo Diego, who consciously identified himself with *creacionismo.*

Ultraísta manifestos revealed a generally iconoclastic attitude toward art rather than any coherent aesthetic or any specific definition of goals or styles. (The first manifesto noted, in fact, that all novel tendencies would be admissible until later definitions were worked out.) Yet certain concepts kept appearing in these documents: the primacy of metaphor, the function of art as play, the need to free poetry from the bonds of reality and of linguistic rules (Videla 33–34, 47–48, 63).

Gerardo Diego and other writers who identified themselves with *creacionismo* sought a more specific poetics. It grew out of Huidobro's statements: the Chilean had exhorted poets to stop imitating nature and instead to parallel its workings, constructing poems just as nature constructs trees (Videla 101). On examination, this statement may be less radical than it seems and may merely constitute an advocacy of less realistic metaphors.

Diego, however, took Huidobro's notion one important step further, toward indeterminacy. In an essay published in *Cervantes* in 1919, he advocated "multiple images" that would mean different things to different people. Such images would make poetry like music, which, he stated, has no meaning of its own ("no quiere decir nada") and is there so that everyone can give it his or her own meaning (quoted in Geist 1980, 57; and Videla 109).[3] Ingenuous as this idea might seem to a music critic, it suggests an overtly antisymbolist stance. Such a stance is also implied in a statement by Diego in his anthology of modern Spanish poetry, which ends "crear lo que nunca veremos, esto es la Poesía" (Diego 1962, 379). {"To create that which we will never see, that is Poetry."}[4]

Only one other poet included in Diego's anthology described the poem as indeterminate. Mauricio Bacarisse, by no means a member of avant-garde circles (he was an essayist, secondary school literature teacher, and insurance company representative), boldly asserted that a poetic text, and more specifically a poetic image, was not "inert" but was free to develop meaning on its own: "Las metáforas . . . cobran existencia y viven su vida" (Diego 1962, 245). {"Metaphors . . . gain existence and live their lives."} This view added one more note to the strain of indeterminacy.

The *ultraísta* and *creacionista* perspective differed significantly from the one prevailing among the Generation of 1927 poets, who, along with some older canonical figures, dominated Diego's anthology. Wanting to counteract the commonplaces of *modernista* verse and the literalism of realistic prose, the avant-garde poets adopted a nihilistic attitude and an antiestablishment posture. If later statements are to be believed, most of them advocated a separation of politics and art (Buckley and Crispin 394–413). Yet as Juan Cano Ballesta has noted, some of them professed revolutionary politics; almost all of them rebelled against lyric subjectivism as well as bourgeois complacency (see Cano Ballesta 1981, chaps. 3–4). This involved in many cases an idealization of modern cosmopolitanism and technology, parallel to that of the Italian futurists (ibid. 97–109).[5]

Most important from my viewpoint, these poets rejected logocentrism and the symbolist tenet that artistic language should enshrine some cohesive set of meanings. Such rejection links them to the French avant-garde. Perloff, using Marcel Duchamp's *Large Glass* as an example, indicated how the avant-garde visual arts resisted resolution in favor of performance: "Art becomes play, endlessly frustrating our longing for certainty" (34). Likewise, dadaist and early surrealist writings used dismemberment, contrary clues, and elliptical word order to foreground the materiality of verbal expression and to stress the irreducibility of language.

The Generation of 1927 poets, on the other hand, immersed themselves in their literary tradition, fitted themselves into the dominant poetic represented by Juan Ramón Jiménez, and, rather slowly, wrote their poetry and criticism. Their first major books (and their contributions to Ortega's *Revista de Occidente*) generally appeared in 1924 or later, when vanguardism was fading away. Their writings initiated, as we have already seen, years of major poetic achievements.

There were, to be sure, significant connections between these two worlds of Spanish poetics and poetry. Several prominent writers participated in both. Gerardo Diego played a major part in vanguard activities while also working assiduously on his criticism and writing traditional as well as experimental verse. Alonso and Lorca had vanguard contacts, and the former praised Diego's vanguard writing. Pedro Salinas was in contact with the avant-garde: he published poems in *Prometeo* in 1911, was obviously influenced by Gómez de la Serna (whose effect is readily apparent in Salinas's fiction), and was affected by, and consciously responded to, *creacionismo* (see Silver 1985, 127–28). Most of the other poets of the Generation of 1927 also had connections with Gómez de la Serna. The vanguardists' emphasis on metaphor fed into the generation's quest for meaning through the creation of original imagery. All of these poets, from both strands of modernity, asserted art's vitality, importance, and independence from daily reality. All of them reacted against the literalism of prior realistic writing and the clichés of second-rate *modernistas*. One group did so by resurrecting Góngora, the other by vanguard manifestos. All avoided anecdote and sentimentality.

One cannot find clear historical and social reasons for the two strands of modernity I have outlined. Most of the poets related to symbolism came from comfortable middle-class backgrounds, were able to travel abroad and expand their cultural horizons, and developed solid academic careers. But the background of those participating in the "isms" was hardly different. What distinctions we do find between them seem based more on attitude and inclination than on social imperatives: a preference for reading and writing in one's study and attending lectures at the Residencia versus participating in a shocking *ultra* event and spending time at vanguard cafés; an inclination to build traditions and give form to meanings versus an impulse to destroy them and undercut determinacy. Some writers combined both tendencies. The second one did at times involve a protest against bourgeois society and market forces (see Geist 1992). Neither tendency motivated a significant interest in social revolution (see Cano Ballesta 1981, 127–28). I cannot see building a social history of literature out of these two strands.

Despite the posture of the Spanish *ultraístas* and *creacionistas,* the actual poems written by them do not reveal many examples of open texts. The images constructed by Pedro Garfias, Juan Larrea, Guillermo de Torre, and others are surprising in their combination of natural and mechanical elements and in their use of what Carlos Bousoño calls "visionary metaphors," whose planes are related by subjective rather than objective links (see Bousoño 1966, 106–14). But surprise does not necessitate indeterminacy: in most cases these images produce a general effect on which different readers will agree. The poetic practice of these writers thus seems to belie their theoretical postures, although some of Bacarisse's poems, which contain widely disparate metaphors and levels of discourse, do approach indeterminacy (see Diego 1962, 246).

Some *creacionista* poems by Gerardo Diego also combine widely disparate elements and seem to lack a central focus. The following lines come from "Ahogo" ("Drowning" or "Choking"; note the absence of punctuation):

> Déjame hacer un árbol con tus trenzas
> Mañana me hallarán ahorcado
> en el nudo celeste de tus venas
> Se va a casar la novia
>   del marinerito
> Haré una gran pajarita
> con sus cartas cruzadas
>   Y luego romperé
>   la luna de una pedrada
> Neurastenia, dice el doctor [Videla 129]

{Let me make a tree from your braids   Tomorrow they will find me hanged on the celestial knot of your veins   The bride of the little sailor will be married   I will make a great paper airplane with their crossed letters   And then I will crack the moon with a stone's throw   Neurasthenia, says the doctor.}

For the most part, however, this poet's surprising images still convey identifiable emotive meanings and force the reader to work out, intellectually, connections and implications. (Even the text quoted above acquires a certain justification via the reference to a doctor who seemingly explains the speaker's confusion.) Reading these poems does call for a process different from that required to understand the Machado and Guillén texts discussed in the previous chapter: it still suggests, however, that the process will yield, at the end, an identifiable experience and/or set of meanings.

This suggestion is substantiated by the history of Diego's publications. He wrote and published vanguard and traditional verse simultaneously and used both kinds to deal with similar themes. His poetic production thus forms two parallel sets of books: vanguardist writing appeared in *Imagen* ("Image," poems written between 1918 and 1921), *Manual de espumas* ("Manual of Foam," 1922), and *Biografía incompleta* ("Incomplete Biography"); more traditional forms and a poetry that verges on sentimentality were included in *El romancero de la novia* ("The Bride's Ballads," 1918), *Versos humanos* ("Human Verses," written between 1919 and 1925), and others. Different as the poems of each set may seem, both kinds use poetic techniques for similar ends. In both, a personal and often emotive theme (individual solitude, lost love), which might have led to sentimentality, is objectified via poetic form and metaphor (see Debicki 1981, 308–28). Both kinds ultimately support the symbolist goal of elevating and objectifying experience, despite Diego's denial of that goal in his statements about *creacionismo*. The very fact that Diego, like Huidobro, put such an emphasis on metaphor as a means of establishing connections and resolutions may also have kept his verse anchored to symbolism. Though seeking novelty, he kept striving for some level of determinacy, much like the other Spanish vanguardists.

The actual creative work produced by these movements was limited. Except for Diego, the Spanish *ultraístas* and *creacionistas* wrote little verse, and most of them never came close to entering the canon. Unlike Guillén or Lorca, they seemed more interested in asserting a stance than in building a body of poetry. One senses that despite the presence of some antisymbolist postures, the aesthetic climate of the decade, the pervading set of attitudes to art and its role, was not receptive to indeterminacy and hence could not be translated into many poems. Perhaps this explains why most of the Spanish *ultraístas* vanished from the literary scene by the middle of the decade, just when the Generation of 1927 was gaining prominence.

Paradoxically but not surprisingly, it was the most academic member of the Generation of 1927 who wrote, later in this decade, several books of poetry that fit within the strand of indeterminacy: Pedro Salinas, who obtained a professorship in Spanish literature at the University of Seville in 1918. As we saw in chapter 1, Salinas's poetics, with its emphasis on the poet's role in confirming reality and embodying experience, is generally consistent with a symbolist stance. Yet Salinas also saw reality as ambiguous and incomplete and viewed poetry as a means of extending it. This attitude, apparent throughout his book *Reality and the Poet in Spanish Poetry*, also motivated some studies that allude to the indeterminacy of literature (and anticipate post-structuralist criticism). In an essay written in 1935, Salinas praised Gómez de la Serna for producing "the play with realities

that do not exist"; in a later lecture on *Don Quijote,* he noted the indeter-
minacy of that novel and consequently the reader's freedom to extend it
(Salinas 1983, 1: 143, and 3: 64). All this reminds us of the relationships
between Salinas and the vanguardists and also connects with Salinas's in-
terest in Freudian psychology and in some later currents of psychological
criticism.

Salinas's attitude has direct relevance to his poetry. John Crispin has
shown that the first five poems of Salinas's initial book of verse, *Presagios*
("Presages," 1923 [1924]), are a kind of poetic creed based on the enig-
matic nature of things (41–46). Salinas's next two books, *Seguro azar*
(1924–1928) ("Certain Chance," 1929) and *Fábula y signo* ("Fable and
Sign," 1931), contain a variety of attempts at deciphering and encompass-
ing this elusive reality. They are the most indeterminate poetic texts writ-
ten in Spain at this time.

Both of these books are filled with playful evocations of modern ob-
jects, viewed with a mixture of delight and irony by the speaker (Stixrude
63–68); in both, the act of naming these objects produces multifaceted
perspectives and invites different and contradictory readings. A good ex-
ample comes from "35 bujías" ("35 Watts") in *Seguro azar.* In this poem an
unusual metaphor engenders an interplay between different interpreta-
tions of reality:

> Sí. Cuando quiera yo
> la soltaré. Está presa
> aquí arriba, invisible.
> Yo la veo en su claro
> castillo de cristal, y la vigilan
> —cien mil lanzas—los rayos
> —cien mil rayos—del sol. Pero de noche,
> cerradas las ventanas
> para que no la vean
> —guiñadoras espías—las estrellas,
> la soltaré. (Apretar un botón.)
> Caerá toda de arriba
> a besarme, a envolverme
> de bendición, de claro, de amor, pura.
> En el cuarto ella y yo no más, amantes
> eternos, ella mi iluminadora
> musa dócil en contra
> de secretos en masa de la noche
> —afuera—
> desciframos formas leves, signos,
> perseguidos en mares de blancura
> por mí, por ella, artificial princesa,
> amada eléctrica. [Salinas 1975, 136]

{Yes. When I want to, I will release her. She is imprisoned, here above, invisible. I see her in her clear crystal [or glass] castle, watched over by—a hundred thousand lances—the rays—a hundred thousand rays—of the sun. But at night, when the windows are closed so that the stars, the blinking spies, will not see her, I will release her. She will fall from above, pure, to kiss me, to surround me with blessings, with clarity, with love. In the room she and I alone, eternal lovers, she, my illumina-tor, docile muse against the massed secrets of the night outside, we will decipher light forms, signs, to be pursued in seas of whiteness by me, by her, artificial princess, electric beloved.}

The correspondence established here between lightbulb and princess contradicts our normal perspective, according to which modern artifacts belong to one realm and fairy tales and fables to another. The poem's metaphors insistently draw connections and bridges between the two realms: the light within the bulb's glass is a princess imprisoned in a castle, the flow of light a kiss, the closed windows a protection from the enemy. Salinas uses specific words that fit in either realm but acquire different meanings in each: *envolverme* and *iluminadora* can point to either, but with very different effects. Both the contrast between the stock fairy tale and the literal reality as well as the speaker's insistence on connecting them force us to notice the far-fetched nature of the metaphor.[6]

A traditional reading of this poem might seek a central meaning behind its underlying metaphor. We might suggest that modern life and chivalric romance are not totally separate, that in our ordinary reality we can find beauty and romance. Yet such a reading seems incomplete and unsatisfac-tory. It ignores the incongruity of the comparison and the humorous effect that it is bound to produce. A purely ironic reading, on the other hand, would have to ignore the speaker's (and the poem's) obvious delight at the comparison. To my mind, the poem refuses to take a single attitude to its subject, and critics who try to establish such an attitude can only construct incomplete and contradictory formulations.[7]

If we resist the temptation to find a resolution of the tensions and an underlying single attitude in "35 bujías," we can read the text in a more in-teresting light. Let us consider the dominant metaphor as a fanciful fiction, calculated to engender play and multiple levels of signification, not to seek a resolved meaning. The following three layers, as well as others, are then simultaneously possible: (1) By making the light like a princess, the speaker and the poem idealize a common scene and find romance in the everyday. (2) The speaker reveals a superior (sexist?) attitude, and his use of the fairy-tale motif reveals his view of woman as simultaneously idealized and placed under his control. (3) The poem, parodying its romance metaphor, invites the reader to laugh at the process—and perhaps at a speaker so mesmerized by the modern that he turns a lightbulb into an archetypal beloved.

Once we have thus questioned the poem's central figure, we notice other unresolved conflicts present in it. The speaker's fantasy at the end, in which the beloved joins him in his quest against darkness, undermines and is undermined by her compliant way of obeying him. Her ambiguity is reflected in the term "electric beloved": *electric* suggests vitality on the one hand, mechanical passivity on the other. *Beloved* makes us see the woman passionately descending upon the speaker, but it also conjures up the image of the compliant princess in the tower. Together with the equally ambiguous phrase "artificial princess," "electric beloved" reinforces the conflicts within the speaker and the poem.

The lack of resolution in the poem's main attitude and metaphor undercuts its ending, in which the speaker asserts a triumphant battle against darkness. "We will decipher light forms, signs," suggests a quest for meaning through textual interpretation, and a possible metapoetic bent. But given the poem's enigmas, we are more likely to judge the speaker's quest as a futile hunting for clues, which takes place in "seas of whiteness," suggesting further enigmas. Everything finally unravels, creating a play of differences and an ultimately undetermined text.[8]

The best overviews of Salinas's first three books of poetry have stressed, quite correctly, the poet's constant search for meanings hidden behind things—behind nature (in *Presagios*), behind modern artifacts (*Seguro azar* and *Fábula y signo*), behind the countenance and the appearance of the beloved (in all these books, and later in *La voz a ti debida* ["The Voice Owed to You," 1933]).[9] This search relates to the symbolist quest for ultimate meanings in poetry, which Salinas the writer, critic, and man of letters would represent and favor. Yet, rather paradoxically, many of Salinas's actual poems convey, above all, the impossibility of this quest and the undecidable nature of what we see, experience, and seek. Such an attitude toward reality also underlies Salinas's short stories written in this period, many of which appeared in the *Revista de Occidente* and all of which constitute the volume *Víspera del gozo* ("The Day before Joy," 1926). Counterposing pragmatic, causal reality to imaginary and invented ones, these stories suggest the indeterminacy of our surroundings.

The indeterminacy we find in Salinas's work constitutes an exception in the poetry of the 1920s. Once the posture of revolt that the "isms" introduced to Spanish letters had subsided, a coherent aesthetic in the symbolist tradition became prevalent, and there was no role for the vanguard (Cano Ballesta 1972, 11–12). The shift occurred, as Ramón Buckley and John Crispin note, around 1925; for quite a few years afterward, most poets sought a new "vital concept" and espoused the poetics of high modernity (10). Gómez de la Serna and other former vanguardists published in the *Revista de Occidente;* Guillermo de Torre was one of the founders of the *Gac-*

eta Literaria, which from 1927 to 1932 reported and reflected the most important European literary and artistic developments. (Its 123 issues, with many surveys and symposia on aesthetic currents and movements, document Spanish interest in such developments.) The literary mainstream in poetry was best represented by the ongoing work of Juan Ramón Jiménez and by an impressive list of books by Generation of 1927 poets, books that came to dominate the canon: Guillén's *Cántico,* Lorca's *Poema del cante jondo, Canciones,* and *Romancero gitano,* four by Alberti, and three by Salinas. With the then-unnoticed exception of the latter, all fit into the symbolist tradition.[10]

Yet even though its presence in canonical texts can barely be discerned, the strand of indeterminacy in the 1920s in Spain obviously affected thought and conversation about literature, then and later on. By pushing at the edges of current aesthetic theory, the vanguardists—and Salinas—raised major issues regarding a work's status: If the poem has independent status, how far does that extend? Can it be independent of any meaning, as well as of external reality? These issues, though relegated to the background by other historical and literary currents of the later 1920s, 1930s, and 1940s, eventually reappeared. They are related to shifts within and beyond modernity.

A Loss of Purity: Spanish Modernity, 1929–1936

A major shift within Spanish modernity did occur at the end of the 1920s; it connects with both aesthetic and politicoeconomic developments at that time. To understand it, however, one needs to step back and take into account one more element of the antisymbolist strand, which also had its origins in the early 1920s but affected Spanish letters primarily after 1928.

Surrealism had actually become familiar to most Spanish writers soon after, and in some cases even before, André Breton issued his famous manifesto in France in 1924. We know of a series of events and contacts: Breton visited Barcelona in 1922; Louis Aragon lectured in Madrid in 1925; Lorca, Luis Buñuel, and Salvador Dalí had contact with each other at the Residencia de Estudiantes; artistic exhibitions and debates took place; and essays and surveys were published in the *Gaceta Literaria,* the *Revista de Occidente,* and many small magazines (Siebenmann 330–32; Morris 12–21, 32–34; García de la Concha 1987, 1: 30–37). The effect of surrealism was more immediate in art and cinema than in literature. Nevertheless, the movement in general was well known to writers and poets. Yet overtly surrealist texts by Spanish writers before 1929 were few: a novel by José María Hinojosa (*La flor de California*), poems by Juan Larrea (despite his later denials of surrealist connections), writings by the Catalan Josep Vicens Foix. Attacked by many, portrayed inaccurately as unfamiliar by others, surrealism seems to have remained dormant and uninfluential for most of a decade, only to affect the later writings of Lorca, Alberti, Cernuda, and Aleixandre.

This should not seem surprising. As Anthony Geist has noted, the classicist impulse of the Generation of 1927 poets would make them react negatively to surrealist doctrines, above all to the concept of automatic writing, which indeed drew explicit rejection (1980, 176–78). The symbolist perspective so central to canonical Spanish poetry of the 1920s, which had become totally dominant by mid-decade as the vanguard strand faded, emphasized the goal of giving form to experience through timeless art and hence contradicted the possibilities of a surrealist poetics and poetry. This becomes evident as we look at published discussions about surrealism. Fernando Vela, in a widely mentioned essay in the *Revista de Occidente* in 1924, mixed perceptive insights on Breton's manifesto with irritated comments criticizing its advocacy of disorder.[11] Several essays in the *Gaceta Literaria* also expressed clear reservations about the movement's value (Morris 18–19; García de la Concha 1987, 1: 30).

By 1929 or so, however, the Spanish literary scene was changing, right along with Spanish history. An economic depression present throughout the West since 1929, and political and economic turmoil in Spain—leading to the fall of the monarchy and the creation of the Republic in 1931, the revolution in Asturias in 1934, and finally the outbreak of the Civil War in 1936—shattered the prior stability and ended an aesthetic climate in which writers had been able to focus on the idealistic goals of giving form to universal meanings. Literary and life issues could no longer be kept separate (see Geist 1993). Simultaneously, a natural reaction against the way in which these goals had been expressed was taking place among poets and critics. Even Dámaso Alonso, the leading figure in the canonization of Góngora, indicated in 1928 that Góngora's poetry was too abstract for the times and too lacking in vital themes. In 1927 Alonso had referred to surrealism as "una vuelta—que ya era necesaria—hacia la raíz subterránea de la inspiración poética" {"a return, which was now necessary, to the subterranean source of poetic inspiration"} (Alonso 1960, 113, 588). A few years later Alonso praised Aleixandre for bringing emotional expression back into Spanish poetry in *Espadas como labios* (Alonso 1952, 282–93). We see here a pulling away from the implicit notion that form, logically discernible structure, and order are the vehicles for poetic embodiment.

The year 1929 seems particularly crucial in marking this aesthetic shift. A renewed interest in Goya's art (motivated in 1928 by the centenary of his death), as well as the initial showing of Luis Buñuel's surrealist film *Un chien andalou,* dovetailed with the publication of Alberti's *Sobre los ángeles* and the writing of Lorca's *Poeta en Nueva York* and of Aleixandre's early poetry. All of them suggest the importance of a subjective attitude connected to surrealism.[12] As we will see, however, the poetry of this time combined surrealist

Harris's hybrid of s t & r

ist features with definable themes and meanings and did not contain inde-
terminate texts. It still followed the modernist-symbolist goal of embodying
meanings in words. The primary shift was one of style and mood: a newly
adopted form of expression emphasized newly important emotive and non-
logical areas of meaning.

This tendency intensified in the mid-1930s, as the concept of "pure po-
etry" came under attack from various sources (see Cano Ballesta 1972,
202–27). Pablo Neruda's arrival in Spain in 1934 created interest in the flow-
ing verse of his *Residencia en la tierra* ("Residence on Earth") and in the pos-
sibilities of an emotively charged poetry that would combine, in seeming
disorder, references to all levels of reality. The magazine *Caballo Verde para
la Poesía*, founded by Neruda and others in 1935, became the vehicle for ad-
vocates of an "impure" poetry, open to all dimensions of human life and es-
pecially to the expression of emotions. The polemic between the supporters
of this new mode and the defenders of purity in poetry, the latter grouped
around the magazine *Nueva Poesía* and around Juan Ramón Jiménez as their
ideal, reveals the growing shift in sensibility to a more subjective view of art.
The specific attacks on surrealism in *Nueva Poesía* indicate the establish-
ment's growing defensiveness (ibid. 213).

As Anthony Geist has indicated, this shift in mood and attitude reflected
on the one hand a personal sense of crisis, very apparent in Lorca's and Al-
berti's alienated views of modern urban life, and on the other a conscious-
ness of social breakdown and the seeds of a posture of revolt (see Geist
1993). The resulting poetry marked a subversion of the preceding idealism
of modernist art and also, at least subconsciously, of the poetics and dis-
course of high modernity.[13]

This shift in sensibility and the use of surrealist techniques was often √
combined, however, with a rejection of the surrealist label. Lorca explicitly
stated that his poems were not surrealist because they contained "poetic
logic" (Siebenmann 333).[14] Aleixandre rejected automatic writing and as-
serted his belief in the poet's conscious creation; Cernuda minimized sur-
realism's effect on him (both quoted in Morris 243, 250). These two poets
spoke from within a prevailing symbolist perspective, even as their work pre-
saged its erosion. As Juan Cano Ballesta indicated, surveys and critical essays
published in the *Gaceta Literaria* and the *Hoja Literaria* in the 1930s kept
stressing poetry's independence and transcendence; Juan Ramón Jiménez
and Paul Valéry were considered the great poets of the time (1972, 107–12).

Surrealist aesthetics, if fully accepted, would have explicitly contra-
dicted the symbolist ideal. The emphasis on the subconscious, the exercise
of automatic writing, and the delight in chance that underlie the surrealists'
view of art stand in clear opposition to symbolism. In the 1930s, however,
there were few and evasive examples of an explicit rejection of this ideal, √
and surrealist elements appeared mostly as a means of producing a more

emotively oriented verse that undermined but did not overtly contradict the symbolist tradition.

Vicente Aleixandre's work may offer the best example. Though born in 1898, the same year as Lorca, Aleixandre wrote his important work later than did his contemporaries: his first book of poetry, *Ambito* ("Milieu"), appeared in 1928. It was *Espadas como labios* ("Swords or/as Lips," 1932), *Pasión de la tierra* ("Passion of the Earth," published in 1935, though written in 1928–29), and *La destrucción o el amor* ("Destruction or/as Love," 1935), however, that really established him as an innovative poet. All of these books contain features that link them with surrealism: fantastic and nightmarish scenes, constructed from a mixture of real and invented figures; visionary metaphors based on subjective and seemingly arbitrary, rather than objective, correspondences between planes; long sentences that detour and fragment; poems in which the referent is left behind by a chain of images (see Debicki 1981, 369–72). José Olivio Jiménez has shown, however, that all these features are a means of expressing a consistent vision of life, based on the theme of a loving union and a fusion of elements. The poet endeavors to create a text that reaches beyond logic to demonstrate and hence become such a vision (Jiménez 1982, 33–39).

This does differentiate Aleixandre's poems from those of Juan Ramón or of Guillén in their break with logical patterns, their focus on the irrational and the subjective, and their nostalgic search for a unity and an origin to human life that lie beyond conscious discovery. Those traits connect Aleixandre, as José Olivio Jiménez and Manuel Durán have noted, with a mode of writing that originates in romanticism (Jiménez 1982, 36). They confirm the reaction against the conceptual and logical nature of 1920s writing, and a privileging of feeling over form. We can see these characteristics in the first three stanzas of "Unidad en ella," from *La destrucción o el amor:*

Cuerpo feliz que fluye entre mis manos,
rostro amado donde contemplo el mundo,
donde graciosos pájaros se copian fugitivos,
volando a la región donde nada se olvida.

Tu forma externa, diamante o rubí duro,
brillo de un sol que entre mis manos deslumbra,
cráter que me convoca con su música íntima,
con esa indescifrable llamada de tus dientes.

Muero porque me arrojo, porque quiero morir,
porque quiero vivir en el fuego, porque este aire de fuera
no es mío, sino el caliente aliento
que si me acerco quema y dora mis labios desde un fondo.
                                                    [Jiménez 1982, 160]

{Happy body that flows between my hands, beloved face in which I contemplate the world, where graceful fleeting birds are copied, flying to the region where nothing is forgotten. Your outward form, diamond or hard ruby, the shining of a sun that dazzles between my hands, crater that invites me with its intimate music, with this unexplainable summons of your teeth. I die because I thrust forth, because I wish to die, because I want to live in fire, because this air outside is not mine, but rather the warm breath that, if I come near, burns and gilds my lips from inside.}

The beloved disintegrates into a series of metaphors that depersonalize her. Most of them are "visionary," in Bousoño's definition: the qualities of hardness, brilliance, fieriness, and cosmic size are based not on objective features but on the subjective effects created upon the speaker (Bousoño 1966, 106–14). The images of flow and crater, while more specific in their sexual connotations, also produce something of a visionary effect. And the way in which the first stanza expands its initial image of the beloved as *cuerpo* and *rostro* into a fantastic scene of birds reflecting themselves and flying off directs us away from any rational scheme, into a mood of lush fantasy. Stanza 3 operates as a kind of *visión* (ibid. 123–33), a scene functioning as an irrational correlative of a mood.

Yet everything in these lines contributes to a single mood: the speaker presents his compenetration with the beloved as a reaching beyond his individual self, as a loss of individual life and identity, and as a fusion within natural patterns. He thus directs us to the main theme of the book, according to which love becomes an image (could we say icon?) of an elemental drive to union with the cosmos. The very title of the book points to this theme: destruction and love are synonyms, two names for the same impulse.[15] The same theme will dominate Aleixandre's poetry through *Sombra del paraíso* ("Shadows of Paradise," 1944).

This reading of Aleixandre's work situates it primarily within the symbolist strand of Spanish modernity: oriented to emotive and irrational visions though it may be, it exhibits a degree of determinacy similar to Guillén's "Perfección," and far greater than Salinas's "35 bujías." The same could be said of Lorca's *Poeta en Nueva York*, written in 1929 and 1930. Though long the subject of critical debates—it was published posthumously, and the organization of its material has been questioned—this book has recently drawn some consensus among critics. Although it contains many irrational images and nightmarish scenes, all of them finally produce a definable experience: they embody an unnatural and mechanized existence, implicitly contrasted to natural ideals (see Díez de Revenga, 1987, 178–80). *Poeta en Nueva York* does incorporate multiple tensions and contradictory voices and makes clear Lorca's loss of confidence in the poetic quest as well as in modern society (Soufas 194–98). But it does not strike one as indeterminate, as explicitly open to conflicting readings. Once we look beyond the irrationality of individual images and procedures, this book, like those by Aleixandre, fits within the symbolist canon, though it implies some erosion of the modernist vision of poetry as reflecting life's values.[16]

Something similar could be said about Rafael Alberti's *Sobre los ángeles* (1929). Here again visionary images serve to engender intense, subjective impressions of a world in decay. Ultimately, these images, and especially the unusual angels that populate the book, are correlatives for all kinds of human moods and feelings. In Alberti's *Sermones y moradas* ("Sermons and Dwellings"), written in 1929 and 1930, strings of nightmarish images dominate, and connections with surrealist notions and techniques are even more obvious. The following excerpt from "Sermón de los rayos y los relámpagos" ("Sermon of Lightning Rays") gives an example:

La ciudad que conoce la precipitación de la sangre hacia el ocaso de las coronas, se inclina del lado izquierdo de la muerte.
¡A ver!
Todas las afueras de un alma son ya ataúdes para los astros que en un segundo de lejanía prefirieron achicharrarse los rostros a revivir la última pulsación del Universo en el arrebato frío de las espadas. [Alberti 190]

{The city that knows the precipitation of blood toward the dusk of crowns, leans to the left side of death. Let's see! All the outside areas of a soul are now coffins for stars that in a second of distance preferred to burn their faces, rather than relive the last pulsations of the Universe in a cold burst of swords.}

These images operate primarily as a way of verbalizing an emotive view of human life, which expands into a more public concern (Soufas 233). Their irrationality, though it has a definite and determined purpose, does indicate a step beyond the dominant rationalism of the modernist aesthetic.

Luis Cernuda's work written after 1929 can also be related to surrealism. The theme of an unsatisfied longing in the face of an illusory and false reality had dominated Cernuda's verse from its beginnings. Expressed in controlled forms in the 1920s, it is projected into free-flowing images and visionary scenes in *Un río, un amor* ("A River, A Love"), *Los placeres prohibidos* ("Forbidden Pleasures"), and *Donde habite el olvido* ("Where Forgetfulness May Dwell"), all composed between 1929 and 1933. Even more than in the case of Lorca or Alberti, however, this style produces a tensive but very definable verse. Philip Silver has cogently described Cernuda's quest for a romantic sublime and its expression in poems that oscillate between a symbolist, metaphorical rendering and a different allegorical vision (1989, chaps. 3–4). Here we can stress Cernuda's importance in the move to subjectivity and a posture of revolt within Spanish poetry, yet also note that he did not break with the overall tenets of modernity.

Born in 1887, José Moreno Villa had written, in the first decades of the century, sensual poetry reminiscent of the early Juan Ramón Jiménez, followed by some tighter works with echoes of popular Spanish verse. Clearly responding to the spirit of the times, he then published two books filled with surprising, irrational imagery and surrealist echoes: *Jacinta la pelirroja* ("Jacinta the Redhead," 1929) and *Carambas* (1931). The new style seems to reflect an impulse to capture the subjective effects of personal experiences and to fit his work to the prevalent mood.

One other, unjustly neglected poet needs to be mentioned at this point. As I have discussed elsewhere, between 1928 and 1936 Ernestina de Champourcin published three books of poetry in which visionary metaphors, patterns of personification and depersonification, and a mixture of diverse planes of reality produce imaginative and emotive experiences (Debicki 1988). Reviews of her work suggest that its neglect was caused by clichéd assumptions about women's poetry and by a consequent inability of critics to see the originality of her verse.

Pedro Salinas's books of poetry written at this time, *La voz a ti debida* (1933), *Razón de amor* ("Reason for Love," 1936), and *Largo lamento* ("Long Lament," published posthumously), do not have any significant surrealist connections, and in many ways they continue the questioning of reality that defined his prior work. Yet the presence of an underlying love theme and story line suggests a more personal and subjective perspective, an attempt to connect the questioning of things to a specific human reality. At times that questioning exhibits notes of indeterminacy similar to those we saw in "35 bujías." In "Tú no las puedes ver" ("You Cannot See Them") a sense of enigma and incomprehension is produced by veiling the referent (the tears of the beloved) while surrounding it with metaphors (Salinas 1975, 314–15). The poem can be read as an example of the arbitrariness of words and signs.

Jorge Guillén continued work on *Cántico* in the late 1920s and early 1930s. The book's second edition, published in 1936, contains 125 poems, distributed in seven sections, whereas the 1928 first edition had 75 poems in five sections. The process of expanding the work organically makes clear Guillén's continued quest to embody experience in form, though the 1936 edition added several texts that deal with death and with human tensions.[17]

A look at most of the poetry written between 1928 and 1935 by many of the poets of the Generation of 1927 reveals a pattern: visionary images, irrational scenes, and involved syntactical systems, in all likelihood based on or related to surrealist writings, were used to configure emotively charged portrayals of a decaying world and of alienated personae. The subjective perspectives so engendered can be related to historical circumstances, to a pervading loss of confidence in the rationality and order of things, to a drawing away from the impulse to rational and verbal order of the 1920s. They do not indicate an explicit abandonment of the modernist-symbolist poetic, though they do mark a shift in discourse that to some extent undermined certain of its tenets, especially a sense of the order of language as a reflection of the order of life. The strand of indeterminacy that we saw in vanguard postures and writings remained an undercurrent, hardly affecting canonical writing.

One younger poet suggests an exception. The new sensibility I have been outlining also infuses the work of Miguel Hernández, probably the most original Spanish poet to start writing in the 1930s. Born in 1910, he has been traditionally identified with the Generation of 1936, the next one, after that of 1927, in the prevalent scheme. Hernández's first book, *Perito en lunas* ("Expert in Moon Matters," 1932), stands out because of the extraordinary creativity of its metaphors. It is most easily contextualized by recalling the author's combined interest in vanguardist writing, the poetry of Guillén, and the poetry of Góngora, which he read while working as a shepherd. It suggests that this poet started, very much like his elders, seeking the roots for his poetry in the most aesthetically creative, most imagistic verse of the Hispanic tradition.

Perito en lunas, however, already contains several mixtures of planes and irrational connections that fragment reality and motivate dissent (see Debicki 1990, 490–93). The transformation of a toilet into an elaborate art form with religious echoes, for example, produces effects akin to surrealist art and could motivate a variety of responses in a reader. In *El rayo que no cesa* ("Unceasing Ray of Lightning," 1936) and several other texts written in the mid-1930s, Hernández's use of visionary images and his construction of irrational effects are more frequent and more apparent and create a mood of anguish caused by unrequited love. But they also allow for a wide range of readings. The following fragment of a sonnet is illustrative:

> Guiando un tribunal de tiburones,
> Como con dos guadañas eclipsadas,
> con dos cejas tiznadas y cortadas
> de tiznar y cortar los corazones,
> en el mío has entrado, y en él pones
> una red de raíces irritadas . . .
> [Hernández, 229]

{Guiding a tribunal of sharks, as with two eclipsed scythes, with two eyebrows blackened and cut by cutting and blackening hearts, mine have you entered, and in it you place a net of irritated roots . . . }

The metaphor of the beloved's eyebrows as scythes, reflecting her cruelty, is intense and subjective, yet grounded on an understandable correspondence. The sharks, however, cannot be explained rationally. They might serve as what Bousoño calls a *visión,* embodying the destructiveness of the subject, in an emotive rather than logical correspondence. The image of a "tribunal" of sharks seems totally inexplicable; for me, its justification lies in the onomatopoeia ("tribunal de tiburones"), which creates a twisted effect, supporting the poem's mood and leading to another onomatopoeia, in *r,* five lines later. Yet it could evoke a wide range of readings. Maybe more important, it leads our attention away from the poem's referent to the issue of word play: the overt subject of the poem fades away. All of this puts this text, at the very least, at the edge of indeterminacy. It and other poems of Hernández's written in the 1930s come the closest to exemplifying what I have been calling the second strand of modernity in the Spain of this decade (see Debicki 1990, 493–500; and Hernández 276–79). The history of Hernández's rapid shifts in style and focus also recalls vanguardist experimentation. Hernández's poetry stands out in its blend of diverse features of modernity, its incredibly fertile mix of symbolist creativity, evolving imagistic techniques, and aspects of undecidability.

Several other poets who were born, like Hernández, between 1907 and 1915 and who have been classified as members of a Generation of 1936, gained prominence in the 1930s.[18] Their first books reveal, as one might expect, connections with the poetry of the Generation of 1927. Their most original contribution, however, lies in the use of personal experiences as referents and in the expression of emotive attitudes in their verse (see García de la Concha 1987, 1: 51–75). Germán Bleiberg's *El cantar de la noche* ("The Song of Night," 1935), for example, contains carefully crafted nature images that recall those of Guillén; yet the references to a specific love experience are far more prominent, and the overt emotional states of the persona more central. Gabriel Celaya's first book, *Marea del silencio* ("Tide of Silence," 1935), also uses landscapes to reflect various emotions, forging a neoromantic view of life.

Luis Rosales's poetry may be, then and later, the most important and innovative of this group. His *Abril* ("April," 1935) uses nature images and echoes of Spanish Renaissance poetry to present a marveled contemplation of life and love. What most distinguishes this book from earlier ones (Guillén's, for example) is the more specific use of personal referents, a more overtly narrative stance, and the explicit presence of religious feeling and motifs. Remembrances of childhood and attempts to recover past experiences produce an admiring contemplation of life and nature; all this motivates, finally, a song of praise to God. To my mind, this book marked the beginning of a mode of writing that would continue in verse published after the Civil War by Rosales, by his contemporaries, and by several somewhat younger poets.

Leopoldo Panero's poetry started out as the most adventuresome and experimental work of this group. His early texts contain vanguardist traits— lack of punctuation, illogical images—and he published in *Caballo Verde para la Poesía* a poem composed of a string of visionary metaphors (see Cano Ballesta 1972, 248–49). His book *Versos del Guadarrama* ("Verses of the Guadarrama," 1945), containing poetry written throughout the 1930s, uses descriptions for emotive purposes: landscapes embody feelings of longing and melancholy. Again, personal events, including the death of his brother, trigger an intense, emotional poetry, undergirded by a consciousness of the tragic effects of time. By the early 1940s Panero would be publishing excellent religious poetry with a similarly effective use of nature images.

Somewhat similar comments can be made about Luis Felipe Vivanco, whose *Cantos de primavera* ("Songs of Springtime," 1936) marks the beginning of a poetic career that would reach full development in the 1940s and 1950s; about Dionisio Ridruejo, author of carefully crafted sonnets with a predominant love motif; and about the first books of Ildefonso-Manuel Gil and Carmen Conde.

Among the poets of this generational grouping, only Panero and Rosales show surrealist connections and some of the surrealist-based imagery seen before in Lorca, Aleixandre, Alberti, and Champourcin. But all of them highlight, in one way or another, the emotive dimension also apparent in the works of the 1930s by these older poets, and all foreground personal themes and referents. Such referents undoubtedly existed in texts of the early 1920s written by Juan Ramón and by Guillén, but they were overlaid and transformed in the poem's quest to embody the "eternal present." Now they become more central. The shift is confirmed by the literary magazines of the 1930s. *Eco. Revista de España* was founded in 1933, as Juan Cano Ballesta notes, to champion the "rehumanization" of literature; it published essays exhorting poets to reflect their lives and times in accessible verse (1972, 144–48). The more prestigious *Cruz y Raya,* which in many ways replaced the *Revista de Occidente* as the leading literary magazine of Spain, adopted a less aesthetic, more philosophical and even religious perspective in the thirty-nine issues published between 1933 and 1936. A renewed interest in Gustavo Adolfo Bécquer, motivated by many events on the occasion of the centenary of his birth in 1936, as well as in Garcilaso de la Vega, the tercentenary of whose death was celebrated in the same year, confirm the resurgence of a neoromantic perspective (García de la Concha 1987, 1: 44–48).

To complete the picture of Spanish poetry in the 1930s, one must take into account work written during the decade by older writers. Antonio Machado can be only marginally connected to the subjective turn that I have discussed. His *De un cancionero apócrifo* ("From an Apocryphal Book of Lyrics") contains a complex philosophical questioning of life and art in prose and verse, filtered through the voices of several heteronyms and complicated by several levels of perspective play (one of them produced by an anthology of poems by fictitious poets, including one named Antonio Machado but identified as different from the real author). The complexity and the game of mirrors present in this work does not contradict Machado's continued, and very modern, quest to detain time through poetry. But it does suggest some modification of the symbolist perspective of the 1920s, away from the confidence that art can fully embody meaning. Meanwhile the series of poems titled "Canciones a Guiomar" ("Songs to Guiomar"), distinct from the *Cancionero* though included within it, presents an intense love experience against the background of an awareness of time.[19]

One does not find any real development in Juan Ramón Jiménez's poetry in the 1930s: his only new book of the decade, *Canciones*, contains mostly revisions of earlier texts and does not mark new directions. Juan Ramón continued writing and rewriting poems, with an ever-increasing impulse to find perfect expression. His work would later become more overtly philosophical, as we will see in chapter 3. In many ways, however, Juan Ramón was always wedded to a single-minded vision of poetry as iconic, and he remained apart from the aesthetic developments of the 1930s.

The shift to subjectivity, the more direct focus on personal experience, and the variety of ways of engendering emotive and often negative responses to life's circumstances that occurred after 1928 did not take Spanish poetry beyond the main, symbolist strand of modernity. The symbolist ideal of the poem as the objectification of unexplainable meanings and as a "making present" of fleeting experience underlay most poetic stances and led to texts that can be read within its premises. Yet one can sense a certain change, a certain erosion. Even if used by poets within this symbolist tradition, the visionary images of surrealist filiation and the subjective and personal characteristics of so many poems questioned the ideal of text as icon or correlative and the premise that meaning can be fully configured in verbal form. A sense of the loss of personal and social harmony implied, to some extent, a parallel loss of confidence in the harmony of poetic language. Antonio Machado's perspective plays, and maybe even his use of a mixture of verse and narrative, might well have had the same effect. And as a backdrop, Spain had the vanguard echoes, the surrealist formulations of an antisymbolist nature, and the indeterminate texts of Salinas and Hernández. We could speak of clues that point ahead to the end of modernity.

A New Determinism: Committed Poetry

The next shift in sensibility and aesthetic orientation, however, was of a different nature. Some of the same historical factors that supported a move to

greater subjectivity in Spanish poetry of the 1930s also motivated an interest
in a utilitarian and committed art and poetry. Economic depression, politi-
cal turmoil and polarization, the revolution in Asturias and the impending
Civil War focused poets, as well as everyone else, on political and social is-
sues. The first interest in artistic commitment came from the Left. Several
journals, most prominently *Nueva España* (1930–31) and *Octubre* (1933–34),
became vehicles advocating a social and revolutionary value for literature.
Later, during the Civil War, *Hora de España* (1937–39) published verse and
prose committed to the Republican side. All these journals contained attacks
on "pure poetry" and the aesthetic tenets attributed to Ortega and the sym-
bolist tradition, which were now condemned as decadent. The presence in
Madrid of César Vallejo and Vallejo's lectures about Mayakovski and about
art as a political vehicle increased interest in such a perspective (Cano
Ballesta 1972, 94–106; García de la Concha 1987, 1: 80–85). Discussions of
poetry's value in furthering social change produced heated polemics, and a
committed view of art did not become totally dominant until the advent of
the Civil War. But social and political commitment emerged as an important
feature in the works of several major poets.

Sociopolitical orientation was at times linked with surrealist style and
tenets, creating a complex mixture of goals that is not easily understood.
The source of the connection goes back to France, where several surrealist
writers, Louis Aragon among them, wished to make surrealism serve the rev-
olution, against the violent objections of Breton (Cano Ballesta 1972,
138–40). More immediately, Rafael Alberti and Miguel Hernández, having
developed their neosurrealist verse as a way of expressing subjective visions,
then acquired a committed view of art. They began to write socially oriented
verse, still using, in many cases, surrealist imagery and language. Sometimes
such imagery and language helped save their work from extreme didacti-
cism. Pablo Neruda's use of surrealist techniques in his *Residencias,* and the
echoes of surrealism in *Caballo Verde para la Poesía,* also contributed to the
link between surrealism and committed art (see Geist 1993). César Vallejo's
poems might also have furthered the connection.

Rafael Alberti became a catalyst and producer of committed poetry in
Spain. After a visit to the Soviet Union in 1932, Alberti asserted his new
stance through the editorship of *Octubre,* through numerous essays, letters,
and reviews, and through his own verse (Cano Ballesta 1972, 170–76). In a
series of individual poems and small books that all became part of *El poeta
en la calle* (*1931–1936*) ("The Poet in the Street") and *De un momento a otro*
(*1932–1938*) ("From One Moment to Another"), Alberti mounted direct at-
tacks on the establishment, the Church, and the moneyed classes and ad-
vocated a union of the oppressed and a battle against various oppressors. In
most of this verse, a simplistic didacticism impedes any richness of nuance.

Only a small part of it seems readable today; perhaps most telling are several works describing the tragic effects of events during the Civil War. In "Madrid—otoño" ("Madrid—Autumn"), for example, a series of visionary images, in a surrealist mode that might recall Alberti's poetry of the late 1920s, dramatically captures the effects of the bombing of the city (Alberti 232–34). This text, unlike the more propagandistic ones, extends the line of subjective writing that was witnessed in the early 1930s.

Alberti wrote some additional direct poetry right after the Civil War. Almost immediately, however, he began to compose *Entre el clavel y la espada* ("Between the Carnation and the Sword"), in which he consciously returned to an artistic perspective. The prefatory poem of the book asserts a desire for the return of "la palabra precisa, / virgen el verbo exacto con el justo adjetivo" (Alberti 252) {"the exact word / the exact virginal verb with the right adjective"}. The volume contains various types of texts, from sonnets to popular poems, in which images engender a variety of tones and moods.

Miguel Hernández visited the Soviet Union in 1935 and was exposed to the doctrines of social realism. His poetry shifted dramatically to social themes in *Viento del pueblo* ("The Wind of the People"), written in 1936 and 1937 and published in the latter year, and *El hombre acecha* ("Man Lies in Wait"), composed between 1936 and 1939.[20] The direct social messages of the poems, and the strident tone in which many are expressed—they were, we must remember, intended for oral recitation—limits their interest today. Yet these books, especially *El hombre acecha*, contain some compelling texts, in which images, personifications, and *visiones* reflect the emotive effects of human suffering. In "El hambre" ("Hunger"), for example, the abstract subject of hunger is turned into an extended *visión*, very similar to those of Hernández's earlier books, which then fans out into a series of subordinate metaphors and later leads to a first-person meditation. In general, this poetry seems most readable today when it produces, through extended metaphors, telluric visions akin to those of *El rayo que no cesa*.

It is worth noting that Hernández's later *Cancionero y romancero de ausencias* ("Songs and Ballads of Absence"), written between 1938 and 1941, leaves behind the tone and the direct messages of his social verse. Combining tight versification reminiscent of "poesía de tipo tradicional" and visionary images of a surrealist bent, Hernández reflects the tragedies and hopes of life. Social concerns still underlie the work, but they find a very different and more timeless expression. The following section makes the impact clear:

> Todas las casas son ojos
> que resplandecen y acechan.
> Todas las casas son bocas

que escupen, muerden y besan.
Todas las casas son brazos
que se empujan y se estrechan.
. . . .
Ya un grito todas las casas
se asaltan y se despueblan.
Ya un grito todas se aplacan,
y se fecundan, y esperan.
                              [Hernández 450–51]

{All the houses are eyes, which shine and lie in wait. All the houses are mouths, which
spit, bite, and kiss. All the houses are arms, which push and hold each other. . . . And
upon a shout all the houses attack and empty each other. And upon a shout all be-
come quiet, become fecund, and await.}

In the context of his last book, one feels that the predicatory nature of
Hernández's social verse had represented a specific response to historical
circumstances and had worked against the grain of his poetic possibilities.
The same seems true of Alberti, in the light of his later shift in *Entre el clavel
y la espada,* and, one suspects, of many other writers of social and political
verse at the time of the Civil War.

The social turn naturally affected the poetics and poetry of other major
Spanish writers. Antonio Machado, who spoke against poetry's involvement
in politics as late as 1934, ended up writing some committed verse and sup-
porting revolutionary poetry (see Cano Ballesta 1972, 155). Emilio Prados,
a member of the Generation of 1927 whose earlier work had shown a philo-
sophical, introspective bent, wrote a considerable amount of socially ori-
ented poetry between 1930 and 1935, collected in *Andando, andando por el
mundo* ("Walking, Walking throughout the World") and *No podréis* ("You
Shall Not"). Most of it strikes us today as rhetorical on the one hand, senti-
mental on the other. Some of Luis Cernuda's poetry written in this decade
and included in *Las nubes* ("The Clouds") deals with human solidarity.

Many other, lesser-known writers published social verses in magazines
and pamphlets, both before and during the Civil War, and recited them in
public, as poetry became a morale builder and propaganda source among
Republican troops. Social messages and didactic goals predominate, al-
though, as Anthony Geist has noted, the effort to gain the reader's assent
gives some of this poetry a certain intensity (see Geist 1990).

The ideological Right, as one might expect, also produced committed
poetry. García de la Concha traces the beginnings of this movement to
Ramón de Basterra, who in the late 1920s composed dramatic exhortations
to Spain to act as spiritual leader of Europe (1987, 1: 90–91). In 1932 José
María Pemán published his first important book, *Elegía de la tradición de Es-*

paña ("Elegy of Spain's Tradition"). Its long chains of eleven- and seven-syllable lines of verse constructed, in overblown fashion, a picture of the grandeur and glory that Spain should build, drawing on its history. More influential yet was Pemán's *Poema de la Bestia y el Angel* ("Poem of the Beast and the Angel," 1938), an epic in high-sounding tones, praising the spiritual values of Spain. Pemán allegorized the Civil War, making it into a mythic crusade; his poem seems, today, strident and authoritarian.

A considerable amount of rhetorical propaganda verse in this mode, composed by many different authors, was published during and immediately after the Civil War. And as in the case of the political Left, several important poets whose most significant work had been written earlier and in different modes now wrote political poems. The best-known poems include a series of sonnets in honor of José Antonio Primo de Rivera by Luis Rosales; some rather rhetorical verse by Dionisio Ridruejo; and a collective volume titled *Los versos del combatiente* ("The Verses of the Combatant"), which included works by Rosales, Pemán, Ridruejo, Vivanco, and Manuel Machado. García de la Concha noted the volume's explicit hope for a harmoniously united Spain after the war (1987, 1: 243–52).

From today's perspective, the turn to social and political poetry before and during the Civil War had an impoverishing effect. Political concerns became translated, most often, into propaganda. More important perhaps, discourse about poetry degenerated to a simplistic discussion about whether art should or should not serve social aims. This represented, to my mind, a reduction of focus. It did, true enough, challenge the modernist view of the poem as icon, as linguistic objectification of meaning. But that idealistic and ambitious symbolist ideal of enshrining experience in form was already in the process of being questioned and modified, as we have seen. In that sense, surrealist-type poetry with social implications seems to us today more fundamentally revolutionary than overt political verse. The shift to a message-oriented and direct political poetry interrupted the erosion of some of the tenets of modernity that subjective poetry had entailed, just as the Civil War interrupted the cultural development of Spain. It would be some years before the country would again see a rich, nuanced discussion of the role of art.

Hence the political and social turn stands as a deviation and distraction, motivated by external factors. One could argue that this deviation would affect the path of much Spanish poetry and poetics until 1960 or so. From this perspective, the social poetry that emerged in the mid- to late 1940s and extended into the 1950s, and the poetics that accompanied it, were limited by sociopolitical goals and constraints similar to those that became dominant in the late 1930s. Discussions concerning the nature of poetry first had to sort out, defensively at times, political roles and issues.

And the tendency to make poetry convey fairly simple postures and ideas produced a rather direct discourse. To some extent at least, both opponents and proponents of the triumphant regime and structure found themselves writing verse that spoke in the same direct way; they became, unconsciously, collaborators in a dominant notion of language as the direct projection of ideas and ideologies. Only years later would this discourse be undermined, as part of a fundamental move beyond modernity. From this perspective, the idea and practice of social poetry imposed on Spain a detour in the evolution of its modernity and in the move to a postmodern era.

3

After the War, 1940–1965

In many and obvious ways, the Spanish Civil War had a long-term negative effect on the possibilities for poetic production. The destruction of war and the focus on material survival during and after the conflict would naturally make literary activity an irrelevant luxury. In addition, the use of verse as propaganda limited creative goals and possibilities, as we have seen. As the war ended and the Nationalists emerged victorious, the country found itself in a climate of ideological concerns, underpinned by censorship, which likewise limited creativity. Most inhibiting, in many ways, was the prohibition on publishing or importing the work of major poets, including Neruda and Vallejo. A whole generation of writers would grow up in ignorance of some of the most significant works and currents of Western as well as Hispanic letters. In addition, political divisions kept young people from reading works by poets of the "other side" (see Batlló 14).

Equally important, the world of poets residing in Spain had been decimated. Antonio Machado and Federico García Lorca had died, and Miguel Hernández would die in 1942; Juan Ramón Jiménez, Guillén, Alberti, Salinas, Cernuda, Altolaguirre, and Prados, as well as other younger poets, had left the country. It would be years before academic and literary institutions would function freely, effectively, and imaginatively. For all these reasons, the intellectual atmosphere of the 1940s would be a narrow and impoverished one.

Given these circumstances, the very fact that poetry was written and published constituted an achievement. The first poems and books issued had, as one might expect, a nationalistic, morale-building focus. Dionisio Ridruejo's *Poesía en armas* ("Poetry in Arms," 1940) and *Sonetos a la piedra* ("Sonnets to Stone," 1943), an anthology of Spanish heroic poetry edited by Rosales and Vivanco, and much of the poetry that appeared in the magazine *Escorial* from 1940 on continued that line of writing, which we observed before and during the war (see García de la Concha 1987, 1: 319–39). Yet as

García de la Concha has also noted, *Escorial* opened its pages to many kinds of writing; it and other new literary magazines made a conscious effort to transcend partisan concerns. The appearance of a large number of magazines, in several cities, between 1943 and 1950 helped develop an intellectual climate and compensate for the constraints of the literary and political scene and for the loss of leading literary figures (Rubio and Falcó 36–40).

The magazine *Garcilaso* (1943–46) and the work of poets grouped around it constituted the first major effort to restore the art of poetry. An increased interest in the poetry of Garcilaso de la Vega had predated the war and had received some impetus from the three hundredth anniversary of the poet's death in 1936. Garcilaso's figure was reinterpreted, almost mythically, as the times changed. Defined as a prototypical love poet before the war, he was later portrayed as a heroic poet-protagonist of the Spanish empire and as an antidote to decadentism (García de la Concha 1987, 1: 360–69). A group of poets who called themselves Juventud Creadora organized activities around his figure and advocated a traditional poetry, deliberately defined as opposed to vanguard writing, "isms," and the Generation of 1927. A number of these poets collaborated in the founding of the magazine.

The magazine, however, as edited by José García Nieto, espoused the wider goal of fomenting good poetry and enhancing artistic pursuits. It published work by many authors of different ages and directions but emphasized carefully crafted verse, consciously asserting the need for "good taste" in its initial manifesto (García de la Concha 1987, 1: 372). We find in *Garcilaso* polished if at times stilted love lyrics, religious texts, some patriotic works, and even some existentialist ones. Sonnets predominated. The poetry of this magazine is best exemplified by García Nieto's own well-structured sonnets, which via parallelisms and hyperbatons reminiscent of Renaissance verse projected nostalgic evocations and gentle feelings of love. The magazine's focus made it, perhaps unfairly, a target for poets who, shortly thereafter, espoused more realistic writing and social and existential concerns.

Very artful poetry was written in the 1940s by Gerardo Diego. One of the three prominent members of his generation to remain in Spain, Diego contributed to various magazines and presided at gatherings of young poets, thus playing a valuable leadership role. He also published six books of poetry between 1941 and 1944, containing new as well as pre–Civil War texts. Most of the poems correspond to his "traditional" (as opposed to his consciously vanguard) style. They make excellent use of elaborate structural and metaphorical schemes. *Alondra de verdad* ("True Lark," 1941), for example, collects forty-two sonnets on various topics. "Insomnio" ("Insomnia"), written in 1929, contrasts the speaker's turmoil to the placidity of his sleeping beloved through the dominant metaphors of sleep as sailing, wakefulness as

shipwreck. Rhythm, syntax, and image work together perfectly to reflect the
conflict in moods, as we can see in the sonnet's first and last stanzas:

> Tú y tu desnudo sueño. No lo sabes.
> Duermes. No. No lo sabes. Yo en desvelo,
> y tú, inocente, duermes bajo el cielo.
> Tú por el sueño, y por el mar las naves.
> . . . .
> Qué pavorosa esclavitud de isleño,
> yo insomne, loco, en los acantilados;
> las naves por el mar, tú por tu sueño. [Diego 1958, 154]

> {You and your naked sleep. You do not know it.
> You sleep. No. You do not know it. I, sleepless,
> and you, innocent, you sleep under the skies.
> You through sleep and dream, and the ships through the sea.
> . . . .
> What an islander's terrible slavery:
> I sleepless, mad, along the coastline;
> the ships in the sea, you in your sleep and dreams.}

Exemplifying Diego's use of metaphor and form to shape and stylize an
emotive attitude, "Insomnio" continues the path traced out by the poet in
both his vanguardist and his traditional works of the early 1920s. Diego's *Angeles de Compostela* ("Angels of Compostela," 1940) consists of beautifully
crafted texts in various forms and meters, which reflect on the art of the Santiago Cathedral and of various Galician writers, and at least implicitly connect religious and artistic transcendence. Diego also collected many of his
earlier avant-garde poems in *Poemas adrede* ("Purposeful Poems," 1943). All
these publications confirm his standing as an accomplished poet, although
one whose works lie outside the dominant currents of the 1940s and 1950s.
He was respected and read, though his greatest contribution to the future
lay in the help he gave to younger poets.

Other examples of accomplished verse are the books of Adriano del
Valle, whose earlier poetry had involved avant-garde metaphorical experiments. His interest in imagery led him in the 1940s to write complicated
poems, loaded with layers of metaphors and conceits that challenge the
reader (García de la Concha 1987, 1: 351–55). Though one can connect
this verse to 1920s experimental writing, del Valle's images seem, for the
most part, more akin to picture puzzles that can be solved. Together with
the poems of *Garcilasistas* like Rafael Montesinos or Jesús Juan Garcés, they
reflect a quest for value in verbal play alone.

From today's vantage point, the turn to form and tradition in the early
1940s was an understandable if limiting way of reaching beyond the daily

circumstances of a war-torn country, of transcending the propaganda that dominated the public scene, of bringing back a cultural focus to Spain. *Garcilaso* and José García Nieto's work as its editor and, for years thereafter, as editor of the *Estafeta Literaria* helped in the restoration of a literary milieu.

That restoration, nevertheless, was anachronistic. On the one hand, it was based on a simplistic and unexamined version of the modernist view of poetry as rendering experience into form. (This view, as we saw earlier, had already been undergoing modification before the war.) On the other hand, it involved a willful disregard for the destructive effects of the war, the difficult conditions of life, the presence of political tensions and repressions, and the ethical dilemmas posed by all of these. The elegant language in which much of this poetry was written, too, seemed out of place. After diverse efforts in the 1930s to adapt poetic expression to new themes and experiences, a return to classical forms and rhetoric would have to seem regressive. For these reasons, this poetry caused a series of negative reactions by the mid-1940s and was soon superseded by other styles and currents.

One other, slightly later strand of formally oriented poetry needs to be remembered. In the mid-1940s, in the provincial city of Córdoba, a group of young writers began to discuss and to write poetry in the context of the major Spanish authors of modernity from Rubén Darío to the Generation of 1927. After some difficulty in getting recognition for their work, they established the magazine *Cántico*, with obvious echoes of Guillén's book. Their poetic stance was marked by their opposition to what they called the "monotony" of the *Garcilacistas* on the one hand and to the rhetorical excesses of existential and social writing (and of the magazine *Espadaña*) on the other. From 1947 to 1949 *Cántico* had a coherent focus and orientation, and it published primarily poems by Juan Bernier, Ricardo Molina, Pablo García Baena, and Julio Aumente, all born between 1911 and 1924 (see Carnero 1976, esp. 39–51).

The statements made by these poets stressed their search for a language that would render feeling with precision. They made a willful attempt to connect back to the symbolist strand of Spanish modernity, and they echoed the 1920s impulse to "pure poetry." They also evidenced an idealistic interest in music, in the arts, in a cultural and aesthetic attitude that contrasted with the dominant views of the time (María del Pilar Palomo likened them to the Pre-Raphaelites; see Palomo 104). They sought to establish a cultural oasis in a pragmatic world.

A look at the poems written by the *Cántico* group reveals considerable thematic diversity: idealized erotic texts by Bernier that echo Darío and create a mythic, idealized beauty; religious works and homages to nature by García Baena and Molina; melancholic landscapes by Julio Aumente. All of these poets tended to write long lines, skillfully weaving description and image to forge timeless sensorial landscapes. The most compelling, for me, is García Baena, whose *Mientras cantan los pájaros* ("While Birds Sing," 1948) and *Antiguo muchacho* ("Boy of Yore," 1950) contain elaborate images, mixing various motifs—literary, erotic, religious—into a rare combination of sensations.

The *Cántico* poets were viewed as marginal in their time and were almost ignored in historical appraisals of the 1940s and 1950s. They were rescued from oblivion in a 1976 study by Guillermo Carnero, one of the leading poets of the *novísimos* of the 1970s (see Carnero 1976). For Carnero, the group represented a link between the aestheticism of earlier Spanish modernity and that of his own period and presaged the later use of cultural elements and literary intertexts as vehicles for poetic meaning. Carnero is correct in reminding us that an aestheticist strand can be found in Spanish poetry of this time and that an artful perspective to poetry did not vanish completely in the early post–Civil War period. To that extent, the attention paid to this group is a valid and necessary corrective to literary history. To my mind, however, and for all the gracefulness of their verse, the *Cántico* poets point backward more than forward, both in their poetics, which echoes early modernity, and in their verse, which is closer to Darío than to Carnero or Gimferrer.

A New Realistic Poetics, 1944–1960

By 1945 a variety of voices were rejecting the formal turn of the early post–Civil War period. The magazine *Espadaña* was founded in León in 1944 with rather contradictory statements on poetics, including modernist echoes of Valéry and Bécquer (García de la Concha 1987, 1: 451 ff.). Yet it became a vehicle for new and antiformal postures. Concern with contemporary problems and individual suffering, as well as the need to express emotive issues concretely, governed several of its pronouncements.[1] Attacks on escapism and aestheticism appeared in its pages, mostly written by Victoriano Crémer and Eugenio de Nora, and included pointed comments on the need to be freed from the tyranny of the sonnet and also that of political repression (ibid. 458–64; Jiménez 1992, 17–19). Between 1945 and 1951 the magazine published a large volume of verse reflecting existential and social concerns. A similar function was performed by *Corcel*, published in Valencia between 1942 and 1949, and *Proel*, published in Santander from 1944 to 1950, in both of which a number of younger poets led by José Luis Hidalgo and José Hierro advocated a subjective and expressive poetry (García de la Concha 1987, 1: 436–44).

The attitude reflected in *Espadaña* and other similar magazines dominated the Spanish literary scene by the mid-1940s and was clearly expressed by Vicente Aleixandre in a 1955 speech and essay, in which he defined the essential theme of then-current poetry as "el cántico del hombre en cuanto *situado,* es decir en cuanto *localizado;* localizado en un tiempo, en un tiempo que pasa y es irreversible, y localizado en un espacio, en una sociedad determinada, con unos determinados problemas que le son propios" (Aleixandre 1955, 8) {"the canticle of man as *situated,* that is *located;* located in a time, in a time that passes and is irreversible, and located in a place, in a specific society, with specific problems that belong to it"}. Throughout the 1940s and 1950s Aleixandre and others frequently alluded to poetry's role as a means of communication, though the phrase was used to encompass a variety of stances, from a simplistic belief in social messages in verse to a modernist view of the poem as an embodiment of complex meanings. (The latter underlies the theoretical criticism of Carlos Bousoño.)

The impulse to make poetry deal with immediate issues remained dominant for nearly two decades. It is best represented in two anthologies of new poets of this time, Francisco Ribes's *Antología consultada de la joven poesía española* ("Survey Anthology of Young Spanish Poetry," 1952, based on a survey of some sixty writers) and Rafael Millán's *Veinte poetas españoles* ("Twenty Spanish Poets," 1955). The poetry collected in these volumes, the statements on poetics included in the first, and the major works of older poets published in the 1940s all support Carlos Bousoño's 1961 characterization of "postcontemporary poetry." For Bousoño, post–Civil War poetry had effected a necessary break from the universalism and irrationality of prior traditions and was distinguished by a new stress on personal dilemmas and experiences, on concepts, and on social issues. To express these, it developed a whole new style, which involved the use of anecdote, of narrative techniques and characters, of direct address and everyday language (Bousoño 1966, 551–76).

A parallel though somewhat narrower overview of the period appeared in the introduction to José María Castellet's *Veinte años de poesía española: Antología, 1939–1959* ("Twenty Years of Spanish Poetry: Anthology" 1960).[2] Castellet asserted, rather polemically, that this period represented a definitive turn away from the symbolist tradition. He documented his stance by also pointing to the use of everyday language and narrative techniques in verse, but above all by stressing the dominance of a new view of poetry's social function and of an interest in content as opposed to form.[3]

The full impact of the new aesthetic becomes apparent in the statements of poetics in the *Antología consultada.* Victoriano Crémer, for example, attributed to poetry a direct, communicative role: "Poesía es comunicación (Vicente Aleixandre). No resta, pues, sino descubrir el ser al que dirigir nuestro mensaje" (Ribes 1952, 65). {"Poetry is communication (Vicente Aleixandre). All that is left, therefore, is to find the being to whom to send our message."} Eugenio de Nora stated, "Toda poesía es social. La produce, o mejor dicho la escribe, un hombre (que cuando es gran poeta se apoya y alimenta en todo un pueblo), y va destinada a otros hombres" (ibid. 151). {"All poetry is social. A human being (who when he is a great poet depends and feeds on a whole people) produces or rather writes it, and it is destined for other human beings."} Gabriel Celaya began by connecting poetry to everyday expression: "Cantemos como quien respira. Hablemos de lo que cada día nos ocupa. No hagamos poesía como quien se va al quinto cielo o como quien posa para la posteridad. La poesía no es—no puede ser—intemporal, o, como suele decirse un poco alegremente, eterna" (ibid. 43). {"Let us sing as one breathes. Let us speak of what concerns us every day. Let us not make poetry as if we were seeking the fifth heaven or like those who pose for posterity. Poetry is not—it cannot be—timeless, or, as one says a bit too happily, eternal."} He noted that writing poetry "no es convertir en 'cosa' una interioridad, sino dirigirse a otro a través de la cosa-poema" (ibid. 45) {"is not the conversion of inner feelings into 'things,' but rather addressing another through the thing-poem"}.

Blas de Otero, though avoiding a simplistic view, indicated poetry's role in "demostrar hermandad con la tragedia viva, y luego, lo antes posible, intentar superarla" (Ribes 1952, 179) {"showing brotherhood with living tragedy, and afterward, very soon trying to rise above it"}. And José Hierro, while stressing the importance of form, rhythm, and tone and the necessity of creating a coherent work, noted that the poet must reflect current circumstances: "El poeta es obra y artífice de su tiempo. El signo del nuestro es colectivo, social. Nunca como hoy necesitó el poeta ser tan narrativo, porque los males que nos acechan . . . proceden de hechos" (ibid. 107). {"The poet is a work and creature of his time. The sign of our time is collective, social. Never as today did the poet need to be so narrative, because the evils that accost us . . . come from deeds."} Even Rafael Morales noted the need of writing for the majority, *la mayoría* (ibid. 126); only Bousoño and José María Valverde stressed poetry's aesthetic nature. The latter, rather defensively, asserted an old modernist view: "La poesía se compone de poemas, de curiosos objetos como piedras" (ibid. 200). {"Poetry is made up of poems, of curious objects like stones."}[4]

These pronouncements make clear a major change in sensibility since the 1920s and 1930s and obviously raise the issue of whether this era marked a shift away from the premises of modernity. On the one hand, the poetics of this period (and, as we will see, the poetry it engendered) was still based on the notion that a poem conveys something real and unchanging, a notion that was fundamental, with a much less literal emphasis, to the modern aesthetic. This notion was now simplified but also strengthened by social poetry, which advocated the communication of a clear message. In that sense, the social and realistic turn in Spanish poetry may have impeded the development of the personalism and indeterminacy that Jerome Mazzaro saw in American verse of the 1950s (28–29).

Yet in another sense, the new poetics undercut one aspect of the modernist-symbolist view, the concept of the poem as an icon or objective embodiment. By stressing the need to communicate with specific and historically situated readers, the poets of this time abandoned the view of text as unchanging object, as is evident in the words I quoted from Celaya. In that sense, the new attitude deflated the idealistic notion of a poem as "eternal present." This led to a less transcendent view of poetry's function and can be clearly related to traits in the poetry of the time that Bousoño stressed in his study of "postcontemporary poetry" (loss of belief in originality and universality, nontranscendent perspectives), and also to its narrative techniques and dimensions. The goal of embodying universal experiences had given way to the communication of specific feelings and of social views. The result was a more particularized, perspectival, and narrative poetry that pointed to the erosion of an important aspect of modernity.[5]

Some of the other new magazines that appeared in Spain in the 1940s and 1950s reveal a broader outlook than *Espadaña* (or the *Antología consultada*). The most important was *Insula,* which from its founding in 1946 published critical and creative work that shed light on the best work of new as well as established writers. Particularly noteworthy were its special issues honoring Machado, Juan Ramón, the Generation of 1927 poets, and others. Its liberal cast made it, indeed, a precarious island on the Madrid scene. More tied to the establishment in its early years, *Cuadernos Hispanoamericanos* also published important studies and poetic works and stressed contacts between Spanish and Spanish American literatures. One also should mention the important contributions of the *Estafeta Literaria, Clavileño,* and *Indice.*[6]

In studying the actual poetry written in the 1940s and 1950s, one has difficulty defining main styles and currents. Víctor García de la Concha's authoritative history identifies numerous strands, using categories such as "neoromantic," "existentialist," "Generation of 1936," "rooted and unrooted," and "intrahistorical," as well as "social." Since authors of different ages wrote similar poetry, the generational scheme becomes even less helpful in distinguishing poets and currents (Bousoño 1966, 566–69).[7] All of this reflects the erosion of a coherent universalist vision of poetry, and the multiple directions that become possible when poets seek to move away from past canons.

In this situation I find it necessary to seek broader characteristics that will help us gain some unifying perspectives. José Hierro's concept of "testimonial poetry" is very useful. Refusing to separate poetry by theme (social, personal, etc.), Hierro stressed, instead, the poet's way of focusing on a subject. By his definition, testimonial poetry explores in depth and from personal perspectives relevant issues, individual or collective, that crucially affect the human life of the time. It differs from aesthetic verse, which is oriented to form and beauty alone, and from political poetry, which is oriented to advocating doctrinaire solutions (see Hierro 1962, 6–10). The term helps explain how Spanish poetry sought new forms to overcome the dangers of sentimentality and triteness, which face any literature that deals with the personal and the emotive and that no longer strives to universalize and eternalize experience. Therefore the concept of testimonial poetry will help me examine the degree to which the most interesting works of these decades did and did not modify the premises and possibilities of prior modern writing in Spain, the degree to which they both prepared and delayed a shift to a different era and aesthetic.[8]

Testimonial Poetry, 1944–1960: The Communication of Personal, Religious, and Existential Emotions

Stylistically as well as thematically, what I will call testimonial poetry of a personal and emotive nature runs a wide gamut—from religious works in flowing lines of elegant verse to anguished existential texts written in colloquial idiom and narrative works that strain the limits of traditional genres. The authors of this vein of writing range from members of the Generation of 1927 to authors born in the 1920s. Many of them, from Alonso to Hierro, Hidalgo, and Otero, had to be affected by European existentialist currents of this period. Yet the social and political circumstances in Spain played an equally important part.

In a sense this lyric of the 1940s continued lines that were already present before the Civil War, as modernity had moved away from "pure poetry" and as new ways of configuring irrational concerns had developed. (We will see specific examples of continuity in the works of Aleixandre, Rosales, and Panero.) Yet it also had to take into account the new artistic and social climate and find an idiom that would be seen as accessible and not anachronistic.

One can begin with a book by Vicente Aleixandre titled *Sombra del paraíso* ("Shadows of Paradise") and published in 1944. One of only three established poets of his generation left in Spain, Aleixandre took on the role of mentor and guide to younger writers and had a profound personal effect on most of them for years. His new book was widely read and cited, although its effect on the poetry of others is debatable (Grande 35–36). In any event, *Sombra del paraíso* echoes the style and effect of *La destrucción o el amor* of 1935 and exemplifies a mode of writing of surrealist filiation that presents subjective perspectives fitting to the times. Again, long lines of free verse and complex syntactical patterns weave series of visionary images and engender a pantheistic vision in which human beings fit into a cosmic order. The new book differs from the previous one mainly in its outlook: the harmonious pantheistic universe is now seen as a nostalgically evoked past rather than a hoped-for future (Jiménez 1982, 62). *Sombra del paraíso* also addresses, almost metapoetically, the poet's function in seeking insight (ibid. 172–73). Hence it reflects and responds to the sense of loss and alienation and the need for new paths of the then-current artistic climate.[9]

If Aleixandre's book constituted a thematic response to the times, Dámaso Alonso's *Hijos de la ira* ("Sons of Anger") offered one that also involved formal and stylistic innovations. Likewise published in 1944, this book created an enormous impact. Written in long lines of free verse, it combined colloquial language, shocking descriptions, self-deprecating comments by a first-person speaker, and contemporary allusions, together with visionary metaphors and literary echoes. Its poems are organized into a narrative sequence that traces the speaker's conflictive (and symbolic) search for meaning in a hostile world. Hence *Hijos de la ira* established a new form, almost a new genre, for the expression of an emotive vision in a language that is immediate yet artistically effective. (It undoubtedly served as a model for Bousoño's definition of "postcontemporary poetry.") It was to influence younger writers for years to come.

In some ways *Hijos de la ira* continued Dámaso Alonso's earlier path as poet. Though previously better known as a critic and scholar, Alonso had since the 1920s published verse in which a protagonist develops conflicting views of the prosaic and the poetic, the earthly and the religious (Debicki 1970, 33–51). In *Oscura noticia* ("Dark News"), which was issued in 1944 but contained works written from 1919 on, he used traditional poetic forms to sharpen these conflicts and relate them to human life and love. "Destrucción inminente" ("Imminent Destruction"), for example, portrays a speaker whose desire to crush a twig is suddenly made parallel to God's arbitrary control of humanity (Debicki 1970, 46). In *Hijos de la ira,* these ways of engendering tension and combining narrative and lyrical perspectives were fully developed and combined with a new diction, focus, and structure.

The characteristics of *Hijos de la ira* take it to the limits of modernity. The lead poem of the book, "Insomnio," furnishes perhaps the best example:

Madrid es una ciudad de más de un millón de cadáveres (según las últimas estadísticas).

A veces en la noche yo me revuelvo y me incorporo en este nicho en el que hace 45 años que me pudro,

y paso largas horas oyendo gemir el huracán, o ladrar los perros, o fluir blandamente la luz de la luna.

Y paso largas horas gimiendo como el huracán, ladrando como un perro enfure-
 cido, fluyendo como la leche de la ubre caliente de una gran vaca amarilla.
Y paso largas horas preguntándole a Dios, preguntándole por qué se pudre lenta-
 mente mi alma,
por qué se pudren más de un millón de cadáveres en esta ciudad de Madrid,
por qué mil millones de cadáveres se pudren lentamente en el mundo.
Dime, ¿qué huerto quieres abonar con nuestra podredumbre?
¿Temes que se te sequen los grandes rosales del día, las tristes azucenas letales de
 tus noches?

[Alonso 1958, 13]

{Madrid is a city of more than a million corpses (according to the latest statistics).
At times at night I turn and sit up in this niche in which I have been rotting for
 45 years,
And spend long hours listening to the hurricane moan, or the dogs bark, or the
 light of the moon flow softly.
And I spend long hours moaning like the hurricane, barking like a mad dog, flow-
 ing like the milk from the warm udder of a big yellow cow.
And I spend long hours querying God, asking him why my soul slowly rots away,
Why more than a million corpses rot away in this city of Madrid,
Why a billion corpses rot away slowly in the world.
Tell me, what garden do you want to fertilize with our rot?
Do you fear that your great rosebushes of day, the sad lethal lilies of your nights,
 will dry up?}

Based on a specific historical reality, the poem refers to the fact that Madrid
had grown to a million inhabitants around 1940. It begins by adopting a pro-
saic tone: its first line imitates a newspaper report. The word *cadáveres* breaks
this tone and forces us to see the statement as image rather than news item.
This word also introduces a series of references to death: if the inhabitants
are cadavers, the speaker sleeps in a niche, his life has been a long dying,
and all humans are cadavers. Thus the supposedly prosaic reality with which
the poem began has been extended into metaphor and into allegory, con-
veying a sense of life's meaninglessness. The impact of the pattern, however,
is due to the way in which it rises up, surprisingly and dramatically, out of
everyday expression and reality.

   In lines 3–4 the poem recalls rather clichéd conventions of romantic po-
etry. Sleepless and anguished, the speaker listens to the storm and the dogs,
watches the moonlight, and then echoes nature's emotions. Every detail
evokes a commonplace of romantic writing until the reference to the "warm
udder of a big yellow cow" undercuts and parodies them all. If lines 1–2 led
us from literal reality to allegorical vision, lines 3–4 take us from a declara-
tion of anguish back to parody and literal-minded description.[10]

   In some ways this poem recalls prior traditions: it is a dramatic mono-
logue, a form going all the way back to Browning; it uses intertextuality in

the manner of much modern poetry. It is symbolic in the symbolist sense of the word, since the characters and images it portrays embody basic, complex, logically inexplicable forces (see Debicki 1970, 53–54, 49; also Debicki 1974).[11] Yet there is something fundamentally different about it. The various levels of discourse present do not fit together into a coherent whole. The speaker builds a certain unity through his sense of anguish and alienation and his final conclusion that his purpose is to serve as God's fertilizer. Yet all that does not necessitate, or account for, the different levels of language and effect. The speaker's role as latter-day romantic does not require the switch from newspaper reporting to allegory, or the undercutting of romantic cliché by parody, or the biblical echoes, or the unusual intertextualities. The language shifts serve not to define the speaker but rather to disorient the reader, to invite her or him to step back from the text, to respond to it as a weaving together of diverse realities. They produce something akin to a collage in art, a set of separate layers that are not joined naturally and that to some extent depend on the viewer/reader for their organization.

In this sense, "Insomnio" seems to leave behind the symbolist goal of embodying meaning in text and to produce an indeterminacy. Yet in the context of *Hijos de la ira* as a whole, all the levels of this and other texts (some of which—for example, "Monstruos"—reveal similar layers of discourse) contribute to a coherent view of a grim world, whose inhabitant-poet seeks meaning, through writing, through love, through God. The juxtaposition of conflicting levels is a means, comparable to the use of surprisingly prosaic elements, of conveying this view in a fresh and impactive way, which the readers of the 1940s would recognize as fitted to the circumstances of the time and which also would produce a more active and perhaps varied response on the part of those readers. Thus I see the book as one straining against the limits of a symbolist perspective, especially the view of text as icon, while ultimately operating within its goals of seizing complex meanings in verbal form.

Alonso's *Hombre y Dios* ("Man and God," 1955), though less surprising, creates a similar effect. This book again centers on a conflictive view of reality and pits an idealistically naive point of view—dominant in its first part—against a negatively existential one in the third part. In between, diverse poems engender various resolutions. The dominant one is generated by the image of human beings as destined to provide God (who lacks eyesight) with a chance to see his own universe. As in *Hijos de la ira,* narrative techniques and the play of tone and point of view produce a dramatic rendering of the struggle for meaning in life.

Alonso's poetry of the 1940s and 1950s has been described, appropriately, as opening the way to existentialist and social verse in Spain. Yet its greatest value may lie in stretching the levels of poetic discourse, in bringing narrative techniques, different and contradictory layers of language, and increasingly rich intertextualities to late modern poetry. By introducing this new style, *Hijos de la ira* and *Hombre y Dios* gave lyric expression to issues and postures that might otherwise have remained merely the subject of didactic presentation.

Several poets of the Generation of 1936 published poetry in the 1940s that offered novel responses to a climate in which conventional styles had been rendered suspect. The most interesting might well be *La casa encendida* ("The Well-Lit House") by Luis Rosales, a single, extensive poem first issued in 1949. In some ways, Rosales's work in general and this book in particular could be placed at an opposite pole from *Hijos de la ira:* written by a conservative figure, generally associated with the regime in power, *La casa encendida* projects a more stable and harmonious view.[12] Yet it pursues a parallel goal: the expression of a personal, emotive vision of things, in a form fitting to the times. In that sense it picks up and carries further the drive for a more subjective and referential verse that Rosales and other poets of the Generation of 1936 had initiated before the Civil War.

After describing a beautiful spring day to convey a sense of life's harmony, the book's prologue indicates the poet's goal: to preserve past experiences through his language. What follows—an opening sonnet and five sections of free verse—engenders various feelings, all based on remembrances of places and events in the speaker's house. The long lines of free verse effectively capture the flowing, meandering memories of the speaker. Everyday words predominate, punctuated by repetition and parallelism. Key moments and emotions are crystallized in metaphor. The following excerpt may give some sense of this style:

> Y entonces,
> cuando viene la juventud del agua cuando corre,
> la juventud que pone hormigas niñas en la lengua
> para decir *te quiero,*
> vino ella
> y por primera vez la miraron tus ojos:
> era un don; se había acercado al puesto; sonreía;
> iba entre sus hermanas con la estatura del maizal
> en agosto,
> y miraba una cosa tras otra,
> y miraba sólo para aprender a sonreír. [Rosales 1979, 184]

{And then, when one reaches the youth of running water, the youth that places little ants on one's tongue to say "I love you," she came, and your eyes saw her for the first time: it was a gift; she had come near the place, she smiled, she moved among her sisters with the bearing of a cornfield in August, looking at one thing after another, looking only so as to learn to smile.}

Crucial events of the speaker's life connected with the house—vignettes of his past, the death of a friend—convey the sorrowful experience of past-ness and yet also an affirmation of harmony and hope. This almost Proust-ian mode, in free verse and common idiom, produces a genre somewhere between narrative and formal lyric, akin to the "prose poems" composed by Spanish American *modernistas* and Juan Ramón Jiménez years before, but much more contemporary and unassertive. Its function is ultimately sym-bolic, in a very modernist way: the reality it portrays represents or embodies a deeper, untranslatable sense of life.[13] It offers a way of conveying a com-plex emotive reality without rhetoric; written at a time in which anything verging on aestheticism or formalism had become suspect, *La casa encendida* provided an original poetic answer.

The book evidently put into practice a poetics that Rosales and several fellow authors of the Generation of 1936 consciously evolved in the mid-1940s and expressed in a number of essays (see García de la Concha 1987, 2: 838–45). Rosales, Leopoldo Panero, Luis Felipe Vivanco, and Dionisio Ridruejo in his first phase, though articulate members of the literary estab-lishment, all sought to avoid posturing, rhetoric, or political commitment. They saw vanguard postures as jaded and feared the triteness of both di-dactic and neoromantic writing. Hence they worked to develop a low-key, intimate, yet artful kind of expression in their poems, which, like other po-etry of this time, placed a greater premium on both individual experience and reader involvement. (They largely continued the kind of verse they had started to publish in the late 1930s.) Unfortunately, their influence was lim-ited: many younger writers ignored them simply because of their proregime backgrounds. Later poets, however, would come to appreciate their art.

La casa encendida is the most original reflection of this posture, though by no means the only one. Rosales's *Rimas* ("Rhymes," 1951), composed of poems written from 1937 on, contains many beautifully crafted texts, offer-ing emotive responses to tragic events. This book, like *La casa encendida*, makes use of a much simpler language and more direct tones than Rosales's prewar poetry, confirming his striving for a simple yet artful style.

In *La estancia vacía* ("The Empty Room," 1944), Leopoldo Panero con-structed a lyric narrative of loneliness and a search for religious meaning, against the backdrop of deaths and losses.[14] Like Rosales, he used common language to surprisingly lyric effect, making true poetry out of the most or-dinary materials. Similar effects, though in more varied tones, are produced by Panero's *Escrito a cada instante* ("Written at Every Moment," 1949). Luis Felipe Vivanco, in *Tiempo de dolor* ("Time of Pain," 1940), *Continuación de la vida* ("Life's Continuation," 1949), and *El descampado* ("The Open Field," 1957), turns remembrances of moments and scenes into spiritual insights, in a continuing quest for a positive view of love and life. An equally subjective but more disillusioned portrayal of human existence emerges from Dionisio Ridruejo's *En la soledad del tiempo* ("In the Solitude of Time," 1944), and also from Ildefonso-Manuel Gil's *Poemas de dolor antiguo* ("Poems of Old Sorrows," 1945).

The style and themes of most of Carmen Conde's poetry fit well with those of the authors just discussed. From the late 1930s on, she had been publishing intense subjective poetry, in which an almost mystic search for transcendence balances a sorrowful contemplation of human suffering. *Ansia de la gracia* ("Desire of Grace," 1945) contains intense love poems, in which human passion also blends into a quest for transcendence. From today's perspective, however, Conde's most important book may well be her mythical and revisionist *Mujer sin Edén* ("Woman without Eden," 1947). As Sharon Ugalde has noted, Conde transforms the figure of Eve to reflect, and protest against, the subjugation of woman. Conde's Eve, metamorphosed into other feminine figures, furnished a background and model for later women's poetry in Spain (see Ugalde 1992).

One additional author composed excellent poetry in this vein, although her residency abroad robbed her of recognition. Her books were published in Spain, however, and obtained several prizes. In *Pájaros del nuevo mundo* ("Birds of the New World," 1945), *Dominio del llanto* ("Control of Tears," 1947), *La hermosura sencilla* ("Simple Beauty," 1953), and *El desterrado ensueño* ("Exiled Dream," 1955), Concha Zardoya combined carefully selected everyday language, great formal control, and a wide range of tones to convey nostalgic evocations and a quest for the deeper sense behind life's experiences.

Behind the work of these authors of the Generation of 1936, and of this whole period of Spanish poetry, one senses the renewed presence of Antonio Machado. This should not be in the least surprising. In *Soledades, galerías* and *Campos de Castilla* Machado had used common scenes and ordinary language to reflect, metaphorically and symbolically, perceptions of time and fundamental emotive responses to them. Though left behind by the more consciously artful poetry of the 1920s, his brand of stark image-making obviously offered writers in the 1940s an example of how poetry can be at once comprehensible, low-key, and significant. Machado also offered them a model for the use of narrative sequences to lyric effect. For these reasons and for his posture (somewhat overmythologized) as a representative of national and moral concerns, Machado—together with Hernández, Vallejo, and Neruda—underlies much of the poetry of the 1940s and 1950s, while the work of Juan Ramón and some of the poets of the 1920s was eclipsed.

In a sense, we can see Dámaso Alonso's *Hijos de la ira* and the books of the Generation of 1936 poets as two ends of a spectrum of emotive poetry. The writers of both kinds of verse, faced with the need to express subjective meanings in a language free from artifice and from didacticism, configured new styles out of everyday language, narrative techniques, and symbolic modes. Alonso's perspective play and dramatic tones produced conflictive texts that bring the reader to the edge of indeterminacy; the less assertive poetry of Rosales, Panero, and others projects rich complexes of feeling in a manner more reminiscent of earlier modernity, but with a more personal and subjective focus.

The spectrum framed by Alonso at one end and Rosales at the other is filled out by the works of poets first publishing in the 1940s. One of the most important is José Hierro, also an accomplished critic of literature and art, who played a major role in the magazines *Corcel* and *Proel* and in defining a poetry of personal perspective.[15] His first book of verse, *Tierra sin nosotros* ("Land without Us," 1947), is undergirded by an intense sense of loss and generates a painful view of reality in which normally positive elements (spring, the moon, remembrances of love) ring sorrowful. In *Alegría* ("Happiness," also 1947) the poetic voice asserts the value of life in the face of this sense of loss and of an increasing perception of the terrible effects of time passing. Happiness emerges as an existentialist assertion of vitality in the face of human limitations. *Con las piedras, con el viento* ("With Stones, with Wind," 1950) focuses on love, yet again constructs a nostalgic vision of an eroded past. The effects of time continue underlying Hierro's poetry throughout the 1950s, in *Quinta del 42* ("Class of '42," 1952) and *Cuanto sé de mí* ("What I Know about Myself," 1957). These last books also include poems on Spain, on specific places and figures, on poetry.

Such thematic generalizations cannot define the uniqueness of Hierro's work. It has an extraordinary ability to draw a deeper emotive vision from an apparently anecdotal experience, as in "Las nubes":

> Inútilmente interrogas.
> Tus ojos miran al cielo.
> Buscas, detrás de las nubes,
> huellas que se llevó el viento.
>
> Buscas las manos calientes,
> los rostros de los que fueron,
> el círculo donde yerran
> tocando sus instrumentos.
>
> Nubes que eran ritmo, canto
> sin final y sin comienzo,
> campanas de espumas pálidas
> volteando su secreto,
>
> palmas de mármol, criaturas
> girando al compás del tiempo,

imitándole a la vida
su perpetuo movimiento.

Inútilmente interrogas
desde tus párpados ciegos.
¿Qué haces mirando a las nubes,
José Hierro? [Hierro 1962, 487]

{Uselessly you question. Your eyes look at the sky. You seek, behind the clouds, signs that the wind took away. You seek warm hands, the faces of those gone by, the circle in which they wander, playing their instruments. Clouds that were rhythms, songs without beginning or end, bells of pale foam, pouring out their secret, marble palms, creatures moving in circles to time's rhythm, imitating the timeless movement of life. Uselessly you question from behind your blind eyelids. What are you doing looking up at the clouds, José Hierro?}

The speaker seems to address, conversationally and bluntly, another person, making us witness a prospective dialogue about the questionable value of seeking images of the past in nature. The poem thus first focuses us on a specific, though rather enigmatic, experience and perspective. From this it endeavors to draw a larger vision of life. We soon realize, however, that this speaker is interrogating and contradicting himself. The scene he watches offers him an index of memories, yet one that finally only conveys to him the fragility and temporality of life. The clouds come to symbolize this fragility and temporality, as the poem comes back, at the end, to a specific image of the speaker as he bluntly challenges his whole quest.

   This poem recalls Antonio Machado, who constantly reflected the theme of time passing in natural imagery.[16] Yet Hierro's poetic strategy differs from Machado's. Machado, in classic symbolist fashion, would focus on an objective scene or image and then derive from it a wider pattern. Hierro throws us into a seeming anecdote, and then turns it into a double-voiced monologue in which the speaker, after interrogating himself, shifts attitudes and denies his hopes. The theme of loss emerges from this dramatic, time-specific interplay and from our particular responses to it; we recall Hierro's statement about the need for timeliness in poetry. As a result of all this, the poem remains somewhat open: we can choose to share the speaker's final pessimism (the "second voice") completely or to stand back a little and sympathize with the "first voice" quest.

   We might see in this poem—and in the poetry of this time—an incipient transition from the text as object embodying experience to the text as stimulus to the reader's response. The abandonment of the notion of the poem as an icon preserving an "eternal present" allows for the expansion of the role of the reader, who can now extend the speaker's experience and relate it to his or her own circumstances. The new techniques seen here—especially the "double voicing," to adopt Mikhail Bakhtin's term—whether or not the poet was conscious of them, contribute to these possibilities.

"Las nubes" offers but one example, one of many ways in which Hierro builds his poems out of very specific and apparently anecdotal materials. In some of his works, a particular event sets the foundation for the poem's theme: thus "Canción de cuna para dormir a un preso" ("Lullabye to Put a Prisoner to Sleep"), possibly derived from Hierro's own prison experience, engenders tension between a sense of horror and escapism (Hierro 1962, 48–50).[17] Many times we receive partial views and hints of an anecdote that cannot be completely deciphered but that lay the foundations for the theme, often related to time and suffering. These procedures produce a sense of immediacy and contemporaneity, intensified by the use of colloquial language and by rich nuances of tone, and often add to the leeway available for our interpretations.

In my opinion, Hierro has been excessively identified with social poetry by critics and historians. Too much has been made of one poem, "A un esteta" ("To an Aesthete"), a critique of a formalist poet who might echo Juan Ramón Jiménez. That text does indeed portray the stereotype of an aesthete and by implication of formal poetry and reflects a posture common to most writers of Hierro's generation. Yet it is not, as David Bary has shown, a manifesto for social poetry (1347). Nor do social or political topics and attitudes dominate Hierro's verse or essays.

For all its contemporaneity, and in a sense because of it, Hierro's poetry is highly artful. He makes masterful use of rhythms and verse forms (including rare ones, such as nine-syllable), creating complex cadences that emerge on reading his poems aloud. (We recall his admiration for Gerardo Diego, and Diego's support of his work.) As his poetry develops, Hierro consciously cultivates two styles, which he describes as *reportaje* ("reporting") and *alucinación* ("hallucination"). The former relies on a combination of narrative and rhythmic control to embody emotion; the latter projects feelings in less concrete fashion (see Hierro 1962, 11). This system makes clear Hierro's deliberate program of creating artful poetry from the everyday— and his success in doing so.

Much as Hierro's avoidance of complex metaphor and his use of colloquial elements, anecdote, and narrative devices separate his poetry from that of prior decades, his poetry of the 1940s and 1950s fits for the most part within the modernist quest of making experiences into verbal present. Yet as readers of poems such as "Las nubes," we do experience a freedom, an invitation to participate and maybe even fill out the text, that the Machado of *Campos de Castilla* or the Guillén of *Cántico* did not offer. Poems of the 1960s, including some by Hierro, would expand on that freedom.

A consciousness of time also pervades the poetry of Carlos Bousoño, although Bousoño expresses it in a very different mode. We can look, first, at his *Hacia otra luz* ("Toward Another Light," 1952), which incorporates the previously published *Subida al amor* ("Rising toward Love," 1943) and *Primavera de la muerte* ("Springtime of Death," 1946), as well as poems from the unpublished "En vez del sueño" ("Instead of Sleep") and from the later-to-be-completed *Noche del sentido* ("Night of the Senses"). Most commonly, the poetic persona uses reflections on scenes, places, or moments to suscitate a mood, often a melancholy sense of the passage of time. An individualized, emotional perspective is produced by a melodic rhythm and by emotive images and vocabulary. The following lines from "Duda" ("Doubt") may recall some aspects of Juan Ramón Jiménez and others of Machado. Finally, however, they offer a lower-key, first-person perspective:

> Tal vez la última caricia,
> la última brisa que se expande.
> Por eso triste caminando,
> miro el sol puro de la tarde.
> Alma dormida allá en el fondo
> alma que duerme y que no sabe.
> [Bousoño 1976, 131]

{The last caress, perhaps, the last breeze that flows. Hence I look at the pure sun of afternoon, as I walk sadly. A soul sleeping in the background, a soul that sleeps and does not know it.}

This poetry is probably best classified as religious, since the speaker often seeks God's presence and love. Yet that quest expands into a more general search for value in one's surroundings, which leads to an existentialist posture. (José Olivio Jiménez has noted relationships to Sartre, George Bataille, and Unamuno [1972, 248–51].) By seeing life as a "springtime of death," Bousoño projects on the one hand its limitation and ultimate insignificance and on the other its value as a struggle and affirmation. Pairs of tensive symbols often capture this double view. Yet the final effect produced by most of this poetry is one of melancholic satisfaction. This feeling emerges, to my mind, from the flowing rhythm and the lack of jarring notes. Very much in the spirit of his time, Bousoño focuses on common scenes and objects: Christ, for example, is presented in everyday aspects of life—as adolescent, as one who contemplates a beautiful landscape (Cano 63). This reality is made to convey life's harmony as well as its fragility.

Noche del sentido (1957) offers a gloomier overall perspective. The conflict between an affirmation of life and a reflection on the tragedy of its passing now emphasizes the latter. The first-person perspective seems even more important: the speaker registers his feelings as he highlights elements from his surroundings that correspond to them. Yet this book, like the preceding ones, gives masterful examples of a way in which very personal and ambiguous attitudes can be conveyed in a language at once artful and unassuming.[18]

More traditionally religious is the poetry of José María Valverde, whose *Hombre y Dios* ("Man and God," 1945) consists of evocations and meditations on the persona's youth, on time passing, on a search for a more satisfying view of God. Valverde's poetry gains greater serenity in *La espera* ("The Wait," 1949) and *Versos del Domingo* ("Sunday Verses," 1954). In the latter book, Valverde moves beyond his earlier self-questioning and seeks religious and transcendent values in everyday elements of life, presaging a sort of social spirituality that characterized his work in the 1950s and 1960s.[19]

José Luis Hidalgo, Hierro's collaborator in *Corcel,* began writing under the impact of surrealism; his early poetry, collected in *Raíz* ("Root," 1943), reflects a variety of emotive states via complex images that recall Aleixandre (see García de la Concha 1987, 1: 609–21). A neoromantic strain also underlies *Los animales* ("Animals," 1944), where irrational images combine with elements of a fable, and *Los muertos* ("The Dead"), Hidalgo's most impressive book, completed shortly before his own premature death in 1947. Critics have noted existentialist, pantheist, and stoic aspects in the book (ibid. 621–32). What makes it significant, however, is its imagery. A complex of visionary images and sensorial descriptions projects an intense subjective vision of existence in the light of the awareness of death. In a sense, the book carries to its ultimate possibilities the goal of embodying sentiment in irrationally constructed imagery that had become dominant in Lorca's *Poeta en Nueva York* and in Aleixandre's earlier work.

Although mainly identified as a social poet on account of his later writings, Blas de Otero is also the author of some of the most impressive existential verse in Spain. Brought up in religious schools and trained as a lawyer, Otero published in 1942 a small book of poetry titled *Cántico espiritual* ("Spiritual Canticle"). Drawing on St. John of the Cross and Fray Luis de León, this work already reveals a struggling search for religious peace. The struggle becomes an anguished one in *Angel fieramente humano* ("Fiercely Human Angel," 1950) and *Redoble de conciencia* ("The Tolling of Conscience," 1951), which Otero combines, with thirty-six additional poems, in his 1958 volume *Ancia* (García de la Concha 1987, 1: 549). Otero abandoned law in 1943, moved to Madrid to study literature at the university, and obtained the support and encouragement of Alonso and Aleixandre.

Ancia represents an extraordinary combination of formal virtuosity, ordinary vocabulary, and emphatic direct address. Most of the poems of its first part consist of a frantic and irreverent questioning of God. The subject, vocabulary, and tone recall *Hijos de la ira,* but the forms used are more conventional. "Hombre" ("Man"), for example, is a sonnet, which asserts a desperate wish to reach God and keep him awake in the first eight lines, and then ends as follows:

> Alzo la mano, y tú me la cercenas.
> Abro los ojos: me los sajas vivos.
> Sed tengo, y sal se vuelven tus arenas.
> Esto es ser hombre: horror a manos llenas.
> Ser—y no ser—eternos, fugitivos.
> ¡Angel con grandes alas de cadenas!
> > [Otero 1974, 24]

{I raise my hand, and you cut it off. I open my eyes, and you pluck them live. I am thirsty, and your sands turn to salt. That is to be human: hands full of horror. To be—and to not be—eternal, fleeting. Angel with great wings of chains!}

The combination of horrifying metaphor and formal order (three parallel images, in exact syntactical balance) conveys a sense of controlled anguish that intensifies the poem's impact. Having seen and presented his tragic view, the speaker then moves inexorably to a logical conclusion and definition, reflected in one more vignette ("horror a manos llenas"), then wrapped up conceptually in the next-to-the-last line, and finally embodied in the paradoxical metaphor of the angel. The fact that this angel's wings, the parts that should make it fly, are what chains it down, dramatically highlights the irony of our predicament. Our religious hopes are but the cause of our imprisonment and suffering.

Other poems make use of other devices and forms but always create a great impact. In "Crecida" ("High Tide"), for example, free verse and a chain of long parallel phrases that recall Aleixandre or Neruda reflect the speaker's anguish, while the dominant image of walking through a field of bleeding human beings points to the state of the world. I cite a short excerpt:

> Con la sangre hasta la cintura, algunas veces
> con la sangre hasta el borde de la boca,
> voy
> avanzando
> lentamente, con la sangre hasta el borde de los labios
> algunas veces,
> voy
> avanzando sobre este viejo suelo, sobre
> la tierra hundida en sangre. [Otero 1974, 26]

{With blood up to the waist, sometimes with blood up to the edge of my mouth, I advance slowly, with blood up to the edge of my lips, sometimes I am advancing over this old ground, over the earth sinking in blood.}

Reading this poetry, one admires Otero's ability to control, through form and image, feelings that could have easily engendered sentimental diatribe. He makes use of an ample formal repertoire: a variety of verse forms and tones, diverse rhythmic effects, carefully used intertexts (we hear echoes of Saint John, Quevedo, popular speech), an original use of the shocking metaphor in a poem's last line (as in "Hombre"), modulated sequences of discourse. The love poems of the second part of *Ancia* reflect a similar mastery and effect; the last part of the book introduces the theme of solidarity among humans and points to Otero's later social verse. An everyday vocabulary is used throughout; in many cases Otero foregrounds colloquial address: "Mire usted en la guía telefónica, / o en la Biblia, es fácil que allí encuentre algo" (1974, 38). {"Look in the telephone book, or in the Bible, you're likely to find something there."}

The sense of order and control conveyed by Otero's early work makes us think, paradoxically, of Guillén, of the symbolists. Thematically situated at an opposite pole, Otero's first books nevertheless constitute a way of engendering experience in verbal form that harks back to a basic principle of modernity. In that sense, we might even see the turn to a new, expressively communicative poetry after the Civil War as a "conservative" one. In order to communicate with impact, to impart their testimonial work to the reader, the most successful poets, like Otero, concerned themselves, in very modern fashion, with making form embody feeling. (And many who did not share this concern wrote diatribes or messages in verse.) Yet their focus on personal emotions and on reader communication leaves behind the notion of textual objectivity and points in new directions, though not as clearly as the work of Alonso or Hierro, with their use of monologue and "double voicing."

To gain a complete picture of emotive and testimonial poetry of the 1940s and 1950s one would also have to consider several other authors: Rafael Morales, whose *Poemas del toro* ("Poems of the Bull," 1943), evocative of Miguel Hernández as well as baroque poetry, produce a sense of passion, violence, and beauty; Vicente Gaos, author of excellent meditative and existential sonnets constituting *Arcángel de la noche* ("Archangel of Night," 1944) and of other valuable books; José Luis Cano, who wrote several volumes of well-crafted emotive verse, although he is best known as critic, literary figure, and cofounder of *Insula;* Eugenio de Nora; Luis López Anglada; Ramón de Garcíasol; Julio Maruri; Elena Martín Vivaldi. Beyond a few obvious examples, it is not as easy to distinguish major works and figures from secondary ones for these decades as it was for the 1920s. An aesthetic climate in which much Western literature remained unread, in which the value of style and originality was considered suspect, and in which immediate expression was a main goal undoubtedly contributed to a certain leveling.

Despite this, and despite much mediocre testimonial poetry published at the time (see Jiménez 1992, 20–21), we have seen that many significant works emerged from these decades. I would especially highlight Dámaso Alonso's use of common language, dramatic monologue, and perspective play in the unique style of *Hijos de la ira;* Luis Rosales's mode of imagistic and symbolic narrative in *La casa encendida;* José Hierro's use of voices, perspectives, and rhythms to make simple language convey complex experience; Blas de Otero's structural, dramatic, and imagistic effects. All of these constitute successful responses to a dilemma: how to convey personal and subjective experiences with some objectivity and in a necessarily common and apparently unadorned language.

The very fact that these salient works invent and employ original, discernible, and definable forms sets them, to some extent, within the tenets of modernity. The fundamental goal of using language to seize subjective experiences still underlies Spanish poetics and poetry, as "communication" (in its various meanings) remains an accepted premise. In a paradoxical sense, several aspects of modernity are affirmed by the antiaestheticism of the post–Civil War atmosphere, which denied the option of regarding art as play, as process with no goal in mind, and hence postponed for another decade or so any new poetics of indeterminacy.[20] The view of poetry as realistically expressive itself constitutes a stable convention and consensus.

Yet in the course of developing new ways of conveying their testimonial themes, the poets I have been discussing point to the erosion of modernist determinacy. The stress on irrational subjectivity in Aleixandre's and Hidalgo's texts to some extent undermines the notion of language objectifying experience, extending the increased stress on emotive meaning that we saw from the 1930s on. The tone and perspective changes of *Hijos de la ira* invite conflicting readings; José Hierro's multiple voices and angles of incidence can call logocentric resolutions into question, as they also call any stable view of life and society into question. The implicit notion of the poem as "eternal present" is left behind, and a greater and more varied role is made possible for the reader. Some of the most interesting poetry of these decades is pointing ahead to a time in which any notion of the poem as icon, object, message, or missile will no longer hold.

Notes of Indeterminacy: Postismo, Surrealism

Although almost ignored in their time, a few poetic ventures of the 1940s asserted a vanguardist, consciously antirational attitude. In January 1945 a group of poets and painters issued a manifesto on a new "ism," immediately followed by the publication of a magazine titled *Postismo.* They emphasized the value of imagination and play as a source of beauty: "El retorno a una idea, una frase musical, una o unas palabra-símbolo . . . es *juego;* y la rima es *juego;* y cierta forma de asociación es *juego*" (García de la Concha 1987, 2: 696). {"The return to an idea, a musical phrase, one or more word-symbols`. . . is a *game;* and rhyme is a *game;* and a certain form of associa-tion is a *game.*"} Otherwise, their stance amounted to an advocacy of cre-ativity as against reason, with allusions to authors as disparate as Lorca, Alberti, and Max Ernst and humorous notes. Their stress on free associa-tion and on a logic of the absurd has obvious echoes of surrealism, and their writings make clear their debt to Breton, Tzara, Artaud, and the dadaists. Their very adoption of *postismo,* the "ism" that comes after all the others, suggests a general posture of rebellion against the dominant liter-alism of the time, rather than a narrow and exactly defined aesthetic.

The venture motivated some laughter and some scandal; censorship prevented further issues of *Postismo.* Its participants, led by Eduardo Chicharro, Gabino-Alejandro Carriedo, and Carlos Edmundo de Ory, came out with three more manifestos and one issue of another journal, *La Cer-batana.* They also published elsewhere; Angel Crespo, one of their affiliates, was instrumental in issuing the magazines *El pájaro de paja* and *Deucalión* in the early 1950s.

Chicharro, son of a well-known painter of the same name, himself moved from painting to letters and composed a fairly large volume of po-etry. In the latter, the phonic level—alliteration, internal rhyme, repeti-tion—often takes over the text and overwhelms its initial subject. This is often combined with arbitrary shifts in imagery; both lead to a disintegra-tion of logic, as is apparent in this excerpt quoted by García de la Concha:

> Es la hoguera en la cocina,
> es el hornillo de coque,
> el caballo que desboque
> busca la musa latina,
> busca el choque.[2: 704]

{The kitchen is a campfire, it is the coke stove, the unbridled horse, seeks the Latin muse, seeks shock.}

Carriedo had first published some realistic poetry on social and histor-ical themes; even there, he used language creatively, producing shocking portrayals of his country in *Poema de la condenación de Castilla* ("Poem of the Condemnation of Castile," 1946). García de la Concha has labeled the book *tremendista,* making us think of connections to the impulse and style that produced, in prose, the novels of Camilo José Cela (García de la Con-cha 1987, 2: 682–86). More important for our purposes here, Carriedo in the late 1940s and the 1950s wrote a number of humorous and parodic texts, filled with word play and free association; they are included in *Los animales vivos* ("Live Animals," published in 1965) and *Del mal el menos* ("Of Evil, Take the Least," 1952). María del Pilar Palomo notes that many of these texts recall Gómez de la Serna's *greguerías* (97). They attest, in any event, to the presence of verbally creative impulses in this otherwise sub- ject- and message-oriented time.

Carlos Edmundo de Ory was more fully and obsessively committed to poetry and art, which he saw as ways of trying to redeem a tragic and mean- ingless existence. Grounded in baroque metaphor as well as surrealist liter- ature, his poetry is marked by many levels of play with words, sounds, and images, although his vocabulary and tone are often colloquial. Ory at- tempted to forge various literary movements, from *postismo* to what he called *introrrealismo* in 1951, and to the Atelier de Poésie Ouverte (Workshop of Open Poetry) in 1968 (see Ory 60–78).

Ory's poetry combines anguished and tragic expressions, erotic evoca- tions, and word play. He also composed some visual works he called *poema- collage*. Today we may give more attention to his satires on emotive and confessional poetry, which uncover the imaginative poverty and the trite- ness of so much verse of the 1940s. Palomo cites a very funny example:

> Sin ti soy triste cosa y triste cosa,
> sin ti me lleno de humo, y me extravío,
> sin ti me armo un lío y me armo un lío . . .
> [Palomo 94]

{Without you I'm a sad thing, a sad thing; without you I'm filled with smoke and I get lost, without you I get in trouble, get in trouble . . . }

Ory would have preferred, undoubtedly, that we pay attention to the imag- inativeness and the surprising quality of his metaphors in his more seriously intended poems. He authored a great number of them, many of which deal with amorous and erotic topics and forge unusual perspectives. Yet the imaginative (and imagistic) inventiveness apparent when we read Ory's col- lected poetry are undercut by its discursiveness and confusion; scintillating moments sink in long, apparently meandering texts.

Juan Eduardo Cirlot, though not connected with *postismo*, also provides evidence of a dissident, vanguard strand beneath the surface of the domi- nant post–Civil War pragmatism. Cirlot is generally labeled a surrealist (García de la Concha, 1987, 2: 724–42), in view of his deliberate efforts to develop a theory of subconscious analogies and images.[21] His most interest- ing poems consist of phonic and word plays, often linked with intertextual allusions and transformations. Cirlot's knowledge of music, of culture, and of both Western and Eastern mythologies gave him the background needed for composing this poetry, which I find most interesting as a way of showing that language can be used for playful and creative purposes, quite opposite to the goals of the dominant poetics. Cirlot's *Lilith* (1949) probably holds the best examples of this poetry and of what the author called "permutatory" poetry (see Palomo 102).

Also generally linked with surrealism is the poetry of Miguel Labordeta, author of a number of books of verse that describe, bitterly and ironically, the evils and meaninglessness of the contemporary Spanish world. Labordeta's work does contain interesting verbal play, from lack of punctuation to unusual typographies and visual arrangements, and to that degree connects with the attention to form and sign that I have been noting in this section. But its main goal and effect reside in its stance of social condemnation.

From my perspective, Chicharro, Ory, Carriedo, and Cirlot all need to be remembered because of their efforts to explore the inventive possibilities of poetic language and because they attest to the presence of a ludic poetics and poetry during a time when a much more pragmatic view of art dominated. They reflect a limited presence during these decades of the strain of indeterminacy that we noticed in Spanish poetry since 1915 or so, a presence that current literary histories largely ignored.[22] That strain has been present, to some extent, throughout modernity, counterbalancing the more object-centered, dominant mode of symbolist filiation as well as the later communicative orientation of post–Civil War verse. It will reappear, in other forms, in later writings.

Social and Political Poetry, 1950–1965

Works that deal with social and political themes probably constituted the dominant current of verse in the 1950s. Even more than the testimonial poetry discussed earlier, they reflect the goal of constructing a powerful new realistic literature, suited to the circumstances, that underlay *Espadaña,* the *Antología consultada,* and the whole climate of the time. To some degree, dealing separately with this poetry destroys Hierro's larger "testimonial" grouping and his excellent point that worthwhile social poems have much in common with personal ones and differ greatly from message verse. Yet it is important to look separately at the category of poetry focused on collective concerns. Despite the profusion of work in this vein published in Spain, I will deal with most of it in general terms, since its main impact is historical and social, and its individual and aesthetic implications are limited.

Though envisioned by the statements appearing in *Espadaña* and other journals of the mid-1940s, this kind of poetry became more pervasive about ten years later, between 1950 and 1960. Various explanations can be suggested, both specific and general: Blas de Otero moved to Paris and adopted communism in 1951; Spaniards developed an increased international and

hence social awareness, as the country's isolation from Europe was attenu-
ated when the United States and other countries reestablished diplomatic
relations with Spain; as time went on, "forbidden" texts, Spanish and for-
eign, were more generally available, and writers had a resulting incentive to
follow their lead and compose social verse. Censorship, though still in place,
became less absolute in the 1950s, and poetry seemed to be the one genre
in which postures of protest could be published, as long as explicit attacks
on the regime were avoided.[23] Growing tourism and increased industrial-
ization both opened the country and raised new issues. All of this may have
contributed to a shift in the focus of poetry from personal anguished reac-
tions to larger themes, as well as to some enrichment of the literary scene.

Vicente Aleixandre's *Historia del corazón* ("Story of the Heart," 1954) is
of major importance. At first glance, the book seems a disparate combina-
tion of passionate love poems and texts that portray the need for human sol-
idarity. Yet the themes connect and make us see how *Historia del corazón*
builds on Aleixandre's earlier poetry. What was in *La destrucción o el amor* and
Sombra del paraíso an individual human being's search for harmony in the
beloved and in nature is now extended to include a striving for human har-
mony in society. Still using long chains of free verse that encompass a vari-
ety of images, Aleixandre now builds more explicit symbolic patterns, in
which specific actions reflect larger themes. In "En la plaza" ("In the Plaza"),
for example, the protagonist's joining a crowd reflects his decision to tran-
scend limited goals; as the image shifts into one of a swimmer immersed in
the sea, the theme acquires more cosmic dimensions.

Most remarkable is Aleixandre's use of verse and image to engender his
social theme without reducing his text to a simple message. In "En la plaza"
he draws this vignette of the protagonist:

Hermoso es, hermosamente humilde y confiante, vivificador y profundo,
sentirse bajo el sol, entre los demás, impelido,
llevado, conducido, mezclado, rumorosamente arrastrado.
No es bueno
quedarse en la orilla
como el malecón o como el molusco que quiere calcáreamente imitar a la roca.
Sino que es puro y sereno arrasarse en la dicha
de fluir y perderse,
encontrándose en el movimiento con que el gran corazón de los hombres palpita
　　　extendido. [Aleixandre 1960, 55–56]

{Beautiful it is, beautifully humble and confident, vivifying and profound, to feel, un-
der the sun, among others, impelled, led, mixed-in, soundingly pulled. It is not right
to remain on the shore, like the dike or like the mollusk that stonily tries to imitate a
rock. Rather it is pure and serene to let oneself be carried in the happiness of flowing
and being lost, of finding oneself within the movement with which the great heart of
human beings, extended, palpitates.}

Aleixandre's way of using syntax, vocabulary, and imagery produces a series
of sensations, foregrounding them over the poem's story line and over its
obvious allegorical meaning. It does so by repeating *hermoso* in *hermosamente,*
by clustering four participles that describe sensations in line 3, by overload-
ing adjectives and adverbs, by delaying the flow of each sentence through
parallel constructions. This language involves the reader in the protago-
nist's subjective experience and thus ultimately turns the theme of social
communion into an emotive reality.

At times this process of turning a social theme into a subjective experi-
ence leads to a very unusual combination of narrative and imagery. In "El
viejo y el sol" ("The Old Man and the Sun") a detailed description of an old
man seated on a tree trunk evolves into a magical image of his being distilled
and evaporated into the sunlight, which leads into the theme of harmony
with the universe (Aleixandre 1960, 81–83; see Debicki 1981, 378–80). The
mixture of perspectives and planes makes this theme emerge dramatically
and concretely, avoiding didacticism. From another point of view, this pro-
cedure destroys the initial realistic expectations of the reader, leaving the lat-
ter groping and free to come up with some coherent explanation.[24] In that
sense, it strains the modernist canon of unity and perspectival consistency far
more than Aleixandre's earlier poetry.

Blas de Otero is another social poet of this time whose work seems
nearly as readable today as it was in its time. In *Pido la paz y la palabra* ("I Call
for Peace and the Word," 1955), *En castellano* ("In Castilian," 1960), *Esto no
es un libro* ("This Is Not a Book," 1963), and *Que trata de España* ("Concern-
ing Spain," 1964), Otero again makes use of the ample verbal and formal
repertoire we saw in his earlier books. He thus manages to infuse impact and
originality into his condemnation of oppression and injustice and his call
for a better world. We also find in these books echoes of other works and
traditions; through them Otero gives original twists to old forms and con-
cepts. In "Con nosotros" ("With Us"), for example, he mixes words from a
Rubén Darío poem about Antonio Machado with an ironic evocation of
Machado's figure to draw him as a poet writing for the people:

> En este Café
> se sentaba don Antonio
> Machado.
> Silencioso
> y misterioso, se incorporó
> al pueblo,
> blandió la pluma,
> sacudió la ceniza
> y se fue . . .
>   [Otero 1974, 44]

{In this café don Antonio Machado used to sit. Silent and mysterious, he joined the people, brandished his pen, shook off ashes, and went away . . . }

The realistic focus of the poem is undermined when we are aware that "silencioso y misterioso" repeats the beginning of Rubén Darío's famous poem about Machado. It is undercut in a different way in line 5, when we expected a literal statement ("se incorporó y salió," perhaps) and are given instead a social metaphor. Reality and metaphor mix again in lines 7–8, which counterpose a clichéd image of a poet to a reminiscence of Machado's well-known habit of dropping cigarette ashes on everything. The end result is a playful mixture of texts and allusions and an affectionate view of Machado. Today we may find the theme of "the poet of the people" less interesting than the way in which Otero handles narrative focus and point-of-view play. We will see more of this in his poetry of the later 1960s and 1970s.

I find Gabriel Celaya's poetry much harder to read today than Otero's. Born in 1911, Celaya had begun his career as a writer by composing neoromantic poetry in the early 1930s. Most of his voluminous writing of the 1940s consists of social verse written in everyday language, although it also includes some love poems. Angel González, perhaps Celaya's most perceptive critic, points out the negative effects of Celaya's devotion to poetry of ideas and to his acceptance of the premises of social realism (Celaya 7–8). Many of his works—especially those signed Rafael Múgica, his original name, and Gabriel Celaya, a pseudonym that he made his legal name—read like simplistic messages in verse, or sentimental diatribes. Yet under the pseudonym Juan de Leceta, Celaya wrote some interesting works. Most telling, perhaps, is his way of creating a very consistent persona, a speaker whom González likens to that of Alonso's *Hijos de la ira*. At his best, this persona manages to construct surprisingly powerful images with extremely ordinary, even vulgar materials. In "Telegrama urgente" ("Urgent Telegram") machines are given feelings while men are dehumanized and described through the image of "un sucio olor difuso / a interiores calientes de pereza y de sueño" (ibid. 67) {"a dirty, diffuse smell of warm innards of laziness and sleep"}. Similar effects are achieved in "Escaparate—sorpresa" ("Store Window—Surprise"), climaxed by the vignette of pink corsets in a store window (ibid. 79). Years later we will find similar uses of language, in a lower key and to greater effect, by Gloria Fuertes.

One can find other good poetry in a social vein. Angela Figuera, who by birth date (1902) would be classified as a member of the Generation of 1927, published most of her verse in the 1950s. Her best poems do not seem to call attention to themselves, yet they make ordinary language and images from everyday life capture human suffering. Those poems stand out, by contrast, from much of the rhetorical social verse that pervaded the decade. Victoriano Crémer, sometimes classified as an existentialist or a *tremendista,* is the author of many texts portraying human suffering.[25] While some make skillful use of narrative techniques—exemplified in the vignettes of a widow collecting her husband's pipe in "El pipa"—pathos, overstated sentiment, and a didactic social bent date his work.

In the late 1950s there began to appear books of poetry written by new writers, most of them born after 1925 and generally studied as members of the Generation of the 1950s. Several focused on social themes, though in a different way from many of their older colleagues. An artful, highly original use of various techniques, some of them common to narrative fiction, let these authors present social issues in less direct fashion and establish very different relationships between speaker and reader. Many of these poets dealt with more personal themes in the late 1950s and turned to social ones later, in the 1960s. One can suggest different reasons: the waning of censorship, an increased social consciousness as the country evolved and as writers matured, perhaps a tendency to expand the scope of earlier and more personal writing. These poets, in any event, came to social issues with a sense of form, style, and poetics already formed and tested on more personal topics.

Gloria Fuertes, though born in 1918, published most of her work after 1958 and will thus fit into the innovative currents of the 1960s discussed later. But the theme of social tragedies and injustices pervades her poetry and is expressed with great originality. Particularly noteworthy is Fuertes's ability to create texts that artfully play off colloquial language, societal conventions, or social premises. Quite often, she will introduce an unexpected form or intertext to produce jarring effects. The best example might be the following poem, written and presented as a file card in a hospital record:

> *Ficha ingreso Hospital General*
>
> Nombre: Antonio Martínez Cruz.
> Domicilio: Vivía en una alcantarilla.
> Profesión: Obrero sin trabajo.
> OBSERVACIONES: Le encontraron moribundo.
> Padecía: Hambre. [Fuertes 135]

> {*Admission Index Card, General Hospital*
>
> Name: Antonio Martínez Cruz.
> Address: He lived in a sewer.
> Profession: Unemployed laborer.
> OBSERVATIONS: He was found moribund.
> Disease: Hunger.}

The very fact of reading a poem in the form of a file card jars us, making us pay more attention to its awful implications. Furthermore, the form seems singularly suited to convey such a tragedy starkly, dramatically, without any didactic intrusion.

Eladio Cabañero's *Desde el sol y la anchura* ("From Sun and Expanse," 1956) draws vignettes of rural Spaniards yet manages to transcend the didacticism dominant in much of Celaya and Crémer. The following lines from "El segador" ("The Reaper") give an example:

> Empuñando la hoz, porificando
> la sangre, enmadejada, endurecida,
> a contra fauces gira las dos manos
> tronchando cañas y venciendo espigas.
> Los ojos dilatados y el resuello
> pegándose en la carne y la camisa.
>   Cabañero 32–33]

{Grasping the sickle, letting hardened blood, rolled into a skein, flow through his pores, he turns his two hands with set jaws, felling canes and beating down wheat. His eyes are dilated, his breath sticks to his flesh and shirt.}

Language and imagery artfully dehumanize the harvester. Describing in detail his holding of the sickle and the movement of his hands, the poem makes his actions mechanical; the image of his blood rolled up in a skein focuses on him as though he were an object. The reference to the man's dilated eyes and the image of his breath sticking to him accent his effort, but only in physical terms. The whole description focuses on the harvester as a physical type and makes concrete the mechanized, inadequate sense of his life. Our negative view of this life is later developed by the imagery of his reaping as a wounding and the vignette of the harvester as bowed down (*curvado*) against the sterile land.

The way in which a subjective vision is produced in this text recalls the poetry of Lorca or Hernández far more than that of the typical social poet of the 1950s. Cabañero makes experience emerge from word and form. He does so throughout this book as well as in his next one, *Una señal de amor* ("A Sign of Love," 1958), in which the theme of love is combined with a quest for social order. Visual imagery is again central, though Cabañero makes greater use of symbolic and archetypal patterns to configure his themes (see Debicki 1982, 170–73). What is most telling, however, is the poet's artful control of language and form.

That same artful control is apparent in some of the early work of Angel González, José Agustín Goytisolo, Jaime Gil de Biedma, and José Angel Valente. Most of these poets dealt predominantly with themes other than social ones, yet they have written significant social poems. Angel González, after dealing with more individual experiences in his first two books, constructed in *Grado elemental* ("Elementary Grade," 1962), *Palabra sobre palabra* ("Word

upon Word," 1965), and *Tratado de urbanismo* ("Treatise of Urbanism," 1967)
critical vignettes of modern Spanish life and society. A subtle use of individ-
ualized speakers and of various tones dramatizes the tawdriness of that world
and its dehumanizing effects. "Nota necrológica" ("Necrological Note"),
from *Grado elemental,* does so via an understated, distanced description of the
limited life of a submissive clerk, which the reader finds more shocking than
the speaker (González 1986, 158–60). "Lecciones de buen amor" ("Lessons
of Good Love"), from *Tratado,* draws an ironic picture of a couple that is sup-
posed to serve as a model of love:

> Se amaban.
> No demasiado jóvenes ni hermosos,
> algo marcados ya por la fatiga
> de convivir durante aquellos años,
> una alimentación con excedentes
> de azúcar y de grasa había dañado
> su silueta,
> . . . .
> y ese estar cotidiano sin tocarse,
> repito, pero juntos,
> irreparablemente, tenazmente próximos
> como mandan la Epístola y las Leyes,
> acreditaba ahora ante los hombres,
> lo que un distante día
> había consagrado un sacramento
> . . . .
> del volumen, decía, de su carne
> húmeda y abundante, trasladadà
> solemnemente por las piernas
> cortas hasta el asiento
> delantero de un coche americano . . .
> [González 1986, 199–201]

{They loved each other. Not too young or handsome, somewhat marked already by
the tiredness of living together for all those years, a diet with too much sugar and fat
had ruined their figures . . . and this togetherness without touching, I repeat, but to-
gether, irreparably, tenaciously joined like the Epistle and the Laws decree, now
manifested to people what a sacrament had consecrated long before. . . . Of the vol-
ume, he said, of her flesh, moist and abundant, transferred solemnly by her short
legs to the front seat of an American car . . . }

    The contrast between the idea of this couple as a model of love, stressed
by the repetition of "se amaban" (with possible echoes of a neoromantic
poem by Aleixandre and its refrain "se querían"), and their tawdry and
grotesque existence suggests the corruption of a whole society. González
combines an ironic speaker, echoes that parody conventional situations and

other literary texts, and even the device of a series of lines printed as a footnote, which points out how the characters actually despise one another. Combining techniques normally used in poetry, narrative fiction, and expository writing, he invents a fresh way of communicating a strongly negative view of a society while avoiding any didacticism.

José Agustín Goytisolo's second book of poetry, *Salmos al viento* ("Psalms to the Wind," 1958), likewise uses carefully controlled narrative techniques to convey the decadence and hypocrisy of post–Civil War Spanish society. Some of these poems are monologues placed in the mouths of unreliable speakers, who praise, with grandiloquent pomposity, a sheltered bourgeois existence, pure poetry, hypocritical behavior. Others reflect, with gentler irony, the perspective of those living muted and resigned lives, as in "Autobiografía," which ends as follows:

> De tristeza en tristeza
> caí por los peldaños
> de la vida. Y un día
> la muchacha que amo
> me dijo y era alegre:
> no sirves para nada.
> Ahora vivo con ella
> voy limpio y bien peinado.
> Tenemos una niña
> a la que a veces digo
> también con alegría:
> no sirves para nada.
> [Goytisolo 54]

{From sadness to sadness, I fell down the steps of life. And one day, the girl that I love said—pleasantly: you are good for nothing. Now I live with her, I am clean, and my hair is combed. We have a daughter, to whom I say, also pleasantly: you are good for nothing.}

Throughout this book, various levels of irony produce dramatic portrayals of a society in decay. Often Goytisolo, like González, makes ironic use of clichéd phrases and situations from the society of the time; at other times he recasts and parodies conventions of traditional genres—a psalm, a hymn of praise, a story with a moral. In all cases, and in contrast with much of earlier social poetry, he creates forms that give original, artful, and nuanced expression to his themes. As is true of González, Goytisolo's best social poems are dramatic monologues that capture the complexity as well as the intensity of their issues by unfolding specific points of view and characters and by eliciting concrete responses to these on the part of the reader. The latter's negative attitude to social ills is formed by those responses rather than solicited directly by the poem's message.[26]

Gil de Biedma's *Compañeros de viaje* ("Fellow Travelers," 1959) also reveals an artful use of various tones and perspectives, which often evoke the limitations of an idle middle-class existence and the way in which illusions turn into cliché. Some of the most important texts in this volume constitute, again, dramatic monologues whose speakers reflect complex visions of social limitations. And José Angel Valente's *A modo de esperanza* ("In Hopeful Fashion," 1955) and *Poemas a Lázaro* ("Poems to Lazarus," 1960) contain several texts that highlight social ills and problems, from poverty to impersonality and lack of individuality. Social issues and themes had to be prominent to any Spaniard in the 1950s and continued to have impact in the 1960s; hence even those poets who focused primarily on other issues dealt with them. This becomes apparent when reading over Leopoldo de Luis's anthology *Poesía social* ("Social Poetry"), first published in 1965, which combines works of the most prominent social poets of the 1940s and 1950s with those by many younger writers for whom social themes were secondary. (In addition to the ones already mentioned, it includes works by Carlos Sahagún, Angel Crespo, and Manuel Vázquez Montalbán.)

The continued presence of social issues in poetry at a time in which new aesthetic directions were developing, in the late 1950s and the 1960s, has helped justify the organization of this book in overlapping periods. The new poetics that underlie the thought and work of the generation born in the late 1920s and the 1930s, as well as the more personal poetry that will be most directly related to it, will be discussed in chapter 4 and will point to directions that Spanish poetry would pursue into the 1970s. Yet it has been important to examine here the continuing social current extending at least until the mid-1960s and to note, above all, that the social poetry written by younger poets and published after the mid-1950s reveals new forms and styles and the same artfulness and manner of involving reader participation that we will see in the personal poetry in the next chapter.

In assessing the general significance of social poetry in Spain in this whole period, one has to stress the negatives, which become even more apparent when considering the average poem published in a magazine or even a book, rather than an excellent one by Otero or Figuera. A very large number of unexciting works were produced, many of which seem almost interchangeable. Perhaps they should be considered as part of social rather than literary history: in the face of censorship and repression, they did take a stand for freedom and social consciousness. Yet their dominance, together with other forms of realistic poetry, led to what later poets would rightly call a different kind of censorship, an imposition of the need to write directly, to avoid anything smacking of complexity and concern with language for its own sake. This produced an atmosphere in which language was devalued, reduced to its simplest meanings, and in which simplistic messages were ex-

pressed in clichéd verbiage. In an aesthetic sense, such writing, regardless
of its ideology, is reactionary: it ignores creativity and papers over (rather
than affirming, confronting, or modifying) the deeper issues about poetry's
value and uniqueness that had been underlying in the poetry of modernity.

The picture is different if we focus on a minority of good poems.
Aleixandre, Otero, and several younger poets used the circumstances of this
time as an opportunity for new poetic solutions. By juxtaposing the literal
and the imagined, the concrete and the symbolic, Aleixandre wrote social
poems that actually challenged mimetic premises of modernity; through
form, tone, echo, and intertext, Otero escaped the limits of didacticism.
Similar procedures and effects helped younger authors deal creatively with
social themes, even as they began to leave behind both the social doctrine
of the text as message and the whole symbolist conception of determinacy.

Poets in Exile

Between 1940 and 1960 many Spanish poets who had left their country
during the Civil War continued writing and publishing. Yet their work
needs to be considered separately from that produced by their compatriots
in Spain, since they were completely isolated from life in their native land
and since their works, in turn, did not circulate in that land until toward
the end of this period.[27] The poetry of the émigrés was also affected by dif-
ferent circumstances.

Juan Ramón Jiménez spent periods of time in Spanish America and the
continental United States but essentially settled in Puerto Rico until his
death in 1958. He wrote a considerable amount of poetry and prose poems.
He also kept revising and rewriting all of his work while letting relatively lit-
tle be published. Thus, very different versions are available: regular lyrical
verse printed in a 1957 edition of *Libros de poesía* ("Books of Poetry") turns
into prose poems in the manuscripts of *Leyenda* ("Legend," posthumously
published in 1978). The bulk of Juan Ramón's new work is collected in
books, most of which were never published separately: *En el otro costado* ("On
the Other Side," texts from 1936 to 1942), *Una colina meridiana* ("A Midday
Hill," from 1942 to 1950), *Dios deseado y deseante* ("Desired and Desiring
God," 1949), and *Ríos que se van* ("Rivers That Depart," from 1951 to 1953).

This poetry continues Juan Ramón's search for beauty, his desire to em-
body life's essences in verbal form. The desire becomes more and more ex-
plicit, involving a conscious quest by the speaker-poet to overcome time. In
the process, the poetry becomes increasingly and overtly philosophical and
develops something like a pantheistic mysticism. In the "Romances de Coral
Gables" ("Coral Gables Ballads"), from *En el otro costado,* specific scenes in
tightly controlled verse project a personified nature and the speaker's

search for its vital principles. In *Dios deseado y deseante* the style shifts to long lines of free verse (which become poetic prose in later versions). The speaker addresses directly a divinity identified with nature and with life forces; by contemplating and naming these forces, he seeks harmony and completion. In the second part, "Animal de fondo" ("Innermost Animal"), he focuses more on himself and his relationship to nature and divinity and seeks a form of harmony and permanence against the obvious backdrop of his aging.

Juan Ramón's ever more philosophical bent is linked, as Francisco Díez de Revenga has noted, to a sense of aging (1988, 51–53). But it also bears some likeness to developments in the work of other modernist poets, whose attempts to endow life experiences with "presentness" gave way to more subjective and more transcendent views: Aleixandre's cosmic visions of the 1930s, Cernuda's quest for a romantic sublime, and Pedro Salinas's *El contemplado* ("The Contemplated One").

After his arrival in the United States in 1936, Pedro Salinas spent four years teaching at Wellesley College and then joined the faculty of Johns Hopkins University until his death; for three years (1943–46) he was on leave, teaching at the University of Puerto Rico. All these years are marked by his extraordinary productivity as a critic, highlighted by books about Rubén Darío and Jorge Manrique and by *Reality and the Poet in Spanish Poetry*. This work undoubtedly intensified his concern with the poetic process.

Written in Puerto Rico between 1943 and 1945, *El contemplado* (1946) is a cohesive set of fifteen poems in which the speaker addresses the sea he is watching. The book has a metapoetic dimension: the speaker-poet's search for key meanings in nature leads to the very process of its writing. As this process develops, the sea in turn moves from passive subject to active collaborator with the poet; between the two, they construct a new way of seeing that may presage salvation: "Y de tanto mirarte, nos salvemos" (Salinas 1975, 649). {"And by looking at you so much, we may both be saved."}

To my mind, *El contemplado* is the cornerstone of Salinas's poetry. It marks the culmination of his constant, questioning search for what lies behind the appearance of things. The book does suggest a final affirmation; its poems lack the obvious indeterminacy that we saw in "35 bujías." Yet *El contemplado* portrays a world whose elements are constantly reversed and transformed: the passive sea and the active speaker change places, and natural rhythms are inverted. In "Variación II," for example, dawn is ingeniously metaphorized as instant springtime:

> ¡Tantos que van abriéndose, jardines,
>   celestes, y en el agua!
> Por el azul, espumas, nubecillas,

¡tantas corolas blancas!
Presente, este vergel, ¿de dónde brota,
  si anoche aquí no estaba?
Antes que llegue el día, labradora,
  la aurora se levanta,
y empieza su quehacer: urdir futuros.
  Estrellas rezagadas,
las luces que aún recoge por los cielos
  por el mar va a sembrarlas.
Nacen con el albor olas y nubes,
  ¡Primavera, qué rápida! [Salinas 1975, 614]

{So many celestial, skylike gardens that are opening up, and in the water! Through the blueness, foam, small clouds, so many white corollas! This garden, present before us, where does it come from—since last night it was not here? Before the day's arrival, dawn, the gardener, arises and begins her work: to create futures. The lights that she still finds in the skies, stars that have fallen behind, she sows in the sea. With the dawn, waves and clouds are born—what rapid spring!}

Based on the visual similarity between the waves' crests and the shimmering sunlight on the one hand, and a field of flowers on the other, the poem constructs an elaborate picture of dawn as a gardener who produces a speeded-up spring. This ultimately makes us feel the sheer creative power of poetic language and imagination: what finally matters is not what reality is but what poetry can make out of it. The process does not collapse into a simplistic philosophical affirmation. In that sense, this poem, and the book, continue the line pursued in Salinas's earlier verse. The poet's task is a battle to forge meaning in the face of time's limits.

This view of poetry in *El contemplado* relates it to Salinas's major critical works of this period, most notably *Reality and the Poet in Spanish Poetry* (1940). There and, more implicitly, in his books on Darío and Manrique, Salinas explores ways in which poetic language deals, penetratingly yet inconclusively, with an enigmatic world. Though grounded in the analytic criticism that we now see as the hallmark of modernity, Salinas's studies point ahead to later post-structuralist and reader-response criticism (see Debicki 1992).

Todo más claro y otros poemas ("Everything Clearer and Other Poems," 1949) contains poems written by Salinas in the United States in the 1940s. Many of them portray elements of modern civilization, recalling in this *Seguro azar* and *Fábula y signo*. But these elements are now seen in a negative light, as examples of the triviality of modern civilization. The poems in which they appear take a more narrative and discursive perspective. In "Nocturno de los avisos" ("Nocturne of Advertisements") an ironic speaker whimsically contemplates the advertisements in Times Square, seeing in them evidence of a world in which myths have been debased (Salinas 1975,

717–20). In some ways, such poems parallel the posture of narrative poetry that was being composed in Spain during the same decade. Both mark a retreat from the imaginative, vanguardist perspective on modern civilization, though Salinas's playfulness imparts notes of ambiguity and indeterminacy that differentiate him from the literalism of social poetry and again presages a later postmodernity.[28]

The title poem of *Todo más claro,* however, consists of four sections in which the speaker, fascinated by reality, seeks to get behind its appearances and seize its mysteries through language. His efforts culminate in "El poema" (title of section 4), which is portrayed as a means of improving reality to such a degree that it is astounded by the results (Salinas 1975, 667). This gives an affirmative, seemingly logocentric answer to the fundamental questioning of reality that underlies Salinas's verse, yet some of the playful openness and ambiguity of his earlier books remain in the vignette of a rose, a stone, and a bird amazed at their portrayal in the poetic text.[29] This poem's metapoetic perspective as it contemplates its own effects also presages postmodern attitudes.

After emigrating to France in 1938, Luis Cernuda spent several years in England, taught in the United States in the late 1940s and early 1950s, and definitively settled in Mexico in 1952. Cernuda's *Las nubes* ("The Clouds"), written between 1937 and 1940, channels the romantic longing that underlay his prior work in a metaphysical direction. The book's underlying persona uses past memories and natural scenes to seek some lasting meaning for his life. (This search takes on ethical implications as he considers his role in the world.) The search leads at times to a vision bordering on pantheism, in which natural beauty freezes time and fits the human self into a larger order. Combining an ordinary (though never colloquial) vocabulary with flowing, controlled rhythmic effects, the poems of *Las nubes* lead the reader along the speaker's evolving feelings, making us share his striving for harmony in the face of the limitations of time and death.[30]

In this striving, reality plays a role akin to that of art. In "La fuente," the fountain is described as a perennial artist, superior to human sculptors, which overcomes time:

> Al pie de las estatuas por el tiempo vencidas,
> Mientras copio su piedra, cuyo encanto ha fijado
> Mi trémulo esculpir de líquidos momentos,
> Unica entre las cosas, muero y renazco siempre.
> . . . .
> El hechizo del agua detiene los instantes:
> Soy divino rescate a la pena del hombre,
> Forma de lo que huye de la luz a la sombra,
> Confusión de la muerte resuelta en melodía.
>   [Cernuda 1964, 143–44]

{At the foot of statues destroyed by time, while I copy their stone, whose enchantment my tremulous sculpture of liquid moments has caught, unique among all things, I always die and am reborn. . . . The magic of water stops instants of time; I am a divine rescue for human suffering, the form of that which escapes from light to shadows, the confusion of death resolved into melody.}

Though virtually unknown in Spain at the time of its first publication, *Las nubes* would become very influential on later Spanish poets: its meditative tone, its artful use of common vocabulary, and its way of weaving larger visions of life and art would offer models for the "poesía del conocimiento," the "poetry of discovery," that would deepen Spanish verse in the 1960s.

Cernuda wrote several other important books after *Las nubes: Como quien espera el alba* ("As One Who Awaits the Dawn"), *Vivir sin estar viviendo* ("Life without Living"), and *Con las horas contadas* ("The Hours Have Been Counted") are all included in the 1958 edition of his collected works, *La realidad y el deseo* ("Reality and Desire"). The meditative contemplation of nature, the metaphysical bent, and the search for answers in the face of time continue in these works. But the comforting pantheistic solution underlying the prior book has faded, and a more complex, often tragic vision emerges. The persona now looks to culture as well as nature. Some of the most impressive poems assert an existential will to continue life and poetry. In this fashion, "Otros aires" ("Other Airs") ends thus:

> No mires atrás y sigue
> Hasta cuando permita el sino,
> Ahora que por los aires
> Una promesa ¿oyes?
> Acaso está sonando con las hojas nacientes . . .
> [Cernuda 1964, 262]

{Do not look back, continue, as long as fate permits, now that through the air, a promise—do you hear it? Perhaps it sounds with the newly born leaves . . . }

In these books poetry and art become, once again, an answer to life's limitations. In "Góngora" poetry offers the Golden Age author not only beauty but also a reason for living and a way of reaching beyond his physical death (Cernuda 1964, 192–94). In "A un poeta futuro" ("To a Poet"), the speaker envisions his own poetry as a way of reaching a future poet, and hence as a justification for his life (ibid. 200–201). Cernuda's style and focus expand somewhat: we see a range from the melodious lyrical works seen in *Las nubes* to longer, more narrative texts on the one hand and to short, sharp, single-image poems on the other. Yet this poetry keeps expressing, in various registers, a struggle to make sense of things and to assert life. Its ethical and aesthetic implications will make Cernuda an example for later Spanish poets.

Jorge Guillén came to the United States in 1938 and taught at Welles-
ley College from 1940 until his retirement in 1957. Throughout most of the
1940s he was writing additional poems for *Cántico,* whose third edition, con-
taining 270 poems, was published in Mexico City in 1945. The fourth edi-
tion, with 334 poems, appeared in Buenos Aires in 1950. Guillén's process
of inserting new poems into the same organic work makes clear a consis-
tency of goals, and *Cántico,* in its newer versions, keeps offering the reader
texts that seize diverse human experiences in a language that attempts to
preserve and affirm their value. Yet Jaime Gil de Biedma has shown that
Guillén's poems written after 1945 are on the whole longer, more narrative,
and more discursive. They refer to specific circumstances and also offer
more philosophical commentary (Gil de Biedma 1960, 177–84). Guillén
seemed to be leaving behind the way of forging verbal realities that we saw
exemplified in "Perfección." By the end of the 1940s he was writing poems
that would be part of *Clamor.*

The first volume of *Clamor,* titled *Maremágnum,* was published in
1957; . . . *Que van a dar en la mar* (" . . . That Lead into the Sea") appeared
in 1960, and *A la altura de las circunstancias* ("In Keeping with One's Cir-
cumstances") in 1963. By giving the whole work the subtitle *Tiempo de his-
toria* ("Historical Time"), contrasting with *Cántico's Fe de vida* ("Testimony
to Life"), Guillén consciously switches from a timeless to a time-grounded
and place-specific perspective. Vignettes of modern life appear, though
they are often played off against mythic echoes. Varied verse forms are
used, from tight stanzas to free verse verging on prose, as are a variety of
stylistic techniques. Concha Zardoya has pinned down the use of person-
ification, dehumanization, sound effects, synesthesia, light and color
play, and other devices in the book (1974, 2: 229–72). For all its apparent
realism, *Maremágnum* takes a fundamentally symbolic focus: the events it
describes both embody and evoke larger patterns. At times this is done
whimsically, as when a holdup in a Boston hotel represents middle-class
materialism ("Los atracadores" ["The Holdup Men"]; Guillén 1987, 2:
167). At other times, as in "Tren con sol naciente" ("Train with Rising
Sun"), the narration slowly configures a panorama that leads to a wider
theme (ibid. 26–30). In this particular text, the vignettes of passengers on
a train bring us to a sense of life's order emerging from chaos:

> Batahola de pista
> Circense nunca falta. ¡Cuánto vario pelaje!
> Más de una solterona, tres marinos,
> Un mozo bien barbado, probablemente artista,
> Un francés sin mirada hacia el paisaje,
> —Ah, les États Unis, rien à voir, rien à voir—
> Dos torvos y robustos con manos de asesinos . . .

El mundo es un vagón. Interminable lista,
Cuento de no acabar,
Confuso, baladí, maravilloso,
. . . .
Maremágnum veloz como un estruendo
De tren.
Y el tren hacia su meta lanzándose, corriendo
—Mirad, escuchad bien—
Acaba por fundirse en armonía,
Por sumarse, puntual, sutil, exacto,
Al ajuste de fuerzas imperiosas,
Al rigor de las cosas,
A su final, superviviente pacto. [Guillén 1987, 2: 29–30]

{The ruckus of a circus ring is never missing. What mixed plumage! More than one spinster, three sailors, a well-bearded youth, probably an artist, a Frenchman who does not notice the landscape—Ah, the United States, nothing worth seeing, nothing worth seeing—two grim toughs with assassins' hands . . . The world is a train car. Endless list, unending story, confused, trivial, marvelous . . . Speedy maremagnum like the noise of a train. And the train running, casting itself toward its goal—look, listen carefully—ends up fusing in harmony, to add up, punctual, subtle, exact, to the adjustment of imperious forces, to the rigor of things, to their final, surviving order.}

Detailed linguistic techniques configure tone and perspective in innovative fashion, producing a genre somewhere between lyric, drama, and narrative. "Reencarnación" ("Rebirth") offers another example:

Son las seis. Cesante el farol,
Va infundiéndose dulcemente
La madrugada alentadora,
Que en mí todavía no cree.
Ya el cielo y sus brumas se alejan
Con la vaguedad y sus huéspedes.
Hasta algún rey casi dormido
Se reanima en su estatua ecuestre,
Y por los huecos de los arcos
El aire, tan cortés, ya es célebre.
[Guillén 1987, 2: 100]

{It is six o'clock. The lantern is unemployed, and the encouraging dawn that does not yet believe in me is sweetly spreading [its light]. The skies and their darkness move away, together with vagueness and its guests. Even some almost asleep king stirs on his statue on horseback, and through the openings of the arches the air, so courteous, is now famous.}

The personifications of lantern and statue, aside from giving impact to the setting, create a specific point of view: everyday, low-key, ironic. Calling the lantern "unemployed" links physical setting and middle-class bureaucracy; presenting the statue as if it were a waking indigent deflates the conventional grandiosity of sculpture. All of this makes the poem an ironic recasting of the traditional theme, so central to *Cántico,* of dawn as rebirth. Yet that theme is ultimately reaffirmed, as the speaker moves from his initial separation from nature (dawn "does not believe" in him), to a final awareness that this moment is after all invigorating and significant. The poem has been for him a "rebirth," a rediscovery of value amid pragmatic reality.

In "El mastodonte" ("The Mastodon") Guillén sets up a counterpoint between two voices, that of a child who views a mastodon skeleton as if it were alive and that of an initially ironic poet (Guillén 1987, 2: 173; see Debicki 1973, 238–40). Playing off the two and even using intertextual echoes of popular ballads, the poem again moves to a merging of perspectives and to a positive view at the end. In *Maremágnum* Guillén has forged a type of narrative poetry through which to affirm life in the face of contemporary limitations.

Having emigrated to Argentina and later moving to Italy, Rafael Alberti also continued writing and publishing. Some of his varied poetic production marks a return to the short, traditional-style lyrics of his first poems; some seems more incidental and anecdotal. Perhaps his most important book is *A la pintura* ("To Painting," 1952), which consciously attempts to reflect in words the effects of painting in poems focused on specific artists, on techniques, on procedures. Emilio Prados was also active in his Mexican exile, writing a number of philosophical poems centered on the effects of solitude, time, and death. And Manuel Altolaguirre, also in Mexico, composed a number of well-crafted poems on various themes ranging from love to nature and portrayals of specific places. León Felipe, whose *Versos y oraciones del caminante* had kept a strand of meditative poetry present in the Spain of the 1920s and 1930s, also published in Mexico a number of important poetic works. So did Juan José Domenchina and Ernestina de Champourcin. In addition, a number of younger Spanish exiles developed poetic careers entirely in Mexico: Luis Rius, Tomás Segovia, and Manuel Durán are probably the most outstanding.[31]

It is the four poets I have discussed more at length, however, who to my mind deserve attention. In very distinctive but parallel ways, and with imaginative stylistic innovations, Juan Ramón, Salinas, and Cernuda made their poetry delve into basic themes of life. In general terms, their work continued the inward movement that modern Spanish poetry took in the 1930s. Thus Juan Ramón's pantheistic mysticism is a personalized and more philosophical version of his earlier attempt to make beauty permanent in the text; the effort to re-create reality poetically in *El contemplado* extends Salinas's previous questioning of things; and Cernuda's later books extend and deepen his romantic vision. This process engendered books of great originality and major significance, precisely at the time when poetry in Spain was limited by immediate concerns, by the restrictions of censorship, by the shortened insights of the debate between formal and social writing, by the aesthetics of the new realism. In that sense, we could say that émigré poetry kept alive poetic modernity. Years later it was read by younger Spanish poets and reflected in their work.

The focus taken by Juan Ramón, Salinas, and Cernuda in this work largely fits the symbolist tradition of modernity and in some ways intensifies it. The attempt to make of poetry an antidote to time and death extends the notion of the text as "eternal present," and the effort to develop appropriate forms of expression is consistent with its logocentric posture. (This posture, as we saw, was being modified and left behind in Spain.) Salinas's work continues to offer exceptions and continues undermining a static vision of reality.

Guillén's new work also continues paths marked earlier: *Clamor* creates a new perspective, a new context from which to affirm human existence, and seems built on the continuing premise that poetry, in whatever form, should embody and preserve human experience. Yet its novel use of language and narrative perspective makes it somewhat akin to Alonso's *Hijos de la ira* in opening new directions for Spanish verse.

4

New Directions for Spanish Poetry, 1956–1970

A New Era, a New Poetics

Because of the preponderance of direct (largely social) verse in Spain after 1944 and of criticism describing a turn to realism after the Civil War, literary historians have often treated postwar Spanish poetry until the late 1960s as the production of one long and almost monolithic period. This organization may seem justified by the continued use of everyday language, as well as by the continued presence of personal and historical referents. Yet from today's vantage point, we need to divide the postwar era and pay attention to the novelty of poetic outlooks that developed during the late 1950s. These new outlooks are related to new directions in the actual poetry being written, directions that gradually overlapped, dwarfed, and replaced the realistic and social poetry that had been dominant from the 1940s on. They also marked the continued shift beyond modernism that we noted earlier and presaged even more fundamental shifts in the 1970s.

Important changes occurred in the social and political climate of the country during this period. Spain became much more open to European and world currents; in 1956 it joined the United Nations. From the late 1950s on, significant economic development took place under governments committed to technological progress. Such development brought with it a growing foreign business presence, largely from the United States. This presence, and the growing tourist industry, contributed to the introduction of foreign cultural phenomena, most notably cinema and popular music. Their impact was intensified by the growth of population centers and of the industrial middle class.

Meanwhile, censorship was significantly relaxed throughout the period, most dramatically under new laws of the press instituted in 1966. Foreign literature, classic and current, highbrow and lowbrow, as well as works by previously censored Spanish writers and émigré writers, became more readily available. New magazines and poetry series appeared, increasing publication outlets. The Adonais series and prize, which had been instituted in 1943 to stimulate poetry, had become a prestigious source and incentive for younger poets. It is against this backdrop that new attitudes toward poetry developed, although the changing cultural scene had varying effects on different writers.

To delineate the main characteristics of the new poetics, I will focus on the ideas of a specific generation—that of poets born roughly between 1924 and 1939. Later on, when discussing the actual poetry produced in the period, I will also treat works by older and younger writers, since all of these help characterize the era. But the members of this one generation, because they became adults at precisely this time of change, best define a newly emerging outlook, motivating new directions in poetry.[1] Many older writers, because of their experiences, were still wedded to a simpler, socially oriented perspective during this time, especially in the first years of the period. (This may account for the overlap of the poetic currents discussed here with the social poetry previously examined.)

The members of the new generation, though born before or during the Civil War, experienced it personally as children, as victims rather than actors. They lived their adolescence in a time of limited cultural horizons, though several expanded them later through foreign residence. Their formative years were also greatly affected by the rigidity and hypocrisy of the first post–Civil War decades. They completed university studies—most of them in law or letters—and began to write during the period of realistic, social, and testimonial currents, in which it was assumed that only ordinary language could be used if poetry was to be contemporary. This was also, as José Batlló noted, a period in which everything in Spain was simplistically polarized between conservative (Francoist) and leftist (Republican) perspectives (12).[2]

As they reached adulthood and expanded their cultural experiences, these poets sought to deal with the murky world in which they had grown up. At the same time they became aware of the limitations and simplifications of prior social visions, poetics, and poetic currents and strove to overcome them. Hence they sought new ways to use ordinary language artfully, and through it to produce work of greater subtlety and originality. Their ideas as well as their poetry are often marked by ambiguities and tensions, involving the simultaneous affirmation and questioning of preceding patterns.

Many of these poets published one or more books each in the late 1950s, tracing innovative directions. But their works did not become dominant in Spanish poetry until the 1960s, when most of them also issued explicit statements on their art. In 1963 Francisco Ribes's anthology *Poesía última* ("Latest Poetry") included works by five of them—Eladio Cabañero, Angel González, Claudio Rodríguez, Carlos Sahagún, and José Angel Valente—and printed significant declarations on poetics in conjunction with their verse. It thus publicized the importance both of their work and of the new views of art that underlay it. Since then their influence has increased apace. In 1968 their work (and their statements about poetry) formed the core of Luis Batlló's *Antología de la nueva poesía española* ("Anthology of the New Spanish Poetry"), which added Jaime Gil de Biedma, Carlos Barral, and Francisco Brines, among others, to the ones included by Ribes. By that time this poetic generation had become the most visible one in Spain and was defining the canon, as almost every member published collected works and major critical studies of them appeared.[3]

Most noteworthy is the reaction of all of these poets against the previously dominant notion of poetry as "communication." As early as 1953, Carlos Barral published in the magazine *Laye* an essay titled "Poesía no es comunicación" ("Poetry Is Not Communication"), in which he condemned the emphasis on theme and message that had pervaded the Spanish poetry of the preceding years. More important, Barral questioned even the more complex theories of poetic communication (and specifically that of Bousoño). He then went on to deny the existence of any meaning prior to the text's composition and projection and posited a view of the poem as discovery (Provencio 1: 66–68). Barral's essay, though mainly read in its time by his generational colleagues, was the first of several formulations that grew into a whole poetics of the text as an act of discovery. Enrique Badosa, another member of this generation, stated in 1958: "En la poesía el poeta se conoce a sí mismo y a las cosas, gracias a su poema, e—igual que el lector—tiene ocasión de hallarse en una nueva experiencia" (Badosa, no. 29, pp. 149–50). {"In poetry the poet comes to know himself and things, thanks to the poem, and like the reader, he has the opportunity of finding himself in a new experience."} José Angel Valente's article "Conocimiento y comunicación" ("Discovery and Communication"), first published in Ribes's anthology in 1963 and reprinted as the cornerstone of Valente's critical work *Las palabras de la tribu* ("The Words of the Tribe") in 1971, asserted:

Todo poema es, pues, una exploración del material de experiencia no previamente conocido que constituye su objeto. El conocimiento más o menos pleno del poema supone la existencia más o menos plena del poema en cuestión. De ahí que el proceso de la creación poética sea un movimiento de indagación y tanteo . . . porque todo poema es un conocimiento "haciéndose." [Provencio 1: 98][4]

{Every poem is, therefore, an exploration of the matter of experience not previously known, which constitutes its goal. The more or less complete knowledge of the poem supposes the more or less complete existence of the poem in question. Hence the process of poetic creation is a process of investigation and testing . . . because all poem is a knowledge in process of "becoming."}

Claudio Rodríguez spoke, in his poetics in the Ribes anthology, of a "partici-
pación que el poeta establece entre las cosas y su experiencia poética de ellas, a
través del lenguaje" (Provencio 1: 168) {"participation that the poet establishes
between things and his poetic experience of them, via language"}. Carlos Sa-
hagún also saw the poet, though somewhat concerned with communication, as
more interested in gaining knowledge and in affirming himself via an "inda-
gación en lo oscuro" (ibid. 196) {"investigation amid darkness"}.[5]

This view of the poem as an act of discovery not only contradicted the
facile definition of poetry as message that had been prevalent in Spain but
also undermined a long-standing modern poetics of the literary work.[6] It de-
nied the notion of a determined, previously existent meaning embodied in
the work. Badosa asserted the text's independence when he noted: "Cuando
hablo del conocimiento poético lo hago sin tener para nada en cuenta al
poeta . . . sino la aprehensión y el conocimiento que surgen cuando ya ni el
poeta es dueño de modificarlos" (no. 28, p. 39). {"When I speak of poetic
discovery I do it without taking into account the poet at all . . . but only the
understanding and the discovery that take place when not even the poet is
able to modify them."}

The notion of the poem's independence led these writers to some skep-
ticism regarding its value: in "La mentira" ("The Lie," from *Poemas a Lázaro*,
1960), Valente described words as empty balloons, uselessly attempting to
embody meanings (Valente 1980, 125–26); both González and Brines ex-
pressed, at times, a loss of confidence in their art (Provencio 1: 39, 145). But
above all, this view of the poem's independence let them privilege the role
of the reader to an extent never envisioned by prior modernists. Barral had
already stated, in his 1953 article:

El poeta ignora el contenido lírico del poema hasta que el poema existé. Del mismo
modo en la lectura el poema adquiere del lector su total compendio lírico a partir
de un esfuerzo de colaboración que vierte sobre él sus vivencias propias y el matiz
de su propio mundo poético. La lectura poética consiste en un verdadero acto
poético, como el del creador. [Provencio 1: 67–68]

{The poet ignores the lyric content of the poem until the poem exists. In the same
fashion, in the process of reading, the poem acquires from the reader its total lyri-
cal compendium, based on the latter's collaborative effort, by which he pours into
it his own life experiences and the shadings of his own poetic world. The reading of
poetry consists in a true poetic act, like that of the creator.}

Gil de Biedma elaborated on this idea on several occasions, developing
the notion of the poem as interplay between poet and reader (see Proven-
cio 1: 114, 119–20, 121–22). The reader's role as cocreator also underlies
Valente's view of the poem as developing in time (ibid. 98), as well as

Brines's sense that a text can produce a new and intense existence for its audience (ibid. 146). The attribution of a new, active role to the reader makes the poem's meaning contingent on the circumstances in which it is experienced, rather than immutable.

As I noted in chapter 3, the modernist-symbolist definition of the poem as an icon that embodies human experience had already been weakened in the late 1930s, the 1940s, and the 1950s. The emotive and personal poetry of these decades had left behind the ideal of literature as "eternal present"; the social poets of the 1950s had adopted a utilitarian stance, stressing more immediate communication. But the premise that a poem constituted a stable entity, and one that privileged the author, still remained behind the ideas and the poems of these decades. This premise was now completely undermined by the poetics of the new generation.

"Postmodernity" is an extremely elusive concept and has been quoted in so many ways and in so many frames of reference—literary, cultural, architectural, social—that it has almost lost any common denominator of meaning. The term must therefore be used cautiously. Yet it seems important that the poetics of this generation reflected a number of concepts that have been cited by many different critics as characteristics of postmodernity. These Spanish poets stressed the indeterminacy of the poetic text, which is a cornerstone of Calinescu's and Hassan's definitions of the postmodern (Calinescu 298; Hassan 27, 54). They saw both reading and writing as a continuous process of creation and re-creation, and the poem as the source of events rather than a product, pointing ahead to Lyotard's view (81). They suggested the text's potential for parody and self-reflexivity (Hassan 46; Pérez Firmat 1986, chap. 1). They also accepted the premise that poems should not be considered independent units, but rather parts of a process of "textualization" of reality (Hutcheon 93–94). They reacted against the view of writing as a career and a form of individual production (Jameson 305–7). The number of ways in which this generation's poetics dovetailed with formulations about postmodernity make clear, at the very least, that it represented a fundamental change in outlook and moved poetics beyond many agreed-upon notions that pervaded the era of modernity.

We have observed that strands of indeterminacy had appeared in avant-garde poetics since 1918 and could be discerned in the poems of Miguel Hernández, Pedro Salinas, and perhaps Dámaso Alonso and Vicente Aleixandre. Yet that had occurred within a prevailing aesthetic climate of determinacy, in eras in which the concept of a work as containing stable meaning still held sway among most writers and readers. Furthermore, avant-garde statements and postures, though arguing poetry's irreducibility, had never developed a consistent view of the poetic experience as a continuous and open process, in which the written text is, in a sense, but a pre-text for unfolding meanings, and in which the reader acts as cocreator. For these reasons, the

poetics of the 1960s that I have been examining really move toward a new way
of looking at art, marking at least a first step beyond modernity. The actual
poetry written by these authors, and by others at this time, likewise reveals fun-
damentally new characteristics, although it remains more bounded by tradi-
tional premises of modernity than the poetics.

For all their skepticism regarding the poem's coherence, or maybe even
because of it, these writers placed renewed emphasis on style and poetic lan-
guage. Claudio Rodríguez wrote, in Ribes's anthology: "Las palabras funcio-
nan en el poema, no sólo con su natural capacidad de decir o significar, sino,
además, en un grado fundamental, en el sentido de su actividad en el con-
junto de los versos. Por eso son insustituíbles" (Provencio 1: 168). {"Words
function in the poem, not only with their natural capacity to say or signify,
but, in addition, to a fundamental degree, in the way in which they act within
the body of lines of verse. For this reason they are irreplaceable."} Carlos Sa-
hagún noted: "Un poema sólo es válido cuando el sentimiento que le ha
dado origen, además de ser auténtico, va unido a una expresión única e in-
sustituíble" (ibid. 199). {"A poem is only valid when the sentiment that orig-
inated it, besides being authentic, is linked to a unique and irreplaceable
expression."} The approach of these poets to the relationship between form
and content was far deeper and more subtle than that of their predecessors
of the 1940s: they viewed an emphasis on theme alone as equally sterile as
empty formalism (see Valente in Provencio 1: 101).

At first glance, this stress on stylistic precision seems to be in conflict
with a view of the poem as evolving rather than static. Yet these authors'
sense of poetry as process and discovery did not negate its meaning in con-
text or make it arbitrary and subjective. The text's particular experience
might be contingent on the moment and the reader and develop differently
at another moment, for another reader. But at one particular moment, for
one particular reader, the exact form of the text would produce one given
experience. Attention to style and meaning could be consistent, therefore,
with a view of the text as subject to evolution (see Smith 1–16, for an excel-
lent discussion of contingent versus subjective meaning).

Most of these writers envisioned a social role for good poetry, though
only if it was coupled to successful poetic expression. Thus Sahagún related
authenticity of attitude to effectiveness and originality of expression. Carlos
Barral also ascribed a social function to poetry (Barral 45). Though it seems
to contradict his rejection of communication, this stance fits Barral's so-
phisticated view of poetry as a way of creating new, and hence possibly rev-
olutionary, perspectives. Gil de Biedma also saw beyond simplistic doctrines
of social communication and envisioned poetry's social role as emerging
from a "conversation" or interplay between poet and reader (Provencio
1: 119–20). Angel González, in his comments in Luis Batlló's anthology,
both accepted the importance of social issues in his and his era's poetry and

criticized a simplistic definition of poetry as either social or not social (ibid. 342). All in all, these poets transcended the commonplace poetics preceding them and handled the relationship of subject and form in deeper and more subtle ways. As José Olivio Jiménez indicated, they wrote with the awareness that poetry "is a personalized modification of language, an individualized empowering of common speech" establishing complex relationships between sender and receiver (1992, 23). And their poetry, as we will see later, uses apparently ordinary language in novel and artistic ways, overcoming the inertia of much previous verse.

Several of these poets saw a moral dimension to their task. In Ribes's anthology, Rodríguez spoke of poetry as a way of participating in existence, of gaining knowledge of it, and of revealing the essence of humanity, adding, "Soy partidario del sentido moral del arte" (Provencio 1: 168–69). {"I support the moral sense of art."} Angel González has consistently described his—and his colleagues'—ethical stance in poetry (ibid. 28). The concept of poetry as a way of knowing that underlies the generation's views implies, in one fashion or another, a quest for the betterment of humankind. Historically grounded in the reaction of these poets against the tawdriness of the environment in which they grew up, an ethical posture also supports their view of the poem as act rather than product.

On the surface, the posture of these poets would seem less socially or culturally "revolutionary" than that of their predecessors, since it did not center on poetry as a weapon for earthly reform. But in a more significant sense, their search for higher moral goals links them to a rebellion against the limitations of the society in which they were raised. In yet another sense, their reaction against prior notions of language as static and univocal constitutes a rebellion against determinism. We could say that many prior modes of writing—the modernist icon, the Falangist manifesto, the social poem—all had in common the goal of conveying meanings that must be received as they were intended. They have to be read within their frame of authority. The poetics I have been examining envisioned, perhaps for the first time in Spain, the possibility of allowing readers a freedom from such rules and implicitly suggested a resistance to the old notion of language as authoritative communication (just as their authors resisted the moral climate of their upbringing).[7] We can relate this new stance to many of the social and historical events of the next decades and to some important developments in poetry, which would become even more evident in later decades.

Experience and Discovery by the New Castilian Poets

When we read poems written in the 1950s and 1960s by authors of the new generation, we often notice that the referent is a specific underlying event, in many cases reflecting the speaker's (and often, presumably, the poet's) personal experience. Critics have noted that this poetry involves a shift from cosmic and collective topics to more individual ones and that these poets give importance to remembrances of their particular pasts.[8] Yet such specific referents and the anecdotes that lie behind individual texts are never important in themselves: they function, rather, as bases for new visions and experiences. To some degree, these poems recall Hierro's "Las nubes"; they use anecdote and point of view to explore wider themes. But in most cases the specific experiences seem even more individual, while, simultaneously, their implications reach further beyond the literal level. Often they produce new perceptions of fundamental issues: life's value in the face of time, the quest for illusions, love. What is new, and most important, is that these wider implications are intertwined with a consciousness of the very process of exploring reality poetically. Many poems of this time lead the reader to a concern with the way in which they (and often poetry in general) seek meaning in experience, rather than just with the universals that can be found amid the particulars of life. Such poems, which became more prevalent as the 1960s unfolded, create new kinds of reading experience.

Connections between specific experiences and larger themes (including that of poetization) are established in various ways. At times patterns of imagery or symbolic schemes are used. More often, however, these poems reveal innovative ways of organizing systems of vocabulary, structuring narrative material, employing tone and point of view, and constructing intertextual correspondences. In the process they often cross traditional genre frontiers, blending narrational, novelistic techniques with imagistic ones. As a result, they form a body of poetry in everyday language that is immeasurably richer and more varied than that produced in prior decades.

The consciousness of poetic creation that underlies much of this work often invites a greater involvement on the part of the reader. Witnessing in the poem's speaker (and often, therefore, in the implied author) an awareness that his or her words constitute a creative process, and a resultant act of discovery, the reader will see the text as dynamic rather than static. To some degree at least, it will offer an invitation to continue its process rather than just to contemplate its form or receive its message. This will, in turn, make the meanings conveyed more subject to change, more contingent on the reader's background and stance.

Given the way in which the poetry of this time is anchored in the specific, it makes sense to study it with some attention to its authors' location and experience. Many of them, though born in different parts of Spain, received their education and took their first literary steps in Madrid. This city had become the center of all political, social, and cultural activity of the establishment in previous decades; any important cultural phenomena (including

social poetry) had to develop there to gain prominence. A number of the po-
ets of the new generation studied and met at its university, obtained help
from writers living in Madrid (most prominently Aleixandre and Bousoño),
and started publishing there (several in the Adonais series). Some, though
not all, reflect an urban setting in their work.

José Angel Valente is one of the most important writers of his time. His
early poetry marked new ways of leading the reader to deeper visions of
life.[9] In both *A modo de esperanza* (1955) and *Poemas a Lázaro* (1960), the
themes of time's passing and death's threat emerge from specific, mostly
first-person, narratives, which at first glance seem very realistic. "El espejo"
("The Mirror"), from the first book, is a good example:

> Hoy he visto mi rostro tan ajeno,
> tan caído y sin par
> en este espejo.
> Está duro y tan otro con sus años,
> su palidez, sus pómulos agudos,
> su nariz afilada entre los dientes,
> sus cristales domésticos cansados,
> su costumbre sin fe, sólo costumbre.
> He tocado sus sienes: aún latía
> un ser allí. Latía. ¡Oh vida, vida!
> Me he puesto a caminar. También fue niño
> este rostro, otra vez, con madre al fondo.
> De frágiles juguetes fue tan niño,
> en la casa lluviosa y trajinada,
> . . . .
> Pero ahora me mira—mudo asombro,
> glacial asombro en este espejo solo—
> y ¿dónde estoy—me digo—
> y quién me mira
> desde este rostro, máscara de nadie?
>   [Valente 1980, 15]

{Today I have seen my face so foreign, so droopy and strange, in this mirror. It is harsh
and so different with its years of age, its pallor, its sharp cheekbones, its pointed nose
amid its teeth, its tired domestic windows, its habits devoid of faith. I have touched its
temples: a being still throbbed there. It did throb. Oh life, life! I have started walking.
This face, too, was once a child, with a mother in the background. It was a child with
fragile toys in the rainy and bustling house. . . . But now it looks at me: mute amaze-
ment, glacial amazement in this lonely mirror, and I say to myself, where am I? and
who looks at me from within this face, this mask of nobody?}

This poem, like many of Valente's, alludes to losses caused by time and
implicitly presages death. This subject, which had led earlier poets to gen-
eral moods of existential anguish, is here handled in an understated man-

ner. Valente immerses us in the immediacy of a specific scene; from it he draws the speaker's perception of time and mortality.

Yet as we read and reread the poem, we pay increasing attention to the larger pattern of alienation and dehumanization that is reflected in its vocabulary and imagery. The speaker's face is "foreign" to him; it is described as "strange"; his eyes are dehumanized when they are called "domestic windows." His description of himself suddenly changes to the third person. The resulting picture of his dehumanized and objectified face in the present ("este rostro," and later "máscara de nadie") is contrasted with the living image of himself as a child in the past.

This apparently easy and realistic poem turns out to be, therefore, an artful construction: the elements I noted form a pattern of signs, portraying a present lack of individuality. This pattern contrasts with another, which reveals a past vital existence (and is represented by the vignette of the child playing and by the words *child* and *mother*). The two worlds come together in the middle of the poem, when the speaker touches his temples and still feels life: he stands, as it were, at a crossroads between past and present, between live child and lifeless mask. His process of organizing experience into sets of signs—hence handling it poetically—is a major part of his inquiry into his past.

This way of combining a specific referent and an intricately controlled pattern of common language and using them to evoke a fundamental life experience also characterizes most of *Poemas a Lázaro,* though in this book the theme of death becomes even more dominant. In "La llamada" ("The Call"), for example, an anecdotal description of a telephone call suggests a foreboding of death and finitude (Valente 1980, 79). Again a series of words and images constitutes a pattern—we might say a code—pointing to a transcendent theme. This procedure allows the poet to build larger visions from common words and specific referents, to achieve a new poetic significance and originality while grounding the text in particular events and in a realistic mode of writing.

In another sense, these poems reflect Valente's, and his contemporaries', quest for a poetry that reaches beyond simple communication to the discovery of new meanings. This is especially evident in "La llamada" and the response it evokes in the reader. As Margaret Persin has shown, the speaker's struggle to understand the mysterious phone call is paralleled by the reader's struggle to relate the literal and symbolic levels of the text. The former's process suggests or echoes the poet's task in seeking meaning. The reader thus becomes something of a collaborator of the speaker, and implicitly of the poet (see Persin 1980, 32–34).[10]

In *La memoria y los signos* ("Memory and Signs," 1966), the poet's social and historical context is much more prominent. Many poems are grounded on reminiscences of the Civil War; some deal with human relationships in the light of social circumstances and with specific family tragedies and events. Again, however, individual events evoke larger patterns. And more evidently than in his prior books, Valente foregrounds the subject of poetic creation, of poetry interpreting human experience. In "El moribundo" ("The Dying"), for example, what begins as a description of a man's dying turns into a poem about the process of preserving and recording life (see Debicki 1982, 116–17). Here and in other works, references to the poetic process make us connect the story within the poem to the topic of textualizing life. At times, as in "Un canto" ("A Song"), a search for the goals of poetry becomes the explicit topic of the text (see Valente 1980, 227–29). In these ways, Valente draws the reader more explicitly into the act of discovery reflected in the poems (see Jiménez 1972, 241–42).

In the latter 1960s Valente's poetry moved beyond the apparent directness of his first books, perhaps reflecting the poet's critical, intellectual, and international concerns. *Siete representaciones* ("Seven Representations,"1967) and *Breve son* ("Brief Song," 1968) make increased use of literary allusions. Valente counterposes and contrasts his texts to prior ones: he shocks us with a negative vision of God's anger, reversing a biblical echo, in *Siete representaciones* (Valente 1980, 252) and writes in the manner of traditional Spanish poetry in *Breve son.* (See "Mar de Muxía," which also alludes to a specific traditional-type poem by Alberti [ibid. 266].) These books still use specific events and stories, presented in clear language, for larger visions. But they make their readers even more conscious of the process of poetization.

Francisco Brines's early poetry, like that of Valente, centers on the passing of time and builds its visions out of specific events. Initially, Brines's poems seem much less intense than Valente's; they unfold slowly and indirectly, through detailed descriptions of past remembrances. Their impact and original effect derive from a gradual and yet precise weaving of a mood. The following text from *Las brasas* ("The Embers," 1960) is part of a long description of the protagonist looking at old pictures:

> Está en la penumbra el cuarto, lo ha invadido
> la inclinación del sol, las luces rojas
> que en el cristal cambian el huerto, y alguien
> que es un bulto de sombra está sentado.
> Sobre la mesa los cartones muestran
> retratos de ciudad, mojados bosques
> de helechos, infinitas playas, rotas
> columnas: cuantas cosas, como un puerto,
> le estremecieron de muchacho. Antes . . .
> [Brines 1984, 20]

{The room is in shadows, the setting of the sun has invaded it, and the red lights that change the garden in the windows; someone who is a bundle is seated. On the table, the boxes show pictures of the city, wet forests of ferns, endless beaches, broken columns; all those things that, like a port, shook him when he was a child. Before . . . }

An unusual mood is created by describing the protagonist as though he were an object, while making the things around him dynamic, personified: the sun invades, the lights transform appearances, the boxes "show" pictures. This inversion of roles turns an apparently neutral description into an intense perception of a human being's passivity on the one hand, and of life's continuity on the other. This leads us to the poem's themes: nostalgia for a lost past and the inevitability of death. The poem exemplifies the highly original way in which Brines combines imagery and narration to create a specific perspective, which in turn evokes a mood and a philosophical attitude underlying it.

Hence Brines's narrative poems operate symbolically, in what Bousoño characterized as "bisemic" fashion: a philosophical layer, subtly highlighted by the text's details, undergirds its narration (Brines 1974, 60–63). This procedure is another example of the artful and profound use of common language and referents. It also illustrates the blending of traditionally lyric and narrative devices that we often find in Spanish literature of the period.

Brines's *Palabras a la oscuridad* ("Words unto Darkness," 1966) expands and enriches the themes and the procedures of his earlier book. The speaker's point of view, generally presented in the first person, is often stressed; symbolic underpinnings are less obvious (see Jiménez 1972, 177). Yet the speaker's experiences always convey deeper perceptions regarding the effects of time and communicate a sense of vitality in the face of time's destructiveness. As I have noted elsewhere, Brines often uses shifts and reversals in attitude to draw varied responses and to involve us within the tensions of the text (Debicki 1987, 30–31). In *Aun no* ("Not Yet," 1971) Brines transforms and defamiliarizes external reality to an even greater degree. Events and places are used symbolically to portray a negative view of our world. The theme of poetry becomes more explicit, and many texts are self-referential.

Claudio Rodríguez's poetry reveals even more surprising ways of generating symbolic and allegorical meanings from concrete referents. In 1953 Rodríguez, then nineteen years old, obtained the Adonais Prize for his first book, *Don de la ebriedad* ("The Gift of Intoxication"). The book motivated both praise and surprise from readers accustomed to the direct style of the early 1950s and marked some of the most important new directions in Spanish poetry.

The book should be read as a single unit, a sustained exploration of reality on the part of a speaker, which simultaneously constitutes a questioning of its own poetic process. Its language is filled with rural referents rather than the urban ones of many of Rodríguez's contemporaries. It concretely anchors the book, on one level, in the poet's native landscape in the province of Zamora. On another level, it sets this poetry in a literary tradition of nature poetry: we recall the idealized scenes of Fray Luis de León's poetry, and the topos of landscape as reflection of life's essences. The persona's search, and some of the vocabulary used, also bring to mind echoes of St. John of the Cross's mystic poetry.[11] An unusual allegorical relationship is established as the book develops, and specific moments and places convey larger themes (see Bousoño in Rodríguez 1971, 11–12).

The sustained exploration of reality in this book is, simultaneously, a demonstration and an exploration of the poetic process. The persona's state of perception (linked with *ebriedad,* literally "intoxication") reflects an almost sacramental communion with nature and exaltation of life, but also an awareness of destruction. Simultaneously, it suggests the possibilities and the limitations of poetic expression. The persona's hopes are undercut by a skepticism about the possibilities of transcendence, just as his own images and discourse become undermined as the poem develops. Jonathan Mayhew and Martha La Follette Miller have explored this double process (see Mayhew 1990, chap. 2; and Miller), which is apparent from the beginning of the book:

> Siempre la claridad viene del cielo;
> es un don: no se halla entre las cosas
> sino muy por encima, y las ocupa
> haciendo de ello vida y labor propias.
> Así amanece el día; así la noche
> cierra el gran aposento de sus sombras.
> Y esto es un don. ¿Quién hace menos creados
> cada vez a los seres? ¿Qué alta bóveda
> los contiene en su amor? . . .
> . . . .
> Si tú la luz la has llevado toda,
> ¿cómo voy a esperar nada del alba?
> Y, sin embargo—esto es un don—mi boca
> espera, y mi alma espera, y tú me esperas
> ebria persecución, claridad sola
> mortal como el abrazo de las hoces,
> pero abrazo hasta el fin que nunca afloja.
>   [Rodríguez 1983, 33]

{Clarity always comes from the sky [heaven]; it is a gift, not to be found among things, but much above them, and occupies them, making of it its own life and work. Thus the day dawns; thus the night closes the great room of its shadows. And this is a gift. Who does make things each time less created? What high vault holds them in its love? . . . If you have taken away all light, how am I to hope for anything from dawn? Nevertheless—and this is a gift—my mouth awaits [hopes], and my soul awaits [hopes], and you await me, intoxicated persecution, only clarity, mortal like the embrace of sickles, but an embrace that never loosens until the end.}

The initial affirmation and the normally positive sense of *gift* are modified and undermined, though never eliminated, as the speaker develops his poetic inquiry. As a result, in Jonathan Mayhew's words, "the poet—a reader within the poem—moves from a transcendent, eternalizing vision toward an unmediated participation in time and nature" (1990, 55). Thus a parallel tension between acceptance and questioning is produced in the reader of the poem.

Rodríguez's *Conjuros* ("Spells," 1958) is more accessible but no less complex or ambiguous. The book describes explicit scenes and events of rural life and connects them to wider issues. Thus, in "A mi ropa tendida" ("To My Spread-Out Clothes") the washing of a shirt evokes spiritual purification (the poem is subtitled "El alma" ["The Soul"]):

> Me la están refregando, alguien la aclara.
> ¡Yo que desde aquel día
> la eché a lo sucio para siempre, para
> ya no lavarla más, y me servía!
> ¡Si hasta me está más justa! No la he puesto
> pero ahí la véis todos, ahí, tendida,
> ropa tendida al sol. ¿Quién es? ¿Qué es eso?
> ¿Qué lejía inmortal, y qué perdida
> jabonadura vuelve, qué blancura?
> [Rodríguez 1983, 83]

{They are scrubbing it, someone is cleaning it. And I who from that day on threw it into the trash forever, not to wash it again, although it was useful to me! It even fits me better! I haven't put it on, but you all see it there, stretched out, clothes stretched out in the sun. Who is it? What is this? What immortal bleach, what lost soap bubbles return, what whiteness?}

Unlike traditional (say, medieval) allegory, the kind created by Rodríguez never collapses the real and allegorical planes into single meanings. Instead, the planes form parallel and coexistent layers, which are related but also set in conflict with each other. "A mi ropa tendida" contains some words that link literal washing to purification, others that merely describe the washing, others that only refer to the purification. It creates surprising juxtapositions ("immortal bleach") and, later on, descriptions (a rooster stepping on the shirt, a praise of the shirt by the people) that make the whole scene strange, unfamiliar, and even humorous.[12] The net effect is to make the reader perceive the correspondence between concrete reality and wider patterns of life as something important but also perplexing, full of tensions, not easy to understand.[13]

Jonathan Mayhew has seen in *Conjuros* a desire to explore the relationships between the poet and society (1990, 58–59). Yet, and in total contrast to the typical social poems of the time, this book produces not clear messages and ideas, but surprising juxtapositions and tensions. In "El baile de Aguedas" ("The Dance of St. Agatha's Feast") a village dance both evokes a sense of harmony in daily life and makes us feel an inevitable conflict between the everyday and the transcendent. The interplay of levels and codes makes this book a unique blend of specific referents and wider themes. It also constitutes a demonstration of poetry's struggle to relate the two levels and its ability to involve the reader in its questioning.

José Olivio Jiménez has noted that in *Alianza y condena* ("Alliance and Condemnation," 1965) Rodríguez's vision broadens again: the quest for patterns in nature now turns into a more fundamental exploration of human life (1972, 146). It centers on a dialectical tension between *alianza*, representing the search for union with others, and *condena*, standing for the negative forces of our existence. The overt juxtapositions and interplays of *Conjuros* now give way to more enigmatic scenes: as Bousoño has noted, we are confronted with puzzling realities, which only make sense after we have discovered an underlying theme (Rodríguez 1971, 17–22). In "Brujas a mediodía" ("Witches at Noon"), for example, a long description of witchcraft weaves into a larger sense of the mystery of reality, of its opacity that deters our efforts at understanding. In the second part, the emphasis falls more on the speaker-poet's reactions to this mystery. He asks a series of cosmic questions, not obtaining any answers; yet he affirms the sense of life that this unexplainable experience has offered:

> La vida no es reflejo
> pero, ¿cuál es su imagen?
> Un cuerpo encima de otro
> ¿siente resurrección o muerte? ¿Cómo
> envenenar, lavar
> este aire que no es nuestro pulmón?
> . . . .
> Pero nosotros nunca
> tocaremos la sutura,
> esa costura (a veces un remiendo,
> a veces un bordado),
> entre nuestros sentidos y las cosas,
> . . . .
> Esto es cosa de bobos. Un delito
> común este de andar entre pellizcos
> de brujas. Porque ellas

no estudian sino bailan
y mean, son amigas
de bodegas. Y ahora,
a mediodía,
si ellas nos besan desde tantas cosas,
¿dónde estará su noche,
dónde sus labios, dónde nuestra boca
para aceptar tanta mentira y tanto
amor? [Rodríguez 1983, 129–30]

{Life is not a reflection, but what is its image? Does a body upon another feel resurrection or death? How can one poison, wash this air that is not of our lungs? . . . But we never touch the suture, this needlework (sometimes a patch, sometimes an embroidery), between our senses and things. . . . This is fools' work, a common failing, this walking amid witches' pinchings. Because they do not study, but dance and piss, they are friends of taverns. And now, at noon, if they kiss us from so many things, where can their night be, where can their lips be, where can our mouth be, to accept so many lies and so much love?}

We may see this text, with Mayhew, as an overtly metapoetic exploration on the part of a self-conscious poet or as a quest for meaning that, though never answered, leads to an existential affirmation (1990, 85–89). In either case, "Brujas a mediodía" involves us in a process of struggling with its enigmatic referents and images, uselessly seeking a message, and finally contemplating (and I think sharing) an affirmation, which the speaker makes despite the lack of answers to the questions he has posed.

Similar experiences are produced by other poems in the book. In "Espuma" ("Foam") the foam caused by waves breaking on the coast evokes various aspects of life: allusions to nature, love, and sexual fertility all point to the theme of regeneration and to the poem's ending, in which the protagonist paradoxically both drowns and feels renewed in life's patterns (Rodríguez 1983, 151). Throughout the book, the desire to affirm life is intertwined with a will to poetic expression.

These three books by Claudio Rodríguez may demonstrate, better than any others of this period, the implications of the new poetics of discovery. Free from the constrictions of didactic verse, endowed with an extraordinary ability to find transcendence in the immediate, and able to create a highly original form of allegorical writing, Rodríguez led Spanish poetry to unsuspected levels of originality. This originality is to a large extent founded in this poetry's self-consciousness. Rodríguez's books represent, as a result, his generation's fundamental revolution against the prior conventions of post–Civil War poetry.

Angel González's early poetry seems clearer and easier than that of Rodríguez. Placed in urban rather than rural settings, it evokes specific events and places, presented in a direct language. But again the perspective and the reactions of the speaker are more revealing than the referents themselves, and the reader is led to wider themes and to a consciousness of the poetic process.

Written mostly in Madrid in the 1950s, where González, after growing up in Oviedo, lived as a student and government employee—and where he met Valente and other members of the generation at the university—*Aspero mundo* ("Harsh World," 1956) portrays a conflict between illusions and a matter-of-fact, often wry realization of life's limitations. Particularly noteworthy is the careful manipulation of tone and point of view, in poems describing specific events or moments. Such manipulation transforms those events, casting them in very unusual perspectives. In "Muerte en el olvido" ("Death in Forgetting"), for example, the speaker addresses his beloved in such a way that he changes our normal frame of reference and triggers a surprisingly strong view of idealized love. This speaker begins by stating that his own physical existence depends on the beloved's attention:

> Yo sé que existo
> porque tú me imaginas.
> Soy alto porque tú me crees
> alto, y limpio porque tú me miras
> con buenos ojos,
> . . . .
>   Pero si tú me olvidas
> quedaré muerto sin que nadie
> lo sepa. Verán viva
> mi carne, pero será otro hombre
> —oscuro, torpe, malo—el que la habita . . .
>   [González 1986, 19]

{I know that I exist, because you imagine me. I am tall because you believe me to be tall, and clean because you look at me with kindly eyes. . . . But if you forget me, I will be dead, even though no one will know it. They will see my flesh alive, but it will be another man—dark, clumsy, evil—that will inhabit it . . . }

The speaker denies a basic law of reality, in accordance with which our age and physical and mental properties are objective truths. Instead he makes his beloved the causal agent for his life, and her love the determinant of his nature and his characteristics. In a sense, this distortion of reality is an extended metaphor, by which the beloved is made as important to the speaker as if she were his creator. Through this metaphor he conveys to us the depth of his love and dependence.

The language, seemingly so plain, effectively emphasizes the transformation and its effect. First-person verbs in the present tense that foreground the speaker ("I know," "I exist," "I am") contrast with third-person ones, which portray acts of the beloved ("you imagine me," "you look at me," "you forget me"). The dramatic interplay heightens the connection between the two persons, leading to a final step in which the speaker switches point of view and thus allows the beloved, hypothetically, to kill him. (At the end he sees himself from the outside, as another: "It will be another man.") All the elements of this short and unpretentious poem contribute to highlight the romantic, vulnerable illusion. Implicitly at least, they make us aware of how poetic language creates—and does not simply reflect—human reality.

Sin esperanza, con convencimiento ("Without Hope, with Determination," 1961) again portrays a tension between idealism and disillusion, though now more explicitly related to a sense of waste and weariness in the face of time passing. Most of the poems center on the feelings and responses of a first-person speaker—to concrete situations, to moods, to objects that serve as symbols (such as a spider, whose destructiveness represents the futility of hope). In "Ayer" ("Yesterday"), the speaker transforms the day just past from Wednesday to Monday in order to portray, first, his sense of tedium, and then his rebellion against it, in which he fantasizes an escape from work (González 1986, 84). Transformations of common events and referents such as this one, and the use of perspective play and ironic commentary, help González engender complex, ambiguous visions of life from seemingly ordinary materials and call into question our normal ways of seeing reality. At least implicitly, they allude to the process of rewriting reality through poetic composition. The finding of new interpretations of life is tied to the finding of new forms of poetic expression; by implication, reading reality anew is related to reading the poem creatively. Occasionally in this book, unusual perspectives are used, ironically, to convey a social theme: "Discurso a los jóvenes" ("Speech to the Youthful") consists of a speech by a leader who, repeating clichés of the Franco regime, encourages his followers to be inhuman and thus makes us feel the unnaturalness of his system (ibid. 110–12).

Social themes become more prominent in two of González's next books, *Grado elemental* and *Tratado de urbanismo*. González's concern with social issues was undoubtedly strengthened by his readings of Celaya, Hierro, and Otero and by his contacts in the late 1950s with poets of the school of Barcelona.[14] As we saw in "Lecciones de buen amor," discussed in chapter 3, his poems in a social vein make skillful use of irony, tonal play, and allusion to produce experiences far richer, and more open to reader participation, than the typical social verse of the early 1950s. They exemplify the absorption of social poetry into the growing dominant stream of a poetry in which individual experience and common language artfully reflect a complex existence.

Although born in Alicante, Carlos Sahagún also studied and lived in Madrid before moving on to teach in Segovia and Barcelona (he was in

England in 1960–61). His poetry is written in an everyday but elegant, flowing language and centers on memories of past experiences. In *Profecías del agua* ("Prophesies of Water," 1958) the speaker evokes a positive view of his childhood, contrasted to later discoveries of life's limitations. Similar memories appear in *Como si hubiera muerto un niño* ("As If a Child Had Died," 1961), although nostalgia for childhood ideals is more balanced by remembrances of subsequent disillusionment.[15] Most important, and original, are Sahagún's ways of turning memories of specific events into compelling experiences for the reader. Vignettes of the past are expanded metaphorically, as in "Río" ("River"), from the first book:

> Le llamaron posguerra a este trozo de río,
> a este bancal de muertos, a la ciudad aquella
> doblada como un árbol viejo, clavada siempre
> en la tierra lo mismo que una cruz. Y gritaron:
> "¡Alegría! ¡Alegría!"
> 　　　　　　　Yo era un río naciente,
> era un hombre naciente, con la tristeza abierta. . .
> 　　　　　　　　　　　　　　[Sahagún 24]

{They called this section of river, this plot of dead people, that city twisted like an old tree, always nailed in the earth like a cross, "postwar." And they shouted: "Joy! Joy!" I was a newly born river, I was a newly born man, with open sadness.}

Sahagún develops and expands a traditional metaphor of a river as life, making it refer first to a period of Spanish history and then to the protagonist's personal biography. He uses it as the cornerstone of a continuing process in which moments of time are presented as places; this dominant metaphorical technique imparts vividness to events and attitudes. It is repeated in his later books; in *Como si hubiera* descriptions and patterns of images are turned into stories, which come to represent the speaker's past experiences. In "Hacia la infancia" ("Toward Infancy"), for example, a speaker well aware of his role as poet uses a walk through gates and into a garden to dramatize a coming to terms with memories of youth (see Debicki 1987, 148–50). This conscious molding of metaphor into metonymy produces a highly effective combination of narrative flow and lyric immediacy. And it leaves us with another, very distinct example of how individual episodes are turned into significant experiences by seemingly simple language, while also calling attention to the process of poetization.

　　At first glance, the poetry of Gloria Fuertes provides a jarring contrast to that of Sahagún, Rodríguez, or even Valente: written in highly colloquial idiom, it is populated by everyday objects and events—buses, bargain basements, street encounters, trivial mishaps. This and the presence of social themes has led some critics to dismiss her work as superficial.[16] Nothing could be further from the truth. Although an attitude of rebellion against social systems does underlie much of her poetry, this poetry handles its materials with extraordinary linguistic and technical skill and thus produces vivid, unsettling experiences dealing with individual as well as social issues.

Much of this poetry's effect is achieved by the surprising use of intertexts (colloquial and artistic) and of unpoetic forms of expression. In chapter 3 we saw how a poem written in the form of a hospital file card gave a jarring sense of a starving worker's suffering. We also find in Fuertes's work texts presented as telegrams, prayers, advertisements, letters, and even as an arithmetic equation. Frequently she parodies literary topics, from the convention of using cypresses to evoke sadness to the transcendence of St. John's verse (see Fuertes 202, 220). While not militantly feminist, her poetry conveys the limitations and vicissitudes of a woman's role in Spanish society, linking them often to other inequities. On other occasions, she constructs unexpected symbolic patterns from common referents to portray more personal subjects. In "Galerías Preciadas" ("Prized Department Store") an effort to try to find an item of clothing that fits the speaker in a specific Madrid store (called Galerías Preciados in real life) becomes a fresh, surprising, and modern symbol for the difficulty of finding a love companion (ibid. 192). And a man's tragic loss of composure over an attractive woman is unexpectedly presented through the metaphor of a car accident:

> En aquella primavera se le aflojaron los tornillos;
> en unas curvas peligrosas
> se le rompió la dirección.
> Los testigos afirmaron que se lanzó al bello, precipicio
> —como a sabiendas. [Fuertes, "Extraño accidente," 195]

{That spring his screws loosened; his sense of direction crashed on some dangerous curves. The witnesses testified that he threw himself into the beautiful precipice—as if knowingly.}

Fuertes's best poetry is exceptionally successful in using apparently trivial materials to create experiences of great impact. The skillful and surprising manipulation of such materials involves the reader not only in the particular text and its theme but also in a larger perception of the dissolution and transformation of genres, levels of expression, modes of speech and writing. As we read Fuertes's work text by text, we transcend all conventional premises and start redefining the nature of poetry. This work foregrounds and highlights its own process of demythification.

Several other writers who appeared on the Madrid literary scene in the late 1950s also exemplify new ways of making poetry with common language. Angel Crespo, who had been a part of the *postista* movement in 1945, published several excellent books in the 1950s and 1960s. Crespo's most telling poems often begin with an enigmatic description, leaving the reader puzzled; the poem's ending offers an interpretation that points to some deeper perception. Thus, in "Los pequeños objetos" ("Small Objects"), a collection of everyday objects guides the reader to an awareness of the connections that we make, in our lives, between things and emotional attitudes (see Debicki 1982, 184).[17]

Eladio Cabañero, most of whose works deal with social themes, also wrote excellent love poems in which rural vignettes dramatize emotive attitudes. These poems were published in *Marisa Sabia y otros poemas* ("Wise Marisa and Other Poems," 1963). Especially interesting is the metapoetic dimension of some of these works; the book's protagonist explicitly comments on his way of turning his experience into poetry, giving a new dimension to a traditional vision of transcendent love.

Also notable for its use of colloquial language and allusion, as well as for its shocking intensity, is the poetry of Félix Grande. Born in 1937, Grande is the author of six books written in the 1960s. His poetry, influenced by César Vallejo, evokes dramatic scenes and characters to portray, sometimes with obvious symbolism, injustices and tragedies of human life and of historical and political events. Grande, together with the well-known critic and poet Joaquín Marco (b. 1935), author of two forceful books of social poetry in the 1960s, and Jesús Hilario Tundidor (b. 1935) and Diego Jesús Jiménez (b. 1942), is classified by María del Pilar Palomo and other historians as part of a "bridge" group or generation, between Valente, Rodríguez, Brines, and Sahagún on the one hand and the later *novísimos* on the other (Palomo 147–48). It seems to me both unsound and confusing to talk of these writers as a separate generation, since three of them have birth dates falling within the range of the earlier one, and the other is close in age to the *novísimos*. It is better to think of them simply as poets who shared a stronger orientation to social poetry than most of their contemporaries, yet who also (much in keeping with the times) sought to write this poetry with care and stylistic effectiveness. With the possible exception of Grande's, these poets' verse seems less important than that of authors previously discussed. Another accomplished poet of this generation, unjustly ignored (perhaps because of her residence in the United States) is Ana María Fagundo, author of a substantial body of verse that artfully explores the implications of various experiences and emotive states.

Andalusian Poets, 1956–1970

A number of new poets from Andalusia published important works during this period, revealing an accomplished and creative use of language paral-

lel to that of the Castilians. Whether influenced by the long history of for-
mal excellence and cultural refinement in the poetry of this region, or by
the precedents of poets and magazines of the 1920s, or by the *Cántico* group,
or by other factors, the Andalusian poets tended to produce even more styl-
ized work. Yet like the Castilians, they revealed, above all, new ways of con-
structing carefully crafted texts that established new kinds of relationships
with their readers.

Especially notable in this respect is the poetry of José Manuel Caballero
Bonald, who was born and raised in Andalusia, although he has studied and
lived in Madrid. His first books, published in the early 1950s, explore the
speaker's memories, seeking to obtain deeper insights and to come to
terms with past questions and enigmas. Caballero Bonald's language,
though in no way archaic, is more dense than that of most of his contem-
poraries. It is characterized by free verse, long passages with subordinate
clauses, and a rich gamut of vocabulary items and syntactical constructions,
often worked into a meandering first-person "stream of consciousness."
María del Pilar Palomo finds its roots in the baroque, while connecting it
to the poet's attempts to uncover new dimensions of reality (142). The ef-
fect of this language is evident in "No sé de dónde vienes" ("I Do Not Know
from whence You Come") from *Memorias de poco tiempo* ("Memoirs of Little
Time," 1954), in which the speaker tries to recall the essence of his brother,
possibly his alter ego:

> Ahora recuerdo el agua pronunciable
> que caía debajo de tu nombre, la casa en cuyo reino
> andaba el agrio día escarceando
> por las claras paredes maternales.
> Lo recuerdo muy junto aunque, no sé,
> hay algo que se escapa, como un resto
> de luz, como una tenue sensación de ausencia,
> algo que se me olvida y que comprendo
> que es lo más decisorio. Y de repente
> ya no recuerdo nada, ya no sé nada tuyo.
> [Caballero Bonald 88]

{Now I remember the speakable river that flowed below your name, the house in
whose kingdom the bitter day walked, meandering around the clear maternal walls.
I remember it all together, although, I don't know, something escapes me, like a
remnant of light, like a sense of absence, something that I forget and yet understand
that it is most decisive. And suddenly I no longer remember anything, I no longer
know anything of yours.}

Las horas muertas ("Dead Hours," 1959) and succeeding books by Ca-
ballero Bonald foreground an explicit consciousness of the poetic task. The
effort to come to terms with past realities is now tied to the act of turning

experience into poetry. "Defiéndeme Dios de mí" ("May God Defend Me from Myself"), for example, uses the image of a battle against oneself to portray a speaker-poet's anguished search for self-expression. *Pliegos de cordel* ("Strands of Rope," 1963) combines evocations of the past with a critical vision of Spanish society. All of Caballero Bonald's verse gives another, more consciously artful example of his generation's, and his period's, use of language in a process of discovery and clarification, which the reader is invited to join.

Also telling is the multifaceted poetry of Manuel Mantero, whose life and work are deeply rooted in his native Seville, despite years spent teaching in the United States. Mantero's first books, *Mínimas del ciprés y los labios* ("Minimal Texts of the Cypress and the Lips," 1958) and *Tiempo del hombre* ("Man's Time," 1960), use common objects and anecdotal situations in original, metaphoric ways: the beloved's tennis ball evokes her traits and effects; a Madrid subway station reflects moods and limitations of life. In each case, literary echoes and intertexts are used to expand and enrich the theme and effect and to turn everyday materials into complex, learned works. Intertexts play even more crucial roles in *Misa solemne* ("Solemn Mass," 1966), which places Christ in a modern setting and deals with issues of contemporary life in texts structured as parts of the mass, and in several later books containing many literary allusions.

More dense and consciously artful, but perhaps less important, are the poems of Miguel Fernández, filled with language play and mythical echoes, and of Fernando Quiñones, who frequently re-creates historical and literary figures and motifs. One should also mention the allusive but visually forceful verse of Luis Jiménez Martos, filled with unusual images affirming life's intensity.

The School of Barcelona

By the mid-1950s the city of Barcelona rivaled and indeed eclipsed Madrid in a number of ways. Long a center of business, Barcelona grew and developed significantly during Spain's industrial expansion of the 1950s. Always more focused on Western Europe than Madrid, it reflected even more quickly the cultural currents that entered Spain as it prospered and opened to the outside world. Above all, the city developed into a major cultural and publishing center, less constrained than Madrid by the regime in power. Especially noteworthy were the activities of the Seix Barral publishing house, which introduced new French, Italian, and German fiction into Spain and also made available major works of modern European fiction, thought, and criticism. In the 1960s Seix Barral almost single-handedly created the "boom" of Spanish American fiction by publishing the major works of that fiction and highlighting their importance through the Premio Biblioteca Breve. It was also responsible for the publication of major works of Spanish "critical realism."

The city was the home of several important poets writing in Spanish, who have come to be considered together and called the school of Barcelona, generally seen as a subset of the generation that also included Valente, Rodríguez, González, and Brines.[18] The three most prominent ones, Jaime Gil de Biedma, Carlos Barral, and José Agustín Goytisolo, together with the critic José María Castellet and the poet Gabriel Ferrater, who wrote in Catalan, all grew up as friends and colleagues. Members of the upper middle class, they went to Catholic (mostly Jesuit) schools and experienced as teenagers the closed and somewhat hypocritical world of the 1940s (they were born, we remember, in the late 1920s). But later they had the opportunity to travel abroad, and because of their background and means, they acquired a sophisticated cultural education and perspective. They also developed a strong political consciousness and adopted leftist attitudes. This mixture of influences and orientations helps explain their interest in social writing as well as in a more cosmopolitan and creative view of literature.[19]

These poets met as students at the University of Barcelona in the late 1940s and crystallized as a group in a series of *tertulias* in the 1950s. They controlled the magazine *Laye* between 1951 and 1955, and in it they reflected their cosmopolitan outlook. In 1959 they were the driving force behind an homage to Antonio Machado in Collioure (where he had died in exile), which put them in contact with other writers. In the same year Barral, Gil de Biedma, and Goytisolo held a poetry reading in Madrid, sponsored by Hierro and introduced by Bousoño. They collaborated in the construction of Castellet's anthology in 1960. In 1961 they created a poetry series named Colliure, which published, in inexpensive editions, books by González, Celaya, Fuertes, Valente, Caballero Bonald, and the members of the group.[20]

Carlos Barral's poetry has, rather unfortunately, been eclipsed by his other literary activities. A man of exceptional learning and ability, Barral, having inherited the publishing house of his name, was the major force in its success and influence. He was an important essayist and critic and also authored fiction, as well as three volumes of memoirs that give an excellent picture of the cultural milieu in which he grew up.[21] His first book of poetry, *Metropolitano* ("Metropolitan," 1957) is unique in Spain for its artful, stylized way of reflecting the effects—marvelous and horrific—produced by a complex urban environment. Barral pays extraordinary attention to language: he wrings double and triple meanings from words by their etymologies, combines the values thus produced with unexpected metaphors, complements them with echoes of other writers, and thus creates rich layers of significance and mood. The first lines of the title poem give an excellent example. Echoing both *city* and *subway* in his title, Barral moves from a quote of T.S. Eliot's *Four Quartets* to a complex of metaphor, image, and monologue:

> Metropolitano
> "Un lugar desafecto"
>
> *Here is a place of disaffection*
>
> Penetraré la cueva
> del bisonte y raíl riguroso,
> la piedra decimal que nunca
> conoce.
>   Soy urgente
> y frágil, de alabastro
>
> Iré.
>   Iré al angosto
> pasadizo sin dolor que habitan
> y por la larga espalda de las sombras
> sobre un viento de vidrio. [Barral 81]

{Metropolitan, "A Disaffected Place." *Here is a place of disaffection.* I shall enter the cave of the bison and rigorous [hard] rail, the decimal stone that never understands. I am urgent and fragile, made of alabaster. I shall go. I shall go to the narrow passage without suffering that they inhabit, and via the long backs of the shadows, over a glass wind.}

On the one hand, the image of the cave links city and subway with darkness and primitive chaos; on the other, it—especially via the word *bisonte*—alludes to caves in which early art was written (see Riera in Barral 81). Upon entering this world, the speaker starts a process of experiencing, comprehending, and ultimately expressing artistically his disaffected world. The Eliot quote situates this speaker-poet within the tradition of poets who attempted to present and decipher the enigmas of urban modernity.

In succeeding poems, the speakers, with varying voices, focus on different places and situations (automatic gates and doors, telephones, failed dialogues) to portray the disharmony of this modern world. Yet they also strive to bring order to it by organizing it poetically. In this sense, the consciously artful language used, the intertextual references, and the levels of meaning reflect the underlying striving for value amid a debased world.

As Carme Riera has noted, basing herself on Barral's own comments (Barral 33–35), the book is a series of dramatic monologues embodying several paths in a general search.[22] In that sense, it continues the tradition of Dámaso Alonso's *Hijos de la ira* as well as Eliot's *Waste Land,* and their speak-

ers' quest for meaning among modern decay. It also foregrounds its own art-
ful use of language and its own process of poetically transforming reality, ex-
emplifying the self-conscious art of this and the following period.[23]

Diecinueve figuras de mi historia civil ("Nineteen Figures of My Civil His-
tory," 1961), Barral's next book of poetry, is written in much more direct
language and is based on remembrances of youthful experiences. It obvi-
ously indicates a desire to use common language poetically and reflects the
Barcelona group's search for a socially conscious and accessible verse. Bar-
ral combines narrative sequences that include descriptive details to evoke
past experiences with various personal as well as social echoes; in "Primer
amor" ("First Love"), for example, this style conveys the tawdriness of a pros-
titute's life as well as the complex of feelings of the speaker, which include
a search for ideals (Barral 134–36).

In later poems, included—together with his previous work—in *Usuras
y figuraciones* ("Usuries and Figurations," 1973), Barral goes back to the lin-
guistic play and complexity already seen in *Metropolitano* and creates elabo-
rate metaphorical transformations of reality that can make us think of
Góngora. These serve, above all, to convert modern realities (often city
scenes) into aesthetic experiences, although they also reflect at times a
sense of the contemporary world's degradation.[24]

In contrast to many of Barral's poems, those of Jaime Gil de Biedma come
across on first reading as clear and "realistic." Most of them evoke specific
episodes, narrated by first-person speakers who also offer commentaries. A
second reading, however, makes us aware that, for all their apparent realism,
the scenes and events portrayed are but the basis for subjective interpretations
and experiences and lead to complex perceptions on subjects as basic as a
sense of loss, the limitations of middle-class existence, and human temporal-
ity and mortality. *Compañeros de viaje* ("Fellow Travelers," 1959), Gil de
Biedma's first major book, is centered on the passage of time, fitting a gen-
eral current of Spanish poetry in the 1950s.

The effects of this poetry are produced by a most effective use of tone
and of narrative techniques and by the juxtaposition of opposing atti-
tudes. Often the speaker will recall a series of events, simultaneously evok-
ing and undercutting their value and suggesting underlying issues. In
"Infancia y confesiones" ("Childhood and Confessions") the speaker's ap-
parently casual narration of his youth points much deeper:

> Cuando yo era más joven
> (bueno, en realidad, será mejor decir
> muy joven)
>   algunos años antes
> de conocernos y
> recién llegado a la ciudad,

a menudo pensaba en la vida.
        Mi familia
era bastante rica y yo estudiante.
Mi infancia eran recuerdos de una casa
con escuela y despensa y llave en el ropero,
de cuando las familias
acomodadas,
                como su nombre indica
veraneaban infinitamente
en *Villa Estefanía* o en *La Torre*
del Mirador
            y más allá continuaba el mundo
con senderos de grava y cenadores
rústicos, decorado de hortensias pomposas.
                [Gil de Biedma 1982, 49]

{When I was younger (well, truly, it would be better to say very young), some years before we met, and had just arrived in the city, I often thought about life. My family was quite rich, and I was a student. My youth was memories of a house, with a school and a pantry and keys in the closets, from the days in which well-heeled families, as their names indicated, vacationed endlessly in Villa Stephanie or The Tower of the Balcony, and beyond them the world stretched out in gravel [garden] paths, rustic outdoor dining areas, decorations of pompous hortensias.}

The speaker calls attention to himself, "correcting" himself and adopting a casual tone that casts us in the role of friendly listeners of idle reminiscences. He thus creates a situation, and a role for himself as a character; having done so, he develops an ambiguous vision of his past. The apparently positive view of leisurely comfort is undercut by details suggesting purposeless idleness ("veraneaban infinitamente"), pretentiousness ("hortensias pomposas"), materialism. The softly ironic tone makes us read lines like "a menudo pensaba en la vida" ambiguously: they point to seriousness and also pretentiousness. An intertextual echo of a poem by Antonio Machado ("Mis infancia eran recuerdos de un patio de Sevilla" from "Retrato") suggests that we read an otherwise straight line with some irony: Gil de Biedma's somewhat jaded speaker contrasts, ironically, with Machado's idealistic one.

One could read this poem as a social commentary on the middle class— a topic that is indeed important in *Compañeros de viaje*; it also exemplifies an ethical concern, which indeed underlies Gil de Biedma's and his generation's work. Yet its skillful use of narration, tone, and intertext turns it into a multifaceted and complex portrayal of illusions and limitations, which, without preaching, makes the reader sense the shortcomings of this world. The form of the dramatic monologue is perfectly suited to convey, simultaneously, a variety of attitudes. The rich families display their limited illusions in their estates; the speaker asserts his own illusions as he condemns their idleness and triteness, while apologizing for being trapped within them. At the end he confesses, somewhat ironically, his persistent search of illusions:

> De mi pequeño reino afortunado
> me quedó esta costumbre de calor
> y una imposible propensión al mito.
> [Gil de Biedma 1982, 50]

{From my small, fortunate reign I kept this habit of warmth, and an impossible tendency to mythify.}

Moralidades ("Moralities," 1966) creates an even greater impression of objectivity than *Compañeros de viaje:* it refers to specific episodes in the speaker's life, offers fewer commentaries, and integrates perceptions more into the presentation of events. Yet the speaker's tone and complex point of view produce highly subjective and ambiguous visions. In "París, postal del cielo" ("Paris, Postcard of Heaven") the remembrance of a past love affair is idealistic on the one hand, conventional and almost trite on the other. In "De aquí a la eternidad" ("From Here to Eternity") the speaker's illusions are ironically undercut by an awareness of a city's banality.

Gil de Biedma exploits point of view, tone, and narrative devices even more fully in *Poemas póstumos* ("Posthumous Poems," 1968). In two key poems, he divides himself into two characters and plays one self against the other. In "Contra Jaime Gil de Biedma" ("Against Jaime Gil de Biedma"), a sober speaker attacks his bohemian alter ego, yet ends up joining him in a paradoxical mix of love and hate. In "Después de la muerte de Jaime Gil de Biedma" ("After the Death of Jaime Gil de Biedma") a survivor mourns the loss of his more idealistic and poetic other self, yet finds survival by writing poetry. The book constitutes, perhaps, the most artful and complex use of tone and point of view in recent Spanish poetry, combined with an underlying metapoetic consciousness.

José Agustín Goytisolo's poetry, like that of Gil de Biedma, uses narratives of events and situations to construct a view of a society and its members. We saw in chapter 3 how in his *Salmos al viento* ironic speakers project the triviality of conventional existence. In other books—*El retorno* ("The Return," 1955), *Claridad* ("Clarity," 1961), *Algo sucede* ("Something Happens," 1968)—Goytisolo takes a somewhat more individual perspective. Vignettes of past events and places convey various moods and seem most effective when capturing nuances of the tawdry, routine-driven existence of the Spanish 1940s and 1950s. Common images and symbols— such as time as a rag, in "Mis habitaciones" ("My Rooms")—effectively highlight the poems' moods. Even the act of writing poetry emerges, at times, as limited and debased by contemporary circumstances. Somewhat similar effects are produced by the works of Jaime Ferrán, a poet educated in Barcelona and associated with the group, though mostly resident in the United States (see Castellet 1960, 291–92, 403).

The works of the Barcelona poets of this era share traits already seen in their Castilian and Andalusian contemporaries: an artful use of everyday language to make individual experiences evoke wider themes, an underlying ethical concern, an explicit self-consciousness of the poetic process. They reveal an even greater use of narrative, tonal, and point of view techniques, often within the frame of dramatic monologues; they also make use of frequent intertextual echoes, which we can relate to the poets' literary sophistication. At the same time they show an underlying social consciousness, generally integrated into more philosophical visions. Behind this poetry lies a vision of the poetic act as a process of discovery and of the text as an evolving reality, which the reader can not only receive but also share and perhaps continue. All of this situates the poetry and poetics of this time beyond the basic outlooks and the aesthetic of European modernity.

Older Poets, New Consciousness, New Forms

The characteristics that I have been tracing in Spanish poetry after the mid-1950s are also reflected in books published at this time by older writers. Many of them appeared in a major new work by José Hierro, who had previously established himself as perhaps the leading testimonial poet of the previous decade. Hierro had developed, by the time of *Cuanto sé de mí* (1957) two poetic modes—he called them "reporting" and "hallucination"—using them to give more realistic and a more complex and subjective expression to the sense of loss and the mood of nostalgia related to it, which underlie his whole work. *Cuánto sé de mí* also reflected the speaker's consciousness of his role as poet.

Hierro's *Libro de las alucinaciones* ("Book of Hallucinations," 1964) significantly extended his poetic manner, connecting it with that of several younger poets, as José Olivio Jiménez has noted (1972, 173). The neat juxtaposition of "reportings" and "hallucinations" is no longer evident, having been replaced by a more coherent, combined mode, though focus and approach do vary from poem to poem. The outlook of the "hallucinations" is obviously dominant, but the narrative sequences and devices of the "reportings" are also important. A sense of artful manipulation of reality becomes more explicit in this book and is often related to the theme of art's conflicts with reality. One of the most colloquial texts, "Yepes cocktail," juxtaposes Saint John's poetry to modern trivia (Hierro 1964, 41–42).

As we read the poems in sequence, we experience versions of a single search for ways of confronting time, overcoming meaninglessness, and asserting life's intensity. Hierro combines a narrative flow with the repeated use of key images to trace this search. In "Alucinación en Salamanca" ("Hallucination in Salamanca") the speaker works through his memories of the city to move poetically from the uncertainty represented by *sombra* {"shadow"} to the affirmation of a color, a memory, and a striving for poetry; his hopes seem to fade at the end. Shifts and contradictions in attitude within the text leave it somewhat unresolved, open to various readings. The speaker does claim to have lost his "word" at the end, but he has also created, in earlier sections, key images that make us feel that he has seized and preserved an experience. I quote a few sections of this long poem:

> ¿En dónde estás, por dónde
> te hallaré, sombra, sombra,
> sombra?
>   Pisé las piedras,
> las modelé con sol
> y con tristeza. Supe
> que había allí un secreto
> . . . .
>   Azul:
> en el azul estaba,
> en la hoguera celeste,
> en la pulpa del día,
> la clave. Ahora recuerdo:
> he vuelto a Italia. *Azul*
> *azul, azul:* era ésa
> la palabra (no *sombra,*
> . . . .
> Quién sabe qué decían
> las olas de esta piedra.
> Quién sabe lo que hubiera
> —antes—dicho esta piedra
> si yo hubiese acertado
> la palabra precisa.
>   [Hierro 1964, 16–19]

{Where are you, where will I find you, shadow, shadow, shadow? I stepped on stones, I carved them with sunlight and sadness. I knew that there was a secret there. . . . Blue: the key was in the blue, in the campfire of the sky, in the pulp of the day. Now I remember: I have come back to Italy. *Blue, blue, blue:* that was the word (not shadow, . . . Who knows what the waves of this stone were saying. Who knows what this stone would have said, earlier, if I had found the exact word.}

This text, and the book, combine narrative technique, the use of a shifting first-person perspective, and patterns of image and symbol to create a tensive, multidimensional exploration of a basic theme of life.[25] This combination produces a work at once artful and profound, yet built from common language, specific referents, and clear narrative. It also specifically incorporates and emphasizes the theme of a poetic quest within the overall search for meaning and invites us to fill out the poem, making our process of reading reflect and extend the speaker's process of seeing, interpreting, and writing.

Carlos Bousoño's *Invasión de la realidad* ("Invasion of Reality," 1962) is based, like his prior books, on the paradoxical view of life as the "springtime of death." The book begins with a positive assertion of reality's value and with an explicit affirmation of the poet's task in proclaiming it. Succeeding sections convey absence and doubt, only to give way, at the end, to an existential praise of life and language in the face of its temporality. The book's style recalls Bousoño's earlier books in its use of everyday language, first-person meditations, and symbolic scenes. Yet greater formal control and variety and the use of verbal patterns (especially internal rhyme) now combine with the explicit treatment of poetry as a way of preserving life.

Though thematically consistent with his previous books, *Oda en la ceniza* ("Ode amid the Ashes," 1967) marks, as Bousoño himself has noted, a major stylistic change in his poetry (Bousoño 1980, 25–27).[26] Many of its poems seem enigmatic: they contain apparent descriptions, exhortations, and queries but give the reader insufficient clues to discern their context. Ironic reversals and tensions within texts make it difficult to define a central outlook. Images point in several directions at once. Long lines of free verse, and long sentences, predominate, often producing complex visions that double back on themselves. Rhythmic and syntactical patterns govern, but also confuse, our search for a poem's focus.

These tensions are stressed, to my mind, by the theme of poetry that underlies the whole book. Its very title suggests that poetic writing is a paradoxical assertion in the face of nothingness: amid the ashes of existence, the poet offers an ode, a poem of praise. In thus making his speaker a poet who fights against oblivion, and the act of writing a way of seeking meaning, Bousoño gives his poetry a focus and a vividness not present in his earlier work. He also involves the reader in the speaker's process, as the former has to grapple with contradictory perspectives: both seek some solution, through the language of the text, to meaninglessness and disintegration. In the following segment of the title poem, the speaker's plea can be read, in context, as an exhortation to a reader or fellow poet to join him in a quest against vacuity:

> dame la mano en la desolación,
> dame la mano en la incredulidad y en el viento,

dame la mano en el arrancado sollozo, en el lóbrego cántico.
Dame la mano para creer, puesto que tú no sabes,
dame la mano para existir, puesto que sombra eres y ceniza,
dame la mano hacia arriba, hacia el vertical puerto, hacia la cresta súbita.
Ayúdame a subir, puesto que no es posible la llegada,
el arribo, el encuentro.
Ayúdame a subir puesto que caes, puesto que acaso
todo es posible en la imposibilidad. [Bousoño 1980, 103]

{Give me your hand in the midst of desolation, give me your hand among disbelief and wind, give me your hand in the whimper, in the gloomy canticle. Give me your hand to believe, since you do not know, give me your hand to exist, since you are shadow and ashes, give me your hand upward, to the vertical haven, to the sudden crest. Help me to rise, since arrival and encounter are not possible. Help me rise since you are falling, since perhaps all is possible within impossibility.}

José Olivio Jiménez has correctly noted the negative vision that dominates this text (1972, 271–72). Yet by expressing this vision while constructing a poem (note the reference to a "canticle"), the speaker works toward an affirmation: unable to find achievement in life, he does find it in art, illuminating the poem's paradox in which falling has led to elevation.

In this poem, and in all of *Oda en la ceniza,* Bousoño reveals new ways of using narrative structures, speaker perspective, image, and paradox to engender an enigmatic view of life. As he does so, he places more explicit emphasis on poetry as a vehicle for meaning. All this connects him to the members of the newer generation and confirms our sense of the emergence of a new and important mode of writing by the mid-1960s.[27]

Blas de Otero continued writing social poetry throughout the 1960s. Many of his individual poems recall those of the previous decade and again demonstrate his exceptional ability for handling ideological topics in a creative and original way. Yet Otero's work also reveals a new dimension in this period, which becomes apparent when we have read a number of texts and books. Again and again Otero evokes prior poetry and art: *En castellano* (1960) and *Que trata de España* (1964) are filled with homages to poets, references to works, and poems recalling earlier styles (see, for example, "Cantar de amigo" ["Friend's Song"] in *En castellano*). In *Esto no es un libro* ("This Is Not a Book," 1963) Otero collects a number of his previously published poems that evoke names of people—mostly authors and literary characters. The title of the book undermines the conventional expectations of a poetry reader of modernity and questions the concept of a stable work. The title, the book, and the act of collecting intertextual works suggest Otero's interest in the continuity of the creative process. This interest connects him to the self-consciousness of poetic writing that we have seen emerging at this time—and points ahead to his later collage poems and metapoetic texts.

Concha Zardoya, resident in the United States and generally identified with the Generation of 1936, wrote, at this time, seven books of poetry that also connect with a poetics of discovery and suggest a heightened sense of artistic consciousness. Perhaps the most outstanding is *Corral de vivos y muertos* ("Yard of the Living and the Dead," 1965), which evokes places, themes, and literary and artistic works reflecting essences of Spain. Specific reminiscences provide the basis for intense images and personifications, which portray the speaker's discovery of essential values. Zardoya masterfully alternates a variety of forms and styles, from popular poetry to the sonnet. Her most impressive poems may be those dealing with painting, such as "Toledo visto por El Greco" ("Toledo Seen by El Greco"):

> Negras rocas llagadas por relámpagos
> el cielo negro-azul dispara en chispas,
> tremendos, hoscos cuévanos eléctricos
> que honduras estelares, ay, erizan.
> La luz combate, viva, con la sombra:
> el paisaje desciende, no lo humilla,
> y las peñas se elevan y traslucen
> en un pasmo de nubes encendidas.
>   [Zardoya 1988, 146]

{The blue-black sky shoots out, in sparks, black rocks wounded by rays of lightning, dark electric baskets that, oh, make starlike depths stand up on end. Light battles, alive, against the shadows; the landscape comes down, does not humiliate it, and the rocks rise and shimmer, in a marvel of lit clouds.}

The poem vivifies, personifies, and hence intensifies the details of the description, which in turn reflects a specific painting of a specific city. The art of the poet, superimposed upon that of the painter, gives greater life and intensity to the reality of a place and invites the reader to perceive art as a way of heightening life. Similar effects are achieved in *Mirar al cielo es tu condena* ("To Look Heavenward Is Your Fate," 1957), in which Michelangelo's painting gains new life thanks to poetic form.[28]

Three poets of the Generation of 1927 published, in this period, works that reflect some of the characteristics I have observed among younger writers. Jorge Guillén's *Clamor* makes effective use of narrative sequences and techniques to present a search for harmony and affirmation among the details and problems of modern existence. Especially in its third volume, *A la altura de las circunstancias* ("In Keeping with One's Circumstances," 1963), Guillén finds in life's everyday events evidence of wider patterns, often making explicit reference to the role of poetry in discovering such patterns (see Debicki 1973, 81–88). This theme becomes dominant in Guillén's third major work, *Homenaje* ("Homage"), first published in 1967. If *Cántico* viewed human existence from a timeless perspective and *Clamor* related it to a particular place and time, *Homenaje* places it in the context of prior works and literary traditions. Many of its poems highlight the contemporary relevance of past literary works or portray a modern reader who discovers the impact of such a work. Thus in "Al margen del Poema del Cid" ("On the Margin of the Poem of the Cid") a modern youngster enthusiastically identifies with the hero as he listens to the poem being read. At times the theme of poetry is handled directly: in "Sospecha de foca" ("A Seal Suspected") the poet -protagonist's sighting of a black dot leads to the construction of a beautiful image of a seal and a resultant commentary on how poetry weaves beauty from reality (see also ibid. 47–49). The poem ends as follows:

> Ondulación de oleaje
> Sobre el dorso de una foca.
> ¿Encontré lo que yo traje?
> A la realidad ya toca
> Con su potencia el lenguaje.
> [Guillén 1987, 3: 151]

{Undulation of the waves on the back of a seal. Did I find that which I brought with me? Language, with its power, now touches reality.}

Guillén's search for life's essences though language has led to a conscious commentary on the poetic process as act of discovery—and an implicit invitation to his reader to continue that process—connecting his work with that of younger authors.

Dámaso Alonso wrote, at this time, poems that form the book *Gozos de la vista* ("The Joys of Sight"), although he only published them individually, in magazines; the book as a whole came out only in 1981. One of these poems, titled "Visión de los monstruos (scherzo)" ("Vision of Monsters [Scherzo]"), is a dramatic monologue whose speaker begins by asserting the superiority of human sight over that of all other creatures, only to convince himself, ironically, of his limitations. The poem ends with great comic impact, as the speaker cannot even convince us of his superiority over a grotesque imaginary slug that he himself had invented. The blend of poetry and narrative, the speaker's self-consciousness of his poetic task, and the final undermining of traditional views about poetic and human superiority connect this work with the prevailing mode of its time.[29]

Vicente Aleixandre's two books of poetry of this period also connect, in different ways, with those of younger authors. *En un vasto dominio* ("In a Vast Dominion," 1962), as José Olivio Jiménez has indicated, combines a cosmic perspective with the focus on human solidarity we noted in *Historia del corazón* (Jiménez 1982, 83–91). The result is a somewhat preachy tone and a book devoid of the nuances of Aleixandre's previous work.

More interesting from our point of view are Aleixandre's *Poemas de la consumación* ("Poems of Consummation," 1968). Constructed around conflicting images of youth and old age, these poems capture both the intensity of life and the tragedy of death. For the first time in his long trajectory as poet, Aleixandre wrote mostly short, sharply structured texts, placing some of them in the mouths of specific speakers. The use of narrative situations and specific points of view may fit this poetry in its time. The book's most telling feature, however, is its self-consciousness. Its initial text, "Las palabras del poeta" ("The Poet's Words"), already sets human life within the frame of the act of poetic naming: life is identified with the language through which it is remembered, and death is defined as the loss of that language (Jiménez 1982, 11–13). The whole book shares the self-awareness of much of the poetry of its time. It is made most evident by Aleixandre's repeated use of lines taken from his earlier poetry (see ibid. 99–100). The reader, as a result, reads the poems not as static messages but as part of an evolving process begun much earlier, as steps in a continuing search.

One additional poet whose birth date (1906) would place him somewhere between the Generation of 1927 and that of 1936, but who was virtually unknown previously, gained importance during the 1960s. Juan Gil-Albert, exiled from Spain right after the Civil War, had published one book of verse in Buenos Aires and several in Spain between 1943 and 1968. His *La trama inextricable* ("The Inextricable Plot," 1968) and *Los homenajes* ("The Homages," 1968) brought him to the attention of critics and fellow poets, and interest in his work kept growing, leading eventually to the publication of his complete works in 1981. One reason for this interest may be Gil-Albert's way of exploring an underlying philosophical theme—freedom of choice and the search for spirituality—by means of a language at once discursive, meditative, and lyrical. Using a flexible free verse and everyday vocabulary, Gil-Albert combines slowly unfolding natural imagery with first-person reflections. In *Los homenajes* he projects, through different voices, various outlooks on life. In many ways his poems resemble those of Brines or Cernuda (see Jiménez 1972, 395–405). His discovery during the 1960s, to my mind, is further evidence of the interest at this time in poetic language as a way of exploring, with both precision and originality, the main issues of life.

Poetry's role as a means of discovery clearly underpins this whole period, affecting the works of authors including the youngest members of the new generation as well as those of the Generation of 1927. It underlies a body of poetry very conscious of its own creative tasks, which artfully configures particular, individual experiences into new visions.[30] Through various and innovative ways—including point of view and narrative techniques—such experiences and an apparently ordinary language produce significant works.

This poetry marks a continued erosion of the modernist-symbolist poetic tradition. Some of the underpinnings of that tradition, most notably the quest for a form that would embody experience, universalizing it in an "eternal present," had already been dismantled by the subjectivism and the play of multiple perspectives in the earlier work of Alonso, Aleixandre, and Hierro and even, to some extent, by social poetry. They are even more clearly negated by the major poems of this period. The very stress on individual experience in these poems, emphasized even more by narrative techniques, partially constitutes such a negation. More important, the speakers' (and poets') consciousness of the act of poetization, and their comments on that act, turn the reader's attention to the poem as process rather than product. Derived no doubt from the new poetics of this time, the simultaneously narrative and self-conscious texts that typify it invite us to focus on their progressive manipulation of reality and language and, to some extent, to share and continue it. As they do so, they form part of a rebellion against the notion of language as static and authoritarian, and hence against the prevalent discourse preceding them.

Does all this make the poems in question postmodern? Any answer depends, I suspect, on one's definition. We can call them that if we see postmodernity, with Lyotard and Hutcheon, as based on the view of the poem as a source of events rather than a product, or as a "textualization" of reality (Hutcheon 93–94; Lyotard 81). If, on the other hand, we define the postmodern text as necessarily plurisignificant or indeterminate, and stress its arbitrariness and avoidance of any stable meanings, the term may not quite fit. Most of this poetry, grounded in individual experience and philosophical meanings, still reflects some quest for closure. In this sense we might say that the poetry of this era is more modern than its authors' underlying poetics, which move beyond the premises of modernity. During the 1970s the fundamental shifts that occurred in the poetry would move Spanish poetry onto clearly new ground. We can call this new poetry truly postmodern, according to certain uses and definitions.

5

The Postmodern Time of the
Novísimos, *1966–1980*

A Poetics of Language

A new mode of poetry, founded on new attitudes to literary language, developed in Spain in the late 1960s. Stylistically, it constituted a more dramatic shift than any that had occurred for decades, probably since the 1920s. Its novelty was quickly perceived, and its impact was intensified by the reactions of critics and above all by a widely read anthology, José María Castellet's *Nueve novísimos poetas españoles* ("Nine Newest Spanish Poets," 1970). This poetry placed renewed and intense emphasis on creativity through language and on the primacy—and, at times, independence—of linguistic form. Its aestheticism is related to historical and cultural currents of the time and points to a new artistic era that fits most definitions of postmodernity.

Social changes in Spain intensified as the 1960s wore on and gave way to the next decade. Economic development and increased opening to Western European and United States currents brought with them the popular culture exemplified by movies, rock music, detective fiction, and fashion magazines. Youths growing up at this time were exposed to the mythic premises of such genres, the mood of sensorial gratification, and the fantasies of sexual freedom represented by the Swedish tourists arriving at Spain's beaches (the *suecas* became a myth of Spanish movies).[1] These developments fed a thirst for contemporaneity and for the acceptance of Western cultural phenomena among younger Spaniards, who saw their country as still relatively backward and repressed.

The irruption of popular culture and the thirst for contemporaneity evoked contradictory responses among poets and writers. On the one hand, popular culture furnished materials for new forms of expression. These materials became almost a signal of the search for less conventional, less authoritarian, and more open forms of expression, opposed to prior idioms. Popular culture also represented, on the other hand, a target against which some authors reacted in striving for a higher art. We will see the effects of this tension as we examine the poetry of the decade: some poets combined contradictory attitudes to the popular, creating ambiguity and indeterminacy. All in all, the idiom of popular culture was related to a breakdown of previous styles and modes of communication and furnished a stimulus to rethink the nature of writing, of genres, and of the identity of the text (the Marshall McLuhan vision of "the medium as the message" pervaded the environment).

In any event, the new circumstances helped the new poets develop an attitude according to which the prior doctrines of realistic writing and the concept of social poetry became anathema or, as Castellet put it, a "nightmare" from which to escape (see 1970, 17–21).[2] These poets had been born between 1939 and the early 1950s: they had no personal experience of the Civil War and little if any memory of the polarization and repression that followed. Their own education was far broader than that of their predecessors, and at the university, it was far better: most of them studied literature and linguistics with the likes of Rafael Lapesa, Dámaso Alonso, José Manuel Blecua, and Francisco Ynduráin. Several of them became leading literary scholars. The grim tenets, and the language, of prior social poets struck them as simplistic and irrelevant to their world and its modes of expression. Most of them also rejected any notion of the poem as an icon of meaning. They did connect better with the poetics and the idiom of immediately preceding poets, especially Valente, Gil de Biedma, and Brines, but did not always appreciate sufficiently their importance and innovativeness, at least in part because they wished to define themselves as the innovators.

Yet this generation too had to become aware of the social issues and events of its time. The *novísimo* poets witnessed, as young adults, the student movements of France in the summer of 1968; the United States and world reactions to the war in Vietnam and the general climate of disillusion that resulted; activism and strikes in Spanish universities; and the growing frustration with Spain's relative backwardness, coupled with expectations of change as the Franco regime moved to an inevitable end. (For some of them, as for older writers, this end seemed to be frustratingly delayed.) All this intensified, in fact, their sense that issues of the Civil War and the old social poetry were passé, irrelevant. Their postures and responses varied, far more than those of prior groups of writers: they ran the gamut from Guillermo Carnero's elitist conservatism to Jenaro Talens's idiosyncratic neo-Marxism.[3] As a result they dealt with the changes taking place after Franco's death in 1975 in diverse ways, though all of them transcended the old polarizations of the 1940s. This generation's one common denominator, however, was an intense emphasis on innovative language in poetry and on the primacy of medium, discourse, and form over theme and referent.

Several of these poets published books between 1965 and 1970, some of which—one by Carnero, two by Gimferrer—came to be seen, retrospectively, as major accomplishments. Three of these poets were included in José Batlló's 1968 anthology, which highlighted the major poets of the prior era. But it was Castellet's 1970 anthology and its rather polemical introduction that made readers and critics notice their work and call attention to its innovativeness, its mass-media orientation, its cultural exoticism, and its vision of decadence and decay, which has roots in the Spanish baroque (see García de la Concha 1986, 19). By coming out when this poetic era was just defining itself and by including its early works, Castellet's anthology did accent its more superficial innovations, which later literary historians probably overemphasized.[4] It also omitted some important figures.

By the late 1970s the *novísimos* were clearly the most talked-about poets in Spain, although the literary canon, as defined by textbook anthologies and editions of complete works, by major prizes, and by mention in histories, still stressed older authors—mainly Otero, Hierro, Rodríguez, Valente, González, Brines, and Gil de Biedma. Poets who had not appeared in Castellet's anthology had been added to the *novísimos* by critics; some of the original participants evolved in new directions, and others faded from sight. New strands of writing became evident, enriching the original definitions: a way of relating aestheticism to personal experiences and attitudes, illustrated by Luis Antonio de Villena and, differently, by José María Alvarez; a freer-flowing and more easily readable neoromantic vein identified with Antonio Colinas; a denser, more sparse, more essentialist verse, based on a "poetics of silence" and best represented by Jaime Siles; and a turn to intellectual writing, which produced poems organized like essays, exemplified by Carnero's fourth and fifth books and by the metapoetic work of Pere Gimferrer, Jenaro Talens, and others. The diversity and richness of this poetic generation's work was represented in two anthologies, Concepción Moral and Rosa María Pereda's *Joven poesía española* and José Luis García Martín's *Las voces y los ecos*, both of which, coming out in 1980, could serve as compendiums in a way in which Castellet's anthology or Enrique Martín Pardo's *Nueva poesía española* (1970) could not.[5]

When in the following sections I discuss the actual poetry written between 1970 and 1980, we will see that many of the features of *novísimo* writing also appeared in texts composed by older poets, especially by several members of the preceding generation. These writers had become disillusioned with the ability of poetry to deal with life's problems and with social issues, and they shifted toward more limited and formal poetic goals, bringing them closer to the skepticism of the *novísimos*. They thus moved from a stress on self-discovery to more consciously artful, intertextual, and metapoetic styles. Aestheticism and self-consciousness, which pervaded the whole

period, allow us to define a continuing, and now more absolute, move be-
yond modernity in Spanish poetry. Because they illustrate explicitly the new
aesthetic consciousness, however, the overt statements on poetics by the
new generation will give us the clearest sense of the innovations in outlook.

The *novísimos* held varying views on many issues and never formed a
group or established tight contacts. This makes the similarity in attitudes to
poetry among them very telling. All of them maintained the urgency of
transcending direct expression and the exclusive use of colloquial lan-
guage, and the necessity of restoring creativity, innovation, and artfulness
to poetry. Pere Gimferrer, in Batlló's 1968 anthology, wrote about attempt-
ing "una serie de experimentos en diversas direcciones, encaminadas a un
intento de renovar en lo posible el inerte lenguaje poético español"
(Provencio 2: 116) {"a series of experiments in several directions, aimed in
an effort to renew as much as possible the inert Spanish poetic language"}.[6]
Guillermo Carnero, in 1974, specifically defined his generation as having
"una única característica común: el propósito de restaurar la primacía del
lenguaje" (ibid. 179) {"a single common characteristic: the purpose of
restoring the primacy of language"}. Antonio Colinas stressed the need for
beauty and harmony in poetic expression and emphasized the importance
of suggestiveness as opposed to literal meaning (ibid. 136). Jaime Siles
claimed that poetry needed to produce a new semantic flowering, and An-
tonio Martínez Sarrión, in noting the limitations of social verse, vehe-
mently asserted the necessity of making poetic expression creative and
independent (ibid. 205, 28).

Implicitly or explicitly, these poets accepted the view of poetry as dis-
covery that had been formulated by Valente and other predecessors:
Gimferrer specifically quoted Valente in calling poetry a "tarea de
conocimiento por la palabra" (Provencio 2: 121) {"task of discovery
through the word"}, while Jenaro Talens stated that "la obra no comunica
. . . sino expresa, permitiendo ser significada" (ibid. 169) {"the work does
not communicate . . . but rather expresses, allowing itself to be made
meaningful"}. Yet this view of poetry as discovery led most of the *novísimos*
in a direction different from their predecessors. Whereas the older writ-
ers had used their poetry to examine and reconstruct, artistically, personal
experiences and themes in a search of self-discovery, the *novísimos* began
by avoiding the personal and the anecdotal, sought their referents in prior
literary and cultural texts, and constructed linguistic and formal struc-
tures to reflect their themes. Alvarez declared flatly that he disbelieved in
the importance of personal feelings for poetic creation and that material
taken from personal experience was no more valid than any other as a ba-
sis for poetry (ibid. 64). Hence these poets foregrounded art and culture,
as Alvarez made clear: "Afirmamos la Literatura, el Arte como nuestra

única patria y nuestro único idioma" (Alvarez 1989, 17). {"We affirm Literature, Art, as our only nation and our only language."}

The view of the relationship of art to life held by the *novísimos* is tellingly explained in a 1992 essay by Carnero, titled "Culturalism and the 'New' Poetry." Examining a poem by Gimferrer, he indicates how a prior literary text—in this case an early modern short story—serves as an analogue for the experience being created. For Carnero, the use of such analogues or correlatives lets the poets of his generation create experiences while avoiding confessionalism and self-referentiality. It thus helps them overcome the limitations of prior romantic and social realistic traditions and produce purer and more independent experiences. In one sense, this formulation recalls the aesthetic idealism of high modernity, since it makes poetry a striving for objectification (we think of Guillén's notion of the poem as embodied meaning). In another sense, however, it points to a postmodern notion of the text's independence from author and referent and suggests that its meanings will be contingent rather than stable.

The goal of the *novísimos* to emphasize the creative power of language in their verse relates to their belief in the independence of the sign in poetry. A comment by Carnero, first published in 1974, deserves attention:

El lenguaje poético se distingue de otros sistemas semiológicos en que pretende poner de relieve el valor autónomo, y no instrumental, del signo. . . . La finalidad de la poesía, y su función en una sociedad que rebaja al nivel de instrumentos lo que heredó como ideas, es luchar por devolver dignidad y libertad al signo lingüístico. [Provencio 2: 180]

{Poetic language is distinguished from other semiological systems in that it tries to highlight the autonomous, not the instrumental, value of the sign. . . . The goal of poetry, and its function in a society that reduces what it inherited as ideas down to the level of instruments, is to struggle in order to give dignity and freedom back to the linguistic sign.}

Leaving behind the notion of language as mere agent (even as agent of self-discovery), Carnero makes it more independent, freeing it not only from intention and message but also from any necessary connection to real experience. By implication at least, poetic language becomes arbitrary. This suggestion is repeated later in the essay, when Carnero calls the poem "un mensaje polisémico finito" {"a finite polysemous message"}, although he goes on to talk about the poet's power to control it, revealing a certain tension between logocentric and antilogocentric attitudes.

A view of the sign as free-floating also underlies Siles's statement that "los signos no son *mundos*, sino *significad*. Significidad y no significado parece ser la condición de un *tiempo*, que a sí mismo se niega como *historia* y se busca en la copia de un disfraz: la de la máscara" (Provencio 2: 209). {"Signs are not worlds, but rather signicity. Signicity and not meaning seems to be the condition of a time, which denies itself as history and seeks its identity in a copy of a disguise: that of a mask."} A like view is apparent in Leopoldo María Panero's description of the poem as a denial of grammar and a destruction of language (ibid. 198). It signals the most extreme separation that we have seen in this century between verbal and literal reality in Spanish poetics. Such separation was used by some, such as Carnero, to stress the poem's way of creating new realities, but also, by others, such as Panero, Félix de Azúa, Martínez Sarrión, Alvarez, and Siles, to define it as an open, malleable, perhaps even meaningless entity. By 1984 Siles adopted a deconstructive perspective and wrote about the text as negation and the sign as operating under erasure: "El signo, que se escribe, no se escribe: se borra" (ibid. 208–9). {"The sign that is written is not written: it is erased."}

This view of the sign's independence helps explain the increased stress on the reader as cocreator of the text. Panero declared, "La poesía, es verdad, no es nada en sí misma . . . no es nada sin la lectura" (Provencio 2: 198). {"The poem, truly, is nothing by itself . . . it is nothing without its reading."} Talens noted that the work of art has meaning only because it is received by an audience (ibid., 163). Siles, in a study of the poetics of the *novísimos,* indicated that they coincided with Jauss and other German aesthetic reception critics in making the reader a producer of meanings and that this represented a revolutionary attitude to language (1988, 126).

All of this suggests that the *novísimos* carried much further the premises of indeterminacy, and of the poetic text as process rather than product, which had been presaged by the previous generation. In making the poetic sign independent, developing further the role of the reader, and abandoning the goal of self-expression and self-discovery that still underlay that generation's attitude, the *novísimos* moved Spanish poetry fully beyond the tenets of modernity.

In line with these developments, some members of this generation recalled ideas and forms harking back to early modernism, vanguardism, and surrealism. Luis Antonio de Villena echoed some fin de siècle notions when he spoke of "el arte que teatraliza la vida—el arte como realidad—y la vida que se vive como arte—la realidad como imaginada" (Provencio 2: 218) {"art that turns life into theater—art as reality—and life that is lived as art—reality as imagined"}. Martínez Sarrión confessed his dependence on Breton and Benjamin Peret and wrote texts that resembled the *poema-collage* (ibid. 30–32; cf. García de la Concha 1986, 21; and Castellet 1970, 34). Panero's and Azúa's poetry also contain surrealist echoes, as does Azúa's definition of poetry as a solution to the malady of reason (Provencio 2: 97). Though his poetics is highly rational, Gimferrer's lyrics have a surrealist filiation, related to his sense of poetry as a way of exploring life's mysteries: he calls poetry "presencia que, de súbito, estalla ante nuestros ojos" (ibid. 122–23) {"a presence that suddenly bursts before our eyes"}. As Siles has indicated, surrealism denied poetic language the function of defining or explaining reality (1982, 14–15); this helps explain the interest of the *novísimos* in surrealist art and aesthetics.

Whether these surrealist connections came directly or filtered through Octavio Paz, José Lezama Lima, or other Spanish American writers whom the novísimos admired does not matter. In one fashion or another, these poets found roots that supported their view of writing as separate from reason, coherent meaning, or even self-discovery.[7] For some, this led to a vision of writing as play (see Castellet 1970, 42). Others developed a neoromantic vision of poetry as a source of mysterious insights; Colinas noted that "cada verso debe traer consigo un bagaje de deslumbradoras y evocadoras sugerencias" (Provencio 2: 136) {"each line of verse should produce a load of dazzling and evocative suggestions"}.

The notion of poetry's indeterminacy is related, in my opinion, to a pessimism about the possibility of seizing meaning through art that underlies the work of many of these poets (especially Carnero and Gimferrer), as well as the writings of older poets during the 1970s. This pessimism, as García de la Concha has indicated, harks back to the Spanish baroque, which fascinated many of the *novísimos* (García de la Concha 1986, 18–19).[8] The baroque poets' and artists' efforts to create artful forms with which to battle time, decay, and disillusion represented, for some of the *novísimos,* both a model to follow and the frightening precedent of an impossible quest.

The attitude of the *novísimos* to language and much of their poetics constitute a profoundly revolutionary posture, again taking further one that had been initiated by their immediate predecessors. Intensifying the previous decade's view of poetry as process and as the textualization of reality, but leaving behind completely any quest for closure, the *novísimos* subverted the notion of language as univalent and authoritarian—a notion that underlay the discourse of the Franco dictatorship as well as that of social poetry and even, to some extent, of the high modern poetry of the 1920s. As Siles has indicated, the language of the new poets, buttressed by a poetics of the free-floating sign, introduced a new rhetoric, which implies a restructuring of one's whole view of reality and meaning (Siles 1988, 126; see also Gimferrer 1971, 95–97; and Bousoño in Carnero 1979, 27–30).

The most specific example of this revolutionary change is metapoetry, which, as we will see, is a key form of this time in texts written by both new and older poets. By referring to its own process of poetization and by blurring the traditional lines of demarcation between the fiction within the text and the reality outside, a self-referential poem denies the expectations of a reader who seeks a stable message, applicable to the real world. Readers are immersed, instead, in a world of uncertain boundaries; sign is foregrounded over significance, process over product. Now situated within this created realm rather than at its outside edge, the readers play roles more akin to those of the implied author and are invited to participate in and to extend the text.

Art as Elevation and Refuge:
Gimferrer, Carnero, Azúa, Cuenca

Though by no means the oldest of the *novísimos*, Pere Gimferrer was one of the first to publish books of poetry, and he has remained a productive and influential member of his generation.[9] In his statement in Castellet's anthology (1970, 155–56), Gimferrer noted that his youth was spent finding refuge in art and literature, reading eight hours a day and concentrating on *modernismo,* surrealism, Spanish poetry of 1927, St. John Perse, Eliot, and Pound. He also developed interest in cinema and jazz. All this underscores his total devotion to the arts and the aesthetic experience as vehicles for seeking insight.[10]

In Gimferrer's *Arde el mar* ("The Sea Burns," 1966), personal experiences are changed by imagery and by artistic intertexts. "Oda a Venecia ante el mar de los teatros" ("Ode to Venice in Front of the Sea of Theaters") offers an excellent example. Most of it consists of the speaker's reminiscences of his adolescence in Venice, presented as though in a dream:

> Asciende una marea, rosas equilibristas
> sobre el arco voltaico de la noche en Venecia
> aquel año de mi adolescencia perdida,
> mármol en la Dogana como observaba Pound
> y la masa de un féretro en los densos canales.
> Id más allá, muy lejos aún, hondo en la noche,
> sobre el tapiz del Dux, sombras entretejidas,
> príncipes o nereidas que el tiempo destruyó.
> [Gimferrer 1979, 19–20]

{A tide rises, acrobat roses over the voltaic arc of the Venetian night during that year of my lost youth: marble in the Dogana, as Pound noted, and the mass of a funeral procession in the dense canals. Go further, much further, deep into the night, on the tapestry of the Dux, weaved shadows, princes or nymphs destroyed by time.}

While creating images of archetypal beauty, the speaker stylizes, extends, and intensifies the scene through allusions to literature and art. In addition, he sets the world he describes a second level back from reality: it is not a place in the real city, but rather a theater scaffold representing a Venetian sea scene, into which the speaker fits his recollections and allusions. Meanwhile this speaker-poet also moves from nostalgic remembrance to a meditation about the process of poetic composition, about the value of artistically recasting reality. He attempts to superimpose a world of art on that of common reality, questions his own task, and ends up pessimistically witnessing the loss of everything—of his memories, of his attempts to compose a poem, and of his very effort to find value in poetry. Yet he conveys to us his quest for the transcendence of self through art. As a result, we as readers may come to sense the beauty he unsuccessfully sought. The poem, therefore, may function more as a stimulus to our own working out of the relationships between reality and its artistic transformations, rather than as a repository of meanings.

Similar experiences are produced by other poems in the book. In "Mazurka en este día" ("Mazurka on This Day") details of a Spanish medieval legend are superimposed on the story of a modern student in Salamanca by means of elaborate literary devices—stylized images, personifications, a symbolic portrayal of the fading of a scepter:

> ¡Trompetas del poniente!
> Por un portillo, bárbaro,
> huidiza la capa, Urraca arriba, el cuévano
> se teñía de rojo entre sus dedos ásperos,
> desleíase el cetro bordado en su justillo,
> quieta estaba la luz en sus ojos de corza
> sobre el rumor del río lamiendo el farellón.
> [Gimferrer 1979, 17]

{Trumpets at dusk! Through a barbarous gate, the fleeting cape—Urraca above—the basket turned red amid her rough fingers, the scepter embroidered on her jerkin faded, and the light was quiet in her doelike eyes, above the murmur of the river licking the cliff.}

The sustained and complex stylization of all these medieval elements makes us read them not as anecdote or referent but rather as literature—as artistic elaborations of motifs derived from other, prior artistic works. These elaborations, together with other literary allusions, overshadow the supposed referent of the Salamanca student, who is first mentioned halfway through the poem and then again left behind at the end. The poem offers us, ultimately, a mazurka, an artistic dance rather than a realistic story, and an example of ways in which art transforms life.

Somewhat similarly, Gimferrer uses allusions to a story by Antonio Hoyos y Vinent as correlatives of a vision of exoticism, luxury, and decay in "Cascabeles" ("Bells"); this is the text through which Carnero defined culturalist poetry. In "Julio de 1965" ("July 1965") he overtly imitates the style of Jorge Guillén's *Cántico* to situate his own text within a prior, modernist affirmation of life. In all these works, literary intertexts communicate the vitality that art can bring to life.[11] Thus *Arde el mar* illustrates the aestheticist vision of the *novísimos,* as well as their manner of foregrounding literature over literal reality and of creating poems that invite elaboration on the part of the reader.

Gimferrer has indicated that *La muerte en Beverly Hills* ("Death in Beverly Hills," 1967) is a single long poem, based on a "personal event" and presenting a sad vision of love (1979, 13). What stands out for the reader, however, is the way in which vignettes, evocations of famous actresses and scenes from movies, and nature images flow into each other, producing emotive, nostalgic experiences. As in *Arde el mar,* any real-life referents are submerged under layers of image and allusion, though the latter now come from a popular more than a learned medium. But the procedure of making experience rise out of intertexts is similar. Free verse, frequent in the prior book, is now used exclusively: long lines that verge on poetic prose weave rich scenes evoking paradoxical combinations of sensuality, nostalgia, and impending death and decay. Occasional lighter notes (also via movie references) only add to this neodecadent mood:

¡Sonrisas de Jean Harlow! El bungalow al alba y el mar centelleante.
Música por toda la olvidada estación del deseo. Palmeras, giratoria luminosidad de
   la playa encendiéndose
. . . .
Ya conozco tus uñas pintadas de rojo, el óvalo hechicero de tu cara, tu sonrisa pas-
   tosa y húmeda de *nymphette,*
estos vestidos negros, estas mallas, tus guantes hasta el codo, el encaje de los pechos,
esta espalda que vibra y palpita como una columna de mercurio.
Cuando amanezca me encontrarán muerto y llamarán a Charlie Chan.
                                                                 [Gimferrer 1979, 55]

{Jean Harlow's smiles! The bungalow at dawn and the shining sea. Music throughout the forgotten station of desire. Palm groves, the circling brightness of the lit-up beach. . . . I know your fingernails painted red, the bewitching oval of your face, your pasty and humid *nymphette* smile, those black dresses, those mesh stockings, your gloves right up to your elbows, the lace at your bust, the back that shimmers and throbs like a mercury column. When dawn comes they will find me dead and call Charlie Chan.}

In 1968 Gimferrer composed *Extraña fruta* ("Strange Fruit"), which he described as an experimental work he decided not to publish (1979, 13). The poems from that book and a few other texts of the period that he did include in his *Poemas, 1963–1969* again juxtapose vignettes, images, and allusions—to music, to writers, to movies—and often create nostalgic moods. A new note is introduced by references to the Vietnam War and other historical events; these too, however, contribute to the subjective mood of decadence and disillusion.

Beginning in 1970 Gimferrer wrote his poetry in Catalan, although he published it together with Spanish translations.[12] The decision marked a personal commitment to a native language that had been marginalized by the Franco regime, but it is also linked to some shifts in attitude. Castellet has noted the poet's growing sense of reality's evanescence and incomprehensibility, accompanied by a continued interest in the subconscious (Gimferrer 1978, 9–11). These are apparent in *Els miralls / Los espejos* ("The Mirrors," 1970) as well as *Hora foscant / Hora oscurecida* ("The Darkened Hour," 1972) and *Foc cec / Fuego ciego* ("Blind Fire," 1973).

In the first of these books, as Margaret Persin has indicated, the dominant image of the mirror signals a skeptical vision of both poetry and human life. The work considers, self-consciously, the topic of poetic composition, and some of its texts are overtly metapoetic.[13] Images of mirrors and reflections not only represent the undecidability of things and the unreliability of any one perspective but also create a series of snares for the reader, who finds the poems' speakers undermining their own attitudes (Persin 1992, 113–18). References to and examples from different poets weave complex nets, and a specific allusion to collage makes us see art as a set of multiple layers.

Els miralls illustrates both the self-consciousness and the self-questioning that pervade much of the new poetry of the time, as well as a turn to more theoretically oriented creative writing that several of the *novísimos* took by the mid-1970s. Having from the outset emphasized creativity, the primacy of poetic language, and the independence of the sign, these poets gradually adopted more reflective and self-conscious postures. By commenting on its own production, much of *Els miralls,* almost paradoxically, "decenters the authorial voice" (Persin 1992, 122) and involves the reader in its own fictional worlds. *Hora foscant* and *Foc sec* do not exhibit such self-consciousness, but present a gloomy vision of human existence as illusive and transitory, harking back to a baroque tension between disillusion and affirmation (see Castellet in Gimferrer 1978, 12–18).

The stylized way in which Guillermo Carnero's *Dibujo de la muerte* ("A Drawing of Death," 1967) presents reality, as well as its complex imagery and its constant use of artistic allusions, could make us focus entirely on its formal aspects. Yet those aspects are used to convey a significant philosophical theme. The book presents a conflict between the transcendent beauty of art and human decay and mortality. This tension, which in a modernist poem might have led to some (perhaps paradoxical) solution, is never resolved: it motivates a series of contradictory experiences for the reader, and perhaps an invitation to extend and continue the subject.

All this is exemplified in "Avila," which opens with the description of a specific funerary monument in the city:[14]

En Avila la piedra tiene cincelados pequeños corazones de nácar
y pájaros de ojos vacíos, como si hubiera sido el hierro martilleado por Fancelli,
buril de pluma, y no corre por sus heridas ni ha corrido nunca la sangre,
lo mismo que de sus cuellos tronchados sólo brota el mismo mármol que se entre-
    laza al borde de los dedos
en un contenido despliegue de pétalos y ramas,
en delgados cráneos casi transparentes en la penumbra de las bóvedas.

[Carnero 1979, 77]

{In Avila the stone reveals small, sculpted mother-of-pearl hearts, and empty-eyed birds, as if the iron hammered by Fancelli had been a feather burin; and blood does not flow nor has ever flowed through its wounds, just as from its severed necks there only flows the same marble that interweaves at the tips of its fingers, in a controlled unfolding of petals and branches, in thin skulls, almost transparent in the shadows of the vaults.}

Initially, descriptions of parts of the monument are combined with metaphorical transformations: taken together, they evoke a sense of the monument—and, by extension, of Avila—as a single, contradictory entity. On the one hand, it has never lived and is still lifeless: marble and not blood flows from it, it seems artfully unreal, and later it is populated by children "nacidos al mármol para la muerte" {"born to marble for death"} and by a body "demasiado hermoso para haber vivido" {"too beautiful to have lived"}. The beauty of the monument comes at the price of its being removed from life, elevated above but therefore separated from the reality of the viewer.

On the other hand, the elements of the monument are given cadaver-like qualities and produce an effect of morbidity that culminates in the image of a skull and the vignette of a dog " muerto en la piedra" {"dead within stone."} By representing people and animals who lived and died, the monument echoes and reflects their fleetingness and mortality. As a result, the poem offers us two simultaneous and contradictory perspectives on art: Its perfection elevates it above and also beyond mortal life, but its grounding in human reality makes it reflect the temporality and mortality of our world.

In the face of this contradiction, the speaker loses hope: he names fragments of art works and finds himself unable even to "reconstruct its death." He seems to be seeking some aesthetic beauty and also to be stressing the mortality of art insofar as it reflects life. An allusion to a modern bar in which a record plays suggests a descent into a trivial literal reality (see Carnero 1979, 78). The poem ends metapoetically, as the speaker describes his inability to gather together even a "fistful of words" or any memories through which to "imagine that someday we will be able to have invented ourselves, that we have finally lived" (ibid. 79). A failure to resolve his view or to find comfort has engendered in the speaker—but not in Carnero the poet—a failure to write a successful poem.

The reader, following the speaker's path, is submerged in the latter's contradictions, feeling both the value of art as raised above and away from life and also its morbid contamination by life. Each perspective is finally pessimistic: the first one makes art lasting but remote and unreal, while the second makes it fleeting. When the speaker-poet comments on his own process at the end, his artistic quest seems to us as paradoxical and limited as that of the monuments he has described.[15] And it may even trigger in us a parallel paradoxical and limited view of what we can accomplish when we view art and read poetry.

"Avila" thus exemplifies the most salient theme and experience of all *Dibujo de la muerte:* a desire to rise above mortality through art, and the limitation and failure of that desire. Crucial to this poem and to the whole book is the use of aesthetic materials to represent this aesthetic quest. Somewhat like Gimferrer, Carnero makes art works, literary intertèxts, eighteenth-century aestheticism, and the contemplation of art into correlatives of his themes: his poems' narrative level is mostly limited to the story of finding meaning in art and literature. This produces a mode of writing quite different from that typical of the 1950s and early 1960s, in which narrative led to a more realistic process of self-discovery. Use of artistic referents is supported by elegant, refined metaphors and descriptions, by a rhythmically flowing free verse, and by an ample descriptive vocabulary, with effective use of adjectives and adverbs. The resultant style makes the medium of beauty part of the message of its quest.

These stylistic features invite us to connect Carnero's verse back to modernity, comprising both *modernismo* and the Generation of 1927. In one sense, the connection is useful, because it highlights the return to a poetry consciously removed from the colloquial, from everyday perspectives, from narrative premises. In another sense, however, it is misleading. Carnero's work is far removed from modernity in at least one basic way. Whereas the modern poet—say, Guillén—saw form and sign as a means of embodying meaning, Carnero viewed them as autonomous, as the source of an ongoing process, as ultimately antirationalistic (see Bousoño in Carnero 1979, 59). Likewise, whereas a poem like "Perfección" seemed to construct a block of images to jell experience consciously into form, "Avila" immerses us in an unfolding experience of artistic quest.

Carnero's *El sueño de Escipión* ("Scipio's Dream," 1971) takes a further step in an antirealistic, antirationalistic path. Bousoño has aptly noted the book's lack of any sentimentalism, the extreme degree to which it stylizes all descriptions, and its increased metapoetic vein (Carnero 1979, 53–66). These features all come from the way it reaches beyond its overt themes and referents and privileges, instead, the very process of poetization. "Jardín

inglés" ("English Garden") furnishes an example. It begins by moving us be-
yond its stated subject:

> Disposición convencional
> y materia vigente, acreditada
> prosodia: ilustraciones
> que es sabio intercalar tanto en la vida misma
> como el discurso del poema. Darles
> un ingrediente de ternura. [Carnero 1979, 129]

{Conventional arrangement, and real matter, sound prosody; examples that it is as
wise to work into life as into the poem's discourse. To give them an ingredient of
tenderness.}

Carnero inverts the normal relationship between theme and proce-
dure, foregrounding the latter over the former. The inversion is empha-
sized by the contrasts between the poem's realistic title and the slow
meditation of the speaker-poet about his process of writing, and between
the lack of detail about the garden and the profusion of images illustrating
the poet's work. All this makes us feel that the garden is but a means to an-
other theme. We soon find out that it indeed evokes for the speaker images
of a past love:

> Los árboles sin savia y los cuerpos sin luz
> dan en las alamedas ya borradas
> al viento su rigor, y la inmortalidad
> es patrimonio firme de lo muerto.
> Así tu cuerpo fue. Y recordarlo ahora
> es un mundo sin eco, una ciudad vacía
> donde sólo su carne
> tuviera realidad, como esta tierra ausente
> [Carnero 1979, 130]

{The sapless trees and the bodies without light amid the fading elm groves give rigor
to the wind, and a feeling of immortality is patrimony of the dead. Thus was your
body. And remembering it now, is an echoless world, an empty city where only its
flesh was real, like this absent land}

Love and garden share, above all, a sense of unreality and the way in
which they have faded away for the speaker-poet. He describes them both via
lifeless images, yet ones that are linked to the processes of art. This leads him
to the same theme that we saw in "Avila": the awareness that the attempt to
turn human life into art cannot eliminate the destructive effects of time. Later
on in the poem, the reality remembered and contemplated is presented as
though it were a painting. (We begin to wonder if the referent might not be
a painting of the garden.) Subject and theme are thus subordinated to the

process of turning them into poetry. The speaker ends by rephrasing his paradoxical view of art as limited yet valuable: "Y en la ficción del aire / y en su nítido trazo hay un signo de gloria" (Carnero 1979, 133). {"And in air's fiction, and in its clear sketch, there is a sign of glory."}

At this point the reader may even wonder if there ever was a garden or even a painting of a garden, or if the garden was only an image created by the speaker-poet to come to terms with his memory of past love. Maybe even the love was imaginary. What ultimately matters, however, is that all reality and all referents have been set back. The poem foregrounds the process of turning life into poetry and, ultimately, the value and limitation of art.

By doing this, "Jardín inglés," and the book from which it comes, break with the canonical, modernist premise of the work of art as a separate entity and immerse us in a process in which theme, technique, and commentary are fused and confused and in which text, implied author, and reader can collaborate in various ways. This moves poetry into what Jean-François Lyotard described as an event: mistrustful of the possibility of forging meanings, the poet emphasizes the process of writing and invites us to concentrate on the process of reading (Lyotard 72 ff.). Carnero's metapoetic bent, and the attempt to find value in the poetic process in the face of a lack of confidence in any poetic product, mark a marginalization of reality and a search for refuge in language, which fit him and his contemporaries within the most prevalent definitions of postmodernity, though they also connect with some avant-garde postures (see Calinescu 171 ff., 221).

Carnero's next two books of verse, *Variaciones y figuras sobre un tema de La Bruyère* ("Variations and Figures on a Theme from La Bruyère," 1974) and *El azar objetivo* ("Objective Chance," 1975) constitute a change that takes Carnero's poetry to the very edge of the genre. Adopting an overtly discursive tone and often structuring their presentation in the form of rational arguments, most of the poems in these books explore various facets and paradoxes of poetic expression, and the whole issue of relationships between reality and its interpretation through language. Their apparently rational manner, however, conceals a complex and twisted outlook: the arguments presented often double back on themselves and undermine their apparent stance. In that sense, these books become explicit examples of Carnero's views about the freedom of the sign, the contingency of meaning, and the simultaneous necessity and impossibility of elevating life in art.

Félix de Azúa has taken a less rational view of poetry than Carnero and has even spoken of it, referring to Novalis, as a "droga que sana las heridas producidas por la razón" {"cure for the wounds produced by reason"} (Provencio 2: 97). Yet behind his ironic manner lies a serious belief in poetry as a unique form of expression. In the preface to his 1989 collected verse, he distinguished poetic "signification," which produces new and open meanings, from the reproductive or instrumental value of reportorial discourse (Azúa 9–10).

In consonance with this attitude, Azúa's poetry uses echoes from both life and literature to generate complex, enigmatic experiences. Most of his texts abound in all kinds of sensorial images, in a rich variety of rhythms and line patterns. Literary, historical, and philosophical allusions are frequent, though not as common as in Carnero or Gimferrer. In "Giorgione," from *Edgar en Stéphane* (1971), an Italian painting motivates a mixture of images of a storm, a mood of fear, and presages Christ's future life:

> . . . gime la tempestad,
> pero la uva prensada y el furor de septiembre
> como un arcángel ebrio
> nos conduce a los hielos y a la Crucifixión. [Azúa 85]

{The storm moans, but the pressed grapes and the September fury, like a drunk archangel, lead us to ice and to the Cross.}

The Renaissance intertext thus operates, simultaneously, as a correlative for the poem's emotion and as an enigmatic pretext for a variety of subjective reactions by the reader. One could interpret this procedure as a motif for play.

At times Azúa juxtaposes allusions to a variety of works, places, and events to create something akin to a collage of echoes and moods. "Café danzante" ("Cabaret"), from *El velo en el rostro de Agamenón* ("The Veil on Agamemnon's Face," 1970), mixes two characters from *The Three Musketeers,* Estonia, and l'Orangerie into a comic strip–like scene (Azúa 53). On other occasions Azúa combines a profusion of sensorial remembrances and images: "Sexta elegía" ("Sixth Elegy"), from the same book, uses this technique to evoke the memories of a schoolboy:

> Escuela, hace ya mucho que percibo tu significación:
> perfecto idiota entarimado en tiza de alma de pez de lago
> rubicunda mejilla anafeitada y verbo maloliente
> cólera y estulticia como cetro, oh madres de los héroes,
> como paraguas sobre los cuellos rígidos
> sobre el rebaño modelado a pupitre y banquillo de reo;
> pizarra como velo del templo como sucia cortina de ducha
> . . . .
> pluma tintero regla cuaderno libro y goma de borrar
> reglamento castigo penitencia filas interno externo medio- pensionista
> domesticado vendido al rey de la pocilga. [Azúa 42]

{School, I have perceived your meaning for a long time: a perfect idiot tabled on chalk of soul of lake fish, rosy unshaved cheeks and ill-smelling expression, anger and stupidity like a scepter, oh mothers of heroes, like umbrellas upon stiff necks, on the sheep flock configured by desk and prisoner's bench; blackboard like temple veil like dirty shower curtain . . . pen inkwell ruler notebook book eraser rules punishment penitence lines boarder day student half-boarder, domesticated sold to the king of the pigsty}

This accretion of schoolboy vignettes, attitudes, and objects merges a number of details and reactions that recall the speaker's petty daily life and fragments of subjects that he studied. This gives it a certain narrative appearance. In contrast to an earlier poem by Sahagún or Brines (or even to a contemporary one by Villena), however, the speaker of this poem does not attempt to interpret his past. Childhood memories are simply a vehicle for the verbal embodiment of diverse sensations, for the creation of new experiences, perhaps for play. In this sense Azúa's poetry, like that of Gimferrer and Carnero, illustrates the drive of the *novísimos* (and of the 1970s generally) to foreground literary language, the effects it can produce, and the stimulus it can offer for the reader's continued process of poetic re-creation.

Even more learned and allusive is the poetry of Luis Alberto de Cuenca. Born in 1950, Cuenca began to publish after the appearance of Castellet's anthology, and he is sometimes classified in a later generation. Yet his work fits perfectly the aestheticism of the first *novísimos*, for it consistently foregrounds literary and aesthetic experience. Most of his poems are written in long free verses, which combine a variety of intertextual echoes—from literature, art, cinema, detective writing—with ample visual images. The result is a rich sensorial effect that at first glance might recall nineteenth-century *modernismo* but that ultimately leads the reader to focus not on the sensations themselves but rather on the creativity of the language and form used. Though not explicitly metapoetic, such poems end up making the process of artistic creation displace their overt subject. At times sound and visual effects overwhelm any narrative or logical sense. Thus "Germania Victrix," though it deals with barbarian invasions and their effects, seems primarily to use these subjects as a pretext for incredibly elaborate synesthesias and metaphors and for a striking mixture (we might say collage) of words and intertexts:

> Mi amiga es una perla disuelta en vino rubio
> bélica está mi alma su zócalo de mármol
> las torres de silencio que guardan los cadáveres
> legiones inmoladas revólveres perdidos
> en el trascoro tibio de un paisaje infernal. [Cuenca 27]

{My friend is a pearl dissolved in blond wine, my soul is warlike in its marble square, the towers of silence that cadavers guard, immolated legions, lost revolvers, in the tepid antechamber of the choir, of an infernal landscape.}

By emphasizing sign over signification, Cuenca's poetry invites us to take an attitude that several theorists would call postmodern. We focus not on deriving a definite or finite meaning but rather on contemplating and enjoying the very textuality of the writing, and perhaps on extending that writing through our own imagination—of sharing and continuing its process.[16] A similar effect is produced by the poems of Antonio Carvajal, which foreground rich imagery as well as elaborate words and forms recalling baroque verse, often obscuring their referent. All of the *novísimos* discussed so far exemplify a shift in art that corresponds to a major change in the reading process.[17]

Popular Culture, the Irrational, Surrealism

Another version of the shift away from rationally comprehensible meanings is exemplified by the poetry of Antonio Martínez Sarrión, Leopoldo María Panero, and some other members of the generation. Martínez Sarrión's work adopts a more everyday idiom than that of Carnero or Cuenca, uses more contemporary allusions and more intertexts from popular culture, and engenders patterns of irrationality that hark back to the surrealists. As Jenaro Talens has noted, the referent in this poetry serves as a jumping-off point for a new creation and for an invitation to a process of play and transformation of reality (in Martínez Sarrión 21–22).

Martínez Sarrión's first book, *Teatro de operaciones* ("Theater of Operations," 1967), uses childhood memories to create disparate visual and sensorial vignettes. "Vals del viudo" ("Widower's Waltz") turns what would normally be an emotional topic into a kaleidoscope of sensations and picture fragments:

> lo más bello del mundo es una fila de platos vacíos
> ah lo más bello del mundo
> un rayo de sol silencioso en la alcoba cargada
> de su perfume
>   cuánta tierra tapiándole los ojos
> qué camino más lóbrego el del tinte
> el color de sus guantes qué indeciso
> qué olor a pulimento en su ataúd de dorados apliques.
>   [Martínez Sarrión 61]

{most beautiful in the world is a row of empty plates, ah, most beautiful in the world, a ray of sunlight, silent in the bedroom full of her perfume, so much earth covering her eyes, what lugubrious path, that of dark stain [color], how indecisive the color of her gloves, what a smell of polish in her gilded coffin}

Synesthesias combine with images and fragments to create this mix of sensations. Lack of any background and plot order, meandering free verse, and absence of punctuation highlight the effect of verbal-visual representation, instead of any possible communication of feeling. References to cinema appear frequently in this book, which in fact produces some of the effect of a detached, artful movie. In "mari pili en casa de manolo" ("Mary Pili in Manolo's House") remembrances of a woman's childhood playing of long ago are first related to a movie, and then metaphorized as a movie that the reader has been watching and that ends abruptly (Martínez Sarrión 48). Life is but a pretext for performance, for theater, for art.

A similar outlook underlies *Pautas para conjurados* ("Rules for Conspirators," 1970) but is now related to a theme new to Martínez Sarrión's writing, the disintegration and decay of art and of human efforts to make meaning through art. The poet continues juxtaposing fragmentary images in free verse, devoid of punctuation. But he now uses longer lines and longer texts, producing more ample and complicated collections of impressions. He combines historical, popular, and cultural allusions with flash images with even greater frequency. In the two pages of "Requisitoria general por la muerte de una rubia" ("General Requisitory on the Death of a Blond"), the death of Marilyn Monroe motivates a dreamlike sequence of vignettes, images, and allusions to various modern figures, producing a disquieting sense of decadence (Martínez Sarrión 106–7). By implication, the decay and disintegration of life and of modern culture is connected to the disintegration of linguistic meaning.

Music, especially contemporary popular music, constitutes the dominant element of *Una tromba mortal para los balleneros* ("A Mortal Waterspout for Whalers," 1975). As Talens has noted, it becomes a focusing device or organizing principle rather than a referent (Martínez Sarrión 29). By building poems around echoes of popular songs, Martínez Sarrión avoids plot, narrative sequence, or thematic message of any kind. Musical compositions cause a profusion of sensations, images, and vignettes that overwhelm the reader with a variety of effects. This carries further—perhaps to its ultimate possibilities—the conversion of elements taken from reality into sensation, into art, and into play that we saw in *Teatro de operaciones*. In "Ummagumma—Pink Floyd" the performance of a specific song motivates an abundance of images, literary and cultural echoes, and nightmarish visions (ibid. 160–63). The book also contains some shorter texts in which a variety of experiences—from music, from reading, and even from daily life—are the source of verbal elaboration and play. In "Obsequio" ("Gift") the sex act is the basis for a text composed of eleven nouns, arranged into a long visual diagram on the page (ibid. 181).

Martínez Sarrión's poems share the surrealists' rejection of logical bonds and sequences and their striving to transcend the bounds of consciousness, to move poetry in the direction of verbal and sensorial play (see

Siles 1982, 14–15). They can also be related to the foregrounding of language and to the undecidability that we saw, many years before, in the neo-surrealist works of Miguel Hernández. They thus give us another example of a historical pattern in twentieth-century Spanish letters, in which surrealist tactics are recalled and revived when literature moves away from rational goals. Yet most of these poems, unlike those of Hernández or Aleixandre, avoid the effort to communicate a defined emotional content.

Also full of references to popular culture, often mixed with literary allusions and extended in long, collage-style texts, is the poetry of Manuel Vázquez Montalbán, who gained much early attention through his inclusion in Castellet's book, his books and essays analyzing the period, and some interesting experimental fiction. Especially in *Movimientos sin éxito* ("Unsuccessful Movements," 1969) and *A la sombra de las muchachas en flor* ("In the Shadow of Ripe Girls," 1973), he created dramatic portrayals of contemporary moods and scenes, consciously demythifying literary topics and conventions. Today his poetry seems to me more dated than that of other *novísimos*, more valuable as a conscious (at times labored) illustration of the less personal, nondiscursive writing that he saw rising out of the era of mass media and camp sensibility in the Spain of the times.

For Leopoldo María Panero, poetry became a means of expressing his alienation from routine, orderly middle-class existence and from the use of language to convey rational and experiential meaning. His work, especially that collected in *Así se fundó Carnaby Street* ("Thus Carnaby Street Was Founded," 1970) and *Teoría* ("Theory," 1973), is composed of a variety of texts, many of them written in poetic prose, which combine multiple allusions to cinema, detective fiction, fables, and modern history. Panero often inverts traditional themes and interpretations or reduces them to comic vignettes, drained of any serious theme or emotive meaning, which recall pop art. Thus Snow White offers trite good-byes to the Seven Dwarfs, while a classic intertext motivates shockingly obscene images ("Homenaje a Catulo" ["Homage to Catullus"]) and traditional elegiac themes are inserted into grotesque, caricatured images ("Vanitas vanitatum" ["Vanity of Vanities"]) (Panero 1986, 50, 97–98, 107–11). Panero combines fragments of image and allusion somewhat like Martínez Sarrión, and with a similar effect: the reality presented loses any emotive significance or referential value, standing merely as text. Many of the poems refer back to childhood memories, especially memories of fear and alienation: these do not serve, however, to explore or explain the past.

A good example of Panero's fragmentation and textualization of reality is "Pasadizo secreto" ("Secret Passage"), composed of a list of nouns and a few adjectives not bound into any plot or action. Further fragmentation is achieved by repeating and dividing two words through line breaks and by playing some words against similar ones (*mueve / nieve*). Some of the terms may evoke for us known fables or topoi (elements from vampire stories and gothic romance abound); some may recall scenes we saw in real life, in movies, or in books. Yet all that, for me, has to be supplied by the reader. The poem foregrounds only its words, its textuality. All else remains indeterminate:

> Oscuridad nieve buitres desespero oscuridad mueve buitres nieve
> buitres castillos (murciélagos) os
> curidad nueve buitres deses
> pero nieve lobos casas
> abandonadas ratas desespero o
> scuridad nueve buitres des . . . [Panero, 1986 94]

{Darkness snow vultures desperation darkness move vultures snow / vultures castles bats dark- / -ness nine vultures des- / -peration snow wolves houses abandoned rats desperation d- / -arkness nine vultures des- . . . }

In Panero's case, more than in Martínez's Sarrión's, those fragmented, depersonalized texts seem part of a consistent effort to negate or parody traditional premises of discourse, both poetic and expository. Allusions, including references to sadism, incest, and homosexuality, are used to shock rather than to mean. Images often reflect the enigmatic incomprehensibility of language. We can see this work as an extreme form of rebellion against the dominant, rational discourse of the previous three decades, which encompassed forms as diverse as Francoist propaganda and social protest poetry. Panero's verse can also be linked to a tradition of marginal, irrational, alienated poetry that we could trace all the way back to Rimbaud and that would also include some vanguardist writing of the early twentieth century.[18] Much of this effect continues in *Narciso en el acorde último de las flautas* ("Narcissus in the Ultimate Harmony of Flutes," 1979), although many poems of this book reveal an underlying persona and a more focused theme.

Several other poets of this generation also move beyond theme and referent to verbal construction and sensorial effect. José Luis Jover turns referent into visual spectacle: word plays and surreal images combine to create unusual sensations. Dreamlike sequences, often populated by figures from popular culture, likewise produce subjective impact in the works of José Luis Giménez Frontín. Ana María Moix, one of the original *novísimos*, who published little poetry in later years, weaves stylized mood pictures with allusions to popular culture. And José Miguel Ullán combines fragments of plot and allusion with visual designs—geometric patterns of words, collages, photographs of hieroglyphs—to suscitate reactions.[19] Together with Panero, Martínez Sarrión, Azúa, and even Gimferrer in some of his work, they illus-

trate various ways in which the foregrounding of language and form during
the 1970s took Spanish poetry beyond rational values or premises. When re-
lated to the foregrounding of language and text in Carnero, Azúa, and Gim-
ferrer, the move beyond referentiality that I have examined in this section
makes clear a fundamental shift in Spanish poetry, which we will also see
confirmed in works by older authors.

Return to the Personal: Alvarez, Villena, Colinas

Several other *novísimos*, however, modified the directions that I have been
tracing and helped define, in the mid- and late 1970s, a shift in the poetry
of the decade. In this second phase, as Siles has noted, personal experience
is more integrated with themes and referents from literature and art, and
even intertextual artistic play leads to the communication of emotive visions
(1988, 127; see also García de la Concha 1986). Luis Antonio de Villena has
suggested that as this occurs, learned and classical elements are used in a
more integrated way, in the context of larger cultural and personal mean-
ings (1986a, 36).

An important poet in this phase is José María Alvarez, who after starting
out as a social writer shifted completely, rejected his first works, and spent
the 1970s building a book titled *Museo de cera: Manual de exploradores* ("Wax
Museum: Explorer's Manual," 1974, expanded in 1978). At first glance, its
poems seem archetypally culturalist, since they center around quotations
from poems, novels, and essays of diverse centuries: often these quotations
take up more space than Alvarez's text, making the work indeed resemble
a museum. Alvarez has also consciously and artfully structured his works in
sections and subsections (see Alvarez 1971, 29). Yet this construct of forms
and intertexts is used to convey personal attitudes.

A good example of Alvarez's poetry is "Melancholy Baby." A four-line
poem by Jorge Guillén occupies the top of the page just below the title and
is balanced, at the bottom, by five lines in which Alvarez emphasizes a sense
of loss, I quote three of them:

> Vamos perdiendo a las personas
> amadas. Loco viento
> las lleva . . . [Alvarez 1971, 51]

{We keep losing loved ones, carried off by the mad wind . . . }

The Guillén text, describing a traveler's estrangement, connects with, ob-
jectifies, and expands what might otherwise have seemed a sentimental ex-
pression. The title, alluding presumably to a current popular song, serves a
similar purpose. All three components function as if they were woven to-
gether and constitute an exploration of loss and alienation.

On other occasions the quotations are less dominant, and Alvarez's texts are longer: they range from narrations interspersed with lyric images to collagelike compilations of bits of commentary, narration, and description. In most cases, however, events and experiences are stylized and textualized, so that they transcend confessionalism on the part of their speaker and become, instead, a basis for the reader's reactions and elaborations.[20] Rather than drain their referents of emotive impact and turn them into verbal form and play, as Martínez Sarrión did, these poems extend and heighten their subjective implications.

Another poet who uses intertexts and cultural evocations to recast personal themes and experiences is Luis Antonio de Villena himself, who gained much prominence by the mid-1970s. His richly allusive *Sublime solarium* appeared in 1971 and was followed by the even more important *Hymnica* (1975, expanded in 1979), which portrays a quest for beauty through sensual experience. In *El viaje a Bizancio* ("The Trip to Byzantium," 1976) Villena draws emotive and sensorial sketches based on literary allusions.

Villena's aestheticism is founded on his belief in art's value as a means of theatricalizing life, of intensifying human experience. It thus differs from the total rejection of anecdote and referent by Carnero and Gimferrer; in some ways it parallels Rubén Darío's drive at the turn of the century to aestheticize, and thus elevate, what had been in real life intranscendent erotic experiences.

This process is often achieved, in *Hymnica,* by evoking historical or mythical figures and artistic objects and making them represent the goal of turning life into art. Thus the Oriental character Ogata Korin, having lived a life of wealth and elegant debauchery, battles against time by creating decorations:

> Creó lacas y biombos. Le hizo célebre
> la perfección, el refinamiento de su
> arte—lirios, ciruelos, dioses—decorativo.
> Debió morir fascinado en la belleza,
> rodeado por una seda extraña, tranquilo.
> Fue afortunado, en verdad, Ogata Korin;
> su vida fue un culto a la efímera
> sensación de la belleza. Al placer y al arte.
> [Villena 1983, 143–44]

{He created lacquers and screens. His perfection, the refinement of his decorative art—lilies, plum trees, gods—made him famous. He must have died happy, fascinated by beauty, surrounded by strange silk. Ogata Korin was indeed fortunate: his life was a cult to the fleeting sensation of beauty, to pleasure and to art.}

The elegance of Villena's expression, in flowing free verse, contributes to the sensorial beauty evoked by these texts. At times the poet combines modern and classical allusions: in "Omnibus de estética" ("Aesthetic Omnibus") the title's double meaning helps fuse the evocations of Persian beauty and a modern seduction on a bus (Villena 1983, 146–47). Occasionally the speaker portrays and comments on the urge to convert action to art: in "El poema es un acto de cuerpo" ("The Poem Is an Act of Flesh") sexual desire becomes textual art:

> porque nada hay como poner la mano
> del amor, sobre la joven llanura de un cuerpo.
> Y hacer la hoguera en ese arte del texto.

> [Villena 1983, 140]

{Because nothing is like placing the hand of love on the young plane of a body, and making a fire in this textual art.}[21]

Again recalling Darío, Villena draws vignettes of decadent elegance, reflecting the aesthetization of sensuality. In "Un arte de vida" ("An Art of Life") he alludes to Verlaine and draws the picture of a fin de siècle dandy as an image of idle existence, implicitly counterposed to the pedestrian pragmatism of ordinary modern life (Villena 1983, 158). Throughout the book, a number of basic metaphors—love as sea, as fire and burning, statues as bodies, precious stones—are used to build a stylized mood of beauty, underscored by the flowing rhythm and elegant expression. A perception of beauty's fragility adds a note of melancholy and even tragedy to some texts (ibid. 185), yet beauty and sensuality remain the best goals for which to strive.

This description of Villena's work might make him seem a throwback to nineteenth-century *modernismo* (see Calinescu 141–61). Yet for all the similarities with Darío and all the echoes of fin de siècle dandyism, Villena's poetry reveals an underlying, explicit, and most contemporary consciousness of the poetic process. The speakers who aestheticize sensuality are presented as conscious artists, as masks or correlatives of the poet's self-conscious endeavor. This provides a metapoetic underlay that situates Villena very much within the decade of the 1970s.

At the same time, his use of the "I" and of first-person experiences does modify the avoidance of anecdote and referent by the first of the *novísimos*. His way of making experience into theater, unlike that of Martínez Sarrión, for example, contextualizes emotive meanings and attitudes. It thus exemplifies the return to the expression of personal emotion in the mid-1970s noted by Siles.

The poetry of Antonio Colinas likewise reveals a more personalized aestheticism, though with a style and vision at opposite poles from those of Villena. Its dominant mode is a harmonious lyrical expression, most often used to record meditations on natural beauty, on its timelessness, and on the tension between human fleetingness and natural continuity. In *Poemas de la tierra y de la sangre* ("Poems of Earth and Blood," written in 1967), Colinas alludes to scenes and landscapes and through images, personifications, and smoothly flowing (often fourteen-syllable) lines captures the harmony of natural cycles:

> Pero ahora que la noche de invierno se avecina
> sólo dura la piedra, sólo vencen los hielos,
> sólo se escucha el silbo del viento en las mamparas.
> De puro frío quema la piedra en nuestras cúpulas
> en las torres tronchadas de cada iglesia vieja. [Colinas 57]

{But now that winter night comes near, only stone endures, only ice triumphs, one only hears the whistling wind amid the screens. The stone of the domes of the cut towers of each old church is so cold that it burns.}

Preludios a una noche total ("Preludes to Total Night," 1969), though based on a specific love plot, creates a romantic, universalized vision of human love. José Olivio Jiménez has noted echoes of Hölderlin and Novalis in this book and has indicated how Colinas has built within it a mysterious cosmic outlook (Colinas 18–19). At times the vision of love expands into a pantheistic sense of natural order:

> Dos cuerpos laten en la misma sombra
> Saben de amor los labios que se besan
> y los brazos abrazan todo el mundo. [Colinas 66]

{Two bodies shimmer in a single shadow. The kissing lips taste of love, and arms embrace the whole universe.}

Colinas's most important books, however, are to my mind *Truenos y flautas en un templo* ("Thunder and Flutes in a Temple," 1972), *Sepulcro en Tarquinia* ("Sepulchre in Tarquinia," 1975), and *Astrolabio* ("Astrolabe," 1979). In them the poet makes greater use of literary references and varied rhythms. By juxtaposing natural scenes and artistic echoes, he vividly conveys the timeless beauty of landscapes and the sensual joy that nature evokes in his persona. Careful vocabulary selection and the use of hyperbatons and run-on lines contribute to the smooth effect. In contrast to most of his generation, Colinas focuses on rural rather than urban landscapes. His view of the countryside, though concrete, is elevated and stylized, and also removed from the literal via artistic echoes. We see it in "Bucólica" ("Bucolic"):

> Soy el pastor de estos paganos prados.
> Veo entre los ciruelos los centauros
> y en las torres enanos de ojos verdes.
> De Tiziano y de Rubens los colores

> de esta ciudad: el oro de los muros,
> el fuego azul del campanil, las rosas. [Colinas 93]

{I am the shepherd of these pagan fields; I see the centaurs amid the plum trees, and on the towers, green-eyed gnomes. The colors of the city are Titian's, and Rubens's: the gold walls, the blue fire of the bell tower, the roses.}

Each detail and artistic echo adds to the mood of harmony and to the dreamlike evocation of an idealized paradise. Such scenes and moments of beauty become the poet's antidote to his consciousness of temporality and mortality. The reader, however, most admires Colinas's ability to combine stylized landscapes, aestheticist echoes, and emotive themes in a poetry that is at once elevated, pleasurable, and accessible. This poetry may appear less part of the postmodern scene than that of other *novísimos,* yet its way of producing emotive participation and continuation on the part of the reader situates it beyond the modernist aesthetic.

Contained Form, Silence, Self-Referentiality

An increased tendency to sparseness and control, and to self-reflexivity, became evident among younger poets as the decade of the 1970s wore on. In a sense, such a tendency was to be expected, given the primacy that the *novísimos* attributed to poetic language and expression: their aesthetic would inevitably lead them, and those who followed them, to keep heightening, ennobling, and reflecting upon their art. We have already seen evidence of the first of these tendencies in the increased stylization in Carnero's poetry in *El sueño de Escipión,* the gradually tightening expression of Alvarez's *Museo de cera,* and the artfulness of Gimferrer's Catalan verse. The increasing self-reflexivity of *novísimo* writing is even more apparent when we recall Carnero's metapoetic focus in *El sueño,* his almost essaylike commentaries in succeeding books, the self-consciousness of Gimferrer's *Els miralls,* and the self-conscious allusiveness of Cuenca and Villena. All these traits are even clearer, with a somewhat different nuance, in the work of poets who gained prominence later—and especially in Jaime Siles.

Important characteristics of Siles's verse are its formal perfection and control, and what José Olivio Jiménez has called its essentiality: its way of capturing basic themes in form, freeing them from anecdote and realistic detail (Amorós 1985, 93). From the outset, Siles's work is devoid of the decorative aspects and the irrationality of many other *novísimo* texts.

Génesis de la luz ("Genesis of Light," 1969) contains some visionary metaphors that may recall surrealism. But it also uses words and visual images with precision, reflecting its speaker's attempts to define himself and his surroundings. In *Biografía sola* ("Lone Biography," 1970), the style

changes: the book is composed of short, tightly constructed texts that bring
to mind Guillén or Juan Ramón Jiménez. Siles's poems, however, are more
concentrated on the one hand, more open on the other. One is titled "Si-
lencio" ("Silence"):

> Equilibrio de luz
> en el sosiego.
> Mínima tromba.
> Ensoñación. Quietud.
> Todo:
> un espacio sin voz
> hacia lo hondo oculto. [Siles 1992, 32]

{Equilibrium of light amid the quiet. Minimal waterspout. Dreaminess. Quiet. All: a
voiceless space, toward hidden depths.}

The text is not built on a concrete scene like those of Guillén's *Cántico*,
but rather on an elusive concept. The first two lines, apparently descriptive,
are in fact a symbol embodying this concept of silence, which is also repre-
sented by three elements, not connected into any plot: the image of a wa-
terspout, the nouns in line 4, and the final image of the last lines. The poem
is ultimately less "realistic," and more artfully creative, than a prototypical
modern one: it uses language not to narrate or describe but to circumscribe,
elaborate on, and re-create in several ways an abstraction, to give it a verbal
identity that, by itself, it lacks.

Siles's next book, *Canon* (1973) continues the process of essentializa-
tion, and of elimination of the "I," that started in *Biografía sola*. Its poems re-
flect an underlying tension between two perspectives: one portrays the
concreteness and vitality of reality, and the other searches, behind it, for
more stylized, essential, absolute visions. In "Convento de las Dueñas"
("Dueñas' Convent"), for example, the speaker focuses on a specific con-
vent as well as on a poem by Wordsworth. Yet these trigger a process of
metaphorical transformation that gradually turns the referent into a sign for
harmony, silence, duration, and transcendent order:

> Y queda un resplandor, una callada imagen,
> un fragmento de tiempo que impreciso se ahonda
> y nunca más se ha sido: se está siendo
> porque en su dimensión la forma dura. [Siles 1992, 59]

{A radiance remains, a quiet image, a fragment of imprecise time that deepens, and
one has never been again, because one keeps on being, because in this dimension
form endures.}

Poetic language becomes a way of constructing experience out of reality, of
making concrete elements point beyond themselves.

In his next book, *Alegoría* ("Allegory," 1977), Siles again questions and re-creates reality. More philosophically complex, this book alludes to Greek philosophers, who appear as characters, and juxtaposes various attitudes to poetic expression. Several poems explicitly question the poetic process. A tension between an impulse to sound and verbal expression and an impulse to concentration and silence underlies the quest.

This ever deepening, ever more essential questioning of reality through poetry, and of poetry itself through poetry, culminates in *Música de agua* ("Water Music"), published in 1983 but written between 1979 and 1981. Precisely organized in five parts, the book traces the reduction of reality to more and more essential elements, culminating in sign and silence. We see this in the following text from its second part, titled "La materia del tiempo, que es forma del lugar, realiza en los ecos plurales su sentido" ("Matter of Time, Which Is a Form of Place, Realizes Its Meaning in Plural Echoes"):

> El espacio ha quedado
> reducido a su centro,
>
> al ala que conduce
> la luz hacia su centro,
>
> al hueco que comprime
> la voz dentro del centro,
>
> al centro que proyecta
> el iris a su centro,
>
> al centro de ese centro
> que anula toda voz. [Siles 1992, 131]

{Space has remained reduced to its center; to the wing that leads the light to its center; to the void that compresses voice within center; to the center that projects the iris to its center; to the center of this center that suppresses all voice.}

The first stanza, which already seems to constrict reality to an essence represented by the "center," is but the first step of a repeated process of reduction, through which we move from more concrete to more abstract elements (from "wing" and "light" to "void"), ending with just a condensation of "center." This reduction, together with the rhyme and repetition of the word *centro*, denies any rational explanation and leaves us with just the reverberation of that one word. Thus we repeat the experience of the speaker: we create a "dis-signification" that leaves us with a pure sign.

This is repeated throughout the book, in variant modes of reduction of life to form. The third part, "Grafemas," highlights the writing process in order to almost eliminate its real referent; the fourth inverts this order, making night (perhaps the most abstract element of reality) an active force that "writes" (and thus de-anecdotizes) the poems' speaker. By the last part, language has been reduced to absolute essence:

> El invisible punto
> ya ha llegado.
> Ya sólo en ti
>   final
> la transparencia. [Siles 1992, 174]

{The invisible point has come: only in you, final, transparency.}

    Siles's *Música de agua* thus carries to its ultimate conclusion the goal of the *novísimos* to highlight art over referent, although this gives us, paradoxically, a more accessible work, free from the decorativeness of some earlier texts. Similarly free from decorativeness and also essentialist in its own way is the verse of Alejandro Duque Amusco, whose *Esencias de los días* ("Essences of Days," 1976) and *El sol en Sagitario* ("The Sun in Sagittarius," 1978) are composed of highly concentrated poems, in which images from nature reflect a sense of life's order as well as the poet's confidence in poetic expression. Although no other *novísimo* follows a like path of essentialization—Ullán might come closest in his visual structures—Siles's and Duque Amusco's verse presages important later works, by both younger and older writers. Many of them, including some by Siles, will give a more affirmative and philosophical cast to the quest for essence and purity.

    The self-consciousness apparent in Siles's poetry is also reflected, in different ways, in metapoetic works by Jenaro Talens, as well as by other poets discussed earlier. An important critic who had examined the undermining of prevailing discourses by the poetry of this time (see Talens 1989), he also published a significant body of verse, most of it self-referential. Some of his most compelling texts invert the traditional relationship of poet and referent: in "Nombres quemados por el sol" ("Names Burnt by the Sun") natural elements act, speak, and indeed think the speaker-poet (Talens 1991, 86). This invites us to reexamine the relationships of subject and interpreter, of living and writing, of writing and reading. In "Autobiografía" ("Autobiography") a simple list of words, mostly verbs, artfully immerses us in a puzzling set of inversions, in which the speaker seems to be writing, finally, about his reader:

> somos, en tí me
> reconstruyo, (lo
> reconstruyes), me
> digo, siempre
> que he hablado, te hablaba. [Talens 1991, 63]

{We are, in you I reconstruct myself (you reconstruct it), I say to myself, every time that I have spoken, I spoke to you.}

Though it produced rather different practical results, ranging from the complex discursivity of Carnero's *El sueño de Escipión* to the disorienting self-referentiality of Gimferrer and Talens and the sparse essentiality of Siles, the self-conscious vein is a most important and revealing feature of *novísimo* writing in the later 1970s. By breaking traditional conventions and lines of demarcation, according to which the fiction of art lies separate from the reality of life (and of the reader), it invited a questioning of prior discourses and of prior notions of a text's integrity. It thus ushered us fully into a world in which the poem's meanings tend to lose their determinacy and in which reading and writing begin to conflate—a world that many theoretical critics, from various viewpoints, have called postmodern.

Established Poets, New Directions

The change in outlook that we saw exemplified by the *novísimos,* and its consequences for poetry, are equally apparent in the writings of the 1970s by the most important established poets of Spain. For Angel González, the decade marked a loss of hope in the practical effects of writing, a conscious desire to leave behind the poetic persona of his earlier books, and an accompanying emphasis on techniques (*procedimientos*) and on poems growing out of structural concerns rather than personal experiences (González 1982, 21–22).[22] Because González's earlier poetry had exemplified the communication of emotive experiences in everyday language, and because it had increasingly demonstrated social concerns in the 1960s (in *Grado elemental* and *Tratado de urbanismo*), this shift to a type of formalism is very significant.

The implications of González's new attitude are apparent in *Breves acotaciones para una biografía* ("Brief Annotations to a Biography," 1971), *Procedimientos narrativos* ("Narrative Techniques," 1972), and *Muestra, corregida y aumentada, de algunos procedimientos narrativos y de las actitudes sentimentales que habitualmente comportan* ("Corrected and Amplified Sample of Some Narrative Techniques and of the Emotive Attitudes That They Normally Convey," 1977).[23] In most texts, the speaker is highly self-conscious of his role as poet, and his narratives, seemingly foregrounded, are overlaid (or displaced) by the theme of writing. In "Meriendo algunas tardes" ("I Snack Some Afternoons"), from the first of these books, the speaker plays on the title's double meaning. Taking a literal perspective and making *meriendo* allude to the eating of afternoons, rather than to eating during afternoon hours, he constructs extravagant images and envisions himself devouring clouds, minutes, seagulls, and even bathers (González 1986, 240). Though some critics have dismissed this text as a joke, it offers a wonderful example of linguistic undecidability and collapse and also marks a displacement and parody of a human situation as well as of the conventions of descriptive poetry. Somewhat similarly, in "Eso era amor" ("That Really Was Love") a sexual encounter is presented in language normally used to order a meal, thus ironically modifying both a human situation and the conventions of love poetry (ibid. 241).

In both of these examples, we are asked to question not only our normal perspective on events but also the language in which these events are narrated. Such questioning is even more evident in "Empleo de la nostalgia" ("The Use of Nostalgia"), from *Procedimientos narrativos* (González 1986, 247–48). This text is arranged in several sections, offering contrasting perspectives of women students on a university campus. At one point, an idealistic view in lines printed at the left of the page is undercut by literal images on the right; at another, allusions to the study of languages are subverted by sexual imagery, and echoes of the *beatus ille* are undercut by modern details. Through this juxtaposition and fragmentation, the poem invites the reader to consider the issue of perspective, and the ways in which language actually creates and transforms experience.

The same topic is even more central to *Muestra:* the book contains a whole section titled "Metapoesía," with some highly original and unconventional perspectives on poetry, as well as several texts playfully elaborating and twisting various common expressions. Most revealing, perhaps, is "Calambur" ("Word Play"), which begins with a conventional image of feminine beauty in a baroque style:

> La axila vegetal, la piel de leche,
> espumosa y floral, desnuda y sola,
> niegas tu cuerpo al mar, ola tras ola,
> y lo entregas al sol: que le aproveche. [González 1986, 298]

> {The vegetable axilla, the milky skin,
> foamy and floral, naked, alone,
> you deny your body to the sea, wave after wave,
> and deed it to the sun: may he enjoy.}

The title warns us to expect word play rather than a straight lyric text. Yet the language and imagery, and the form of hendecasyllabic quartets, almost lull us into just appreciating the flow of conventional verse. We do note a tension between elevated style and (common) subject: the poem, after all, describes a woman who prefers sunning herself to swimming. That tension continues in the next stanzas, intensified by the juxtaposition of stylized love imagery to a common scene. It leads, in the last stanza, to the *calambur,* as the poem's imagery collapses into verb play:

dore mi sol así las olas y la
espuma que en tu cuerpo canta, canta
—más por tus senos que por tu garganta—
do re mi sol la si la sol la si la. [González 1986, 298]

{let my sun gild thus the waves and the
foam in which your body sings, sings
—more by its bosom than by its throat—
do re mi sol la si la sol la si la.}

The promised (and long-awaited) pun turns the image of gilding and the sounds of earlier lines into a version of the musical scale. This foregrounds technique over theme and inverts traditional expectations, in which the technique of a poem is just a means of conveying its subject. When related to the earlier tension between the conventional theme and language on the one hand, and the modern story of a sunbather on the other, this ending makes the whole text a jumble of perspectives, never resolved by the speaker. The reader is free to organize and relate them at will—or merely to contemplate the confusion. (Is this mostly a parody of baroque verse? Of women? Of poetry writing?)

Angel González's focus on the poetic process produced, in the 1970s, texts that immerse the reader in their verbal play and invite him or her to continue it. They confirm the tendency to self-referentiality and indeterminacy, and to the foregrounding of language, which we saw in younger poets. That does not make González's work akin to that of the *novísimos*. Except when deliberately parodying baroque verse, González, as he did in the 1960s, uses a rather plain vocabulary and constructs vignettes that discover, behind everyday scenes, larger and ambiguous perceptions—about modern love encounters, daily habits, and attempts to write poetry. He also satirizes the aestheticism of the *novísimos* in a poem of *Muestra* titled "Oda a los nuevos bardos" ("Ode to the New Bards") (González 1986, 310). In these ways he reflects his own generation and basic style. But he does so, now, in the framework of a new, self-conscious focus, fitted to the times.

A similar change occurred in the poetry of Carlos Barral. After shifting from the more complex style of *Metropolitano* to the more common language and social concerns of *Diecinueve figuras de mi historia civil,* Barral composed, in the late 1960s and the 1970s, highly artful poems that foreground language and technique. As Carme Riera has indicated (Barral 53–66), these poems are directed at sophisticated readers and reveal a deliberate attempt to experiment with complex forms, traditions, and registers of discourse, including colloquialisms, now combined with "learned" language. An excellent example is "Informe personal sobre el alba y acerca de algunas auroras particulares" ("Personal Report on Dawn and Some Specific Daybreaks," 1970), later collected in *Usuras y figuraciones* ("Usuries and Figurations," 1973). A very old poetic tradition is here exploited for a variety of effects, by

using allusions, incredibly complex metaphors and word play, and nightmar-
ish visions. The pervading negative view of reality reflects, as Riera noted, Bar-
ral's growing pessimism, but the work's import lies in its verbal virtuosity.[24]

But Barral's most fascinating poem of this period may well be "La dame
à la licorne" ("The Lady and the Unicorn"), first published in 1966 and in-
cluded in *Usuras y figuraciones*. Recasting the medieval myth, and its repre-
sentation in the tapestries of the Cluny Museum, Barral describes a girl who
gets off a bicycle and removes her blue jeans. This modern referent, how-
ever, is transformed by incredibly elaborate metaphors and by intertextual
echoes of baroque poems. Literal reality (including genital references) is
thus converted into highly artful beauty, and the work constitutes a demon-
stration of how language and imagery can be foregrounded while they turn
ordinary reality into aesthetic effects. The poem constitutes, in this sense,
an echo and a repetition of Góngora's transformation of—and escape
from—reality. It connects Barral's work with that of Gimferrer and other
novísimos, with whom he had frequent personal contact.

Jaime Gil de Biedma published few new poems in the 1970s. But it is well
to remember that his *Poemas póstumos* of the later 1960s combined the artful
use of point of view with an underlying metapoetic consciousness, reflecting
a turn parallel to that of González and Barral. Gil de Biedma also wrote in
this decade a major volume of criticism, *El pie de la letra* ("The Literal of Let-
ters," 1980), and a sophisticated, self-reflexive book of memoirs titled *Diario
de un artista seriamente enfermo* ("Diary of a Seriously Ill Artist," 1974).[25]

The poetry of Claudio Rodríguez did not change as obviously as that of
Barral or even González, but it does reveal a new and important artistic con-
sciousness and a new use of intertextuality. More than most of his genera-
tional colleagues, Rodríguez had already related the exploration of reality
to that of the poetic process in his earlier books. His one new volume of
verse published in this period, *El vuelo de la celebración* ("The Flight of Cele-
bration," 1976), goes a step further.[26] A sense of the arbitrariness of poetic
language and the elusiveness of reality underlies it and turns many of its po-
ems into attacks on meaning, leading to ambiguous and contradictory re-
sults. These poems make us think explicitly about the possibilities and
limitations of artistic communication (see Mayhew 1990, 123). Very often,
they make intertextual references to other works of literature and art, in-
cluding Rodríguez's earlier texts, and thus foreground their themes and
their process (ibid. 114). "Hilando" ("Weaving") begins with an allusion to
a specific Velázquez painting:

> (*La hilandera, de espaldas,* del cuadro de Velázquez)
>
> Tanta serenidad es ya dolor.
> Junto a la luz del aire

la camisa es ya música, y está recién lavada,
aclarada,
bien ceñida al escorzo
risueño y torneado de la espalda,
con su feraz cosecha,
con el amanecer nunca tardío
de la ropa y la obra. Este es el campo
del milagro: helo aquí,
en el alba del brazo,
en el destello de estas manos, tan acariciadoras
                    [Rodríguez 1983, 230]

{(The weaver, her back turned, from Velázquez's painting.) So much serenity is now pain. Next to the air's light, the blouse [shirt] is now music, and is just washed, clarified, tightly bound to the joyous and rounded foreshortening of the back, with its fecund harvest, with the never delayed dawning of clothes and work. This is the zone of miracles: here it is, in the dawn of the arm, in the shimmer of these hands, so caressing}

At its most obvious level, the poem is an homage to the vitality of Velázquez's art, since it describes one figure from his painting and emphasizes its compelling beauty. We must observe, however, the constant references to the artfulness, perhaps even artificiality, of the woman's portrayal. Her back is a "foreshortening," the blouse is "music," the resulting picture is a "miracle." Later on we are told that the picture "sings" and read a very mannered description of the woman's hair. The action described, weaving, is of course also an artistic endeavor. All of this produces a seemingly contradictory view of lifelike qualities produced by artifice; it thus makes us think about the paradoxical relationship of life and art.

This sends us back to the enigmatic first line and its curious link between calm and suffering. The latter could refer to the fact that the weaver is described at a moment of great stress; the former could allude to her graceful portrayal by Velázquez. Thus the line may again reflect the tensive relation of life and art. Once we recognize this theme, we must observe another allusion. The description of the *camisa* as "recién lavada" contains a direct reference to an earlier poem of Rodríguez, "A mi ropa tendida" (see chapter 4). This intertextuality cannot help but emphasize the ways in which art plays on life, and the surprising relationships between life and art.

As the poem develops, the figure is described more and more as though she existed outside the painting, making us wonder if the qualities the speaker attributes to her—he talks of her "celebration" and her "service"— come from Velázquez, or from real life, or from his interpretation. The dividing line between art and life blurs for us: are we watching a figure in a painting, a real woman, a character in a poem? In one sense at least, the painting is the most real of the three, since it hangs in the Prado Museum, where we can check its features. In another sense, Rodríguez is making a fictitious character real. The poem does not resolve these tensions, but rather situates us within them, emphasizing the ambiguities and inviting us to continue working with them.

This poem, and *El vuelo de la celebración* as a whole, continues Claudio Rodríguez's way of poetically transforming concrete referents in order to discover within them deeper indices of life patterns. This process, however, has now become more self-conscious, as the poet refers more explicitly to art, to literature, to his own prior work. As this happens and as the lines of demarcation between text and life blur, this poetry also opens the way for more active participation by the reader.

Even the apparently direct narratives of José Angel Valente's first books often related basic life patterns to the poetic quest. By the late 1960s Valente's verse had become more complex and allusive and focused more explicitly on the theme of poetry. This focus intensified by 1970 and was coupled with an increased use of intertextuality. In *Presentación y memorial para un monumento* ("Presentation and Memorial for a Monument," 1970), Valente satirized fanaticism and misguided ideologies by placing his texts in the mouths of various unreliable speakers; he used references to a pastoral letter once issued by Spanish bishops and inverted the text of a prayer to show the twisted effect of a stultified religion. The book also combined popular and learned references, much as did the work of the *novísimos* (see Valente 1980, 306–7, 310).

Literary intertexts are more prominent in *El inocente* ("The Innocent One," 1970), where they generate ambiguous experiences in the reader. In "Reaparición de lo heroico" ("Reappearance of Heroism") Valente alludes to the plot of books 17–18 and 21–22 of the *Odyssey,* in which the returning hero confronts and kills the suitors of Penelope. He initially inverts the epic's point of view, putting in the mouth of the chief suitor Antinous a reasonable-sounding defense of pragmatism and describing the legends of Troy as vague hoaxes. Having thus set up a conflict with the traditional notion of Odysseus as hero, Valente shifts outlooks and describes the killing of Antinous in heroic though very bloody terms (Valente 1980, 352–54; see Debicki 1983). All of this makes every angle of vision suspect and involves the reader in a conflict between pragmatic and heroic attitudes, which the poem leaves unresolved.

In "Estatua ecuestre" ("Equestrian Statue") Valente alludes to a poem of the same title by Jorge Guillén and anteposes a view of disintegration to Guillén's affirmation of human existence:

> Hundióse el monumento.
> No hubo nada.
> Entre los sauces desfiló una orquesta
> con aire de domingo.

                              Y quien tuvo mi imagen
                    se la echó a los perros, con estricta piedad,
                    de la vecina noche. [Valente 1980, 336]

{The monument sank: there was nothing. A band marched between the willows, with festive air. Whoever had my image threw it to the dogs, to neighboring night's strict pity.}

As Margaret Persin has indicated (1987, 143–49), this subversion of Guillén's text, emphasized by Valente's use of some typically Guillén-like stylistic features, leaves the reader with a dramatic contrast between two outlooks on life and art.

Intertextual references are also frequent in *Treinta y siete fragmentos* ("Thirty-seven Fragments," 1972) and *Interior con figuras* ("Interior View with Figures," 1976); their most notable feature, however, is an explicit concern with the process of poetic naming. This poetry reflects the thoughtful attention to literary meaning that also underlies Valente's essays, many of which were collected in the widely read *Las palabras de la tribu* (1971) and *La piedra y el centro* (1982). Valente's essays affected not only his generation—which followed, as we have seen, his notion of the poem as an act of discovery—but also younger writers, who read his later articles and adopted their view of poetry as a form of epiphany, and also were influenced by his skepticism about its ultimate efficacy. The growing questioning, complexity, intertextuality, and self-referentiality of Valente's writing in the 1970s corresponds to, and helps define, the aesthetic climate of the decade.

Something similar can be said about Francisco Brines. *Insistencias en Luzbel* ("Insistences on Lucifer," 1977) continues the gloomy vision of human life that underlay his earlier works and again transforms descriptions and events to convey its moods. In this book, however, this occurs against the backdrop of a world in which basic values have been reversed, in which God is a trickster and Lucifer the apparent hero (although he also stands for forgetfulness). In this world, the speaker seeks various antidotes to a prevailing meaninglessness and oblivion. In the light of the underlying reversal of values, seemingly intranscendent events often become significant: in "Canción de los cuerpos" ("Song of Bodies") a chance erotic encounter stands as an affirmation of life (Brines 1984, 231). The book's final effect is a series of paradoxical experiences, the ultimate resolution of which is left open.

The theme of poetic creation is dealt with explicitly in several of Brines's texts, and the persona's act of writing poetry is a major element of his struggle against temporality and nothingness. By commenting on the process of poetic creation while undertaking it, he invites us both to take part in it and to contemplate it. The poem titled "Al lector" ("To the Reader") begins thus:

En las manos el libro.
Son palabras que rasgan el papel
desde el dolor o la inquietud que soy,
ahora que todavía aliento bajo tu misma noche,
desde el dolor o la inquietud que fui,
a ti que alientas debajo de la noche. [Brines 1984, 215]

{In your hands, the book. These are words that tear the paper, from the pain or rest-lessness that is I, now that I still breathe beneath your very night, from the pain or the restlessness that I was, to you who breathe beneath the night.}

Carlos Sahagún's *Estar contigo* ("Being with You," 1973) contains the same metaphorical transformation of childhood memories as his prior verse and is a continuation of the poet's coming to terms with the past by expressing it in language and image. Sahagún's style acquires greater variety; the book includes some excellent prose poems. Very often, the metaphors used are more complex than in the poet's earlier work and take the focus off the referential values of the scenes portrayed. While still reflecting the poet's (and his generation's) drive to make poetry a means of discovery, this book also shows the greater foregrounding of language and form that characterized the decade.

The poets of the generation born between 1923 and 1938, who formed a major part of the literary establishment in the 1970s, revealed in their works an artistic consciousness, a self-reflexivity, and a shift to intertextual and metapoetic concerns that paralleled those of the younger poets of this time. Such concerns led them to refine, rather than abandon, the use of poetry to uncover life's meanings—in past experiences, in their surroundings. Although here they differed from the antireferential *novísimos,* their works, original and impactive, acquired a new openness.

A few poets, chronologically part of this generation though practically unknown in the previous decade, gained importance in the 1970s. María Victoria Atencia, born in Málaga in 1931, had written some interesting poetry in the 1950s. After a decade or so of silence, she published four important books: *Marta & María* (1976), *Los sueños* ("Dreams," 1976), *El mundo de M.V.* ("The World of M.V.," 1978), and *El coleccionista* ("The Collector," 1979). Atencia, like other poets of her age group, uses a rather everyday vocabulary to present memories and places that evoke basic themes and issues of life. Specific objects and experiences produce perceptions of temporality, of the intensity of life at given moments, of surprising moods and sensations. Quite often, an object, vignette, or element in a story will function symbolically to make common reality point beyond itself; thus in "Con la mesa dispuesta" ("The Table Being Ready") a surprise guest at dinner comes to represent the arrival of death and the speaker's willingness to accept it (Atencia 85).

If the combination of immediacy and wider implications connects Atencia's poetry to her generation, its artfulness ties it to the 1970s and even the *novísimos*. In diverse ways, she uses image, vocabulary, and rhythm to turn ordinary elements into beauty. In the following lines, the speaker's view of a pigeon evokes a surprising sense of color and harmony:

> Reposa tu fatiga un momento en la casa
> mientras hierve en colores la pluma de tu cuello
> y echa luego a volar y vuelve con los tuyos. [Atencia 104]

> {Rest your tiredness for now in the house
> while the plumage of your neck bubbles in color
> and then fly off, go back to your world.}

The rhythmic effects achieved by Atencia's alexandrines and the interplay of image and sound that they produce constitute some of the salient formal achievements of the time. Like many younger poets, Atencia also combines literary references with those taken from cinema; they are used sparingly and tellingly.[27]

Another poet deserving note is Francisca Aguirre, born in 1930, whose first book, *Itaca* ("Ithaca," 1972) presents a feminist rereading of the *Odyssey* from Penelope's point of view. In this and several later books, Aguirre makes artful use of straightforward vocabulary and narrative technique to undercut traditional philosophical attitudes such as the need to organize life around transcendent goals. Her work presages the subversive strand of women's poetry that would appear in Spain in the 1980s.

Two other women poets, whose birth dates but not their styles would group them with the *novísimos,* can be mentioned here. Pureza Canelo (b. 1946) gained a wide readership during the 1970s, writing straightforward and emotive verse that reflected anecdotal events and situations. Canelo's work was to become more self-reflective, and to my mind more significant, in the next decade. Clara Janés (b. 1944), in contrast, did not attract much attention during the 1970s, though her poetry seems to me more important than Canelo's. During the decade she published several books in which she artfully combined everyday language and learned elements to cast new light on various objects and situations. Janés is also the author of some intense erotic poetry, in which human sexuality reflects larger natural patterns. Her work gained greater importance in the 1980s, as we will see in the next chapter.

Carlos Bousoño's *Las monedas contra la losa* ("Coins Fallen to the Pavement," 1973) continued the style introduced in *en la ceniza.* The book's persona combines a discursive mode, in which he questions diverse aspects of reality, with a symbolic presentation, in which objects and actions represent, rather enigmatically, human conditions and dilemmas. The book connects the view of poetry as a way of overcoming temporality and meaninglessness (seen previously in the *Oda*) to the more general existential struggle against death that had pervaded Bousoño's earlier verse. *Las monedas* returns, for example, to the paradoxical image of life as "springtime of death." Different poems reflect different moods, creating a tensive, conflictive whole. A pessimistic perspective predominates: in the title poem, the symbol of coins dropped dramatizes life expended, robbed by a greedy force.

In this setting, poetry and writing are not only a means of asserting one's existence (as they were in *Oda*) but also images of the course of human life. In the title poem the speaker sees himself as the subject of someone else's narration: "Y te sientes contado e infinitamente narrado" (Bousoño 1980, 143). {"And you feel yourself told, and infinitely narrated."} In "Formulación del poema" ("Formulation of the Poem") he weaves together several themes and perspectives: the process of life passing and disintegrating, its symbolic representation as the breaking of porcelain and crystal, the composition of the poem, and, in the last part, a search for light, higher vision, and transcendence. The poem begins as follows:

> Con la vida hecha añicos, despedazado el cántaro;
> rota la soledad como una urna; la alegría
> de aquella fina mañana, junto al mar,
> destrozada porcelana de Sèvres; hermoso
> plato de Talavera, la amistad y el amor,
> hecho trizas aquí:
> fragmentos duros de instantes, ruinas de primaveras, de
>   crepúsculos, polen
> de dicha. . . . [Bousoño 1980, 168]

{With life turned to splinters, the vase broken; solitude broken like an urn; the happiness of that fine morning by the sea turned into broken Sèvres porcelain; friendship and love, beautiful Talavera plate, turned to shreds; hard fragments of moments, ruins of spring, of sunsets, pollen of happiness. . . . }

As often occurs in the book, what may seem like rather straightforward symbolism is not easily explained: if the passing of life is like the breaking of vessels, does the making of poetry in the title reflect the passing, or the attempt to detain its evanescent beauty, or the search for some higher vision, which is described in the last section of the poem? Or some combination of all of these? We have here an example of what Bousoño himself described as an effort to amaze, to break logical expectations and make his text actually reflect (rather than describe) the paradoxical nature of its theme: "Mi estilo como tal aspiraba no sólo a *cantar,* sino a *ser* . . . una 'primavera de la muerte' " (Bousoño 1980, 26). {"My style as such aimed not only to sing but to be . . . a 'springtime of death.' "

Thus *Las monedas contra la losa,* even as it brings together the themes of Bousoño's previous verse, takes the metapoetic focus that had appeared in *Oda en la ceniza* one step further. It textualizes not only the theme of poetry as an answer to life's quest but also the very process and experience of composing the poem. And it makes us see that experience as enigmatic, unresolved. In that sense, it invites us to try to make sense of it, to involve ourselves within in. This way of making the book contingent on the reader situates it, and its author, within the dominant, perhaps postmodern, climate of the 1970s.[28]

More surprising than Bousoño's new bent is the appearance, in 1970, of *Mientras* ("Meanwhile") by Blas de Otero. Thematically, we find in the book some of the same political views that had established Otero as Spain's leading social poet, but these are now presented in a complex and self-reflexive text, quite different from the poet's closed works of the 1950s. Its format is telling: pages in different typefaces alternate with others containing drawings, or just titles, or section numbers, or even apparent commentaries: "El lápiz con que tracé aquella carta a los dioses está gastado, romo, mordisqueuado" (Otero 1970, [122]). {"The pencil with which I scribbled that letter to the gods is worn down, dull, bitten down."}[29] The book establishes a tension between overt impulses to reflect history, describe events, and convey truths on the one hand, and a fanciful wish to make life poetic on the other.

Otero does not abandon his quest for a popular kind of poetry. But where his earlier work had at least implied poetry's didactic nature, *Mientras* personifies it as irreverent, in a text that also seems to mock any solemn poetics:

> ah poesía al fin salió vistióse
> simplemente de hombre
> se restregó las manos escupió
> al pie del papelucho
> y dijo de esta manera
> > soy más valiente que tu
> > manera de hacer poemas [Otero 1970, (53)]

{Ah, Poetry finally came out, dressed simply as a man, rubbed its hands together, spit at the bottom of the paper, and spoke thus: I'm braver than you are, than your way of making poems}

Mientras contains many intertextual references, continuing a tendency that we saw in Otero's earlier *Esto no es un libro.* The poet recasts a work by Bécquer and alludes to Góngora and Goya. He also includes his picture and a copy of several of his handwritten lines; at one point he alludes to the process of writing this very book: "Dejo unas líneas y un papel en blanco. / Líneas que quiero quiebren la desesperanza" (Otero 1970, [45]). {"I leave lines and a blank page; lines that I hope undo desperation."} In this fashion, and also by explicitly referring to the future readers of his poems, he breaks the convention of the book as an independent fictional world and fore-grounds writing and reading. Sylvia Sherno has suggested that references to paper and printing are played off against texts that reveal a mistrust for the written word, producing conflicts of reality and illusion and, ultimately, a very unstable and in that sense postmodern text.

The publication of such a book by an author who best exemplified Spanish social poetry of the 1940s, and its goal of expressing clear truths in accessible language and effective form, is probably the best example of a shift in times, in poetics, in aesthetic sensibility. A traditional generational perspective on Spanish poetry would miss the way in which Otero's work, as well as that of Bousoño and of poets that had emerged in the 1950s and 1960s, reflected the new perspectives of the 1970s.

Less unstable or overtly metapoetic, Concha Zardoya's poetry of this decade nevertheless also illustrates, and contributes to, the aesthetic sensi-bility of the time. Her *Hondo Sur* ("Deep South," 1968), *Los engaños de Tremont* ("The Deceits of Tremont," 1971), and *El corazón y la sombra* ("The Heart and the Shadow," 1977) use a variety of tones and verse forms to draw basic emotions and insights on human nature from scenes, visual images, and literary evocations. "Oda al jazz" ("Ode to Jazz") commences with vio-lent, chaotic imagery, reflecting the contemporary intensity of the music. The speaker, somewhat ironically, then attempts to relate the effects of this art to known myths, images, and natural patterns. The poem's varied im-agery combines with dramatic descriptions to skillfully render all the nu-ances of the subject (Zardoya 1968, 143–50).

We see further evidence of a new era and poetics in Vicente Aleixan-dre's *Diálogos del conocimiento* ("Dialogues of Discovery," 1974). The format of its poems is radically new in Aleixandre's work: they are composed of speeches by diverse characters, who utter dialogue in pairs. In a sense, the book continues Aleixandre's constant, and ever more intense, search for new knowledge about existence through poetry. It also continues the self-consciousness about the poetic process that had developed in his *Poemas de la consumación*, which immediately preceded *Diálogos*. But the new format gives us, instead of the earlier searches for unified perspectives, a frag-mented collection of attitudes and what José Olivio Jiménez has called "una gran escritura abierta, multívola, devorándose insaciablemente a sí misma" {"a great, multivalent text, insatiably devouring itself"} (1982, 99). The critic has also perceptively indicated ways in which Aleixandre makes these texts play off against lines and sections of his own earlier poetry and has noted ways in which he undermines aphorisms and conventional ideas and expressions. All this produces a series of conflicts between an existential and an idealistically metaphysical outlook, which are never resolved logically. Often the speakers of the dialogues seem not to hear each other; instead of responding, they offer opposed perspectives. Aleixandre now gives new meaning to a stylistic device present in his previous verse, the ambiguous conjunction *o* ("or/and"), which in *Diálogos* serves to place the reader squarely within the book's conflicts (ibid. 105).

This shift to new forms, to a consciously intertextual and self-referential writing, and to a form of indeterminacy is particularly telling given Aleixandre's role on the Spanish literary scene. Ever since the 1940s and 1950s, he had acted as mentor and guide to generations of younger poets; almost every one of them had visited his house, offered him poems, and sought his advice, which was always given generously, and with an amazing ability to understand shifting styles and needs. Now the master, in his last major work, reflected the self-conscious and open poetics of his protégés and of the decade.

Jorge Guillén, whose *Cántico* had made him, perhaps, the archetypal poet of Spanish modernity, composed two volumes in this era: . . . *Y otros poemas* (". . . And Other Poems," 1973) and *Final* ("The End," first published in 1981, but including poems written from 1973 on). Both of these books contain many intertextual references, including frequent comments on Guillén's earlier poems; both also make explicit references to the process of writing poetry. In *Final,* this process becomes the dominant theme, and all other subjects—the passage of time, the impulse to assert one's existence in the face of mortality, the value of memory—are subordinated to it. The poet becomes the main example of a human search for vitality; the reader, in turn, is seen as re-creator of the works and hence of the lives of past writers. The text, as a result, evolves constantly:

> El texto del autor, si bien leído,
> Se trueca en otro ser—de tan viviente.
> Las palabras caminan, se transforman,
> Se enriquecen tal vez, se tergiversan.
> Tras la hazaña de origen se suceden
> Las aventuras del lector amigo.
> He ahí revelándose un misterio
> De comunicación entre dos voces
> Mientras los signos gozan, sufren, mueren.
> [Guillén 1987, 5: 63]

{The author's text, if read well, becomes another being, with its own life. Words walk, change, perhaps become richer, are distorted. After the original deed, the adventures of the friendly reader follow. There lies, revealed, a mystery of communication among two voices, while the signs enjoy, suffer, die.}

The poetics so directly presented here are a total departure from the view of poem as icon that could be found in Guillén's statements of prior decades, even as late as the 1960s. Guillén's new attitude is related, in my mind, to the new way in which the poems of this book have to be read. Taken in isolation, many of them may seem rather conceptual, even didactic: the reader accustomed to *Cántico* may miss the intensity of imagery and sensorial experience of that book, as well as the narrative and perspectival play of *Clamor.* But on reading those poems of *Final* that refer to or remake earlier Guillén texts, we will discover a rich play of perspectives and an intriguing invitation to compare styles and to consider all the issues involved in trying to express a theme in poetic language. "En un viaje por mar" ("On a Sea Trip"; Guillén 1987, 5: 89), for example, explicitly refers to a poem titled "El encanto de las sirenas" ("The Sirens' Charm") from *Clamor.* But it develops a series of perspectives very different from those of the earlier text and offers an unresolved debate, in two voices, about the value of illusions. The second and more prosaic voice seems, in addition, to render less attractive (perhaps to parody?) one of the attitudes of the earlier poem. On one level, the new poem criticizes the negative attitude to myths of the earlier one; on another, it opens the subject to a play of multiple outlooks and directs the reader to its process rather than to any possible resolution (see Debicki 1984, 93–94).

Similar readings can be suggested for other poems that refer to earlier works of Guillén. *Final* may be best considered, in fact, a way of reading and rereading Guillén's prior texts, and thus re-creating and extending them in time. It is also revealing that Guillén himself, after the publication of the first edition of *Final,* changed the order and the lines of some poems and actually marked the changes, in pen, in the copies of those who came to see him (see photocopied examples in Debicki 1984, 103–5). One cannot find a better example of a poet focusing on process rather than product, or of an evolution beyond a modernist poetics.

 If Spanish poetics of the previous period, centered largely on the notion of poetry as an act of discovery and on the artistic use of common language to make this act occur, pointed beyond modernity, the poetics and aesthetic climate of 1966–80 seems fully outside the modernist aesthetic. The foregrounding of linguistic creativity and of the poem as an independent world, and the view of literature as intertextual, as self-referential, and as process rather than object constitute a complete reversal of notions that had pervaded Western letters since at least the advent of symbolism.

We can also see the actual poetry from this decade that I have been examining as belonging to an era beyond modernity. Can we call it postmodern? The many definitions of *postmodernity* that have been offered (one is tempted to say "bandied about") make it hard to use the term without elaborate distinctions and qualifications. Yet the Spanish poems of the 1970s have consistently revealed traits stressed by many different studies of the subject. Whether we focus on the tendencies to discontinuity, to irresolution, and to open texts, picking up the ideas of Calinescu, Lyotard, Hassan, and Pérez Firmat; emphasize the textualization, the self-referentiality, and the undermining of conventions from within that are stressed by Hutcheon; or highlight the immanentism and the focus on presence rather than knowledge, as does Altieri, or the revolt against decorum and comprehensibility, as do Lyotard and Pérez Firmat, every one of these perspectives seems applicable to the poetry of the period, whether it is written by younger or older authors. All these perspectives are useful in distinguishing the poetry of the 1970s from that of earlier eras. Many traits that Fredric Jameson uses to define postmodernism within the context of "late capitalism"—a mixture of high and low culture, pastiche, a reshuffling of text fragments, discontinuity—are likewise reflected in these works, although some of Jameson's social conclusions do not seem applicable to Spain.[30]

In one sense at least the poetics and poetic language of this decade have significant cultural and historical implications. I suggested in chapter 4 that the 1960s view of poetry as process rather than product represented a reaction against the static, message-oriented discourse of preceding decades. The more indeterminate, more self-referential and language-centered outlooks of the 1970s, best represented by the *novísimos,* continued and intensified this reaction. And the actual poetry of the decade, whether written by younger or older poets, constitutes a subversion of the notion of literature as communication of univalent meanings, whereas the poetry of the 1960s, for the most part, did not. By breaking the lines of demarcation between text and intertext, by reflecting on their own production, by undermining coherence, and by inviting the active participation of the reader, this poetry subverts, in a fundamental way, a previously dominant view of language as an assertion of power, which underlay forms as diverse as modernist literature, nationalist discourse, and leftist social poetry.[31]

It is both thought-provoking and telling that this major change in poetic outlook and in the nature of the poetry being written occurred—or at least began—before the end of the Franco regime. This order of events calls into question our tendency to see literature as being influenced by, and reflecting, social and historical conditions. It suggests, instead, the validity of an opposite model, brilliantly developed by John Brushwood in his examination of Mexican fiction of approximately the same period. Brushwood relates the traits of that fiction—which include the emphasis on process over product, and openness to reader participation—to a new intellectual attitude, a new state of mind that preceded and presaged later political changes (see Brushwood, esp. 57 ff.). It seems equally valid to suggest that the attitudes underlying the poetics and poetry of the 1970s in Spain presaged (though they could not have caused) the post-Franco world and its various manifestations: the new outlook on life, state of mind, and vision of life and writing were in place, ready to be expressed when circumstances allowed.

6

The Evolution of Postmodern
Poetry, 1978–1990

A Very Immediate Past

Evaluating the last decade of Spanish poetry poses problems: lack of historical perspective, uncertainty regarding the future path of younger authors, and a general difficulty critics have always had in dealing with recent styles and features suggest a need for caution.[1] Even identifying the most important works and poets proves difficult; for that reason, I have taken a larger number of younger authors into account, however briefly.

The new poetry published in Spain in the 1980s seems less obsessed with linguistic creativity, with allusiveness, and with self-reflexivity. The younger poets of the decade adopted less polemical attitudes. Several critics have described them as a "continuing" rather than a revolutionary generation, noting that they reflect trends that go back at least twenty years (see García Martín 1988, 19; and Villena 1986b, 17). Many of these poets skipped back past the 1970s and connected with the 1950s and 1960s, rereading Gil de Biedma, Brines, González, and Valente. Thus they revived the tradition of poetry as discovery and as expression of feelings—whereas the *novísimos* of the 1970s had revived the aestheticist tradition of the 1920s.[2] Regular rhythmic patterns, verse forms, and stanzas were used more frequently throughout the decade, often as part of a search for melodic effects.

However provisionally, we can group individual poets by several main strands of verse. The essentialism, the verbal precision, and the classic bent that gained importance in the mid-1970s are evident in one large group of works of the 1980s, written by both new and established writers. These works also reflect more serious philosophical concerns, suggesting a general thematic deepening of verse. In a separate group or groups, we can gather a number of poets, younger and older, who convey emotive states, often through interior monologues and the creation of various personae. Some do so in straightforward lyrical fashion. For others, especially younger ones, the expression of subjective states fades into irony, which often protects lyric postures from sentimentality and also lessens their intensity, shifting poetry into minor keys. For yet other poets, who can constitute another strand of writing, irony and satire create a play of many perspectives, move poetry toward narrative, and in some cases engender subversive views. All these different strands frequently blend into each other or combine in the work of a given poet (I have made some arbitrary decisions on their placement). Despite their heterogeneity, all of them suggest a renewed interest in expressivity in poetry—as contrasted to linguistic elaboration and experimentation.[3]

From today's (still nearsighted) perspective, the decade seems rich in the production and diffusion of poetry. Several publishing houses specializing in verse (most notably Hiperión, Visor, and Renacimiento) issued many volumes, some of which sold quite well: Hiperión actually publicizes poetry "best-sellers." Collected works by the important poets of all prior generations had become available by the end of the decade. Perhaps more important in the long run, publishing houses in provincial cities increased dramatically their output of poetry, and new magazines that included verse sprang up throughout Spain (making it more difficult to keep up with new developments). Anthologies of new writers, national and regional, appeared in ever greater numbers (see García Martín 1988, 51–66). Many (perhaps too many) poetry prizes were established, sometimes publicizing small communities and ventures. All of this suggests a great vitality. How much of the poetry of this period will be included in a longer-term canon is of course impossible to predict.

One feature of the period is the emergence of important women poets—some, though not all, new to the literary scene. Some of their work illustrates the essentialist line of the decade, or its more lyric strand. Other women's poems, however, exemplify the most innovative subversive styles and attitudes of the time.[4] A disposition to read women's poetry more attentively can be related to the rapid social changes occurring in Spain and to an increasingly international perspective and a new view on gender roles that became evident among younger generations.

The importance of women's poetry was made clear by several widely read books. Ramón Buenaventura's *Las diosas blancas: Antología de la joven poesía española escrita por mujeres* ("White Goddesses: Anthology of Young Spanish Poetry Written by Women," 1985) gained a readership for many younger poets and established, despite the editor's patronizing comments, that poetry by women deserved more serious treatment than it had received. A special issue of the journal *Litoral* titled *Litoral femenino* (1986), edited by Lorenzo Saval and J. García Gallego, called attention to Spanish women poets throughout the century, starting a process of reappraisal. And Sharon Ugalde's *Conversaciones y poemas* (1991) presented, in perceptive interviews supplemented by texts and bibliographies, women's special views and concerns. One matter, raised by several interviewees, deserves note: the productivity of women poets does not follow the generational schemes of men, due often but not exclusively to a juggling of careers and life patterns.

The stylistic features I have noted in the poetry of this period could make it seem regressive, a return to pre-1970 literary situations. Yet this is not the case: the canon and the conditions for poetry had been irremediably changed by the developments of the 1970s. All the poems of the next decade had to be written against the backdrop of the previous self-reflexivity and artful use of language, of the achievements of the *novísimos*, of the poetics of literature as process. When the new poets of the 1980s did not stress linguistic creativity as much as their predecessors had done, they were not erasing a prior trend but merely recognizing, consciously or unconsciously, that the battle for creativity had already been won and did not need to be repeated. Unlike the *novísimos* ten years earlier, who had still felt obliged to counteract tawdry or social verse, authors beginning to write in the late 1970s could turn their attention to the content rather than the form of poetry and develop subjects that mattered to them—whether they were philosophical inquiries, emotive states, or new postures on gender issues. Older poets could do the same, transcending formal and aesthetic concerns that earlier situations had imposed upon them. For this reason thematic issues dominated the decade. As polemical stances on form and on poetics diminished, and as generational distinctions faded, we saw imaginative, original, but not so self-conscious poetry produced by authors in their thirties, forties, fifties, and sixties.[5]

The poetry of this decade was also written against the backdrop of literature as a process open to collaboration by the reader. Such a view was stated explicitly by some poets and assumed by many more. It underlies a number of texts that I shall examine and gives new dimensions to philosophical inquiries or emotive experiences. These texts have now been consciously made open to various readings, in ways that 1930s texts, for example, were not.

It may seem paradoxical that this decade of apparent "continuism" in poetry occurred during a time of deep historical and social change in Spain. Beginning with the death of Francisco Franco in 1975 and with the establishment of the constitutional monarchy, patterns of life underwent dramatic shifts. A mere couple of years separated a very traditional society under censorship from one in which social freedom and a variety of lifestyles prevails, in which many young people live modern and independent lives, in which any verbal or visual expression is allowed. The very fact that the political establishment is now a (rather tame) socialist party, and that many younger persons who had once seen themselves as revolutionaries wield political and economic influence, speaks to the shift. Since all this has led to a significant renaissance of the arts that has made Madrid a unique city, and to some very daring works of fiction, one might have expected a parallel revolution in poetic styles.

To my mind, that would imply an inaccurate model of literary-cultural relationships. I find more compelling one in which, as John Brushwood has suggested, literary language and form presage culture instead of following it (see Brushwood 57 ff.). For me, the stylistic revolution in poetry that should be linked to the new Spanish society had already occurred during the previous decade or two. The prior attacks on the view of literature as message, the new emphasis on linguistic creativity during the 1960s and its foregrounding in the 1970s, and the growing view of poetry as process had already shaken poetic styles out of old molds and thus had preceded social change. By 1980 the new state of mind that had made such shifts possible had been emerging for two decades and was fully in place among poets and readers.

As a result, the poetry of the ensuing decade could be innovative in its themes (more than its forms) and could develop new attitudes about the roles of women, new and deeper insights on personal, social, and philosophical issues, and new ways of reading literary and cultural traditions. (We will see, for example, intertextual plays, serious and parodic, on past forms and conventions.) Alternately, it could be whimsical, playful, and lower-key, offering less intense perspectives.[6] The new social structures of the time, especially the consumer society that has expanded so rapidly in urban Spain, with its attendant signs and symptoms in the media, provided the background to many of these new attitudes.[7]

From Silence to Essence

In an essay published in 1989, Amparo Amorós contrasted the emphasis of the *novísimos* on the language of the poem to a later search, typical of the 1980s, for philosophical meanings that can be unearthed through poetic language. Thus, for Amorós, the "essentialist" poets built on, and used for deeper goals, the notions of creativity that had developed throughout the 1970s.

We can describe the origins of this "essentialist" poetry of the 1980s even more specifically. It grew out of the striving for concision, for exact form, and for the reduction of expression to pure sign that had already appeared during the second phase of the 1970s (Siles 1990) and was best illustrated by Siles's verse. The poetry of the 1980s took this striving further, to a more affirmative and philosophical goal, exemplified by Siles's *Columnae* (1987), by new works by Andrés Sánchez Robayna and María Victoria Atencia, and by the emerging poetry of Amparo Amorós, Clara Janés, María del Carmen

Pallarés, and others (see Ciplijauskaité 1992). José Angel Valente, Guillermo Carnero, Pere Gimferrer, and others followed parallel if somewhat different paths.

The connection between poetic creativity and philosophical inquiry in the work of many of these poets was influenced by the eloquent, almost mystical writings of the philosopher María Zambrano, and especially by her ideas about a *razón poética* {"poetic reason"} and about the symbiosis of poetic and metaphysical modes of inquiry. Zambrano's view of *la mirada* {"the gaze"}, of ways in which creative language instantaneously captures insight, and of the potential transcendence of expression are reflected in many of their works (see Amorós 1982, 1986).

As I indicated in chapter 5, Siles's *Música de agua* had reduced reality to sign and had privileged the word over the referent. *Columnae* presents a more affirmative view of the relationship of life to verbal expression. After referring back to the earlier book's last part, Siles constructs, in "Hortus conclusus" ("Closed Garden"), an homage to life through poetry. Written in rhymed seven- and eleven-syllable *liras,* the poem recasts themes, images, and even tones from Fray Luis de León. Explicitly reflecting on the poetic process, it gradually foregrounds light over darkness, and the poetic naming of reality over empty signs:

> La claridad resuena
> y no de su vacío: de su fronda
> el silencio se llena. [Siles 1992, 186]

{Clarity resounds, and not from emptiness; silence is filled out of its foliage.}

"Textualidad en comas" ("Textuality between commas") exemplifies Siles's new attitude and reveals an increasingly rich and nuanced perspective. It begins by contrasting the emptiness of language to the physicality of human life and love. Yet the poem forges a complicated relationship between sign and experience, as it playfully describes physical love through images of textuality:

> Página de la carne,
> alfabeto del habla,
> único ser acorde
> con la unidad que encarna.
> . . . .
> quiero hoy de tu libro
> releerme sus páginas,
> suprimirles un punto,
> pasar, lentas, las láminas
> y dibujar dos comas

con él sobre la cama
porque busqué el volumen
y vi que ya no estaba. [Siles 1992, 190–91]

{Page of flesh, alphabet of speech, sole being in harmony, with the unity that embodies . . . I wish today to reread the pages of your book, to erase a point, to slowly turn the illustrations, and to draw with it two commas on the bed, because I sought the volume, and saw that it was not there.}

If we take the referent to be the experience of the lovers, it has been metaphorized and stylized to such a point that life has become a text. If, on the other hand, we assume that the subject is the act of writing, it has been transformed into a very physical love relationship. By the end of the poem the speaker himself, who began asserting the value of reality over language, cannot separate one from the other. As a result the poem makes us feel that living and writing (or reading), though in tension, are ultimately bound together; and it does so in a delightfully dramatic and whimsical way.

In this, the poem exemplifies all of *Columnae*. The joyous affirmation that underlies the book arises from a combination of life experiences and verbal discoveries, and from the awareness that they explain and support each other. As a result, the poet's tone and point of view are more complicated than in Siles's previous books, but also earthier and lighter.

The quest for naming human and natural reality and thus discovering its essence continues throughout the volume: in "Blanco y azul: Gaviotas" ("White and Blue: Seagulls") vignettes of the birds that have been reduced to form, textualized, and read by a speaker-poet give him a sense of reality and confidence (Siles 1992, 196–97). Throughout the book, the image of columns foregrounded in its title reminds us of the order of language in poetry, through which human beings strive to organize life and meaning. The speaker-poet's self-consciousness and the stress on his quest as process invite the reader to share and to continue it.

Siles's *Semáforos, semáforos* ("Traffic Signals, Traffic Signals," 1989) takes a different point of view, juggling images of modern life and popular culture with classical and literary allusions. Some poems constitute blatant parodies of modern referents, while others stress language and image play; the book fits within a whole vein of ironic and satiric verse, as we will see later. Yet it also constitutes an exploration of the confrontation between reality and verbal naming and their generation of new perceptions.

María Victoria Atencia's poetry of this decade fits nicely in this section on essentialist verse. *Compás binario* ("Binary Compass," 1984) uses allusion, scene, image, and vignette to reflect basic life patterns, their ambiguities, and their ironies. In the title poem, for example, a vignette formed by a double metaphor defines passionate love as a paradox of delay and speed:

> Tardasteis largo aliento en coronar la cima
> y fuisteis un destello deslumbrante en la noche,
> que en la opuesta ladera se apagó bruscamente.
> [Atencia 150]

{You took long effort to crown the summit, and were a blinding flash in the night, which quickly burned out on the other slope.}

We are made to feel, simultaneously, several aspects of this experience: the duration and struggle of the lovers' effort, the glory of their success, the tragedy of love's brevity and oblivion. Language operates multidimensionally to explore a complex human reality, as Atencia's elegant alexandrines artfully reflect a meditative mood.

In *Paulina o el libro de las aguas* ("Pauline; or, The Book of Waters," 1984) Atencia evokes places and art works in Italy. Much like the images of *Compás binario,* these reflect basic themes, most frequently the fragility and temporality of human life. At times an unusual angle deepens a traditional insight and makes a poem point to several meanings. Thus a Michelangelo statue of a slave simultaneously communicates this particular figure's lethargy, sculpture's way of evoking life, and art's general quest for immortality:

> Para la muerte fuiste engendrado en belleza
> antes de que el cincel descubriera en el mármol
> tu descompuesto escorzo de aburrimiento y sueño.
> [Atencia 167]

{You were engendered in beauty for death, before the chisel discovered in the marble your slovenly foreshortened figure of boredom and death.}

It is left to the reader, as Ciplijauskaité notes (1992, 156–57), to organize, resolve, and pursue these disparate implications. Similar effects are produced by Atencia's more recent poetry, which shows exceptional skill in using details—images, incidents from daily life, echoes of art works—to reflect, without simplifying, major themes. Perhaps for that reason Atencia's works, hitherto unjustly neglected, have gained increased attention in the 1980s.

Another poet who had not received sufficient credit before this decade is Clara Janés, who also fits in this section. Janés, born in 1944, had published several books in the 1960s and 1970s. The selections in her *Antología personal* ("Personal Anthology," 1979) make clear her skill at seizing basic feelings in sharp images and short, tight lines of verse. *Libro de las alienaciones* ("Book of Alienations," 1980) takes a more pessimistic, perhaps even anguished view of human life, expressed via sharp but complex language and via images echoing Spanish baroque verse, especially Quevedo's.[8] Then, in seven more books of the 1980s, Janés published a rich and varied poetry, underpinned by a renewed affirmation of life and art. The motivating subjects vary, ranging from places to individual experiences and sexual and erotic love (generally linked to cosmic patterns), from art, music, and poetry to concrete objects. Some works comment, metapoetically, on their production. Typically, a transforming image or images modify the initial subject, generating a series of feelings and, ultimately, a fresh perspective on reality. For me, perhaps the most interesting of these books of the 1980s is *Lapidario* ("Lapidary," 1988).

Each poem deals with one kind of stone; the verso page gives either a scientific description or some historical background, and the recto one contains Janés's poem. The reader thus must juxtapose a historical or objective view to a poetic creation. Almost always, the latter picks up aspects of the former but elevates it to an original and intense experience. The definition of *opal,* for example, describes the mysterious effect of the stone's glow; the poem then stresses the sensorial effect of this glow and makes the stone represent a life pattern:

> Un secreto en la nube se diluye,
> oval olvido que la luz persigue,
> mas siempre una centella la rescata
> y se ofrece: resquicio del enigma. [Janés 1988, 19]

{A secret dissolves in the cloud, oval forgetfulness that light pursues; but a spark always rescues it, and offers itself: chink [glimmer] of the enigma.}

This poem has combined image and fable to explain the opal's unique shimmer. It has likened the stone to a cloud that hides parts of light from sight, yet allows other parts to come forth, beautifully and mysteriously; thus it has made us feel the presence of life's enigmas, partially revealed. In a few key lines, Janés has reached far beyond her visual referent and has produced a new beauty, as well as a sense of life's mystery.

Kampa (1986) frequently focuses on natural elements and scenes, sharply distilling from them (or endowing them with) sensations and attitudes, which often define love experiences. The book also marks a conscious effort to relate poetic and musical experiences (see Ugalde 1991, 42–43). And in *Creciente fértil* ("Fertile Growth," 1989), Janés recalls ancient Hittite and Sumerian myths to draw, in precisely traced poems, intense, exotic views of regal (and assertive) females and their loves.

Andrés Sánchez Robayna fits generationally, like Janés, among the *novísimos.* His first book, *Clima* ("Climate," 1978), could have been discussed in the previous chapter, since it was written between 1972 and 1976; its metaphysical bent, however, situates it even better in this one. Sánchez Robayna uses natural images and personifications, coupled with a variety of tight, precisely controlled forms, to convey feelings. In "El durmiente que oyó la más difusa música" ("The Sleeper Who Heard the Most Diffuse Music") a sea scene in a dream evokes an almost mystical sense of order. The poem organizes its few images in a rhythmic pattern and connects them with music, working the reader into its mood. Every detail adds something: a series of items joined by *y,* for example, reflects a sense of continuity:

> El mar en esta brisa de verano.
> La más difusa música, en el sueño,
> la visión más intensa,
> las olas prolongadas y el sol y los pinos
> giran con esas olas y ese aire que él sueña.
> [Sánchez Robayna 27]

{The sea in this summer breeze: the most diffuse music, in the dream, the most intense vision, the waves fanning out and the sun and the pine trees all circle within these waves and this air that he dreams.}

In many poems, the visual arrangement of words on the page helps produce its rhythm. And throughout the book, natural patterns are related to human moments and schemes and also to the process of poetic creation.

Sánchez Robayna's *Tinta* (1981) and *Laroca* (1984) contain longer and more varied texts, using more complex imagery and patterns and showing greater self-consciousness on the part of the speaker-poet. (In the former, ink, blackness, and night are related, as natural scenes blend into the experience of writing.) In general terms, these books continue the poet's effort to engender, with precision, essential intuitions.

Also essentialist is the polished, precise poetry of Abelardo Linares. *Espejos* ("Mirrors," 1991) contains some of his most impressive poems. Several love lyrics of the book's second section focus on a single moment and, through a few carefully selected images, capture its intensity. In another section, the scene of a statue of horses is vivified and described as if in motion, thus capturing its aesthetic impact.

As we saw in chapter 5, Alejandro Duque Amusco published two important books of poetry of the 1970s, in which intense nature images offered an affirming view of life and poetry. In 1983 he issued *Del agua, del fuego, y otras purificaciones* ("Concerning Water, Fire, and Other Purifications"). As Ignacio-Javier López has indicated (1990, 89–94), Duque Amusco continues explicitly rejecting the complex allusiveness and decorativeness of early *novísimo* writing and makes poetry a way of transcending time and affirming the beauty of human expression. Meanwhile the younger Juan Manuel Bonet, in *La patria oscura* ("Dark Homeland," 1983), creates brief, suggestive sketches of cities, scenes, and events to evoke specific sensations and moods. Bonet's willing acceptance of the term *impressionism* to describe his work is very telling (García Martín 1988, 97). His poems center on a few visually salient details, modify them with unusual adjectives or personifications, and thus create a novel experience. In "Pamplona," for example, he combines sketches of sad arches and a blind lantern with memories of nineteenth-century revolts, thus suggesting a nostalgic romanticism (Bonet 18).

Very conscious of her goals as poet, Amparo Amorós has been seeking a "poetic thought" that reaches beyond logic, literal meaning, and devalued everyday idiom to discover coherent visions of reality (see Amorós 1982, 1986, 1989). In *Ludia* (1983) Amorós uses language, image, and allusion with great precision to portray, and reflect upon, the artistic experience.[9] In poem 1 from the section "Visiones," prefaced by a quote from St. John of the Cross, the speaker seeks a *tú* identified on the one hand with a lover, on the other with poetic insight (Amorós 1992, 71–82). Much as in the poetry of St. John, the anecdotal level of the relationship is dissolved in language, and the experience is converted into an essential (though sensual) quest.

The interrelationships of life and art are stressed throughout the book: in "Fachada modernista" ("Modernist Facade") a decorative facade attracts the viewer by its artfulness, but also produces a sensorial effect denied to more utilitarian structures:

> Toda línea se aviene a la dulzura,
> se entrega mansamente a la mirada
> reinventa en las horas
> la magia de una forma
> que osa tímidamente un surtidor lascivo.
> [Amorós 1992, 55]

{All lines blend into sweetness, give themselves over to sight, and reinvent the magic of a form that a lascivious fountain timidly dares project.}

We come to feel that the more artful the subject becomes, the more it gains emotional value.

Amorós's *La honda travesía del águila* ("The Deep Path of the Eagle," 1986) continues the line of *Ludia*. The book transforms its referent, evidently a love affair, to stress on the one hand the theme of union, and on the other poetry's role in elevating life. In "Consentiment" ("Assent") a flight of gulls evokes a magic mood of harmony that stops time and points to poetry's transcendental power:

> En su instante perfecto
> no vuelan
> se abandonan en el aire

> entregadas al viento
> las gaviotas. [Amorós 1992, 129]

{In their perfect moment the gulls do not fly: they abandon themselves in air, given over to the wind.}

One precise image and a few key words, presented sparsely and rhythmically, reflect the wider theme. We can hear echoes of Guillén and Juan Ramón in this poem and throughout the book. The open suggestiveness of Amorós's poetry, however, makes it part of the 1980s. The same suggestiveness and the same quest for transcendence underlie her most recent work, *Arboles en la música* ("Trees in Music," 1993), which weaves together images of nature and artful music; each poem is associated with a specific musical composition.

María del Carmen Pallarés's poetry is not easy to categorize: almost all of it offers subjective responses to life's issues and could have been discussed in a later section on expressive verse. Yet its treatment of metaphysical topics with precision and economy situates it within this unit and also underlines its importance.

Del lado de la ausencia ("On the Side of Absence," 1979) and most of *Molino de agua* ("Water Mill," 1980) consist of short, tight poems in which a few images convey feelings. In these poems, objects that metaphorize emotive states, personifications, and actions reflect, precisely and economically, basic and usually pessimistic attitudes to life. In "Abril" ("April") a time normally associated with rebirth evokes sadness: "Como un tren ciego al túnel / la primavera corre a la tristeza" (Pallarés 27). {"Like a blind train toward the tunnel, spring runs toward sadness."} Pallarés has here converted an abstraction and a mood into an object, simultaneously producing a specific feeling and implicitly suggesting life's tragic disintegration. This image is confirmed by a later, allied one of the poem crossing a nightmarish station. Pallarés's poetry is highly visual and tactile, which may relate to her work as painter and sculptor; nouns predominate, and every image is coordinated with the rest.

Beginning with Pallarés's *La llave del grafito* ("The Graphite Key," 1984), poems become longer, tones more varied, and narrative patterns more common. In *La llave* childhood memories objectify a variety of attitudes. In most poems, details are condensed and accumulated to intensify a mood. At times a phrase or syntactical construction is the key to a whole outlook. In "Pero aún hay más" ("But There Is More Yet") the phrase "hay más abajo" {"there is more below"}, recast and rephrased various times, reflects a desperate seeking of greater meaning in life (Pallarés 62). Succeeding books by Pallarés expand the range of reference of this poetry and add the use of different point-of-view techniques. In *El hallazgo de Agrigento*

("The Agrigento Discoveries," 1984) the perspective of primitive human be-
ings offers a unique angle on the theme of our thirst for knowledge. "Por
pasiones así" ("Because of Such Passions"), from the 1987 volume *Cara-
vanserai,* personifies elemental forms of life (ibid. 103–5). Several poems re-
create the effect of paintings, using syntax and word selection to reflect their
impact.

    Biruté Ciplijauskaité has called attention to the poetry of Luis Suñén,
whose *El lugar del aire* ("The Place of Air," 1981) and *Mundo y sí* ("World and
Yes," 1988) use tight nature images to convey a joyous affirmation of life, in
a way reminiscent of Guillén's *Cántico* (Ciplijauskaité 1992, 153–54). Equally
or more important is the work of Jesús Munárriz.[10] In his *Camino de la voz*
("The Path of the Voice," 1988) he deals with basic themes in short lines of
verse, with key nouns and images tightly structured via rhythm, rhyme, and
word order. In "?" for example, a black crow set against the snow is likened
to a question mark, producing an unusual perspective and a suggestion of
nature's enigmas (Munárriz 50). The book makes us feel life's mysteries as
well as poetic achievement. Ciplijauskaité notes (1992, 155) that echoes of
Golden Age poetry give an unexpectedly affirmative view of poetry's worth.
The book's prefatory poem is a good example:

> De la pluma, no es propio que alce el vuelo
> y de la tinta, que recuerdo deje . . .
> . . . .
> Los vientos del azar y del destino
> murallas, templos y palacios siegan,
> versos arrastran, pulen, ciernen, siembran.
>   [Munárriz 7]

{Is it not proper for pen to rise in flight, and for ink to memory leave? . . . The winds
of chance and destiny cut down walls, temples, and palaces, but pull, polish, sift, and
sow lines of verse.}

The main traits of Munárriz's book are typical of much Spanish poetry of
the 1980s: an inquiry into life's mysteries via tightly controlled language,
coupled with a conscious affirmation of the process of writing.
    Ciplijauskaité indicated that the quest for essential meaning in Spanish
poetry of the 1980s, expressed in a language of great economy and preci-
sion, marked a "return towards real experience, towards the concept of the
poem as something that remains" and transcended the linguistic self-con-
sciousness, and the negativity, of the previous decade (1992, 153).[11] Does
this, as she suggests, mark a return to modernity? For me, such a return
would be impossible: the new outlooks and the poetic shifts of the 1970s
place any poetry published in the 1980s in a new context. The new essential
poetry does not arise in the light of Jorge Guillén's or Juan Ramón's view of

the poem as permanent icon, but with a consciousness of the text as evolv- ✓
ing, as a living process in which the reader can collaborate. Rather than a
historical pattern coming back full circle, I see a spiral, in which a renewed
affirmation of poetry emerges against the backdrop of a new poetics.

New Directions, Established Poets:
Expressions of Feeling and Experience

A number of well-known Spanish poets published important new books dur-
ing the 1980s. In most cases, they deal with the age-old topics of time's pass-
ing, life's values and limitations, and quests for meaning; they stress personal,
subjective effects and often relegate metapoetic issues (so common in the
prior decade) to the background. Luis Rosales, who had been writing poetry
steadily throughout the previous decades, published in 1979 *Diario de una res-
urrección,* ("Diary of a Resurrection") a single long text addressed to a beloved
and centered on a quest for insight and transcendence. After that book and
Un puñado de pájaros ("A Handful of Birds"), Rosales began issuing a multi-
volume work he has titled *La carta entera* ("The Whole Letter"). Its form and
style bring to mind Rosales's much earlier *La casa encendida:* the book nar-
rates reminiscences in an ample, flexible free verse verging on poetic prose,
in a style ranging from colloquial to lyric. It continually explores the past,
finding in its events a symbolic reflection of basic themes and insights. The
first volume, *La almadraba* ("The Fishing Net," 1980), sets the mood of ques-
tioning through recall, against the backdrop of the passing of time and the
prospect of death. Particularly impressive is the second volume, *Un rostro en
cada ola* ("A Face on Every Wave," 1982), which includes comments on writ-
ing, on political and social situations, and on various individuals, including
fellow writers. Occasionally caustic in its comments on the Civil War and the
Franco regime, the volume adopts for the most part a meditative stance, with
moving elegiac moments. Recalling friends who have died, the speaker
speaks with them and attempts to preserve their memory. The view of poetry
as means of capturing and illuminating experience implicitly (and at times
explicitly) underlies this volume and also the third, title one (1984), which
combines vignettes recalling the past with a desire for a new birth. The ap-
pearance of *La carta entera* contributed to a renewed interest in Rosales's ear-
lier work, particularly *La casa encendida.*

Concha Zardoya continued publishing, throughout the period, books
that explore fundamental issues through past memories. This more recent
verse of Zardoya and Rosales easily blends with the reminiscent, philosoph-
ical, and often elegiac work of younger poets, letting us see an underlying
current of poetry of exploration and discovery that reemerged throughout
the 1980s, suggesting echoes of the 1950s and 1960s.

Carlos Bousoño's *Metáfora del desafuero* ("Metaphor of Outrage," 1988), like his previous books, is pervaded by a sense of the impending and inevitable tragedy of death. It also contains a number of texts reflecting on the poetic process and several very expressive love poems. The book reveals a variety of tones and verse forms. But Bousoño seems to have left behind the metapoetic play and the effort to amaze and confuse that we saw in *Las monedas contra la losa*. Many poems of *Metáfora del desafuero* present subjective commentaries on life, in direct address and discursive language: their speakers make us feel, more often than not, the horror of life's temporality and death's impending presence. At times a surprising point of view reinforces this view: in "Felipe II y los gusanos" ("Philip II and the Worms") the speakers are worms devouring the king's body and thus acquiring some of his traits and impulses. Ghoulish touches and conversational tone combine and help the poem express a caustic sense of the limitations of human life and glory (Bousoño 1988, 112–13). The other end of the book's tonal scale is represented by a moving elegy to Vicente Aleixandre, which echoes the style of his poetry.

Poetry's task in confronting life's main issues, forging subjective responses in creative language, and thus gaining insight, has been a constant theme of Claudio Rodríguez's work. As Rodríguez's collected poems appeared in 1983, as he was awarded the National Prize for Poetry in 1983 and elected to the Royal Academy in 1987, he became for many the model of the poet who explores life's issues artfully yet emotively. Rodríguez spent the decade writing and rewriting a single book, *Casi una leyenda* ("Almost a Legend"), which was finally published in 1991. In some ways it takes us back to his works of the 1960s: natural scenes and moments of the day trigger meditative comments by the poetic persona. In most poems, long chains of free verse explore life through shifting moods and questions, arriving at paradoxical stances. Verse and rhythmic patterns, though, vary more than in the poet's earlier books.

When a specific event or situation is recalled, it often acquires broad allegorical echoes and becomes a starting point for complex explorations. In "El robo," for example, a thief and thievery evoke the deceit, decay, and evil of a person described and addressed. This long poem unfolds slowly; I quote a short section:

> Ahora es el momento del acoso,
> del asedio en silencio,
> del rincón de la mano con su curva
> y su techumbre de codicia . . .
> . . . .
> Es el recuerdo ruin y luminoso
> y la mano entreabierta con malicia y rapiña

y los dedos astutos ya maduros
con el temblor de su sagacidad.
Es cuando el tacto brilla con asombro y con vicio,
la mirada al trasluz,
la encrucijada a oscuras del dinero. [Rodríguez 1991, 39]

{Now is the moment of assault, of the silent siege, of the hand's edge with its curvature, and its avaricious gesture. . . . It is the despicable yet shiny memory, and the hand open in malice and thievery, and the canny hands now ripe in the tremor of their sagacity. This is when the touch shines with amazement and vice, with a reflected look, at the dark crossroads of money.}

Rather than present a sequenced narrative, the text weaves a few visual details with negative adjectives, a physical characterization, and a judgment. This mix denies any logical development and foregrounds, instead, a mood of emotional evil for the reader. As the poem unfolds, it contrasts this mood to the speaker's exhortation to seek life and light. Ultimately, the text dramatizes a conflict between destructive and constructive life forces. Yet it conveys this theme intensely and intuitively, avoiding any possible reduction to simplistic ideas.

Temporality and death are dominant themes in this volume and furnish the background to the persona's overall quest. Some texts allude specifically to the death of a loved one in the past; in others, finitude is just the setting against which the speaker must construct his attitude. In many poems, he offers a positive response based on the contemplation of harmonious moments in nature and his quest for love and life. At times his affirmation takes on an intensity that blends erotic and mystical qualities, as in "Momento de renuncia" ("Moment of Renunciation"):

. . . Basta sólo
la mañana sin fin que entra y desea
en vuestro cuerpo que es el mío. Basta
la verdad misma, una emanción.
Bajo mi cara más, ya sin distancia.
Hay que limpiar el aire y hay que abrir
el amor sin espacio,
gracia por gracia y oración por vicio. [Rodríguez 1991, 57]

{The endless morning that enters and desires, within your body that is mine, suffices; truth itself, an emanation, suffices; beneath my face, without distance. One must clean the air and open love without space, grace for grace and prayer over vice.}

In "Nuevo día" ("New Day") the sunlit freshness of a new day creates a sense of transcendent beauty that momentarily stops time (Rodríguez 1991, 31–32). Yet overall, the limits of life are more apparent than in Rodríguez's prior books.

The theme of poetry appears in several texts, and poetic inspiration motivates the persona's affirmative attitudes. The frequent use of symbols that had been prominent in Rodríguez's earlier books (including washing, rotation, illumination) also suggests a consciousness of the poetic process and the continued pursuit of a single poetic path. Yet explicit metapoetic references and allusions to other texts are less frequent than they had been in *El vuelo de la celebración,* making the stress fall more on the intense expression of a fundamental life quest.

Temporality is also the underlying theme of Francisco Brines's *El otoño de las rosas* ("Autumn of Roses," 1987). A consciousness of death, of impending annihilation, underlies the whole book. Memories of past experiences (frequently love episodes) are juxtaposed to a perception of life's evanescence. The poet skillfully fits modern referents into timeless settings and into classical poetic traditions. "Collige, virgo, rosas," ("Gather ye rosebuds while ye may"), for example, addresses a modern lover by recasting an old convention, centered on the quest for life in the face of death's inevitability. By using the old symbols of night and day, yet inverting their traditional roles so that the former instead of the latter stands for life, the poem revitalizes the old topic. The speaker's awareness that he will die before his addressee makes his advice all the more poignant:

> Mas aunque así suceda, enciéndete en la noche,
> pues detrás del olvido puede que ella renazca,
> y la recobres pura, y aumentada en belleza,
> si en ella, por azar, que ya será elección,
> sellas la vida en los mejor que tuvo,
> cuando la noche humana se acabe ya del todo,
> y venga esa otra luz, rencorosa y extraña,
> que, antes de tú conozcas, yo ya habré conocido.
>   [Brines 1987, 25]

{But even though it happen thus, do burn in the night, for perhaps it will be reborn from forgetfulness, and you may recover it pure, increased in beauty, if in it, by chance (which will then be choice) you will seal life at its very best, for when human night end completely, and that other strange and rancorous light come, which, before you discover it, I will already have known.}

José Angel Valente's *El fulgor* ("Radiance," 1984) is even more explicitly elegiac, since its thirty-six brief and tight poems form a sequence, lamenting a specific death. The repeated image of the body (*cuerpo*) makes the book develop on a grim note, intensified by images that dramatically evoke disintegration:

> El cuerpo
> caído sobre sí

>   desarbolaba el aire
>   como una torre socavada
>   por armadillos, topos, animales
>   del tiempo,
>   nadie. [Valente 1984, 11]

{The body, fallen on itself, stripped the air like a tower undermined by armadillos, moles, animals of time, no one.}

As the book continues, the speaker recalls different memories and comes to terms with the loss. He combines traditional images—light, night, dawn, fire—with echoes from the Gospels and from Hispanic literature. The economy and exactness of these poems increases their effect and lets the reader share the speaker's acceptance. Another book of poetry by Valente, *Mandorla* (1982), contains mostly tight, terse texts that reflect on form, creativity, and life's patterns. It could be classified with essentialist verse.

A sense of time passing dominates Angel González's *Prosemas o menos* ("Prosems or Less," 1983, expanded in 1985). In one respect, its everyday language, its narrative focus, and its frequent ironic tone make this book very different from the ones by Rodríguez, Brines, and Valente. Yet it offers parallel and compelling views of human life and temporality. In most poems a specific speaker contemplates, from a lucid, complex, and detached perspective, the effects of time and aging on specific events and situations. As the title suggests, this speaker ironically juxtaposes his shrewd and apparently matter-of-fact view to traditional (or clichéd) poetic attitudes to life and death. As he does so, he develops original and often emotional insights and experiences.

To some degree, then, González goes back to the lyricism tinged with irony that we saw in his first books, although the dominant speaker's role as poet is now more evident. This speaker consciously transforms his referents via his language and recalls other authors and other texts, from popular song as well as literature. Yet like Rodríguez, González leaves behind the metapoetic bent and the explicit focus on procedures of the 1970s. This suggests that the awareness of process has become instinctive, and hence backgrounded, for the poet and the period.

"El día se ha ido" ("Day Has Left") exemplifies the book's language, imagery, and point of view. The speaker vivifies a day gone by as a prosaic dog, contrasts it with a stealthy cat (night), and points to the humdrum routine of life's course and to its irretrievability. Insights into life thus come across in understated and fresh fashion, avoiding any possible grandiloquence (González 1986, 329). Similarly, though in a more condensed way, a muted yet intense (almost desperate) desire for life marks the ending of "El conformista" ("The Conformist"):

Cuando era joven quería vivir en una ciudad grande.
Cuando perdí la juventud quería vivir en una ciudad pequeña.
Ahora quiero vivir. [González 1986, 398]

{When I was young I wanted to live in a big city; when I lost my youth I wanted to live in a small city; now I [just] want to live.}

Some poems set up conflicts among contrasting attitudes. In "Canción, glosa y cuestiones" ("Song, Gloss, and Questions") the speaker twists an image from a romantic Mexican song into a cynical portrayal of an unfaithful girlfriend (González 1986, 380); a succeeding text then juxtaposes a highly idealized view, in which the persona's whole life is a brief moment of one love (ibid. 384). A serious poem in homage to Jorge Guillén is balanced by an ironic portrayal of Juan Ramón Jiménez as a compulsive mechanic who cannot resist tampering with a car; some very lyrical evocations of landscapes of New Mexico balance an ironic metaphor of life as an undependable beloved. The end result is a contemporary, complex, and yet coherent view, in which specific angles blend into a larger sense of human life, its satisfactions and limitations.[12]

The theme of temporality had already been present in the earlier works of Rosales, Bousoño, and the writers of the Generation of the 1950s. It had constituted an important facet of the "poetry of discovery" of the 1950s.[13] Yet it becomes even more dominant in the books of the 1980s and engenders a more intensely subjective lyrical expression. To some degree, this could be related to the poets' aging.[14] Yet it also confirms the 1980s return to basic experiences and emotions in poetry, which we also see in older and younger writers. In most poets of this generation, such a return is accompanied by a lessening of the self-reflexivity, the commentary on techniques, and the metapoetry that had developed during the 1970s.

After many years devoted to teaching and criticism, Guillermo Carnero published *Divisibilidad indefinida* ("Indefinite Divisibility") in 1990. It marks a step back from the discursive tone and essaylike style of his two previous books, to a lyrical mode that in some ways recalls *Dibujo de la muerte*. The new book uses tightly controlled forms: it alternates groups of two sonnets with longer poems, mostly in quatrains. Its vocabulary is consistently elegant, almost consciously artful and antique, and underlines the echoes of the Spanish baroque also present in its themes. We note the presence of references to art and literature, including Carnero's earlier texts. Yet as López has noted, the themes of art blend harmoniously into those of life.[15] A consistent tone and the repetition of key images give the work unity and coherence.

On one level, the book's main subject is poetry and art: the speaker deals with their efforts to preserve life and meaning. The dominant note is pessimistic. Again and again, the speaker's efforts to see life preserved in form produce an awareness of emptiness, artificiality, or insufficiency. The ordering impulse of art is countermanded by the accidents and upheavals of life and time. In "Teatro ducal de Parma" ("Theater of the Dukedom of Parma") the theater stage seems to save human forms from death, yet finally offers only an artifice:

> El silencio y la muerte así burlada
> trazan espacios de serena gloria
> y un firmamento plácido y fingido
> como pueblan los reinos de la nada
> la escenificación de la memoria
> y la cartografía del sentido.
> [Carnero 1990, 11]

{Silence and death, thus fooled, draw spaces of serene glory, and a placid and artificial firmament, as the cartography of the senses and the scenification of memory populate the kingdoms of nothingness.}

Art's stability is illusory; it only captures human experience in sterile fashion, and its presence reveals an underlying absence. Here the book's theme becomes the fleetingness of our existence. This theme is also compellingly presented in "Música para fuegos de artificio" ("Music for Fireworks"). The image of fireworks shows how poetry and art construct an overwhelming beauty, yet one that quickly disintegrates in a night symbolically identified with death.

The outlook behind *Divisibilidad,* echoing baroque *desengaño* {"disillusion"}, thus recalls the negative paradoxes of *Dibujo de la muerte*. But the reader's experience differs: rather than being led down many and contradictory paths that foreground art and process, we follow the speaker's single and consistent quest. As we do, and as we see its goals and its failures, we focus on the human dilemma represented: the personal, tragic struggle for permanence and order in a universe, and a language, that offer only a mirage. The consistency of tone and perspective, the imagery, and the spare and telling use of referents contribute to a masterful text.

Changes similar to those in Carnero's poetry occurred in work published during this period by other members of the *novísimo* generation. Félix de Azúa left behind the foregrounding of language and the fragmented style of his earlier books; his *Farra* (1983) is a series of clear narrative poems, set against the background of a seaside village. Sketches of the lives of fishermen mix with different moods and sensations. Leopoldo María Panero also wrote more narrative poetry, with various speakers, in *Last River Together* (1980) and in sections of *Dioscuros* (1982). His last poems include some short texts in the manner of haikus.

Meanwhile the emotive poetry of Leopoldo María's brother, Juan Luis Panero, almost completely ignored in the previous decade, drew attention in the 1980s. His *Juegos para aplazar la muerte* ("Games for Delaying Death," 1984) and *Antes que llegue la noche* ("Before Night Comes," 1985) mix contemporary references and neoromantic, imagery-laden mood pictures focused on death and temporality. The book attracted younger readers and poets, inviting them also to reread his earlier *Los trucos de la muerte* ("The Tricks of Death," 1975). Another member of the *novísimo* generation who drew increased attention in the 1980s was Justo Jorge Padrón (b. 1943), author of emotive poetry that sets human experience in the context of natural patterns.

Several other *novísimos* made their poetry more intense and serious during the 1980s. We note a shift to the more explicit and concentrated expression of emotion in Martínez Sarrión's "El centro inaccesible, 1975–1980" ("The Inaccessible Center"), published in his complete works, similarly titled, in 1981. In the shorter poems of this book, Martínez Sarrión abandoned his earlier tendency to collect disparate sensations and blended mythic and modern elements into coherent moods; love poems became most impressive and important (see "Arribada" ["Arrival"]; Martínez Sarrión, 196). Two later books by the poet reveal an even more direct use of language, and an increasingly narrative manner. Manuel Vázquez Montalbán left behind the playfulness and the ironic view of contemporary culture, moving to an allegorical view of a historical theme in *Praga* ("Prague," 1982). Meanwhile Pureza Canelo, who had published some good (and popular) verse in the 1970s, wrote in the 1980s more penetrating and philosophical works, often reflecting on the poetic process.

Pere Gimferrer, in the bilingual *Apariciones y otros poemas* ("Apparitions and Other Poems," 1982), combined meditative, lyric texts underpinned by a sense of time's passing with homages to Vicente Aleixandre and Antoni Tàpies and with brief, aphoristic texts on topics ranging from winter to poetic art, from destiny to landscape. This last group fits the strand of essentialist poetry.

Both important and telling is the new poetry of Jenaro Talens, whose earlier verse had for the most part focused on metapoetry and the poetic process. Talens's *El largo aprendizaje: Poesía, 1975–1991* ("The Long Apprenticeship," 1991) combines several works, all of them containing very expressive poetry. Narrative texts, in which specific events motivate insights on basic themes, dominate *La mirada extranjera* ("Foreign Perspective") and *Tabula rasa*. In "Mirando unas fotografías" ("Looking at Photographs") a consciousness of time passing makes the speaker develop new perceptions on himself, on meaning, on love and its expression, as he addresses his son:

> Se me han ido los años. Si supieras
> con qué avidez me acerco a tu ternura. Fluyo
> entre libros extraños y lugares sin sol,
> poblando su silencio con palabras
> que no me implican ni me dicen, sólo
> son un mero refugio [Talens 1991, 115]

{My years have gone by. If you only knew with what eagerness I approach your tenderness. I flow amid strange books and sunless places, filling their silence with words that do not reveal or tell me, that are mere refuge}

Many poems in *El sueño del origen y la muerte* ("The Dream of Origins and Death," written 1986–1988) present even more directly, and in a similarly lyrical style, meditations on life, time, and love.

Antonio Colinas's *Noche más allá de la noche* ("Night beyond Night," 1983) continues the expressive line already marked by his prior books. In elegant and smoothly flowing verses, its poems draw natural scenes with mythical echoes, creating a variety of moods ranging from contemplative acceptance to nostalgia and a mournful awareness of time and death. Colinas now achieves increased cohesiveness, immediacy, and unity: the whole book is centered on the image of night, and most of its poems are composed of twenty-eight fourteen-syllable lines, at times in consonant rhyme. The book thus constitutes a focused, archetypal exploration of human life and feelings. The following lines illustrate one of its dominant moods:

> El cuerpo del desierto y el cuerpo de la mar
> se penetran de noche, y oigo derramado,
> allá arriba, un aullido de placer y de muerte
> en el que se desgarran los hombres y los dioses
> que a lo largo del tiempo han sido y serán. [Colinas 248]

{The body of the desert and the body of the sea are filled with night, and I hear the flow, up there, of a cry of pleasure and of death, in which men and gods who have been and will be throughout time become undone.}

From one perspective, *Noche más allá de la noche* is the culmination of Colinas's harmonious neoromantic verse; from another, it exemplifies the emotive and expressive strand of 1980s poetry.

The new poetry of Luis Antonio de Villena also extends the aesthetic and emotive features of his earlier *Hymnica*. His preface to *Huir del invierno* ("Escape from Winter," 1981) explicitly defines the title as symbolic, representing a rejection of puritanism, northern cultures, and monotheistic culture and an inclination to Hellenism, hedonism, and vital forces (Villena 1983, 191). The poems exemplify this outlook, continuing Villena's quest for sensual beauty. Yet new notes appear: the book contains four separate sections stressing diverse moods, from the joyous one of the "Odas" to the thoughtful, at times melancholic "Elegías." Intertexts and artistic references are foregrounded less, and we note a certain shift, emphasizing life experiences over artistic ones.

Dramatic monologues, spoken by diverse and carefully defined speakers, are more in evidence and trigger complex points of view. For the most part, characters or narrators describe variants of a struggle for artistic fulfillment in the face of time. In "Una gran actriz" ("A Great Actress"), for example, an observant companion speaks about the protagonist, making us feel simultaneously her aestheticist vitality and the tragic limitations and erosions of time (Villena 1983, 236–38). Throughout the book, nostalgic notes, based on a consciousness of life's flow, mute the underlying hedonism while increasing its depth and range; the erotic theme, as José Olivio Jiménez has aptly noted, blends into the larger issues of communication and union (ibid. 46). Villena's next book, *La muerte únicamente* ("Only Death," 1984) continues the same path.

The recent poetry of the *novísimos,* then, shows increased stress on emotive meanings and on deeper, more philosophical topics and looks beyond the linguistic concerns of the prior decade. It thus relates to a large body of expressive verse published during this period by younger writers.

Expressive Poetry: New Voices I

Andrés Trapiello is one of several younger poets of this period to express subjective meanings in traditionally lyric ways. These poets can be connected, in that sense, to Rodríguez and Brines, or to Colinas or Villena. From the start, Trapiello's poetry combines exact descriptions that make us visualize drawings with auditory and olfactory images. In *Junto al agua* ("By the Water," 1980) carefully traced details produce contemplative moods, usually centered on an awareness of time. In "Tiempo del aire en Tarifa" ("Time of Air in Tarifa"), for example, the picture of lines made by lights on ships' masts and the smell of the sea make the speaker reflect upon change and continuity (García Martín 1988, 120–21). García Martín has connected Trapiello's verse with the preoccupations and the mood writings of the Generation of 1898, observing that the poet has edited the work of Unamuno (ibid. 36).

The poems of *Las tradiciones* ("Traditions" 1982) and *La vida fácil* ("Easy Life," 1985) transform natural scenes in even more obvious ways, with a more frequent use of metaphor and personification: streets sleep, streetcars have eyes, and an afternoon "asoma, encapotada / a las vitrinas, triste" (ibid. 126) {"sad, hooded, looks into the store windows"}. We note a greater variety of meters and rhythmic effects. But Trapiello continues to evoke moods (often a vague melancholy) through natural scenes and thus to suggest basic themes. His verse is underpinned by his belief that poetry must be spiritual and must portray a poet's search for permanence, and by his preference for concrete symbolism, as it had been defined by the symbolists, to capture life's enigmas (ibid. 118–19).

Alvaro Valverde's poetry produces emotive effects in a straightforward modern idiom. Nature scenes and descriptions, and accompanying first-person reflections, convey a sense of order and contentment that recall the tradition of the *locus amoenus* and of neoplatonic verse. Valverde makes use of a wide repertoire of rhythms and verse forms, always selected to make more attractive the subject and attitude portrayed. Poetry becomes a way of finding harmony in a time-limited world, as exemplified in these lines, whose outlook and tone recall Fray Luis de León's:

> hojas de acanto y rosas,
> una vieja piedra de molino y enramadas,
> —el suelo tejido de una hiedra fresca—
> el dejarse caído cuando la siesta insiste,
>   [García Martín 1988, 187]

{acanthus leaves and roses, an old millstone and thickets, the land carpeted with fresh vines, letting oneself recline when slumber calls,}

Occasional intertexts denote Valverde's poetic self-consciousness. They invite us to see the poetry's theme and moods as part of a whole tradition of Spanish and European verse. Once we do this, we can compare and connect his poems with different versions of similar themes, from different times, and thus in some sense continue Valverde's search for harmony and order through poetry. If we read Valverde's poetry in this fashion, we confirm his own overt belief that the reader must "cerrar el círculo de creación en poesía" (García Martín 1988, 184) {"complete the circle of creation in poetry"}. Valverde's books of poetry include *Territorio* ("Territory," 1985), *Sombra de la memoria* ("Shadow of Memory," 1986), and *Lugar del elogio* ("Place of Praise," 1987).

Harmonious sensory and aesthetic experiences are also produced by the work of José Lupiáñez, who explicitly defined the artist's role as "celebra[r] el mundo, celebra[r] lo que le circunda" (Rossel 212) {"celebrating the world, celebrating what surrounds him"}. Lupiáñez uses decorative visual and sensorial images to reflect the gracefulness that underlies our reality. (This may relate to his Andalusian heritage.) His vocabulary is more elegant than that of Valverde or Trapiello and recalls the learned tradition of Spanish poetry. So do his rhythms and verse forms, which vary, with an increased tendency to long lines of verse, and also his images, which include basic natural elements and forces. At times visionary metaphors are used for intense sensory effects; in "Las manos encendidas" ("Burning Hands") they elevate the lovers' feelings to cosmic dimensions (ibid. 224–25). Lupiáñez is the author of *Ladrón de fuego* ("Thief of Fire," 1975), *Río solar* ("Sun's River," 1978), *El jardín de ópalo* ("The Opal Garden," 1980), and *Amante de gacela* ("Lover of Gazelle," 1980).

Equally elegant, though more gloomy in tone, is the poetry of another Andalusian, José Gutiérrez. His work reflects a melancholic vision of life's temporality and a nostalgic search for beauty in past memories and land-scapes. His polished vocabulary, the musicality of his verse, and the use of classical motifs and allusions recall the latter *novísimo* strain that we saw ex-emplified in Villena and Colinas. Yet much of his poetry refers to everyday scenes and landscapes. Some of his most impressive poems use such scenes to express a tensive combination of tranquility and loss. In "Antiguo Paraíso" ("Ancient Paradise") the return to a village left behind long ago generates a view of life's timeless harmony, but also reveals the speaker's consciousness of alienation and of the losses that life's course entails (Rossel 255–56). *El cerco de la luz* ("The Siege of Light," 1978), *La armadura de sal* ("The Salt Armor [Frame]," 1980), and *El don de la derrota* ("The Gift of De-feat," 1981) contain what I find to be some of Gutiérrez's best poetry.

An intense sensitivity that crystallizes into sensuality pervades the poems of the Valencian Miguel Mas: apparent in the love poetry of *Celebración de un cuerpo horizontal* ("Celebration of a Horizontal Body," 1978; see Rossel 245–46), it is even more evident and significant in the descriptive texts of that and other books. Natural elements reflect the speaker's feelings, very often centered on time's losses. Many visual images, repeated and dramatic personifications of natural moments and forces, and metaphors contribute to the subjective effects. And although Mas uses a normal, modern vocabu-lary, strong adjectives and repeated references to sensations (fire, burning, cold, light) further intensify these effects. The following lines come from "Ocaso" ("Dusk"):

> Caen las espigas sobre el campo, cae la luz
> y arrastra pavesas imposibles.
> Vida,
> qué me das, qué nácar abres
> contra las rocas del aire,
> qué ingenua geometría pretendes devorando
> el brillo tardío de un pecho solitario
> en este incierto atardecer que lentamente me arrebata.
>   [Rossel 242]

{Sheaves fall on the fields, light falls and drags impossible embers. Life, what do you give me, what nacre do you open against the rocks of air, what ingenuous geometry are you seeking by devouring the late shimmer of a solitary chest, on this uncertain dusk that slowly seizes me.}

Some of the same intensity is conveyed by *La hora transparente* ("The Transparent Hour," 1985), although many of its poems also include the speaker's introspective and at times metapoetic comments. We note, too, a more varied use of point of view and an increasingly complex, though still intense and foreboding, view of existence.

Julio Martínez Mesanza, in *Europa y otros poemas (1979–1990)* ("Europe and Other Poems," 1990), uses eleven-syllable blank verse and an almost archaic vocabulary, coupled with frequent historical allusions and settings, to offer mythic, romanticized treatments of basic themes.

Expressive Poetry: New Voices II

Other new figures of this period created a subjective poetry in more mixed tones: romantic feelings frequently shade into irony, real-life concerns combine with parodic echoes. Here circumstances and generational factors do seem to have played a part. Ironic comments protect sentiment from sentimentality; emotive attitudes that in other eras might have produced intense drama are handled in a lower key. Most of this poetry is set in the urban post-Franco world of the *movida* and reflects the cool, laid-back tone of this world. The surrounding climate of popular culture and the consumer atmosphere invited poets to mix artistic and everyday referents, edging toward kitsch (see Mayhew 1992, 401–2; and Calinescu 244). Lyric techniques and devices are often combined with narrative structures and techniques. In its moods, this strand of poetry recalls Gil de Biedma and González more than Rodríguez. Yet as we will see, its expressivity is one of its main features.

Luis García Montero's verse is not only excellent and original but also a good lead into this new poetry. It consists of seven books, running the gamut from prose poems echoing American black fiction to intertextual parodies and subjective reflections. The latter, however, are the most significant and are generally produced by remembrances of places and events from the persona's past.

Tristia (1982), whose title echoes Ovid and derives from "sadness," consists of reminiscences of love. They are presented in a carefully adjusted everyday language, punctuated by suggestive understatement and by effective, surprising images that transform objects and settings. "Homenaje" ("Homage"), on one end of a mood scale, is a nostalgic evocation of a lover who had committed suicide. The low-key tone and the common details intensify the tragedy, which culminates with chilling horror:

Aquí
no es diaria ni justa la existencia.
Bésame y resucita
si es posible. [García Montero 1989, 16]

{Here life is neither everyday nor just; kiss me and resurrect, if that is possible.}

"El lugar del crimen" ("The Place of Crime"), in contrast, uses the metaphor of a holdup to express love's intensity in a humorous way (García Montero 1989, 19). All in all, the book offers a fresh and understated view of love as a quest for affirmation in our world. The three lines of "Ars amandi" ("The Art of Love") best illustrate its attitude and its impact:

En la sombría expectación del tiempo
se trata simplemente de tenerte
sintiéndome la piel sobre la tierra.
                    [García Montero 1989, 29]

{In the somber expectation of time, it is simply a matter of having you feel my skin upon the earth.}

Diario cómplice ("Accomplice Diary," 1987) is again based on remembrances of a beloved. Unusual images point to various moods: the simile of the lover's piled-up clothes as a crouched cat captures a feeling of impending intensity, while the metaphor (perhaps also synesthesia) of the moon as saxophone catches the strange sensuality of a night in Paris (García Montero 1988, 28, 88). The theme of love blends, in this book, with the consciousness of life as a subject for writing, of poetry. In poem 8 the speaker describes his own feelings, vivified as cats, watching him, as he in turn sees life as a yet-unwritten text (ibid. 68–69). This metapoetic level does not take the focus off the book's main themes (as it did in some *novísimo* texts), but rather incorporates the drive to record and preserve experience into the theme of recalling that experience. Its presence supports a more self-deprecating, lower-key outlook, without eliminating emotive meaning.

Somewhat similarly but even less seriously, García Montero uses ironic takeoffs on classic Spanish poets in *Rimado de ciudad* ("Rhymes of the City," 1984) and *Egloga de los dos rascacielos* ("Eclogue of Two Skyscrapers," 1984) and finds in the modern world debased versions of poetic topics such as the passing of time. In perhaps the best example, a Góngora sonnet on life's evanescence is redone with images of a car speeding through a stop sign.

El jardín extranjero ("Foreign Garden," 1983) contains, to my mind, some of García Montero's most impressive poems. It is based on reminiscences of the past and of a city where the persona dwelled and also contains a long work imagining García Lorca's return to New York. In "Paseo marítimo"

("Seaside Promenade [Avenue]") the speaker expresses a low-key nostalgia for the city of his youth. Visionary images and personifications capture a mixture of nuances:

> Será porque el amor tenía entonces
> el color de las lámparas de gas
> y yo tan pocos años que miraba
> caer en las hamacas
> una lenta experiencia de cansado
> septiembre.
> > Era en las tardes últimas,
> > [García Montero 1989, 47]

{It was probably because love was then the color of gas lamps, and I was so young that I saw a slow mood of a tired September fall in the hammocks. It was during the last [late] afternoons.}

The subjective, visionary nature of the images allows for a variety of suggestions: the love evoked via gas lamps seems remote, romantically quaint, innocently laid-back; the speaker's mood, at once tired, unfocused, melancholic, self-deprecating. By personifying a moment as someone falling into a hammock, the poem captures a mood without any logical explanation or narration. (Such use of rather everyday personifications is a repeated feature of this poet's work, and of many others of his generation.) The remainder of this poem continues weaving various images to expand this melancholic but low-key mood. Vignette combines with metaphors, sometimes ambiguous (the woman's eyes are "cansados de café," "tired as/of coffee"—perhaps bored of sitting, perhaps faded brown in color). A complex, subjective effect is produced, with room for the reader to dwell on, perhaps extend, various images and facets.[16]

"Reestreno" ("Repeat Performance") takes reminiscences to another level by converting the action of recalling the past into the performance of a play, which is also described as "esta ciencia ficción de nuestra vida" (García Montero 1989, 59) {"this science fiction of our life"}. This continuing metaphor eliminates any literal perspective, distances and stylizes life and memory, and fuses emotive recall and artistic transformation. It at least implies a metapoetic level—the persona writes/portrays himself—making the nostalgic yet self-deprecating awareness of time past and passing both a pretext for and a reflection of the process of poetization.

Nostalgia overlaid (or undercut) by irony also characterizes the work of Leopoldo Sánchez Torres. Evoking past scenes and moods, the poet expresses feelings of loss and time past in an everyday language, effectively punctuated by images and personifications. His most compelling poems trace specific scenes and images: "Historia de la Noche" ("Story of the

Night") refers to a meeting in a bar; the color play of blue shoes and eyes, the vignettes of hands watched and shouts heard, and the surprising personification of a glass of beer all create a feeling of idle, ultimately intranscendent excitement (García Martín 1988, 287). Sánchez Torre's poems also contain occasional questionings of the speaker's poetic quest, which help balance and protect the sentiments expressed.

Similar tones govern the poetry of the younger Alvaro García, in which sharply drawn sketches evoke moods ranging from discomfort to lethargy and laid-back nostalgia. Often a moment in a narrative seems frozen, highlighted through selected detail, image, and low-key personification, turned into feeling. Modern references and ironic notes add to the understated effect. García's books include *Para quemar el trapecio* ("To Burn the Trapeze," 1985), *La dulce edad* ("The Sweet Age," 1986), and *La noche junto al album* ("The Night by the Album"), which obtained the 1989 Hiperión Prize.

Vicente Gallego, another younger poet, composes richer and more sensorially intense poetry, mixing traditionally poetic images with prosaic physical elements. Some of his love poems combine erotic detail, conventional feeling, and artistic allusion; in his nature poetry he explores the relationship between poet and landscape through very disparate tones and referents, visionary vivifications and personifications, and occasional ironic, self-mocking notes.

Juan Lamillar's poems, in contrast, capture basic, simple moods—joyous love moments, compelling natural scenes, perceptions of the past—yet always avoid conventionalism and rhetorical effects. Emotion is muted or understated. Personifications of nature are compellingly colloquial: the sun is a sneaky traveler, shadows knock on doors and run down paths, facades of houses remembered become austere faces. Unusual metaphors impart unexpected novelty to common situations: in "A punto la tarea" ("Moment for Homework") the lovers' attempts to recall and come to terms with the past are described, with subtle humor, as a homework assignment (Lamillar 44). At times Lamillar converts abstractions into concrete objects, as in "Aún queda amor" ("There Is Still Love Left"):

> Aún queda amor: en el embozo de las sábanas,
> en el café del desayuno,
> en el balcón abierto sobre el barrio,
> en el amor compartido.
> Aún queda amor en las pequeñas cosas. [Lamillar 45]

{There is still love left: in the sheet covers, in the breakfast coffee, in the balcony open to the neighborhood, in the shared mirror. There is still love left in small things.}

This makes feelings very tangible, but also adds a light note, which protects the poem from sentimentality.

Self-conscious comments on the poetic process are frequent in Lamillar's verse, always undercutting solemnity. A vignette of the persona as frustrated writer makes him human and likable (see Lamillar 14). In "A pesar de la fecha" ("In Spite of the Date") a few conventional and almost trite love phrases such as "the thirst of your lips" are suddenly undermined by the comment that the text being written is turning into a bad poem (ibid. 24). This produces a wonderful parody on conventional verse, while it gives new life to the work's theme of a love remembered during an absence.

As a result of these tactics, Lamillar's poetry exemplifies a contemporary, muted way of expressing subjective experiences. He may be at his best in *Muro contra la muerte* ("Wall against Death," 1982), which blends remembrances of love moments and places visited. Similar effects, in somewhat more complex poems of varying lengths, which include specific referents, are achieved in *Interiores* ("Interiors," 1986) and *Las playas* ("The Beaches," 1987). The novelty and understated nature of this poetry makes it fulfill Lamillar's goal: "de rescatar el instante, de construir otra realidad" (García Martín 1988, 150) {"to save the instant, to build another reality"}. It elevates the everyday and confirms his view of poetry as a way of living life twice (see Mayhew 1992, 404).

Felipe Benítez Reyes's work displays a variety of referents and speakers: his poems include the monologue of an ancient warrior, a vignette of a warhorse, a symbolic bookstore, and nature scenes filled with dreamlike images.[17] They reveal a special gift for wringing surprising effects or perspectives from their subjects: "Flor de una noche" ("A Night's Flower") gives an unusual twist to a conventional scene and engenders an ironic attitude to life and illusion (García Martín 1988, 211). "El invierno" ("Winter") combines visual images and evocations of past pageants and battles (perhaps in art works), creating something like a cornucopia of sensation and feeling (ibid. 204–5).

The poetry of Almudena Guzmán is more overtly narrative. In long, flexible lines of verse that can also be read as emotionally punctuated prose, Guzmán traces a mix of moods and attitudes evoked by modern city life. At times her monologues become direct address to places or persons: in "Madrid" the city is thus treated as a lover, making the poem a bittersweet yet ultimately refreshing mix of affection, illusion, irony, and resigned acceptance of tawdriness (Buenaventura 209–10). Everyday details and moments are used for subjective effects. Guzmán's most recent work, *Usted* (1986), is a sustained narrative based on the plot of a woman student's affair with her professor. It makes telling use of detail to reflect attitudes and psychological insights. The work takes a contemporary outlook (with feminist dimensions), which exemplifies the new consciousness of Spain's younger generations.

José Angel Cilleruelo's setting is also a modern city, though the mood and tones of his work are totally different from Guzmán's. The locale of his work comes across as impersonal, forbidding; it may be based on his native Barcelona. Most frequently, his poems portray tawdry sexual encounters, mercenary affairs, and an atmosphere of alienation. This setting motivates an almost romantic sense of isolation and dislocation, though presented in a contemporary perspective and a carefully crafted language that make it all the more effective.

In "Canción triste de cabaret" ("Sad Cabaret Song"), for example, a woman's offer of a one-night stand contrasts with the speaker's search for lasting love (Cilleruelo 48). The contrast between the two attitudes is intensified by the speaker's use of traditionally romantic phrases: "Nos besamos sobre la ciudad encendida" {"We kissed over the lit-up city"}; "los labios que habían sido míos eternamente" {"the lips that had been forever mine"}. Most of Cilleruelo's poems are constructed as narratives; their impact, however, comes from carefully selected words, images, and tone shifts, confirming the author's linguistic virtuosity and precision. In several recent texts titled "Versillos de amigo" ("Little Poems of the Friend"), Cilleruelo adopts the form and dramatic stance of medieval popular verse, adding modern ironic twists (ibid. 127–28). (Some of Cilleruelo's early poems contain verbal play reminiscent of the vanguard, such as a text that repeats, fragments, and rearranges on the page one single name, Mercedes.)

Behind the alienating view of the city and its relationships lies a larger, and effectively understated, lament for the erosion of love and life. In "Cuerpo de nadie" ("Nobody's Body") the speaker asks if love is no more than money or a gift lost two stops back on a bus, and life no more than the coffee shared by two people after a casual encounter (Cilleruelo 111). Taken as a whole, Cilleruelo's poetry compellingly reflects the vacuity of postmodern settings and outlooks.[18]

A parallel sense of the world is present in the poetry of Fanny Rubio, though it is expressed in very different ways. A prominent critic, prose writer, and person of letters, Rubio has written several books that stretch the genre of poetry toward fiction, as they also open it to new ways of reading. In *Acribillado amor* ("Riddled Love," 1970) long lines of verse mix selected and magnified details of modern life with metaphors. These poems create a sense of discomfort and alienation characteristic of the last decades. A similarly critical view underlies much of *Retracciones* ("Retractions," 1981), but this book expresses a wider range of moods in a great variety of forms, ranging from short, almost traditional-type lyrics to prose poems. Rubio also introduces different speakers—most notably Lot's wife, embodying rebellion against cruel destruction—echoes of historical situations and texts, and evocations of artists and writers. Her compellingly lyrical homage to Picasso catches the dynamic quality of his art, its way of reflecting action and life in a stroke or two:

> Aquí su mano expande rítmica.
> Palpita incorporando la materia.
> Aquí su línea avanza, surca espacios,
> se crece la mirada donde ordena.
>   [Rubio 1989, 35]

{Here his hand rhythmically expands; it palpitates incorporating matter. Here his line advances, cuts through space, and the gaze grows where he ordains.}

Reverso (1988) is more uniformly narrative, consisting of prose evocations of situations, both contemporary and historical. The pedantry of academia, the monotony of daily life, and the pathetic loss of ideals in our world are dramatically reflected in details and images: love is motivated by a commercial perfume, the modern version of an epic is a sterile boxed-in existence in sordid routines.

In *Dresde* (1990) Rubio goes back to more varied forms. The unifying thread is the German city, famous for the arts and reduced to rubble in World War II, here a background image for disintegration and human suffering. The texts include prose vignettes, in one of which the speaker, a modern tourist with a Nikon camera, juggles flash images of executions and corpses; succinct poetic sketches, whose precise visual images reflect feelings; and longer lyrics, which generally produce negative moods. The variety of points of view, and the open way in which many texts end, recall (and conform to) Rubio's view of her art as "una *manera* de mirar y ser vista en un juego de espejos, a la manera borgiana o cervantina" (Ugalde 1991, 129) {"a *manner* of seeing and being seen in a game of mirrors, in the manner of Borges or Cervantes"}. This fits Rubio's art, and its author, in the indeterminacy of the new Spain and of the postmodern era.[19]

A few younger poets composed, in the last decade or so, poems that recall surrealism in their way of expressing subconscious states of emotion. Julio Llamazares's work can be best described as poetic prose: in clusters (or long lines?) of one or two sentences, it unfolds sensations, vignettes, and comments that create complex, often irrational moods. Description, sensation, and metaphor combine. At times this procedure forcefully conveys a rich mix of feelings. Llamazares has discussed, in a statement of poetics, the relationship between beauty and horror in art, and its way of reflecting an attraction that "the abyss" holds for humanity (Villena 1986b, 36). This attitude, also reminiscent of some surrealist writings, provides useful background to his work, which includes *La lentitud de los bueyes* ("The Slowness of Oxen," 1979) and *Memoria de la nieve* ("Memory of Snow," 1982).

Blanca Andreu's poetry has produced great impact in Spain since the appearance of *De una niña de provincias que se vino a vivir en un Chagall* ("About a Girl from the Provinces Who Came to Live in a Chagall," 1981), which won the 1980 Adonais Prize. Written in long passages of free verse, its poems unfold a luxuriant view of elemental love and life impulses, blending into morbid apprehensions of death and destruction. Visionary metaphors and *visiones*—in Bousoño's sense of irrational correlatives for states of emotion—are presented, often in parallel phrases that retard the flow of a sentence, and of an idea, and leave the reader contemplating a list of images and effects. As in the earlier poetry of Vicente Aleixandre, this style foregrounds effect over concept and organizes images into clusters of feeling:

> Amor mío de nunca, afiebrado y pacífico,
> versos para el pequeño pulpo de la muerte,
> versos para la muerte rara que hace la travesía de los teléfonos,
> para mi mente debelada versos, para el circuito del violín,
> para el circuito de la garza gaviota,
> para el confín del sur, del sueño,
> versos que no me asilen ni sean causa de vida,
> que no me den la dulce serpiente umbilical
> ni la sala glucosa del útero.
> Amor mío, amor mío, mira mi boca de vitriolo
> y mi garganta de cicuta jónica,
> mira la perdiz de ala rota de carece de casa y muere
> mira los desiertos del tomillo de Rimbaud,
>
> [Andreu 14–15]

{My love of nevermore, feverish and peaceful, verses for the small octopus of death, verses for the strange death that travels through telephones, for my conquered mind, verses, for the violin's circuit, for the circuit of the bluish seagull, for the limits of the south, of dreams, verses that shall not isolate me nor be cause of life, that give me not the sweet umbilical serpent nor the glucose chamber of the uterus. My love, my love, look at my vitriol mouth, and my throat of Ionic hemlock, look at the partridge of broken wing that lacks a home and dies, at the thyme deserts of Rimbaud,}

Both thematically and stylistically, the book thus recalls a line of poetry traceable back to Aleixandre, Neruda, and the whole surrealist vein. It adds a number of contemporary referents, including drugs, which combine with more traditional literary and artistic allusions. Certain images—doves and other birds, day and night, spring and fall, and, prominently, horses—help unify the book, as it molds together a world of irrational fears and impulses and converts it into aesthetic effect. Cosmic imagery creates, at times, a sense of rare beauty. The book's impact on readers and poets suggests a yearning for a new kind of lyrically expressive verse that relates to contemporary feelings.

Quite often in Andreu's work, as in the passage quoted above, an explicit awareness of the poetic process accompanies a consciousness of love's and life's irrational ebbs and flows. Poetic expression offers both a reflection of the irrational and illusive nature of reality and a way of imparting some meaning to that reality.

In *Báculo de Babel* ("Babel's Cane," 1982) a similar view of existence is engendered in an even more flowing style, that for the most part opens into long sentences of poetic prose. Occasional references connect a tragic sense of life to the alienation of the speaker's time and generation. Poetry is often seen as a means of configuring life's mysteries. Then, in *Elphistone* (1988), the mysterious transcendence of poetic expression is foregrounded even more. The poet seeks to recover the lost language of the mythical protagonist while expressing an emotive outlook on reality. We find in this book more concentrated texts, usually using somewhat shorter lines and structural patterns similar to those of *De una niña*.

Luisa Castro, one of the youngest poets mentioned here, constructs a tragic mood of love through effective irrational imagery. A great variety of verse forms and linguistic registers gives impact and originality to her work. Castro combines chillingly prosaic elements with mythic ones and makes frequent use of visionary metaphors. In diverse fashions, she organizes her referents, including common objects, to cause maximum effect, and makes reality into eerie fantasy: ships attack women, bulls fall from the sky, trunks cry, bodies become boxes. Love is seen as a primitive force, and life, often, as a violently unpleasant existence. To my mind, Castro's most impressive book is *Los versos del eunuco* ("The Eunuch's Verses," 1986), for which she obtained the Hiperión Prize. Others include *Odisea definitiva, libro póstumo* ("Definitive Odyssey, Posthumous Book," 1984) and, most recently, *Los hábitos del artillero* ("The Artilleryman's Habits," 1990).

Also impressive is the poetry of Amalia Iglesias, who presents elemental views of physical love in long lines of verse. The style and syntax may recall Andreu, though Iglesias's poems are more dynamic, as well as somewhat more uniform, perhaps more routine. Her *Un lugar para el fuego* ("A Place for Fire," 1985) obtained the Adonais Prize.

From Expression to Satire, Irony, and Subversion

Ana Rossetti, one of the most impressive poets to emerge in the 1980s, is difficult to classify: her work ranges from sensual decorativeness to ironic subversion. Yet that range, aside from giving her poetry value, helps characterize the period. Rossetti's *Los devaneos de Erato* ("Erato's Deliriums," 1980) abounds in sensual portrayals of erotic love. It makes use of literary allusions, of elaborate imagery (flowers are most prominent), and of a carefully selected vocabulary that both alludes to and stylizes physical features. Critics have likened this poetry to Luis Antonio Villena's, and it could be related to a tradition going back to Darío.

This sensual world is shaded and balanced, however, by pragmatic and ironic notes. A play of perspectives develops when a grandmother's advice on sexuality is undercut by her own images (Rossetti 30–31). Vignettes of a sexually aroused seminarian and the homosexual reminiscences of the persona's husband situate erotic sensuality in a contemporary (and comic) context. And what is presented as a mythic view of Cybele among sensual flowers is ironically balanced by the awareness that the referent is a statue in front of the Madrid post office (ibid. 27; see Ugalde 1991, 156). The result is an ambiguous (may we say postmodern?) world, in which intense sensuality coexists with its parody.

Rossetti's *Dioscuros* (1982) is a tighter and more cohesive book. Sensual and sexual imagery is blended with historic and literary references (sometimes to the France of the belle époque). Speakers again vary, point of view is carefully controlled, and poems are sharper (often also shorter). Then, in *Devocionario* ("Devocionary," 1986), Rossetti uses mostly liturgical and religious scenes and images to produce a variety of sensual experiences. We must keep in mind that this echoes a long tradition going back to the mystics, though for Rossetti the liturgical is a vehicle for the sensory.[20]

Indicios vehementes ("Vehement Signs," 1985) is more heterogeneous, though centered, as the title and the explanation make clear, on scenes that reflect hidden moods and fears. It includes an evocation of night as both beautiful and tragic, a suicide's desolation, several perspectives on time and death. A few poems have literary intertexts: one, "Chico Wrangler," seems especially important, even though it may not be representative of the whole volume:

> Dulce corazón mío de súbito asaltado.
> Todo por adorar más de lo permisible.
> Todo porque un cigarro se asienta en una boca
> y en sus jogosas sedas se humedece.
> Porque una camiseta incitante señala,
> de su pecho, el escudo durísimo,
> y un vigoroso brazo de la mínima manga sobresale.
> Todo porque unas piernas, unas perfectas piernas,
> dentro del más ceñido pantalón, frente a mí se separan.
> Se separan. [Rossetti 99]

{Sweet heart of mine, suddenly assaulted. And all because I adored more than is permitted. All because a cigarette sits in a mouth, and moistens gradually in its silkiness. Because a provocative undershirt marks the very sharp shield of his chest, and a strong arm protrudes from the slight sleeve. All because a pair of legs, of perfect legs, inside the tightest pants, spread out before me. They spread out before me.}

The first line could have appeared in a sentimental poem, recalling the emotional, clichéd language a *poetisa* might use. Then the rest of the work denies any such perspective. By line 3 it is obvious that the speaker lusts, in primitive fashion, after a stereotypical male figure. The description alludes in detail to a specific advertisement for Wrangler jeans. Yet its particulars also emphasize the speaker's blatant desire.

An understanding of this text's meaning and effect requires some attention to its context, and specifically to poetic conventions. "Chico Wrangler" is, basically, an upside-down version of a *carpe diem* poem. Rossetti has inverted (and hence subverted) a traditional situation in which a male speaker desires a female. The subversion is accented by the modern elements: the protagonist is the subject of modern advertising, not an idealized shepherd; the woman is a down-to-earth female, not a damsel in distress. Ultimately, this poem turns the tables on a conventional male-female relationship in poetry and hence forces us to reassess our reading habits. Anyone shocked by it will have to consider why he or she was not shocked by Lorca's "Ballad of the Unfaithful Wife" or by poems of Neruda, Paz, Góngora, Quevedo, in which a male speaker desired a female.

We might note that this text, and others like it, leave much to the reader, whose response to the speaker can take several forms—the amused smile of the feminist, the surprised discovery of some traditional readers, even the irritation of a sexist male. A very determined perspective has created an open, and in that sense postmodern, text. Similar readings can be offered of Rossetti's "Calvin Klein, Underdrawers" (Buenaventura 68) and of several ironic poems from her earlier books; all make clear an important dimension of her work. They may also suggest that multiple responses, governed by the reader's background and point of view, are most often triggered by texts that undermine established traditions and conventions.

Similarly subversive is Amparo Amorós's *Quevediana* (1988), which at first glance may surprise the readers of her serious, metaphysical poetry. Composed of a series of sonnets playing off specific Quevedo texts, this work satirizes diverse Spanish scenes and types: a literary gathering, a masochistic boyfriend, an arrogant critic, an advice columnist. In "Soneto burlesco a un Apolo para necias acaloradas" ("Burlesque Sonnet to an Apollo, for Passionate Dumb Girls") Amorós twists Quevedo's poem beginning "Erase un hombre a una nariz pegado" {"There was a man stuck on to a nose"}, starting hers "Erase un hombre a un pito atornillado" {"There was a man screwed on to a prick"}. Quevedo's succeeding images are also shockingly redone, one by one: at the end, the speaker, presumably the "passionate dumb girl" of the title, expresses a crude sexual desire (Amorós 1992, 224). The poem is a parody on several levels, of several discourses and conventions: of Quevedo's text, of the common reading of that text as sexual innuendo, of sexually allusive poetry in general, and perhaps even of contemporary sexually allusive poetry by women (such as Rossetti), and of the whole environment of explicit writing. Therefore this poem, too, can elicit several readings and operates as a stimulus to readers' responses more than as a set of meanings.

It may seem misleading to call Andrea Luca's poetry subversive. Beginning with *En el banquete* ("At the Banquet," 1987), Luca uses elegant and precise language to construct beautiful visions of love, of basic life patterns, and of a human search for intensity and beauty. Luca blends mythic and artistic references with sensual images and works them into narrative sequences. In the very important *El don de Lilith* ("Lilith's Gift," 1990), however, this style is used to build a sustained myth around the biblical figure of Lilith, described as a female figure alternate, and opposite, to Eve. Identified as Adam's first wife, who left him in search of independence, Lilith embodies woman's quest for freedom from man's domination. She also reflects an awareness of life's darker forces and a quest for an ideal androgynous identity. Potent images dramatize different dimensions of woman's fate and goal. Lilith originates from primitive earth; she is not, like Eve, a "costilla maltratada / desenganchado eslabón de la osamenta" (Luca 13) {"mistreated rib, disconnected section of bone"}. She sees herself mythically sailing within the flow of cosmic nature (ibid. 26). Her story, and Luca's work, add a significant dimension—poetic and feminist—to contemporary Spanish literature.[21]

As we have already seen, the expressive poetry written in Spain since the late 1970s often contains a significant ironic thread. In Angel González's *Prosemas o menos,* an ironic mode consistently modifies romantic outlooks and balances lyrical attitudes with more detached ones, leading to a complex view. Luis García Montero uses irony as a foil to nostalgia and as a way of casting a new, critical look at the way classical poets handled traditional themes. For Leopoldo Sánchez Torres, Alvaro García, and Vicente Gallego, ironic tones help express feelings without risking naïveté—much as they did in the earlier work of González and Gil de Biedma, which these younger poets read attentively. And irony fits one prevailing poetic stance of the times, in which the prior decade's intense search for new discourses has been replaced by a complex, lower-key exploration of many issues of life.

Other poets, however, use irony and satire in more dramatic ways, again shedding light on a mood of the times. Luis Alberto de Cuenca, whose earlier poetry had illustrated so well the elaborate linguistic creativity and the foregrounding of verbal effect over referent of *novísimo* writing, includes in *La caja de plata* ("Silver Box," 1985) a unit titled "Serie negra" ("Black Series"), in which sketches resembling sick jokes suggest a gloomy, perhaps desperate, view of life. One text offers brutal advice to a rape victim, and others reflect the shocking outlooks of murderers and a potential rapist. The book also contains a satirical pastiche in sonnet form that combines a classical reference, echoes of a Bogart movie, and a contemporary allusion (Cuenca 126–27).

In *El otro sueño* ("The Other Dream," 1987) Cuenca includes a series of satirical sonnets undermining love and poetic conventions. In "Soneto del amor atómico" ("Sonnet of Atomic Love") a consistent pattern of nuclear war vocabulary ("fission," "bombing," "mined," "missiles," "blown up," etc.) casts ironic light on the genre of conventional love poetry (Cuenca 155). The effect is intensified by what seem to be echoes of a sonnet of Sor Juana Inés de la Cruz: her "no te atormenten más celos tiranos" {"may tyrant jealousies torment you no more"} becomes "no más fisión, amor, no más ojivas" {"no more fission, my love, no more ogives"}.[22] "Cesen con tu victoria los enojos" {"may your anger cease with your victory"} recasts the discourse of baroque poetry in the new atomic context. This produces multiple effects: it makes the conventions of a love sonnet seem humorously stilted, the new poem and its speaker ludicrous, and our whole contemporary world and language trite and debased. Another sonnet of the series creates similar effects by applying baroque syntax and structure to a modern episode in which the "beloved" takes away the speaker's wallet. And the *ubi sunt* convention of medieval verse is parodied in a metapoetic text.

Most interestingly, perhaps, these poems make us step back and contemplate the issue of levels of discourse, their relationships, their possibilities and limitations. Jaime Siles's *Semáforos, semáforos* (1989), already mentioned above, has the same effect. The title poem juxtaposes a modern anecdote—a woman crossing a street by a traffic signal—to a semiotic exploration (Siles 1992, 275–78). Other works mix contemporary language and referents with various literary and traditional echoes. These poems by Siles and Cuenca, and some others that we will see later, invite us to view critically verbal expression and its relationship to human life and communication. Rather than foreground artistic creation, as did the highly aesthetic texts of the 1970s, they invite us to contemplate how we speak, write, and live. Yet this contemplation remains playful and low-key; it does not invite a search for grand discoveries or for a new aesthetics (on the waning of rigor in this decade, see Mayhew 1992, 408–11).

A great sensitivity to levels and forms of discourse underlies the work of Jon Juaristi, one of the major poets of the decade.[23] By juggling diverse levels of expression, allusion, and human experience, Juaristi produces surprising and disquieting perceptions on various topics. The title of his *Diario del poeta recién cansado* ("Diary of the Newly Tired Poet," 1985) echoes a romantic one of Juan Ramón Jiménez but turns it into a whimsically prosaic, laid-back outlook, which leads us perfectly into its complex view of

life. Different voices, tones, and rhythmic patterns express different atti-
tudes ranging from melancholy to savage irony: poems are cast as sermons,
as nostalgic lyrics, as definitions and descriptions, as versions of other
poems. Visual and sensory images and details catch moods precisely: thus
greasy napkins and the smell of mustard convey the debasement of a city,
and of a society.

Literary and social satire combine masterfully in "La casada infiel"
("The Faithless Wife"), based on the Lorca ballad of the same title. Its
speaker repeats lines in which Lorca's gypsy protagonist had described his
discovery that the woman was married and his decision to give her a gift and
leave her, rather than to fall in love. But Juaristi converts the speaker from
a gypsy into a Basque, turns the husband into a Basque partisan, and
changes the gift from a basket into the Basque flag (the famous *icurriña*).
With this switch he produces an incongruous mixture of topics and tones
and a savagely funny poem, parodying the mannered stylization of the Lorca
ballad on the one hand, and the whole world of Basque extremism on the
other (Juaristi 1986, 32). Juaristi's identity as a Basque who is proud of his
origin but bitterly opposed to the terrorist revolution is obviously linked to
some of the tones in his poetry.

A caustic pessimism, expressed through different levels of satire, per-
vades *Suma de varia intención* ("Sum of Diverse Intentions," 1987), one of the
most chilling and impressive volumes of poetry of the decade. Form, image,
and point of view are precisely controlled, as we can see in "Barbara":

> Vuelvo a leer tus cartas de hace un siglo,
> de cuando estaba en el cuartel, ¿recuerdas?
> o en la trena, mi amor, no exactamente
> en la Cárcel de Amor, o en las terribles
> provincias que he olvidado. Amarillean
> los sobres de hilo, corazón. Los sellos
> habrán cobrado algún valor. No en vano
> oro es el tiempo de la filatelia.
> Me hablas de tu fractura de escafoides,
> de tu dolor de muelas, de tu perro,
> de lo mal que lo pasas en agosto,
> de una excursión a Andorra . . . Poco a poco,
> me has vuelto desabrida la nostalgia:
> mi dulce bien, no me quisiste nunca. [Juaristi 1987, 14]

{I read again your letters of a century ago, when I was in the barracks, do you recall?
Or in jail, my love, not exactly in the Cárcel d'Amore, or in the awful provinces that I
have forgotten. The linen envelopes are yellowed. The stamps must have gained some
value. Not in vain is time the gold of stamp-collecting. You speak of your broken hand,
your toothache, your dog, how badly off you are in August, a trip to Andorra . . . Little
by little, you have made insipid my nostalgia: my sweetheart, you never loved me.}

The sonnet form, the conventions of love letters, and even the setting of a romantic rereading of old letters are ironically undermined by the triviality of the matters described, the speaker's literalistic materialism, and the awareness that there was no real illusion in this affair. Echoes of the conventions of love poems—the rhythmically perfect sonnet, the yellowed letters, the phrase "hace un siglo," the form of address "mi dulce bien"—play off against the prosaic facts and attitudes. The end result, for me, is a very telling and serious perception of how the ideals and conventions of a major aspect of life can be absent, or hollow, and a picture of a depressing prosaic world.

Other poems in the book make us feel other limitations of common lives, often from unusual angles: one speaker describes the boring complaints of those who lost the Civil War; another tells how his listening to his lover reading a Gil de Biedma poem gave him a clue to put on his clothes and flee from her. Several poems narrate experiences in poems parodying Vallejo, Martí, and others. A series of texts offers sketches and moods of Mexico; a two-line satire twists a Barthes title; a poem plays with several works by Lope mixed in with contemporary allusions.

Juaristi's *Arte de marear* ("The Art of Causing Seasickness," 1988) also adopts various points of view and tones, ranging from light to heavy: we laugh when Diderot writes his *Encyclopédie* as a consequence of having eaten bad cheese. We respond emotively to several excellent elegiac texts and to a poem that demonstrates an extremely creative and skillful use of Spanish while overtly deprecating the language.[24]

Humor also plays an important part in the poetry of Carlos Marzal, which consistently undercuts traditionally lyric topics, often through parodic echoes of poetic commonplaces. Marzal uses an unusual and successful blend of regular rhythms and colloquial vocabulary to produce a smooth, easy to read, but never facile work. Surprising images and humorous notes also produce sharp insights into modern reality in the poetry of Justo Navarro. Meanwhile Angel Muñoz Petisme mixes contemporary (often explicitly sexual) references, learned echoes, and a mixture of tones to construct an unsettling and often debased world.

It is impossible to encompass, in a few concluding sentences, poems as different as those of Juaristi, Luca, Rossetti, and the other poets I have mentioned here. Yet the wide range of tones and outlooks, coupled with many different ways of modifying and undermining traditional attitudes, conventions, and texts, reveals a will to explore, question, and rephrase all aspects of life. This makes the stylistically "continuist" decade of the 1980s in Spanish poetry both innovative and exciting.

Conclusion

Placing twentieth-century Spanish poetry in the context of European modernism helps clarify some of the principles and goals that underlie it. It also sheds new light on the poems themselves and on their impact.

A view that grew out of symbolist poetics, and that defined a poem as the verbal embodiment of complex, unexplainable experiences, undergirded Spanish verse in the first decades of the century. It helps us understand texts by authors as different as Antonio Machado and Juan Ramón Jiménez and provides a telling context for major books that writers of the Generation of 1927—Federico García Lorca, Jorge Guillén, Pedro Salinas, Rafael Alberti, Vicente Aleixandre, and others—published during the 1920s. It also lets us see the coherence of verse written throughout the first third of the century by poets of diverse ages, and the implications of different stylistic features—structure, imagery, rhythmic effects—prevalent during this time.

Several avant-garde strands formed a less objectivist aesthetic current and undercut, to some extent, the canon of high modernity. They help explain a strain of indeterminacy in a few important authors and works of the 1920s. And they suggest some relationships between vanguard theories and the mood and goal shifts occurring during the 1930s, without negating the continuation of a dominant modernist poetics.

As the 1930s went on, however, significant changes occurred within the modernist aesthetic and presaged even more fundamental developments later. The view of a poem as "verbal icon" and the quest for "pure poetry" were left behind; new forms of expression were coupled with new themes, ranging from unsatisfied love and the alienating effects of the city to a religious questioning. An emphasis on subjective values brought with it a renewed interest in surrealist techniques (though coupled, often, with a rejection of surrealist doctrine): these underlay important new books by Alberti, García Lorca, Aleixandre, and Miguel Hernández. A new generation of poets, best exemplified by Luis Rosales, introduced new ways of turning personal referents into poetry. Finally, socially committed works appeared, as Spain became immersed in the struggles that culminated in the Civil War.

The Civil War and its aftermath marked an obvious (and well-recognized) impoverishment both in poetic production and in thought about poetry. Then, from the mid-1940s on, a realistic poetics and the desire to address immediate issues led to much thematically innovative but formally unchallenging verse. They also delayed the possibility of a more creative evolution in modernist poetics. Yet a few compelling books of poetry were written in the 1940s. Some of them, most notably Alonso's *Hijos de la ira* and several works by Blas de Otero and José Hierro, introduced new styles and new ways of addressing the reader. Meanwhile émigré Spanish authors published some important poetry within the modernist aesthetic.

Thus the realistic poetry and poetics of the 1940s and 1950s seem, from today's perspective and in the light of the development of modernity, less revolutionary than they appeared in their time. The outlooks of younger poets who emerged in the late 1950s, however, now appear important and profoundly innovative. The view of the poem as an evolving process and as a means of discovery, cogently presented by José Angel Valente, Carlos Barral, and others, directed Spanish verse past notions that had been dominant since the advent of modernity. This suggests that we might consider this period the beginning of a new postmodern era.

At the same time important works, written by both younger and older authors, opened new possibilities for Spanish verse. The artistic and original use of everyday language and referents produced poems ranging from the complex and ironic (Angel González, Jaime Gil de Biedma) to the lyrically testimonial (Claudio Rodríguez, José Hierro, Carlos Bousoño). Major books, reflecting new currents, were also written by Jorge Guillén and Vicente Aleixandre. Centered on the goal of reflecting personal experience in verse, the poetry of the late 1950s and the 1960s retained greater connections to the traditions of modernity than did the new concepts of poetics, yet also represented a significantly innovative impulse.

The appearance of a group that was labeled the *novísimos* signaled the emergence of a new aestheticism in the late 1960s. Leaving behind the aim of communicating personal experience, the new poets focused instead on the world of the arts. The views of literary and artistic texts as correlatives for life on the one hand, and vehicles for evasion from literal reality on the other, contributed to the creation of brilliant new works by Guillermo Carnero, Pere Gimferrer, and others. Meanwhile, a tendency to consider form and sign apart from the realities to which they would refer led Jaime Siles and others to a new essentialist poetics and poetry. And most important, works written during the next decade by established older poets signaled a dramatic shift to formal concerns and to self-referentiality. All of this situates this period within several definitions of postmodernity and supports the view that a historically major shift was taking place.

Poetry written in Spain during the 1980s seems less linguistically innovative and also harder to define. The previous stress on verbal creativity and on self-reflexivity gave way to several currents of expressive writing. Spare, essentialist verse was exemplified by new books of Siles, María Victoria Atencia, Amparo Amorós, and others. A poetry of experience and discovery, recalling to some extent the 1950s and 1960s, included work by both new and established writers, by women as well as men. Thematically, however, the poetry of this decade opened important new directions. Most telling, perhaps, is a subversive critique of traditional topics and outlooks, represented by Ana Rossetti, Amparo Amorós, and Jon Juaristi, among others.

A look back at Spanish poetry and poetics since 1915 or so reveals an exciting trajectory. It began at the high point of modernity, marked by an idealistic poetics based on symbolist tenets and by the appearance of masterpieces that parallel, to my mind, the great works of the Golden Age. The evolution of goals and forms of expression toward greater subjectivity and relativity in the 1930s presaged a transition, interrupted and affected by the Civil War, that became most evident from the late 1950s on: it led to new notions of literature that moved Spain beyond the main principles and goals of modernity. Most important, however, it was accompanied by the composition and publication of outstandingly original poems and books of poetry, that both captured the issues and concerns of their world and time and extended their readers' experiences beyond their literal boundaries.

This suggests, in turn, that Spain is in the early stages of a new era, one no longer bound within the logocentric premises of symbolist modernity. The new roles of text and reader, and the relationships between them, are just becoming defined; at the same time, a rich variety of poems is casting new light on the issues and problems that confront Spain at a crucial moment of its history. The increase in poetic production and readership, and the spread of magazines and presses throughout the peninsula, is accompanied by admiration and strong private and public support for the genre. The expectation that poetry will play an even greater role in Spanish life and experience seems amply justified.

Notes

1. The Apogee of Modernity in Spain, 1915–1928

1. The notion that the poem gives permanence to experiences by freezing them, thus stopping time, pervades the poetics of the 1920s. From our perspective today, it is interesting that Franz Roh used the term *magic realism* to define this notion as he described postexpressionism in 1927: "Para él [el post-expresionismo], lo más profundo, el motivo por el cual erige como símbolo ese mundo de cuerpos permanentes, es lo que, por persistente, se contrapone a la eterna fluidez" (285). {"For postexpressionism, the deepest goal, the reason for which this body of permanent things is constructed as symbol, is that it is persistently counterposed to eternal fleetingness."}

2. Baudelaire, "Le peintre de la vie moderne," quoted in De Man 1971, 156. De Man's essay discusses literature's "desire for modernity" as part of an impulse to capture the uniqueness of the moment—we might say of the present—much as that effort may be doomed to failure (153–57).

3. In explaining the title of his major book, *The Verbal Icon*, W.K. Wimsatt, Jr., noted that an icon was "a verbal sign which somehow shares the properties of, or resembles, the objects which it denotes" (x). The term illustrates the modernist and New Critical conception of the poem as a stable correlative for specific meanings and experiences. It connects with the notion of the work as "concrete universal"—this is the title of one of the chapters of Wimsatt's book—as embodiment in form of specific, complex experiences.

4. The best summary of prevalent definitions of *modernismo* can be found in chapter 2 of Ned J. Davison's *Concept of Modernism in Hispanic Criticism*. That chapter makes clear how influential critics from Alberto Zum Felde to Max Henríquez Ureña and Federico de Onís, while contradicting each other in various respects, all helped establish a narrow view of the term. This, from my point of view, isolated the historiography of Hispanic literature from that of other Western literatures.

5. Ezra Pound defined the imagist image thus: "An image is that which presents an intellectual and emotional complex in an instant of time" ("A Retrospect" [1918], quoted in Bradbury and McFarlane 48). This view is clearly parallel to the symbolist conception of the poem as embodying a timeless immediacy.

6. It bears remembering that Spain had a rather small intellectual elite, comprising both career writers and middle-class professionals interested in art and letters (see Blanch 32). As a result, important works, cultural events, and trends had a significant effect.

7. Ortega has been generally classified within a Generation of the 1900s (*novecentismo*) also called the "Generation of 1914," following the more Spain-centered Generation of 1898 and laying the groundwork for the more stylistically innovative Generation of 1927 (Díaz Plaja 1975, chap. 2). So detailed a scheme can be questioned, as I will indicate later. What is important is a larger point: Ortega (born in 1883) and some of his contemporaries championed an opening of Spain to Europe that was continued by younger writers.

8. This view seems contradicted by Machado's own negative view of symbolist poetry, which he deemed excessively concerned with beauty and egotistically lacking in concern for the reader and for coherence of thought (see Castellet 1960, 52–54). I would argue that this merely indicates Machado's lack of insight into the essential goals of modernism; he took elegance of expression to be a driving principle, rather than a by-product of its poetics. Castellet does make an important point in noting Machado's effective use of everyday language; for me, this usage occurs within a modernist framework of verbally configuring timeless values.

9. For a discussion of the complexities of Machado's posture and of the limitations of studies that have tried to reduce them, see Silver 1985, 49–73.

10. To remove this issue from biography and "real author" intentions, we might say that the voice we hear in these poems, or the implied author behind them, has selected discernible patterns of language and form, suggestive of the belief that these produce given correspondences and effects.

11. The affinities between Bécquer and Juan Ramón are convincingly explained by Ciplijauskaité (1966, 182–84), who suggests that Juan Ramón saw in Bécquer the first Spanish symbolist.

12. Silver's perceptive study of this poetry corrects a tendency to see it, biographically, as an egotistic battle for survival; written within our post-structuralist tradition, it also hints at the impossibility of Juan Ramón's (and symbolism's) quest.

13. John C. Wilcox has explored the possibility of reading Juan Ramón's work from both modern and postmodern perspectives; the latter often stress the inadequacy and impossibility of the poetic goals I have described, and hence the crumbling of the modernist ideals. As historians, however, we must remember that the modern persona would have been dominant for 1920s readers, even as the postmodern one attracts us today.

14. Marías (97–98, 169–78) sees a new generation emerging every fifteen years; Arrom (15–20, 223 ff.) spaces generations thirty years apart (with possible subdivisions). Most critics label generations by the median year in which their members reach age thirty. (Hence the Generation of 1927 would include those whose birth dates range, approximately, between 1893 and 1907.) Regardless of the scheme one adopts, it should be used with some reason, regularity, flexibility, and common sense. Critics who arbitrarily create multiple generations at erratic intervals render the method shallow and suspect.

In my opinion, a variant of Arrom's scheme is most useful. A clear distinction in worldview and attitude exists between members of the Generation of 1898, such as Machado, Unamuno, and the younger writers of the Generation of 1927. Those born in between, such as Ortega and Juan Ramón Jiménez, might form a second "wave" of 1898, changing their elders' preoccupation with Spain to a more universal and philosophical outlook. In Marías's scheme, they would form a whole intervening generation of the 1900s or of 1914. Using strict chronological ages, such a generation would also include two writers generally associated with the Generation of 1927, Jorge Guillén and Pedro Salinas. They do reveal, in their essays, some traits justifying their inclusion in the earlier group or their characterization as transitional between 1914 and 1927 generations. Ultimately, however, the very definition of a separate Generation of 1914, and Marías's more fragmentary scheme in general, seem to me less useful than Arrom's broader pattern, which allows us to see clearly the pervasive high modernist aesthetic linking Ortega, Guillén, Lorca, and others.

Since poets generally create significant work at an early age, I would pay particular attention to the outlook and production of those in their twenties and thirties (whereas Marías makes writers into dominant generations when they range from forty-five to sixty). Thus, for me, the Generation of 1927 gains prominence and plays a guiding role through the 1920s and 1930s: this is confirmed by many of its major works (see Debicki 1981, 52–68). Hence its poetics as expressed in this era will give us the best clues about the dominant aesthetic outlooks. It will become a guide for poets of different ages. Thus the poetry actually written both by members of this generation and by older writers will correspond, in general terms, to this poetic.

We will see a similar pattern repeated with later generations. As a new poetic outlook emerges, introduced usually (but not always, and not exclusively) by a new generation, it will affect the work of poets of different ages. (Poems written by "1927" authors in the 1950s, for example, will reveal the effects of the poetics of that time.) For this reason, I have tended to organize my discussion of the poetics and attitudes of a given period around the ideas of the emerging generation and then relate them to the actual poetry written during the period by authors of diverse ages. A careful and sensible discussion of generations among contemporary poets can be found in García Martín 1980, 13–33.

15. Juan Ramón also once telegraphed Guillén, stating that he withdrew his contribution to Guillén's journal, and also his friendship.

16. Most interesting in this respect is Guillén's treatise on the relationship of the work and its author, written in 1917, which espoused a view of the work's transcendence and of the need to study texts independent of their authors, prefiguring a New Critical stance. See Guillén 1990.

17. As Renato Poggioli has written, "The modern mystique of purity aspires to abolish the discursive and syntactical elements, to liberate art from any connection with psychological and empirical reality, to reduce every work to the intimate laws of its own expressive essence" (201).

18. Guillén wrote to Vela: "Como a lo puro lo llamo simple, me decido resueltamente por la poesía compuesta, compleja, por el poema con poesía y otras cosas humanas. En suma, una 'poesía pura' *ma non troppo*" (Diego 1962, 327). {"Since by pure I mean simple, I definitely choose complex, combined poetry, the poem containing poetry as well as other human things. In sum, a 'pure poetry,' but not too much."} He also rejected the notion that poetry requires a special idiom: "Poetry does not require any special poetic language. No word is excluded in advance. . . . The word 'rose' is no more poetic than the word 'politics' " (Guillén 1961, 214).

The debate concerning pure poetry and the stance of Guillén and other Spanish poets are well described in Blanch 198–204, 284–303. Concha Zardoya's extensive study on the relationship of Guillén's work and ideas to Valéry's is most important; see Zardoya 1974, 2: 169–219.

19. *Cántico* grew organically, as the poet added to the volume most of the poems he wrote in the decades of the 1920s, 1930s, and 1940s; the first edition (Madrid: Revista de Occidente, 1928) contained 75 poems, the second (Madrid: Cruz y Raya, 1936) 125, the third (Mexico City: Litoral, 1945) 270, and succeeding ones 334. Many of the poems that became part of the first *Cántico* had been published in earlier versions in *La Pluma* and the *Revista de Occidente* in the early and mid-1920s; see Debicki 1973, 197–216.

20. Claude Vigée has suggested that Guillén takes a characteristic of symbolist poetry one step further, as he transcends an individualized "I" and captures basic human patterns in concrete fashion.

21. Much of Lorca's poetry was published well after its composition, but many of his poems had been read publicly, had circulated, and had appeared in journals. For a succinct description of this issue, see Díez de Revenga 162–66.

22. Dámaso Alonso, in a 1927 essay, used the mythical episode of Scylla and Charybdis to highlight the double line, learned and popular, of the most significant Spanish poetry (Alonso 1960, 11–28). His outlook and this essay would be both influential for and representative of the Generation of 1927.

23. Two additional figures should be mentioned within this generation. Juan José Domenchina, born in 1898, will probably be best remembered as critic, chronicler, and anthologist; his abundant verse traces a path from a rather prosaic *modernismo* to tighter, more conceptually complex poems in the 1920s and 1930s. José Bergamín (b. 1895) played an even more major role as prose writer, critic, essayist, and editor. He founded and directed the key magazine *Cruz y Raya* in the 1930s. Bergamín also wrote verse, though his poetry was only published in recent decades and hence did not form part of the production of this era.

24. This is a place-name, like many of the headings of poems in Alberti's book.

2. Currents in Spanish Modernity, 1915–1939

1. Vanguard writing may have been responding, in various ways, to industrialization and the growth of market economies (though Spain gives only limited evidence of these). It combines a fascination with technological developments with a critical, often ironic response to vulgarization and commercialization. See Geist 1992; and Cano Ballesta 1981, chaps. 3 and 4.

2. In addition to Lyotard's *Postmodern Condition* and chapter 2 of Hassan's *Paracriticisms,* the last section of Calinescu's *Five Faces of Modernity* describes well the concept of indeterminacy as a postmodern literary phenomenon. For further discussion of this issue, see chapters 4–6 below.

3. Very telling are the following excerpts from "Posibilidades creacionistas" ("Creationist Possibilities," *Cervantes,* Oct. 1919, 26–27, as quoted in Videla 109):

"Imagen triple, cuadruple, etc. Advertid como nos vamos alejando de la literatura tradicional. Estas imágenes que se presentan a varias interpretaciones. . . . El creador de imágenes no hace ya prosa disfrazada: empieza a crear por el placer de crear (poeta-creador-niño-dios). . . . La imagen debe aspirar a su definitiva liberación, a su plenitud en el último grado.

"Imagen múltiple. No explica nada; es intraducible a la prosa. Es la Poesía . . . es también la Música. . . . La música no quiere decir nada. . . . Cada uno pone su letra interior a la Música, y es letra imprecisa, varía según el estado emocional. Pues bien: con palabras podemos hacer algo muy semejante a la Música, por medio de imágenes múltiples."

{"Triple metaphor, quadruple metaphor, etc. Note how we are moving beyond traditional literature. Those metaphors that permit various interpretations. . . . The creator of images no longer produces disguised prose: he begins to create for the pleasure of creating (poet-creator-child-god). The image ought to aspire to its definitive liberation, to its plenitude in the greatest degree.

"Multiple image: it explains nothing. It cannot be translated into prose. It is Poetry . . . it is Music. . . . Music means nothing. Everyone imposes his or her own writing on Music, and it is imprecise writing; it varies according to the emotive state. Well, with words we can do something similar to Music, through multiple images."}

It is worth noting that the term *imagen* normally means "metaphor," an implied comparison between two planes. Diego clearly was using it that way, as were most vanguardists. Some Spanish critics differentiate *imagen* from *metáfora* by reserving the latter term for condensed metaphors ("the pearls of her mouth" as opposed to "her teeth were pearls"). But some vanguard writers also used *imagen* rather loosely, as Geist has noted (1980, 52).

4. The presence of indeterminacy in vanguard poetics and poetry during the 1920s supports not only Perloff's view of a second strand of modernity but also Umberto Eco's study of the presence within modernity of "open works," which allow their readers to complete their meanings (see Eco, esp. chap. 3).

5. This stance could be related to historical circumstances, above all to the fact that in Spain industrialization took place relatively late and in a less complete fashion than in other Western countries. Artistic modernity in that sense precedes a full modernization of society. It can view such modernization as a fanciful ideal, not an accomplished state.

6. Here it might be useful to take into account Paul De Man's definition of *metaphor,* which makes it a means of suspending ordinary meaning and "free[zing] hypothesis, or fiction, into fact" (1979, 150–52). For De Man, metaphor does not offer a resolution of the two planes but rather breaks the rules of reality and deliberately asserts what would normally be an "error" in order to engender a process of reading and rereading. Interestingly and paradoxically enough, Salinas's use of metaphor seems to fit this conception better than that of Gerardo Diego, whose work reveals more explicit connections and resolutions.

Carlos Bousoño's contrast between a poetic metaphor and a joke based on an implied comparison is also worth considering. For Bousoño, the two differ primarily in their effect: the metaphor motivates assent, whereas the joke motivates dissent (Bousoño 1966, 120–21, 312–23). Bousoño makes a logocentric assumption: the metaphor points to a meaning to which the reader assents. If we reject this assumption and assume that all metaphors engender play and indeterminacy, we could consider the "serious" metaphors of the 1927 poets as well as the extravagant and the consciously humorous ones of the vanguardists part of the same process.

7. Here the poem functions very much like the "enigma text" by John Ashbery discussed by Perloff, and in contrast to Eliot's *Waste Land* or, for that matter, Guillén's "Perfección" (see Perloff 8–16, 36–37). Its separate tones and levels are not orchestrated into a single attitude.

8. For the truly deconstructive critic, the indeterminacy of this text would not make it radically different from any other, including the Jiménez and Guillén poems

discussed in the previous chapter, because all language is ultimately undetermined. I would nonetheless argue that the undecidability of the Salinas poem is more evident and forces the reader to confront it more quickly and inevitably. While this may not matter so much to the literary theorist seeking ultimate definitions, it is important to me as a practical critic, interested in the experience of the reader.

9. See Stixrude; and Zardoya 1974, 2: 106–48.

10. Here we may have, in fact, the best argument for making the strand of indeterminacy of the 1920s a part of modernity, rather than a sign of incipient postmodernity: it developed an iconoclastic posture within a world (and a universe of readers) that still accepted the possibility of permanent meanings in artistic works.

11. Commenting on the surrealist manner of transcending literal reality and logic, Vela wrote: "No es por los altos caminos de la fantasía y la imaginación, sino a través de un túnel, de un subterráneo: el sueño" (429). {"It is not via the high roads of fantasy and imagination, but through a tunnel, an underground: dreams."} Later on he likened Breton's manifesto to a spiritual fertilizer, commented on the one-sidedness of the surrealist perspective, and complained that for the surrealists art seemed to be a trunk (*baúl*) that is never full because you can always throw something else into it (430–31). Despite Vela's attempt to understand surrealism, a canonical symbolist attitude limited his perspective.

12. It is worth underlining the importance of anniversaries in modern Spanish literary history. The anniversary of an author's birth or death often motivates numerous symposia and publications and, when thus exploited, can influence styles and aesthetic climates. The relatively small size of the literary establishment intensifies the effect.

13. It is important that the optimistic view of modern industry and technology of the early 1920s gave way, at this time, to a predominantly negative one (see Cano Ballesta 1981, 208 ff.).

14. A recent study by Andrew A. Anderson explains and documents Lorca's ambiguous attitude toward surrealism and shows how the poet's sympathy with the goal of expanding imaginativeness was balanced by his symbolist commitment to the discovery of poetic truths. See also García-Posada.

15. Likewise, *Espadas como labios* points to the equivalence of love and destruction. Critics have frequently noted Aleixandre's use of conjunctions to indicate equivalence rather than separation. See J.O. Jiménez 1982, 34.

Carlos Bousoño has defined the surrealist image as inevitably producing dissent in the reader (Bousoño 1979, 69–73, 145–47). Such a definition would clearly exclude Aleixandre from the category.

16. It has been compared with Eliot's *Waste Land* and to my mind is as "determined" (Young 1992). Perloff's analysis of the Eliot poem as symbolically coherent and determined could serve as a model for a study of Lorca's (13–17). But see also note 8 above; any "determinacy" is obviously relative, subject to the limitations of language and of signification.

17. Thus the appearance in the second edition of *Cántico* of texts like "Muerte a lo lejos" ("Death in the Distance") and "Los tres tiempos" ("Three Periods of Time") might support a turn to existential concerns. In general, though, this edition enriches all the aspects, moods, and perspectives of the first.

18. I find the category "Generation of 1936" questionable, especially if it is separated from a succeeding "post–Civil War generation" centered in the early 1940s.

No convincing system can account for a new generation every five to seven years. For me, a more sensible grouping would place both this group of the late 1930s and slightly younger poets emerging after the Civil War (like José Hierro and Blas de Otero) in one generation, and then differentiate their works by publication date, circumstances, theme, and other criteria. All of these poets share a renewed interest in using personal referents as bases for poetry, in creating a testimonial poetry, both artful and accessible, and in embodying subjective meanings in appropriate form.

In Marías's terms, a new generation should emerge fifteen years after 1927 or so, and therefore around 1942; it would include poets born roughly between 1908 and 1922. If we place the appearance of the prior group a little earlier (see Debicki 1981), a new phase could begin in the 1930s and extend into the 1940s. In Arrom's scheme, we would observe then the appearance of a second wave (*promoción*), modifying an earlier major shift. Any generational pattern is obviously related to, and modifiable by, historical circumstances. But the generational link between these prewar and postwar poets is, in my opinion, helpful.

19. Somewhat paradoxically, the use of personal experiences as referents, as well as the concern with the theme of time passing and the use of nature imagery to reflect emotive states, connects the work of the younger poets of this period with Machado's earlier verse, and especially with *Soledades, galerías*. This reflects, to my mind, the turn to subjective perspectives and the erosion of the drive to construct icons universalizing experience.

20. The book's planned publication in 1939 was prevented by the Republican defeat.

3. After the War, 1940–1965

1. Thus, in a poetics in issue number 2, we find: "Y que están muy bien estos versos delicados y sutiles, hechos de imágenes bellas. . . . Pero que todo eso se apaga cuando resuena la voz enérgica y poderosa que nos habla, o nos canta, o nos increpa, desde las más hondas oquedades del hombre" (García de la Concha 1987, 1: 456). {"Those subtle and delicate verses, made of beautiful images, are OK. . . . But all that fades when an energetic and powerful voice sounds, and speaks to us, or sings, or rebukes us from the depths of humanity."}

2. The introduction to Castellet's anthology was the product of discussions and insights developed among a group of writers generally linked to the school of Barcelona of the Generation of the 1950s, including Jaime Gil de Biedma, Angel González, Carlos Barral, and José Agustín Goytisolo. They started with a rather utilitarian view of poetry that their own works transcended in the 1960s.

In 1966 Seix Barral published an updated version titled *Un cuarto de siglo de poesía española*.

3. For an excellent discussion of the poetics of this period (and the succeeding one), see Rubio 1980.

4. A new, more "collective" view of poetry is implicit in the decision to use the opinions of sixty writers to select the poets to be included in the *Antología consultada*. It is dramatized by a graph, showing that the nine finally included were mentioned by 50 to more than 80 percent of those answering (Ribes 1952, 15). One could see an implicit move toward a reader-response orientation here.

5. Bousoño's essay, titled "Poesía contemporánea y poesía postcontemporánea," was written in 1961, first published in 1964, and subsequently included in *Teoría de la expresión poética* (Bousoño 1966, 533–76). It is an important document, testifying to its author's prescience, although it obviously cannot place the period in later contexts. For a critique, see García Martín 1980, 9–20.

6. For an excellent and exhaustive study of the magazines and journals of the post–Civil War period, see Rubio 1976.

7. Bousoño has reexamined the question of generations fully in his later book *Epocas literarias y evolución* and has developed useful insights regarding historical circumstances that affect the degree to which generational concerns come into play (1981, 194–203). For a different perspective, see García Martín 1980, 13–33.

As I noted in the previous chapter, many poets first gaining prominence in the 1940s, including Hierro and Otero, cannot be separated generationally from Rosales, Panero, and the other "1936" writers, though they hold somewhat different attitudes (García Martín, 32–33). Dámaso Alonso, on the other hand, belongs to an earlier generation, yet he published at this time a book that can serve as a model for new "postcontemporary" writing (see Bousoño 1966). Generational distinctions are modified and diminished by historical and social issues.

8. Unlike Hierro, I will subsume religious poetry under the "testimonial" category, since it exhibits similar goals. Hierro, in setting it up as a discrete category, might have been responding to differences that are more ideological than aesthetic.

José Olivio Jiménez, in an excellent overview, has used the categories of reflective, existential, and historical realism (1992, 20); my presentation merges the first two, which allows me to see the subjective vein of the poetry of this time in one focus. Jiménez's third category corresponds to the fifth section of this chapter.

9. Jiménez has also noted that at least one poem of *Sombra del paraíso* suggests the inadequacy of the pantheistic vision and the need for collaboration among men and hence points ahead to Aleixandre's next book, *Historia del corazón* ("Story of the Heart") (Jiménez 1982, 63–64).

10. All this takes place amid intertextual echoes. The images of line 3 evoke the romantic tradition; the view of Madrid as cemetery recalls, as Philip Silver has noted, a well-known work of Larra's (Silver 1970). Line 1 recalls statements made in Madrid newspapers in 1940.

11. Robert Langbaum has suggested that the dramatic monologue conveys particularly well relative judgments and perspectives, anchored in specific social situations; it fits an age in which absolute judgments are difficult (107–8). The form allowed Alonso, in the 1940s, to project his negative vision without succumbing to preaching, as many social poets did.

Traditional dramatic monologues such as Browning's, however, offered unified perspectives of clearly delineated protagonists. Alonso's text seems at least partially to undermine such unity.

12. Here one recalls Dámaso Alonso's division of the poetry of this time into the categories of *arraigada* (rooted) and *desarraigada* (unrooted). Looking at the religious and existential lyric of the times, Alonso uses these terms to emphasize how some poets find harmony while others embody anguish. See Alonso 1952, 366–80.

13. Here one recalls Mallarmé's definition of symbol as a means of suggesting a state of soul ("un état d'âme"). In this sense at least, the poetry of Rosales and other

authors writing at this time seems to fit squarely within the modernist-symbolist tradition, despite its use of everyday language.

14. Religious poetry, almost totally absent in the 1920s in Spain, gained some importance in the 1930s and even more in the 1940s: Rosales, Panero, Vivanco, Bleiberg, García Nieto, and Bousoño are all important religious poets. Whether it was motivated by a search for answers to the horrors of war or by other factors, the growth of religious poetry is an important part of the Spanish shift to testimonial and emotive verse.

15. Born in 1922, Hierro identifies himself with a group named Quinta del 42, containing those subject to military service in that year. He is close in age to Blas de Otero (b. 1916), José Luis Hidalgo (1919), and Carlos Bousoño (1923). As I noted above, these writers are only slightly younger than those of the Generation of 1936 and cannot constitute a completely new generation: if the Generation of 1927 encompasses authors born from around 1893 to 1907, then members of the next generation (Marías) or *promoción* (Arrom) would have been born between 1908 and 1923. For this particular era, however, generational categories seem less important than historical circumstances, as Bousoño has indicated (see note 7 above).

16. I have studied the intertextual correspondences of "Las nubes" and Machado's poem 72; see Debicki 1978.

17. The genre intertext (a lullaby, the experience of a prisoner) sets up a conflict that highlights the tragedy and unnaturalness of the prisoner's existence.

18. I do not think it accidental that the author of this poetry is also the critic who asserted a definition of poetry as the communication of all the emotive, conceptual, and sensory dimensions of an experience, synthetically, via the form and style of the text (Bousoño 1966, 19–24). This highly modernist view of poetry has to be relevant for the reader of Bousoño's verse.

19. Born in 1926 (the year after Angel González), Valverde would seem to belong to a succeeding generation. Yet he began publishing early, and his poetry consistently resembles that of older rather than younger authors. This recalls Arrom's view that authors (especially those at generational margins) can accommodate themselves forward or backward; it also makes us aware of the relativity of generational categories.

20. For Linda Hutcheon, the destabilizing of conventions is a basic condition of a move to the postmodern (23–37); see also Lyotard 81 ff.

21. See García de la Concha's explanation of how Cirlot's ideas parallel and contrast with Breton's posture (1987, 2: 725–26). Cirlot's efforts to systematize a theory of correspondences is made very clear in his *Diccionario de símbolos,* still used by critics.

22. Yet I find exaggerated later efforts to see in these poets the seeds of creative work of the *novísimos* of the 1970s; not only was their poetry largely ignored, but the work of none of these poets seems to offer, even for today's reader, the coherence and consistency that would allow us to define its unique contribution.

23. González noted that poetry, especially ironic poetry, could most easily fool censors (1982, 18–19). In addition, one gets the impression that by allowing criticism in verse, the regime could make a case for its openness in the international forum, while restricting circulation to the minority normally interested in the genre.

24. One's response to this text may be akin to that evoked by later novels of "magic realism" like *Cien años de soledad.*

25. *Tremendismo* is a term used mostly with respect to fiction, but it is occasionally applied to poetry (see García de la Concha 1987, 2: 667–90). Originating in negative criticism, it was accepted to describe works that were seen as shocking, such as Camilo José Cela's *La familia de Pascual Duarte*.

26. See the discussion of Alonso's "Insomnio" above. In the case of the poets discussed here, as in that of Alonso, the dramatic monologue is especially effective in conveying a sense of society's decay without preaching—and in triggering an active involvement on the part of the reader.

27. By 1960 most of these poets were published in Spanish editions, and contacts were more regular. Hence in subsequent chapters I will consider poets living abroad together with those in Spain.

28. On this subject, see Bou; and Crispin in *Pedro Salinas* 1992, 69–71.

29. Additional poems of Salinas's written in this period are included in *Confianza,* edited by Juan Marichal and first published in 1955.

30. García de la Concha has suggested echoes of Wordsworth and Machado in this way of using scenes and descriptions to forge transcendent perspectives (1987, 1: 278–80).

31. Given this book's focus on the poetry of Spain, I do not deal with the work of poets whose careers developed entirely outside the country. On the Spanish exile poets growing up in Mexico, I recommend Susana Rivera's anthology *Ultima voz del exilio* (Madrid: Hiperión, 1990).

4. New Directions for Spanish Poetry, 1956–1970

1. It is interesting that according to Arrom's scheme of thirty-year intervals between generations, the Generation of the 1950s is the first new generation since the one of 1927 (the poets emerging between 1936 and 1948 or so would be a second *promoción* of the latter). This scheme would therefore confirm the innovation of the generation's poetic outlook.

2. Batlló also refers to the very limited intellectual environment that characterized the period in which these new poets were students: as teenagers, they had to read Neruda, Vallejo, Hernández, and Alberti in smuggled editions, and they had few mentors and role models other than Aleixandre, Bousoño, occasionally Alonso and Diego, and some social poets.

3. The most important critical study, which established the still-current view of the period and the new generation, was José Olivio Jiménez's *Diez años de poesía española, 1960–1970,* published in 1972. It remains an excellent source for an understanding of this era. Also useful are Persin's *Recent Spanish Poetry and the Role of the Reader* (1987) and José Luis García Martín's *La segunda generación poética de posguerra* (1986). See also my *Poetry of Discovery* (1982).

4. Rather than citing the original sources for most of the statements on poetics here quoted (which are usually Ribes's anthology or magazines of the time), I refer to Pedro Provencio's *Poéticas españolas contemporáneas,* which collected them, adding useful introductory comments, and made them readily available in a convenient format.

5. As a result, these poets essentially liquidated the prior poetics of social writing; thanks to them, "la batalla contra la poesía socialrealista que los novísimos creyeron librar estaba ya ganada, teóricamente al menos" (Provencio 1: 14). {"The

battle against sociorealist poetry that the novísimos thought they were conducting had already been won, at least in the area of theory."}

6. The term most often employed by these poets, *conocimiento,* is used by them to mean the acquisition of new insights and visions and hence is best translated as "discovery" (rather than "knowledge").

7. Pere Gimferrer has perceptively noted how the inertia and fossilized language of the poetry of the 1940s constituted a linguistic conservatism; the new poetic stances of the 1960s and 1970s represent, in various ways, a more fundamental revolution. By changing the frame and nature of discourse, they also point to a change in attitude and vision (Gimferrer 1971, 95–97; see also Bousoño in Carnero 1979, 27–30.)

One could argue that some earlier works, most notably the neosurrealistic poetry of Lorca, Alberti, and Aleixandre, represented a similar revolutionary stance; see chapter 2 above, and Geist 1993. The revolutionary stance of these texts seems to me, however, less central to the definition of the poetry of their era.

8. Carlos Bousoño suggested that if post–Civil War poetry focused on the role of the self in society, the 1940s and 1950s stressed the social side of the issue, and the 1960s emphasized the situation of the individual (see Carnero 1979, 16).

9. Valente, after studying in Santiago and Madrid, taught Spanish literature at Oxford. In 1958 he moved to Geneva as an official of the United Nations. These experiences, and his work as critic and theorist, could be related to the increasing allusiveness of his poetry.

10. This reading of the poem, especially in conjunction with Valente's poetics of discovery, tempts one to stress the indeterminacy of "La llamada" and see it as postmodern. Yet the text has a coherent structure and an almost allegorical pattern that does not make it that different from works by Hierro, Bousoño, or González (see Debicki 1982, 112–13).

11. Rodríguez has frequently indicated, in conversation, that his growing up in a rural setting, his readings of Spanish classical poetry, and his avoidance of the social verse that dominated the times were important and positive conditions for the development of his own poetic voice.

12. See Debicki 1982, 42–45, for a discussion of the conflicting codes and the "defamiliarization" in this poem.

13. Mayhew writes that this poetry "foregrounds the tension between the literal and the figurative planes of meaning (or between the divisive and unifying functions of metaphor) that is implicit in any use of figurative language" (1990, 71). This foregrounding suggests the way in which Rodríguez's poetry, unlike much that preceded it, offers the reader an invitation to participate in a process of discovery rather than simply to receive the product of prior discoveries.

14. González met Jaime Gil de Biedma, José María Castellet, Carlos Barral, and other Barcelona writers in the late 1950s and remained in close contact with them thereafter. He took an active part in the homage to Antonio Machado in Collioure in 1959 and participated in some of the discussions on the planning of Castellet's anthology and the Colliure publishing venture. See the discussion of the school of Barcelona, below.

15. These books are included in *Memorial de la noche (1957–1975)* ("Memorial of Night"), from which I take my quotations.

16. Fuertes's age (she was born in 1918) and her language also led critics to connect her with earlier social poets. Yet almost all of her poetry was published after

1954, and it reveals the artistic and original use of language characteristic of the late 1950s and the 1960s. One should also note Fuertes's interest and success in reciting her poetry orally: reading her texts aloud often contributes an important dimension to their effect.

17. Crespo's work has been reworked and collected in *En medio del camino: Poesía, 1949–1970,* where it can best be consulted.

18. The term and concept were to a great degree the creation of Carme Riera, through her detailed history *La escuela de Barcelona.* To my mind, it is useful to study these poets together, to take into account special features in their locations and backgrounds, and also to see them in the context of other literature of their time.

19. The two poles of this group's orientation can be seen in Barral's essay on poetry as an act of discovery, and in the introduction to Castellet's anthology, with its emphasis on social poetry and on the dominance of realism. They reflect a tension between a cosmopolitan aesthetic vision and a revolutionary one.

20. Colliure is the Spanish name of the town in which Machado died. For a detailed discussion of this group, see Riera.

21. *Años de penitencia* (Madrid: Alianza Editorial, 1975), *Los años sin excusa* (Barcelona: Ed. Seix Barral, 1978), and *Cuando las horas veloces* (Barcelona: Tusquets Editores, 1988).

22. On the dramatic monologue and its suitability to the poetry of this time, see chapter 3 above, especially note 11. Robert Langbaum's view of the dramatic monologue as "an appropriate form for an empiricist and relativist age, an age in which we consider value as an evolving thing dependant upon the changing individual and social requirements of the historical process" (107–8) suggests that this form's frequent use at this time relates to the new perspective of the text as process.

23. Barral's artistic consciousness, and self-consciousness, are reflected in a detailed diary recording the process of composing *Metropolitano,* titled *Diario de Metropolitano,* later edited by Luis García Montero and published in Granada in 1989.

24. The poetry of *Usuras* will be discussed in chapter 5, but it merits mentioning here in order to give a fuller sense of Barral's work.

25. Jiménez has examined how the key images of this poem, many of which echo earlier works by Hierro, fit into a complex narrative and verbal structure reflecting different dimensions of its search (1972, 128–43).

26. Bousoño indicates that he felt himself freed from the limitations of clarity and "realism" that Spanish poetic traditions had previously imposed upon him, and he sought, in this book, to deliberately disorient the reader in order to embody stylistically the tensions of his theme (1980, 26, 29–30).

27. One must keep in mind that Bousoño became, in the 1960s, one of the most perceptive critics of the poetry of this younger generation, as well as one of its admirers and supporters. His studies of Brines and Rodríguez are still indispensable.

28. One should also at least mention the composition and publication, during this period, of several excellent books of poetry by members of the same generation as Zardoya. Among several by Carmen Conde, I would emphasize *Derribado Arcángel* ("Defeated Archangel," 1960), which uses biblical imagery to reflect human love. Also noteworthy are Leopoldo Panero's *Cándida puerta* ("Candid Door," 1960) and his collected, posthumous poems (1963); Luis Felipe Vivanco's *Lugares vividos* ("Lived Places," 1965); and Luis Rosales's *Canciones* ("Songs," written from 1968 to 1972).

29. "Visión de los monstruos" first appeared in *Clavileño* 7, no. 41 (1956): 65–69.

30. The consciousness of the creative process that we have seen in this poetry can also be found in the fiction of the period: Luis Martín-Santos's *Tiempo de silencio* ("Time of Silence," 1962) may serve as the best example. It also illustrates a way of using apparently realistic materials in an artful fashion and of combining highly creative techniques with a critical view of society.

5. *The Postmodern Time of the* Novísimos, *1966–1980*

1. This background was described by Manuel Vázquez Montalbán in several works, perhaps best in *Crónica sentimental de España* (Barcelona: Lumen, 1971). Vázquez Montalbán was the oldest poet included in Castellet's anthology; his most important later work, however, is in prose.

2. Given the changed circumstances in which they grew up, it makes sense to consider the *novísimos* as a new generation; they would be defined as such in Marías's fifteen-year scheme. In a thirty-year scheme, such as Arrom's, they would be the second wave of a generation whose first wave had been formed by the Valente-Rodríguez-González group. Although this could be justified—they did continue and extend the prior group's notion of poetry as discovery—the poetics and work of the *novísimos* might seem too revolutionary for a mere second wave. It is best, I feel, to accept the relativity and variability of any scheme and note, pragmatically, that a new aesthetic stance developed at this time, ten or fifteen years after another significant change. This new stance, as we will see, illuminates the poetry written by older as well as younger authors.

3. There was during this decade some effort to create a new kind of socially committed poetry, probably best represented by the magazine *Claraboya* of León. In the late 1960s that magazine had been stressing the importance of the 1950s generation in combining social and aesthetic concerns; in 1971 it issued a manifesto favoring a new dialectical poetry and published poems that combined narrative techniques, allusions to popular culture, and ironic commentary. See García de la Concha 1986, 13–14.

4. Some of the poets Castellet included had published little; some stopped publishing soon afterward and faded from view; several poets who would eventually be even more important had not yet surfaced. Later anthologies thus give a more complete picture of the *novísimos;* this one, however, placed them on the map.

5. Very good overviews of the poetry of the *novísimos,* and the era, can be found in García de la Concha 1986; Siles 1988; and Villena 1986a.

6. As in chapter 4, here I take my statements on poetics, whenever possible, from Pedro Provencio's anthology, for which he systematically collected essays and declarations originally published in diverse anthologies and other sources. Many come from the sections on poetics in Castellet's *Nueve novísimos* and in other anthologies.

7. Calinescu has suggested that avant-garde decadence and irrationality can be related to some aspects of the postmodern (141–50).

8. García de la Concha observed that many of them studied with José Manuel Blecua at the university in Barcelona and followed his lead in seeing the creativity of Spanish baroque art and poetry.

9. Castellet's anthology divided its poets into three "seniors," Manuel Vázquez Montalbán (b. 1939), Antonio Martínez Sarrión (1939), and José María Alvarez (1942); and six younger writers, all born between 1945 and 1948: Gimferrer, Félix

de Azúa, Vicente Molina-Foix, Guillermo Carnero, Ana María Moix, and Leopoldo María Panero. From today's perspective, the rather small age difference between groups does not seem significant.

10. Gimferrer's essays and memoirs, as well as his poetry, exemplify his dedication, sophistication, and critical vision. His thirst for knowledge is illustrated by this anecdote: when asked why he was about to start studying Rumanian, Gimferrer told me that it was a demanding Romance language that he did not yet know and that also he did not know its literature. Thus it was next on his program for cultural growth.

11. Intertextuality is thus used by Gimferrer and other *novísimos* to make the reader play off the new text against previous ones. This process makes the reader almost create a new work out of the confrontation between several texts. See Pérez Firmat 1978; and Culler 37–39, 100–108.

12. In a sense, these books should be studied as part of literature in Catalan rather than Spanish. Given the value and importance of this poetry and its relevance to other poets, though, I will deal with them here.

13. Persin quotes Gimferrer as describing the book as follows: "Se trata al mismo tiempo de un libro de poemas y una indagación sobre el sentido de la poesía" (1992, 109). {"It is both a book of poems and an investigation of the meaning of poetry."}

14. As Ignacio-Javier López notes, it is the tomb of the prince Don Juan by Domenico Fancelli, located in the Church of Santo Tomé (1992, 141).

15. As Juan José Lanz has indicated, a baroque consciousness of emptiness (*vacío*) underlies this attitude and poem (1989, 96–103).

16. One could suggest that other kinds of poetry—Góngora's *Soledades*, for example—could be read with the same attitude. This reminds us that antecedents to literary attitudes can usually be found and that all movements, eras, and terms are but approximations and arbitrary creations.

17. The open, unresolved nature of this poetry brings to mind Umberto Eco's notion of a strand of contemporary poetry—which he links with the avant-garde— that deliberately remains unfinished and "cannot be appreciated unless the performer somehow reinvents it in psychological collaboration with the author himself" (4).

18. This would fit Panero very nicely within the "poetics of indeterminacy" that Marjorie Perloff traces from Rimbaud, through Pound, to recent American figures like John Cage and David Antin.

19. As we come closer to the present, it becomes harder for any reader to define with confidence even a personal canon: Jover, Ullán, and Jiménez Frontín may in fact deserve as much attention as Azúa or Leopoldo María Panero. In order to deal with a manageable universe, I have made some choices that probably reveal no more than personal intuitions.

20. The use of language and form to objectify experience was, of course, a main goal of modernist poetry (see chapter 1). For modernity, however, this assumed the goal of forging a static, closed text; for poets like Alvarez it seems to imply compiling a "museum" open to the readers' contemplation and reorganization.

21. The vision of sexuality as aesthetic exoticism obviously harks back to nineteenth-century conceptions of decadence: it bears noting that Villena is the author of a study titled *Introducción al dandysmo (El dandysmo, Barbey, Baudelaire)* (1974). Villena's vision of homosexual love also places him in a tradition of marginal sexuality, recalling not only Gil de Biedma and Cernuda but also Rimbaud and aspects of the *poète maudit*.

22. A loss of hope in the possible social effects of poetry thus brought González to a more formalist attitude, paralleling that of younger poets who rejected social and realistic writing from the start. González's new awareness was also influenced, undoubtedly, by his travels in the United States and Mexico and by his teaching of Spanish literature in the States after 1972.

23. An earlier version appeared in 1976, titled *Breve muestra de algunos.* . . .

24. We must keep in mind Barral's important role as publisher and literary figure. His shift to a more esoteric style and a more aesthetic perspective in the 1970s, after having attempted to combine poetic and social concerns in the 1960s, reflected a pattern applicable to some degree to the whole Barcelona group, and to other Spanish poets like González, Valente, and Caballero Bonald.

25. "El pie de la letra" involves an untranslatable pun on an idiom, "al pie de la letra," which means "literally." The *Diario* obviously echoes James Joyce.

26. Rodríguez's poetic output is sparse, compared with that of his colleagues; he works on a text for years, adding and changing whole sections and combining poems in various ways. The result, however, is one of the most important collections of Spanish poetry of the era.

27. The way in which Atencia's poetry does not fit generational schemes with ease seems typical of women's poetry in Spain, as we will see again in chapter 6. This fact may relate to the recentness of women's acceptance into the canon, and to the way in which they develop their careers and life patterns differently from men.

28. Perhaps this should not surprise us, if we remember that Bousoño, as critic, has offered some of the most perceptive insights on its revolutionary poetics (see his introduction to Carnero 1979; and Bousoño 1984). We must also keep in mind Bousoño's key position on the Spanish literary scene, as well as his contacts with, and helpful attention to, the poets of succeeding generations.

Villena, in an insightful article, observes that Bousoño gives some of the poems of this (ultimately irrational) book the form of an essay or treatise (see Villena 1977). This parallels a procedure used by Carnero in the later 1970s and suggests that this kind of writing grows out of the self-reflective attitudes of the decade.

29. The interplay between text, drawings by Joaquín Alcón, and typographical arrangement thus creates something like an ekphrastic work, one combining the artistic forms of writing and the visual arts. Page numbering is omitted and has to be deduced from the index; for me, that signals an impulse to maintain the visual integrity of an art work.

30. The late development of commodity production and of a consumer society in Spain makes it difficult to argue that postmodern traits result from such conditions. For this reason I find it more useful to discuss the issue of postmodernity in formal and aesthetic terms.

31. See Bousoño in Carnero 1979, 27–30; Gimferrer 1971, 95–97; Siles 1988, 126. The view of discourse here suggested draws on Michel Foucault (see 17–35); see also Hutcheon 96–101.

6. The Evolution of Postmodern Poetry, 1978–1990

1. Our tastes and criteria are inevitably conditioned by past readings, and new forms and styles can seem disorienting. It is useful, and humbling, to recall that reviewers of the early books of Alberti, Guillén, and other Generation of 1927 poets found them enigmatic (or hermetic), apparently because they did not always offer

detailed descriptions, in complete sentences, like the works of poets whom they knew well.

I have again created an overlapping of periods, to allow for works published in the late 1970s that seem to fit new sensibilities. The overlap also addresses ways in which some characteristics of the second phase of *novísimo* writing blend into the new era. Any classification, however, has to be extremely tentative.

2. The renewed interest in the generation of the 1950s and 1960s was aided by the publication of collected and complete works during this period: Valente's *Punto cero: Poesía, 1953–1979* (1980); González's collected works, *Palabra sobre palabra,* in a new expanded edition in 1986, as well as his selected *Poemas* in 1980; Brines's *Poesía, 1960–1981* (1984); Rodríguez's complete works, *Desde mis poemas* (1983); a new edition of Gil de Biedma's *Las personas del verbo* in 1982; and Barral's *Poesía* in 1991. Several of these poets received major prizes. According to generation theory, they were, by this decade, a dominant one (see García Martín 1980, 23–32).

3. Important general studies of the poetry of the 1980s include Siles 1990; Ciplijauskaité 1992; the introductions to Villena 1986b, Barella, and García Martín 1988; and the last parts of Jiménez 1992, Lanz 1991, and Mayhew 1992. In identifying the emerging canon, the García Martín anthology is most useful, though it must be complemented by Villena's, Rossel's, and Buenaventura's, as well as by Ugalde 1991.

Whether it is due to the lack of historical perspective or to the "continuist" nature of the period, generational breakpoints become harder to establish, and many poets have been called younger *novísimos* by some critics and members of a new generation by others. Writers of different ages often show similar characteristics, and many women poets do not readily fit their chronological generations. This inclines me to use generational distinctions more flexibly. Yet we should still note that writers born in the 1960s are maturing in a world different from the Spain of their predecessors: many, for example, have not had a Catholic education, previously common to almost everyone.

The following "new" poets here discussed were born in the 1950s: Andreu, Bonet, García Montero, Gutiérrez, Juaristi, Lamillar, Linares, Lupiáñez, Llamazares, Martínez Mesanza, Mas, Navarro, Pallarés, Rossetti, and Valverde. Born in the 1960s were Benítez Reyes, Castro, Cilleruelo, Gallego, García, Iglesias, Marzal, Muñoz Petisme, and Sánchez Torres. Munárriz was born in 1940, Padrón in 1943, Janés in 1944, Canelo in 1946, and Rubio in 1949.

4. I have deliberately not created a special category of women's poetry, to avoid the danger of marginalizing it—an error to which Spanish critics and anthologists have been too prone.

5. This suggests that by the 1980s, after two decades of effort, the simplistic aesthetics of poetry as message, which had pervaded Spanish letters since the Civil War (bringing together, paradoxically, nationalist propaganda and leftist social verse), had been totally left behind.

6. Jonathan Mayhew has discussed the trivialization of artistic topics, the presence of kitsch, and the resultant diminution of intensity in much of the poetry of this time (1992, 401–5).

7. Again, however, we might note that poetry of the 1970s had already responded to popular culture and to the media—in some cases before their effect on Spanish culture had become widely prevalent. As Brushwood suggests, the writer can be the person most aware of developing cultural patterns.

8. Janés, like many of the *novísimos,* studied baroque poetry with José Manuel Blecua in Barcelona; she attributes her start as a poet to that experience and recognizes the effect of the experience and the poetry. See Ugalde 1991, 39–40.

9. Amorós refuses to reveal her birth date in order not to be identified with her generation (presumably the *novísimos*), from which her attitude and dates of writing separate her. For me, in any event, her poetry is characteristic of a facet of the 1980s, and its publication during this decade very telling.

10. Munárriz, the director of the publishing house Hiperión, is an important critic and advocate for poetry; his attitude and poetics, therefore, are revealing and influential. I should note that, having been born in 1940 and having published poetry in the 1970s, he belongs to the *novísimo* generation. His influence and attitude, however, fit him into the new directions of the 1980s.

11. Ciplijauskaité's insight suggests another parallel: the poets of the 1980s, like those of the 1920s, wrote their affirmative verse in a climate in which the importance of poetic form and artistry has been established by a prior generation. As Guillén and Lorca built on Juan Ramón Jiménez, so the 1980s poets could build on Carnero, Gimferrer, Villena, and Siles.

12. Other poets of this generation also published important works during the 1980s. José Agustín Goytisolo continued the narrative mode of his prior poetry, with, if anything, increased stress on a critical view of middle-class society. *A veces gran amor* ("Sometimes Great Love," 1981) contains some interesting love poems in the tight forms of "poesía de tipo tradicional." Two books by José Manuel Caballero Bonald, *Descrédito del héroe* ("The Discrediting of the Hero," 1977) and *Laberinto de Fortuna* ("Labyrinth of Fortune," 1984), almost point in the opposite direction, being marked by linguistic experimentation, intertextualities, and a subversion of traditional myths. The latter volume, for example, recasts a classical Spanish text by Juan de Mena. Meanwhile, César Simón, chronologically a member of this generation and the author of several books published in the 1970s that did not receive much attention at the time, gained recognition in the 1980s, probably because of the way in which his work portrays emotively charged states.

13. It is revealing that Carlos Bousoño's verse, especially after the dominance of a realistic mode of poetry had subsided, connects with the (younger) poets of the 1950s generation better than with many of his own generational colleagues, reminding us, again, of the relativity of any age scheme.

14. Here Díez de Revenga's theory about a "poetry of aging" would be relevant (1988). His comments on that path of earlier authors might presage, though at later ages, what we have noted here.

15. López notes, correctly, that at this point there was no need for Carnero to react against prior poetic discourses by foregrounding form: "There's no longer an enemy" (López 1992, 146).

16. The following sentence of García Montero's poetics seems relevant: "Las palabras . . . se ponen en movimiento para invitar al lector a circular por un mundo imaginario que necesita ser creado a cada paso" (García Martín 1988, 162). {"Words . . . are put in motion to invite the reader to wander through an imaginary world that needs to be created at every step."}

17. Also Andalusian, Benítez Reyes was born in Cádiz; his books of verse include *Paraíso manuscrito* ("Manuscript Paradise," 1982) and *Los vanos mundos* ("Vain Worlds," 1985).

18. The poetry from several previous books of Cilleruelo's is collected and re-arranged in his *El don impuro* ("The Impure Gift," 1989).

19. Rubio's career (especially when contrasted with that of academics of previous generations) reflects the new Spanish literary scene: she lectures at the university, runs a television program, organizes symposia, writes poetry, fiction, and different kinds of criticism, and is constantly on the move.

20. In her interview with Ugalde, Rossetti stressed the effects of her education in a religious school and of her readings about martyrs; she noted that this sort of background was common in her era (she was born in 1950) but would not affect younger poets. See Ugalde 1991, 151–54.

21. In 1992 Luca published *Canción del samurai* ("Song of the Samurai"), composed of short, intense poems accompanied by ideograms. Oriental motifs and the dominant image of the samurai's sword provide an eerie sensual atmosphere for the treatment of love, death, and poetic creativity.

22. See sonnet 164 in Cruz 636. Since these lines reflect baroque topoi, another source is possible—or a combination of several. A Spanish reader, in any event, would hear parodic echoes of seventeenth-century love poetry.

23. Born in 1951, Juaristi belongs, chronologically, to the *novísimos*. All his books of poetry were published in the 1980s, however, and fit (and also help define) that decade's perspective.

24. This text, "En torno al casticismo" ("About Correctness" [title of a book by Unamuno]; Juaristi 1988, 31–32) thus works on several levels: the speaker-poet accomplishes what he claims the language cannot; he (needlessly) excuses himself for regionalisms and dedicates the poem to a colleague who advised him not to write in Spanish.

Works Cited

Pedro Salinas: Estudios sobre su praxis y teoría de la escritura. 1992. Santander: Sociedad Menéndez Pelayo.

Aguirre, J.M. 1973. *Antonio Machado, poeta simbolista*. Madrid: Taurus.

Alberti, Rafael. 1961. *Poesías completas*. Buenos Aires: Ed. Losada.

Aleixandre, Vicente. 1955. *Algunos caracteres de la nueva poesía española*. Madrid: Instituto de España.

———. 1960. *Historia del corazón*. 2d ed. Madrid: Espasa-Calpe.

Alonso, Dámaso. 1931. "Un poeta y un libro." *Revista de Occidente* year 9, vol. 23, no. 98: 245.

———. 1935. *La lengua poética de Góngora*. Part 1. Madrid: Revista de Filología Española.

———. 1952. *Poetas españoles contemporáneos*. Madrid: Gredos.

———. 1958. *Hijos de la ira: Diario íntimo*. Selecciones Austral, 2d ed. Madrid: Espasa-Calpe.

———. 1960. *Estudios y ensayos gongorinos*. 2d ed. Madrid: Gredos.

Altieri, Charles. 1979. *Enlarging the Temple*. Lewisburg, Pa.: Bucknell UP.

Alvarez, José María. 1971. *87 poemas*. Madrid: Ed. Helios.

———. 1989. "Las rayas del tigre: Introducción a la actual poesía española." Zurgai, pp. 14–17.

Amorós, Amparo. 1982. "La retórica del silencio." *Los Cuadernos del Norte* 3, no. 16: 18–27.

———, ed. 1985. *Palabra, mundo, ser: la poesía de Jaime Siles*. Barcelona; Litoral.

———. 1986. "Una poética de la intensidad." Interview with Antonio Requeni. *La Prensa* (Buenos Aires), April 13.

———. 1989. "Los novísimos y cierra España!" *Insula* 512–13: 63–67.

———. 1992. *Visión y destino: Poesía, 1982–1992*. Madrid: Ed. La Palma.

Anderson, Andrew A. 1991. "Lorca at the Crossroads: 'Imaginación, Inspiración, Evasión' and the 'Novísimas Estéticas.' " *Anales de la Literatura Española Contemporánea* 16: 149–73.

Andreu, Blanca. 1986. *De una niña de provincias que se vino a vivir en un Chagall*. 5th ed. Madrid: Hiperión.

Arrom, José Juan. 1963. *Estudio generacional de las letras hispanoamericanas*. Bogotá: Instituto Caro y Cuervo.

Atencia, María Victoria. 1990. *Antología poética*. Madrid: Ed. Castalia.

Azúa, Félix de. 1989. *Poesía (1968–1988)*. Madrid: Hiperión.

Badosa, Enrique. 1958. "Primero hablemos de Júpiter (La poesía como medio de conocimiento)." *Papeles de Son Armadans* 10, no. 28: 32–46; no. 29: 135–59.

Balakian, Anna. 1969. *El movimiento simbolista.* Madrid: Ed. Guadarrama.

Barella, Julia. 1987. *Después de la modernidad: Poesía española en sus distintas lenguas literarias.* Barcelona: Anthropos.

Barral, Carlos. 1991. *Poesía.* Ed. Carme Riera. Madrid: Cátedra.

Bary, David. 1968. "José Hierro's 'Para un esteta.' " *PMLA* 83: 1347–52.

Batlló, José, ed. 1968. *Antología de la nueva poesía española.* Madrid: El Bardo.

Blanch, Antonio. 1976. *La poesía pura española: Conexiones con la cultura francesa.* Madrid: Gredos.

Bonet, Juan Manuel. 1983. *La patria oscura.* Madrid: Trieste.

Bou, Enric. 1988. "Salinas, al otro lado del océano." *Boletín de la Fundación Federico García Lorca* 3: 38–45.

Bousoño, Carlos. 1966. *Teoría de la expresión poética.* 4th ed. Madrid: Gredos.

———. 1976. *Antología poética, 1945–1973.* Barcelona: Plaza y Janés.

———. 1979. *Superrealismo poético y simbolización.* Madrid: Gredos.

———. 1980. *Selección de mis versos.* Madrid: Cátedra.

———. 1981. *Epocas literarias y evolución.* Madrid: Gredos.

———. 1984. *Poesía postcontemporánea.* Madrid: Júcar.

———. 1988. *Metáfora del desafuero.* Madrid: Visor.

Bradbury, Malcolm, and James McFarlane, eds. 1978. *Modernism: 1890–1930.* 2d ed. Atlantic Highlands, N.J.: Humanities.

Brines, Francisco. 1974. *Poesía, 1960–1971: Ensayo de una despedida.* Barcelona: Plaza y Janés.

———. 1984. *Poesía, 1960–1981.* Madrid: Visor.

———. 1987. *El otoño de las rosas.* Seville: Ed. Renacimiento.

Brushwood, John S. 1989. *Narrative Innovation and Political Change in Mexico.* New York: Lang.

Buckley, Ramón, and John Crispin, eds. 1973. *Los vanguardistas españoles (1925–1935).* Madrid: Alianza Editorial.

Buenaventura, Ramón, ed. 1985. *Las diosas blancas: Antología de la joven poesía española escrita por mujeres.* Madrid: Hiperión.

Caballero Bonald, José Manuel. 1983. *Selección natural.* Madrid: Cátedra.

Cabañero, Eladio. 1970. *Poesía (1956–1970).* Barcelona: Plaza y Janés.

Calinescu, Matei. 1987. *Five Faces of Modernity: Modernism, Avant-Garde, Decadence, Kitsch, Postmodernism.* Durham, N.C.: Duke UP.

Cano, José Luis. 1974. *Poesía española contemporánea: Las generaciones de posguerra.* Madrid: Ed. Guadarrama.

Cano Ballesta, Juan. 1972. *La poesía española entre pureza y revolución (1930–1936).* Madrid: Gredos.

———. 1981. *Literatura y tecnología (Las letras españolas ante la revolución industrial: 1900–1933).* Madrid: Ed. Orígenes.

Carnero, Guillermo, ed. 1976. *El grupo "Cántico" de Córdoba.* Madrid: Editora Nacional.

———. 1979. *Ensayo de una teoría de la visión (Poesía, 1966–1977).* Madrid: Hiperión.

———. 1990. *Divisibilidad indefinida.* Seville: Ed. Renacimiento.

———. 1992. "Culturalism and the 'New' Poetry: A Poem by Pedro Gimferrer, 'Cascabeles' from *Arde el mar.*" *Studies in Twentieth Century Literature* 16: 93–107. (Another version in Ciplijauskaité 1990, 11–23.)

Castellet, José María, ed. 1960. *Veinte años de poesía española: Antología, 1939–1959.* Barcelona: Ed. Seix Barral.

———. 1970. *Nueve novísimos poetas españoles.* Barcelona: Barral Editores.

Castro, Luisa. 1989. *Los versos del eunuco.* 2d ed. Madrid: Hiperión.

Celaya, Gabriel. 1981. Poesía. Ed. Angel González. 3d ed. Madrid: Alianza Editorial.

Cernuda, Luis. 1964. *La realidad y el deseo (1924–1962).* Mexico City: Fondo de Cultura Económica.

———. 1965. *Poesía y literatura.* 2d ed. Barcelona: Ed. Seix Barral.

Cilleruelo, José Angel. 1989. *El don impuro.* Málaga: Puerta del Mar.

Ciplijauskaité, Biruté. 1966. *El poeta y la poesía (Del romanticismo a la poesía social).* Madrid: Insula.

———, ed. 1990. *Novísimos, postnovísimos, clásicos: La poesía de los 80 en España.* Madrid: Orígenes.

———. 1992. "Recent Spanish Poetry and the Essential Word." *Studies in Twentieth Century Literature* 16: 149–63.

Colinas, Antonio. 1984. *Poesía (1967–1984).* Madrid: Visor.

Crespo, Angel. 1971. *En medio del camino: Poesía, 1949–1970.* Barcelona: Ed. Seix Barral.

Crispin, John. 1974. *Pedro Salinas.* New York: Twayne.

Cruz, Sor Juana Inés de. 1976. *Obras selectas.* Ed. Georgina Sabat de Rivers and Elias L. Rivers. Barcelona: Ed. Noguer.

Cuenca, Luis Alberto de. 1990. *Poesía, 1970–1989.* Seville: Ed. Renacimiento.

Culler, Jonathan. 1981. *The Pursuit of Signs.* Ithaca, N.Y.: Cornell UP.

Davison, Ned J. 1966. *The Concept of Modernism in Hispanic Criticism.* Boulder, Colo.: Pruett.

Debicki, Andrew P. 1970. *Dámaso Alonso.* New York: Twayne.

———. 1973. *La poesía de Jorge Guillén.* Madrid: Gredos.

———. 1974. "Satire and Dramatic Monologue in Several Poems of Dámaso Alonso." *Books Abroad* 48: 276–85.

———. 1978. "José Hierro a la luz de Antonio Machado." *Sin Nombre* 9: 41–51.

———. 1981. *Estudios sobre poesía española contemporánea: La generación de 1924–1925.* 2d ed. Madrid: Gredos.

———. 1982. *Poetry of Discovery: The Spanish Generation of 1956–1971.* Lexington: UP of Kentucky.

———. 1983. "Intertextuality and Reader Response in the Poetry of José Angel Valente." *Hispanic Review* 51: 251–67.

———. 1984. " 'Final': Reflejo y reelaboración de la poesía y la poética guillenianas." *Sin Nombre* 14: 85–102.

———. 1987. *Poesía del conocimiento: La generación española de 1956–1971.* Madrid: Júcar.

———. 1988. "Una dimensión olvidada de la poesía española de los 20 y 30: La lírica visionaria de Ernestina de Champourcin." *Ojáncano* 1: 48–60.

———. 1989. *Angel González.* Madrid: Júcar.

———. 1990. "La poesía de Miguel Hernández y el surrealismo." *Hispanic Review* 58: 487–501.

———. 1992. "La crítica de Pedro Salinas: De la modernidad a la postmodernidad." Forthcoming.

Debicki, Andrew P., and Michael J. Doudoroff, eds. 1985. *Azul. Prosas profanas,* by Rubén Darío. Madrid: Ed. Alhambra.

De Man, Paul. 1971. "Literary History and Literary Modernity." *Blindness and Insight: Essays in the Rhetoric of Contemporary Criticism.* New York: Oxford UP. 142–65.

————. 1979. *Allegories of Reading.* New Haven: Yale UP.

Díaz Plaja, Guillermo. 1951. *Modernismo frente a noventa y ocho.* Madrid: Espasa-Calpe.

————. 1975. *Estructura y sentido del novecentismo español.* Madrid: Alianza Editorial.

Diego, Gerardo. 1958. *Primera antología de sus versos.* 5th ed. Madrid: Espasa-Calpe.

————, ed. 1962. *Poesía española contemporánea (Antología).* 3d ed. Madrid: Taurus. (This is a new edition, incorporating Diego's anthologies *Poesía española: Antología, 1915–1931* [1932] and *Poesía española contemporánea* [1934].)

Díez de Revenga, F.J. 1987. *Panorama crítico de la generación del 27.* Madrid: Ed. Castalia.

————. 1988. *Poesía de senectud.* Barcelona: Anthropos.

Eco, Umberto. 1989. *The Open Work.* Trans. Anna Cancogni. Cambridge, Mass.: Harvard UP.

Eliot, T.S. 1953. *Selected Prose.* Ed. John Hayward. Harmondsworth, Middlesex: Penguin.

Eysteinsson, Astradus. 1990. *The Concept of Modernism.* Ithaca, N.Y.: Cornell UP.

Fish, Stanley. 1980. *Is There a Text in This Class?* Cambridge, Mass.: Harvard UP.

Foucault, Michel. 1980. *The History of Sexuality.* Vol. 1. New York: Vintage.

Friedrich, Hugo. 1959. *Estructura de la lírica moderna.* Trans. J. Petit. Barcelona: Ed. Seix Barral.

Fuertes, Gloria. 1977. *Obras incompletas.* 3d ed. Madrid: Cátedra.

García de la Concha, Víctor. 1986. "La renovación estética de los años sesenta." *El estado de las poesías.* Monografía 3. *Los Cuadernos del Norte,* pp. 10–22.

————. 1987. *La poesía española de 1935 a 1975.* Vol. 1, *De la preguerra a los años oscuros, 1935–1944.* Vol. 2, *De la poesía existencial a la poesía social, 1944–1950.* Madrid: Cátedra.

García Lorca, Federico. 1957a. "La imagen poética en don Luis de Góngora." *Obras completas.* Madrid: Aguilar. 65–88.

————. 1957b. *Obras completas.* Madrid: Aguilar.

García Martín, José Luis, ed. 1980. *Las voces y los ecos.* Madrid: Júcar.

————. 1986. *La segunda generación poética de la posguerra.* Badajoz: Diputación.

————, ed. 1988. *La generación de los ochenta.* Valencia: Poesía.

García Montero, Luis. 1988. *Diario cómplice.* 2d ed. Madrid: Hiperión.

————. 1989. *El jardín extranjero; Poemas de "Tristia."* Madrid: Hiperión.

García-Posada, Miguel. 1989. "Lorca y el surrealismo: Una relación conflictiva." *Insula* 515 (Nov.): 7–10.

Geist, Anthony Leo. 1980. *La poética de la generación del 27 y las revistas literarias: De la vanguardia al compromiso (1918–1936).* Barcelona: Ed. Guadarrama.

————. 1990. "El Angel y la Bestia: La poética de la batalla de Madrid en la Guerra Civil." *Texto y sociedad: Problemas de historia literaria,* ed. Bridget Aldaraca, E. Baker, and J. Beverly. Amsterdam: Ed. Rodopi, 245-57.

————. 1992. "Modernidad y postmodernidad en la poesía española contemporánea (1975–1992)." Unpublished.

————. 1993. "Geografía del 27: La diáspora." Unpublished.

Gil de Biedma, Jaime. 1960. *Cántico: El mundo y la poesía de Jorge Guillén.* Barcelona: Ed. Seix Barral.

————. 1982. *Las personas del verbo.* Barcelona: Ed. Seix Barral.

Gimferrer, Pere. 1971. "Notas parciales sobre poesía española de posguerra." *Treinta años de literatura,* by Salvador Clotas and Pere Gimferrer. Barcelona: Ed. Kairós: 91–108.

————. 1978. *Poesía, 1970–1977: Edición bilingue.* Madrid: Visor.

——. 1979. *Poemas, 1963–1969.* Madrid: Visor.

——. 1982. *Apariciones y otros poemas: Edición bilingue.* Madrid: Visor.

González, Angel. 1982. *Poemas.* 2d ed. Madrid: Cátedra.

——. 1986. *Palabra sobre palabra.* Barcelona: Ed. Seix Barral.

Goytisolo, José Agustín. 1980. *Salmos al viento.* 5th ed. Barcelona: Ed. Lumen.

Grande, Félix. 1970. *Apuntes sobre poesía española de posguerra.* Madrid: Taurus.

Guillén, Jorge. 1961. *Language and Poetry: Some Poets of Spain.* Cambridge, Mass.: Harvard UP.

——. 1969. *El argumento de la obra.* Barcelona: Llibres de Sinera.

——. 1980. *Hacia "Cántico": Escritos de los años 20.* Ed. K.M. Sibbald. Barcelona: Ed. Ariel.

——. 1987. *Aire nuestro.* Ed. Claudio Guillén and A. Piedra. 5 vols. Valladolid: Centro de Creación y Estudios Jorge Guillén.

——. 1990. *El hombre y la obra.* [1917.] Ed. K.M. Sibbald. Valladolid: Centro de Creación y Estudios Jorge Guillén.

Gullón, Ricardo. 1958. *Conversaciones con Juan Ramón Jiménez.* Madrid: Taurus.

——. 1971. *Direcciones del modernismo.* Madrid: Gredos.

Hassan, Ihab. 1984. *Paracriticisms: Seven Speculations of the Times.* Urbana: U of Illinois P.

Hernández, Miguel. 1979. *Obra poética completa.* 5th ed. Ed. Leopoldo de Luis and Jorge Urrutia. Madrid: Zero-Zyx.

Hierro, José. 1962. *Poesías completas, 1944–1962.* Madrid: Ediciones Giner.

——. 1964. *Libro de las alucinaciones.* Madrid: Editora Nacional.

Hutcheon, Linda. 1988. *A Poetics of Postmodernism: History, Theory, Fiction.* New York: Routledge.

Jameson, Fredric. 1991. *Postmodernism; or, The Cultural Logic of Late Capitalism.* Durham, N.C.: Duke UP.

Janés, Clara. 1979. *Antología personal (1959–1979).* Madrid: Adonais.

——. 1988. *Lapidario.* Madrid: Hiperión.

Jiménez, José Olivio. 1964. *Cinco poetas del tiempo.* Madrid: Insula.

——. 1972. *Diez años de poesía española, 1960–1970.* Madrid: Insula.

——. 1982. *Vicente Aleixandre: Una aventura hacia el conocimiento.* Madrid: Júcar.

——. 1992. "Fifty Years of Contemporary Spanish Poetry (1939–1989)." *Studies in Twentieth Century Literature* 16: 15–41.

Jiménez, Juan Ramón. 1959. *Libros de poesía.* 2d ed. Madrid: Aguilar.

——. 1978. *Leyenda (1986–1956).* Ed. Antonio Sánchez Romeralo. Madrid: CUPSA Editorial.

Juaristi, Jon. 1986. *Diario del poeta recién cansado.* 2d ed. Pamplona: Pamiela.

——. 1987. *Suma de varia intención.* Pamplona: Pamiela.

——. 1988. *Arte de marear.* Madrid: Hiperión.

Kaplan, E. Ann, ed. 1988. *Postmodernism and Its Discontents.* New York: Verso.

Lamillar, Juan. 1982. *Muro contra la muerte.* Seville: Ed. Renacimiento.

Langbaum, Robert. 1957. *The Poetry of Experience.* New York: Norton.

Lanz, Juan José. 1989. "Rechazo del realismo y del surrealismo: Por una concepción barroca y simbolista de la poesía de Guillermo Carnero." *Zurgai,* pp. 96–103.

——. 1991. "La última poesía española: Un recuento." *El Urogallo,* no. 48: 61–65.

López, Ignacio-Javier. 1990. "Noticia del fuego: La poesía sustantiva de Alejandro Duque Amusco." Ciplijauskaité 1990, 81–94.

———. 1992. "Language and Consciousness in the Poetry of the 'Novísimos': Guillermo Carnero's Latest Poetry." *Studies in Twentieth Century Literature* 16: 127–48.

Luca, Andrea. 1990. *El don de Lilith.* Madrid: Ed. Endymion.

Luis, Leopoldo de, ed. 1969. *Poesía social: Antología (1939–1969).* 2d ed. Madrid: La Palma de la Mano.

Lyotard, Jean-Franois. 1984. *The Postmodern Condition: A Report on Knowledge.* Minneapolis: U of Minnesota P.

Machado, Antonio. 1977. *Poesías completas.* Selecciones Austral, 3d ed. Madrid: Espasa-Calpe.

Mallarmé, Stéphane. 1945. "Sur l'évolution littéraire (enquête de Jules Huret)." *Oeuvres completes.* Paris: Gallimard. 866–72.

Marco, Joaquín. 1986. *Poesía española siglo XX.* Barcelona: Edhasa.

Marías, Julián. 1949. *El método histórico de las generaciones.* Madrid: Revista de Occidente.

Martín Pardo, Enrique. 1970. *Nueva poesía española.* Madrid: Scorpio.

Martínez Sarrión, Antonio. 1981. *El centro inaccesible (Poesía, 1967–1980).* Madrid: Hiperión.

Mayhew, Jonathan. 1990. *Claudio Rodríguez and the Language of Poetic Vision.* Lewisburg, Pa.: Bucknell UP.

———. 1992. "The Twilight of the Avant-Garde: Spanish Poetry of the 1980s." *Hispanic Review* 60: 401–11.

Mazzaro, Jerome. 1980. *Postmodern American Poetry.* Urbana: U of Illinois P.

Millán, Rafael, ed. 1955. *Veinte poetas españoles.* Madrid: Agora.

Miller, Martha La Follette. 1981. "Claudio Rodríguez's Linguistic Skepticism: A Counterpart to Jorge Guillén's Linguistic Faith." *Anales de la Literatura Española Contemporánea* 6: 105–21.

Miró, Emilio. 1980. "La poesía desde 1936." *Historia de la literatura española,* vol. 4, ed. José María Díez Borque. Barcelona: Taurus. 328–79.

Moral, Concepción G., and Rosa María Pereda, eds. 1980. *Joven poesía española.* Madrid: Cátedra.

Morris, C.B. 1972. *Surrealism and Spain, 1920–1936.* Cambridge: Cambridge UP.

Munárriz, Jesús. 1988. *Camino de la voz.* Madrid: Hiperión.

Olson, Paul. 1967. *Circle of Paradox: Time and Essence in the Poetry of Juan Ramón Jiménez.* Baltimore: Johns Hopkins UP.

Ory, Carlos Edmundo de. 1978. *Metanoia.* Ed. Rafael de Cózar. Madrid: Cátedra.

Otero, Blas de. 1970. *Mientras.* Zaragoza: Ediciones Javalambre.

———. 1974. *Verso y prosa.* Madrid: Cátedra.

Pallarés, María del Carmen. 1987. *Antología (1979–1986).* Málaga: Puerta del Mar.

Palomo, María del Pilar. 1988. *La poesía en el siglo XX (desde 1939). Historia crítica de la Literatura Hispánica,* vol. 21. Madrid: Taurus.

Panero, Leopoldo. 1973. *Obras completas.* Vol. 1, *Poesías* (1928–62). Madrid: Editora Nacional.

Panero, Leopoldo María. 1986. *Poesía, 1970–1985.* Madrid: Visor.

Pérez Firmat, Gustavo. 1978. "Apuntes para un modelo de la intertextualidad en la literatura." *Romanic Review* 69: 1–14.

———. 1986. *Literature and Liminality: Festive Readings in the Hispanic Tradition.* Durham, N.C.: Duke UP.

Perloff, Marjorie. 1981. *The Poetics of Indeterminacy: Rimbaud to Cage.* Princeton, N.J.: Princeton UP.

Persin, Margaret H. 1980. "José Angel Valente: Poem as Process." *Taller Literario* 1, no. 1: 24–41.

———. 1987. *Recent Spanish Poetry and the Role of the Reader.* Lewisburg, Pa.: Bucknell UP.

———. 1992. "Snares: Pere Gimferrer's 'Los espejos / Els miralls.' " *Studies in Twentieth Century Literature* 16: 109–26.

Poggioli, Renato. 1968. *The Theory of the Avant-Garde.* Trans. G. Fitzgerald. Cambridge, Mass.: Harvard UP.

Predmore, Michael P. 1973. *La poesía hermética de Juan Ramón Jiménez (El "Diario" como centro de su mundo poético).* Madrid: Gredos.

Provencio, Pedro, ed. 1988. *Poéticas españolas contemporáneas.* Vol. 1, *La generación del 50.* Vol. 2, *La generación del 70.* Madrid: Hiperión.

Ribes, Francisco, ed. 1952. *Antología consultada de la joven poesía española.* Valencia: Distribuciones Mares.

———. 1963. *Poesía última: Selección.* Madrid: Taurus.

Riera, Carme. 1988. *La escuela de Barcelona.* Barcelona: Ed. Anagrama.

Rodríguez, Claudio. 1971. *Poesía, 1953–1966.* Prologue by Carlos Bousoño. Madrid: Plaza y Janés.

———. 1983. *Desde mis poemas.* Madrid: Cátedra.

———. 1991. *Casi una leyenda.* Barcelona: Tusquets Editores.

Roh, Franz. 1927. "Realismo mágico." *Revista de Occidente,* year 5, vol. 16, no. 48: 274–401.

Rosales, Luis. 1979. *Rimas y La casa encendida.* Selecciones Austral. Madrid: Espasa-Calpe.

———. 1982. *Un rostro en cada ola.* Málaga: Rusadir.

Rossel, Elena de Jongh, ed. 1982. *Florilegium: Poesía última española.* Madrid: Espasa-Calpe.

Rossetti, Ana. 1987. *Indicios vehementes (Poesía, 1979–1984).* 3d ed. Madrid: Hiperión.

Rubio, Fanny. 1976. *Las revistas poéticas de España (1939–1975).* Madrid: Ed. Turner.

———. 1980. "Teoría y polémica en la poesía española de posguerra." *Cuadernos Hispanoamericanos* 121, nos. 361–62: 199–214.

———. 1986. "Hacia una constitución de la poesía española en castellano: Un lustro desasosegado (propuesta ficción)." *El estado de las poesías.* Monografía 3. *Los Cuadernos del Norte,* pp. 47–56.

———. 1989. *Retracciones y Reverso.* Madrid: Ed. Endymion.

———. 1990. *Dresde.* Madrid: Devenir.

Rubio, Fanny, and José Luis Falcó, eds. 1982. *Poesía española contemporánea (1939–1980).* 2d ed. Madrid: Ed. Alhambra.

Sahagún, Carlos. 1976. *Memorial de la noche (1957–1975).* Barcelona: Ed. Lumen.

Salinas, Pedro. 1940. *Reality and the Poet in Spanish Poetry.* Baltimore: Johns Hopkins UP.

———. 1961. *La responsabilidad del escritor.* Barcelona: Ed. Seix Barral.

———. 1970 [1941]. *Literatura española siglo XX.* Madrid: Alianza Editorial.

———. 1975. *Poesías completas.* Ed. Soledad Salinas de Marichal. Barcelona: Barral Editores.

———. 1983. *Ensayos completos.* Ed. Solita Salinas de Marichal. 3 vols. Madrid: Taurus.

Salinas de Marichal, Solita. 1968. *El mundo poético de Rafael Alberti.* Madrid: Gredos.

Sánchez Barbudo, Antonio. 1962. *La segunda época de Juan Ramón Jiménez (1916–1953).* Madrid: Gredos.

———. 1967. *Los Poemas de Antonio Machado. Los Temas. El sentimiento y la expresión.* Madison: U of Wisconsin P.

Sánchez Robayna, Andrés. 1978. *Clima (1972–1976).* Barcelona: Edicions del Mall.

Sanz Villanueva, Santos. 1984. *Historia de la literatura española.* 6/2. *El siglo XX: literatura actual.* Barcelona: Ed. Ariel.

Saval, Lorenzo, and J. García Gallego, eds. 1986. *Litoral femenino: Literatura escrita por mujeres en la España contemporánea.* Torremolinos: Revista Litoral.

Schulman, Ivan A. 1966. *Génesis del modernismo.* Mexico City: El Colegio de México and U of Washington P.

Sherno, Sylvia. 1993. "Blas de Otero, Postmodern Poet." Unpublished.

Sibbald, K.M. 1978. "Jorge Guillén: Portrait of the Critic as a Young Man." *Homenaje a Jorge Guillén.* Ed. Wellesley College Department of Spanish. Madrid: Insula. 435–53.

Siebenmann, Gustav. 1973. *Los estilos poéticos en España desde 1900.* Trans. A. San Miguel. Madrid: Gredos.

Siles, Jaime. 1982. *Diversificaciones.* Valencia: Fernando Torres, Editor.

———. 1988. "Los novísimos: La tradición como ruptura, la ruptura como tradición." *Hispanorama* 48: 122–30.

———. 1990. "Ultimísima poesía española escrita en castellano: Rasgos distintivos de un discurso en proceso y ensayo de una posible sistematización." Ciplijauskaité 1990, 141–67. (Also in *Iberroromania,* no. 34 [1991]: 8–31.)

———. 1992. *Poesía, 1969–1990.* Madrid: Visor.

Silver, Philip W. 1970. "Tradition as Originality in 'Hijos de la ira.'" *Bulletin of Hispanic Studies* 47:124–30.

———. 1985. *La casa de Anteo: Estudios de poética hispánica (De Antonio Machado a Claudio Rodríguez).* Madrid: Taurus.

———. 1989. *De la mano de Cernuda.* Madrid: Fundación Juan March and Cátedra.

Smith, Barbara Herrnstein. 1988. *Contingencies of Value: Alternative Perspectives for Critical Theory.* Cambridge, Mass: Harvard UP.

Soufas, C. Christopher. 1989. *Conflict of Light and Wind: The Spanish Generation of 1927 and the Ideology of Poetic Form.* Middletown, Conn.: Wesleyan UP.

Stixrude, David. 1975. *The Early Poetry of Pedro Salinas.* Princeton, and Madrid: Princeton U Dept. of Romance Languages/Castalia.

Talens, Jenaro. 1989. *De la publicidad como fuente historiográfica. La generación poética española de 1970.* Valencia: Centro de Semiótica y Teoría del Espectáculo.

———. 1991. *El largo aprendizaje: Poesía, 1975–1991.* Madrid: Cátedra.

Ugalde, Sharon Keefe. 1991. *Conversaciones y poemas: La nueva poesía femenina española en castellano.* Madrid: Siglo Veintiuno Editores.

———. 1992. "The Feminization of Female Figures in Spanish Women's Poetry of the 1980s." *Studies in Twentieth Century Literature* 16: 165–84.

Valbuena Prat, Angel. 1953. *Historia de la literatura española.* 4th ed. Vol. 3. Barcelona: Ed. Gustavo Gili.

Valente, José Angel. 1971. *Las palabras de la tribu.* Madrid: Siglo XXI de España.

———. 1980. *Punto cero: Poesía, 1953–1979.* Barcelona: Ed. Seix Barral.

———. 1984. *El fulgor.* Madrid: Cátedra.

Vela, Fernando. 1924. "El suprarealismo." *Revista de Occidente,* year 2, vol. 6, no. 18: 428–34.

Videla, Gloria. 1963. *El ultraísmo: Estudios sobre movimientos poéticos de vanguardia en España.* Madrid: Gredos.

Vigée, Claude. 1962. "Jorge Guillén et les poètes symbolistes français." *Révolte et louanges.* Paris: J. Corti. 139–97.

Villena, Luis Antonio de. 1977. "Poesía y autoreflexión de Carlos Bousoño." *Insula,* no. 373: 1, 10.

———. 1983. *Poesía (1970–1982).* Madrid: Visor.

———. 1986a. "Enlaces entre vanguardia y tradición." *El estado de las poesías.* Monografía 3. *Los Cuadernos del Norte,* pp. 32–36.

———, ed. 1986b. *Postnovísimos.* Madrid: Visor.

Wilcox, John C. 1987. *Self and Image in Juan Ramón Jiménez.* Urbana: U of Illinois P.

Wimsatt, W.K., Jr. 1958. *The Verbal Icon: Studies in the Meaning of Poetry.* 2d ed. New York: Noonday.

Young, Howard T. 1980. *The Line in the Margin: Juan Ramón Jiménez and His Readings in Blake, Shelley, and Yeats.* Madison: U of Wisconsin P.

———. 1992. "Sombras fluviales: 'Poeta en Nueva York' y 'The Wasteland.' " *Boletín de la Fundación García Lorca* 10–11: 165–77.

Zardoya, Concha. 1968. *Hondo Sur.* Barcelona: El Bardo.

———. 1974. *Poesía española del siglo XX: Estudios temáticos y estilísticos.* 4 vols. Madrid: Gredos.

———. 1988. *Corral de vivos y muertos.* 2d ed. Madrid: Ed. VOSA.

Zuleta, Emilia de. 1971. *Cinco poetas españoles (Salinas, Guillén, Lorca, Alberti, Cernuda).* Madrid: Gredos.

Index

Note: All poems and books of poetry written by the authors here studied are indexed, as well as the first lines of untitled poems. Titles of critical works mentioned are not indexed, but names of critics (and all other persons) are. The index also includes references to magazines and journals. The notes are indexed only for critics' names and for the poets here studied.

155 1970's poetry beyond referentiality to ↑reason
      foreground lang + form

#163-4, González: "Meciendo algunas tardes"

#165, "Calambur"
166:67. "Hilando" (Rodríguez)
#177 Pollo
190 Luis Guillén
     Jesús Munárriz

237 n 11   1980s → 1920s
            where Lorca, Alberti, etc. built on
            V '80's poets built on Luis Guillén,
            Canero, files, Villena

196 80s verse less metapoetic/self-reflexive
     more subjective + experience based
     than 70s verse (life v. aesthetics)

199 Luis Antonio de Villena
*212 Ana Rossetti: "Chico Wrangler"
214 Since late 70s - irony, more low-key
215 John Navichi: Diario de un poeta recien cansado

82 Otero's social poetry

84 Gloria Fuertes: poesía social
    lenguaje coloquial

86 Angel González: Tratado del urbanismo (1967)

100 1956-70; poesía ≠ comunicación (C. Barral)
                = acto de descubrimiento | conocimien-
                (José Angel Valente) | to

101 reader privileged over author

102 postmod: Brines, Valente, Gil de Biedma, -121
                          106   -124
           A. González, C. Rodríguez, C. Barral
        - indeterminacy (Calinescu, Hassan)
                                    111
        - process over product (Lyotard)
        - parody + self-reflexity (Hassan, Hutcheon)
      (v. a.g ≠ text as open w/ reader role)

104 resistance to authoritative communication

116 Gloria Fuertes

132 1960s- conscious of creative process
            - indiv. experience
            - narrative technique
            - poem as process

135 los novísimos- lang, discourse + form over content, theme
            - metapoetic, irrational
            - less colloquial, more artful
            - less personal & anecdotal, more cultural & literary
            - sign as indep., augment reader role (139)
            - self-conscious (late 70s)

148 meaning is slippery, so process is foregrounded

151 Leopoldo Mª Panero
    Antonio Martínez Sarrión

Gimferrer
137 ,143
144 espejos,
metapoesia

Modernism, fr. Symbolism – verbal configuration of
(339, 18)   timeless values – presentness
                                   (text = icon, correlative)
another modernism = avant-garde
  – process, play, resistance to logic + closure
  – anti-symbolist indeterminacy   Modernist
  (minority voice in 1920s) 374n1   determinacy
                                                      (logocentric)
34 contradiction bet. theory + actual product   vs.
39 Juan Larrea as Surrealist   a.g. pomo
41 S. techniques w/o S. label   indeterminacy
43 Aleix. + PN as Symbolist primarily
44 & sobre los ángeles

60 post-war poetry: personal +   1940s return to
social (anecdote, narrative,   form + tradition
    everyday lang.)   (anachronistic)

62 social, realistic v. inditer-
                        minacy
   poem ≠ icon but
          communication

63 José Hierro + Delicki – poesía + testimonial 144-'60
                        emotiva (76) – communication
                                       everyday lang.
71 1940s-- text = icon of   → reader's
   60s   experience   participation/response
              (objective   (anecdote)
              correlative)

77 post-Civil War atmosphere postponed poetry as play

80 Symbolist object-centered verse
   post war communication
   inventive possibilities of lang (a.g.)

80 1950-65 - dominant = social + political
              collective concerns